MW00809157

Praise for *Outgrowing Capitalism*

"Capitalism is now in crisis, unable to address some of today's great challenges. Chief among these is climate change, an existential threat to life on this planet. Marco Dondi, in this excellent book, offers an important contribution to this examination, focusing on money supply through a new concept of monetism. It is this kind of fresh thinking from the next generation of business leaders that offers hope that we can come to terms with our global challenges, before it is too late."

—**ANDREW J. HOFFMAN,** Holcim (US), professor of sustainable enterprise at the University of Michigan and author of several books on business and sustainability

"At the heart of a bold alternative to capitalism as we know it, *Outgrowing Capitalism* contains the most sophisticated and persuasive plea ever for an unconditional basic income funded by inflation-proof money creation."

—**PHILIPPE VAN PARIJS,** author of Basic Income, professor at the University of Louvain, Hoover Chair of Economic and Social Ethics, and chair of the Advisory Board of the Basic Income Earth Network

"Dondi eloquently makes the case that modern banking actually hinders capitalism's creative forces, whilst a fiat-money-based universal income scheme he calls *monetism* would unleash them, reducing debt and poverty in the process. This book is easy to read, and Dondi's ambitious proposals are grounded in a unique understanding of banking and real-life economics. His excellent arguments deserve serious consideration."

—**STEVE KEEN,** author of *Debunking Economics*, honorary professor University College London, and former head of economics at Kingston University

Outgrowing
CAPITALISM

Outgrowing
CAPITALISM

Rethinking Money *to*
Reshape Society *and* Pursue Purpose

Marco Dondi

FAST
COMPANY
Press

This publication is designed to provide accurate and authoritative information in regard to the subject matter covered. It is sold with the understanding that the publisher and author are not engaged in rendering legal, accounting, or other professional services. Nothing herein shall create an attorney-client relationship, and nothing herein shall constitute legal advice or a solicitation to offer legal advice. If legal advice or other expert assistance is required, the services of a competent professional should be sought.

Fast Company Press
New York, New York
www.fastcompanypress.com

Copyright © 2021 Marco Dondi

All rights reserved.

Thank you for purchasing an authorized edition of this book and for complying with copyright law. No part of this book may be reproduced, stored in a retrieval system, or transmitted by any means, electronic, mechanical, photocopying, recording, or otherwise, without written permission from the copyright holder.

This work is being published under the Fast Company Press imprint by an exclusive arrangement with Fast Company. Fast Company and the Fast Company logo are registered trademarks of Mansueto Ventures, LLC. The Fast Company Press logo is a wholly owned trademark of Mansueto Ventures, LLC.

Distributed by Greenleaf Book Group

For ordering information or special discounts for bulk purchases, please contact Greenleaf Book Group at PO Box 91869, Austin, TX 78709, 512.891.6100.

Design and composition by Greenleaf Book Group
Cover design by Greenleaf Book Group
Cover images used under license from ©Shutterstock.com/rolandtopor; ©Shutterstock.com/Dejan Popovic; ©Shutterstock.com/timquo. Interior images used under license from ©Shutterstock.com/Monkey Business Images; ©Shutterstock.com/Dudarev Mikhail; ©Shutterstock.com/scooperdigital

Publisher's Cataloging-in-Publication data is available.

Print ISBN: 978-1-7354245-7-6

eBook ISBN: 978-1-7354245-8-3

Part of the Tree Neutral® program, which offsets the number of trees consumed in the production and printing of this book by taking proactive steps, such as planting trees in direct proportion to the number of trees used: www.treeneutral.com

Printed in the United States of America on acid-free paper

21 22 23 24 25 26   10 9 8 7 6 5 4 3 2 1

First Edition

CONTENTS

Introduction

You Think Society Is in Danger and Then You Get Donald Trump

It was February 2013 and I was about to start an experience that would refocus my life. I took off for a country I didn't even know existed to volunteer for a pro bono consulting company. My task: to analyze the maize value chain in Swaziland and recommend ways to increase crop yields of small farmers. As the months flew by, the excitement of spending most of my time helping others had become a non-negotiable feature for my life.

Many people come to a similar resolution and end up dedicating their time in the most diverse activities. We each tell ourselves the story of how what we do is the best we can to help others. Myself? As a strategy consultant, I solve problems or define ways to pursue new opportunities. My question was therefore, "What is the most critical problem or untapped opportunity I should focus on as my life mission?"

The Swazi experience nudged me toward helping developing countries achieve Western standards of living. Yet once back in Europe, it became clear that Western economies were in no position to be role models for developing countries. The constant smiles, the simple life, and the close connections of the Swazi communities gave way to the frenzied, stressful, and individualistic life in the north of Italy. I could not tell whether the life of a poor Swazi was more or less enriching than that of the average busy man or woman in the Western world.

Three years later, Brexit and the election of Donald Trump confirmed my intuition. Western economies cannot be held as exemplary targets, and, unless some radical changes happen, they might as well become another historic example of how great empires fall. It is the so-called "developed economies" that show the biggest gap between opportunity and reality, between what life could be and what we seem to have settled for. Solving this conundrum became my life purpose.

And an urgent one at that.

* * *

We face fundamental threats, beyond one American president. But the opportunity is dazzling.

Consider: Around 40 million Americans live in poverty,[1] and 7 million of these are poor even though they are employed. Poverty rates have not changed since the early 1980s.[2] Thirty-nine percent of Americans have no savings and another 18% have less than $1,000.[3] In some respect, the UK fares even worse. Most other high-income countries do only marginally better.

We can end this.

The opportunity to thrive in society is strongly linked to access to quality education, but attending four years of United States (US) colleges includes board cost on average $170k at private colleges and $110k at public ones,[4] with the cost to attend the best universities easily exceeding the $250k mark. On average, students graduate with more than $30k in debts and take more than 10 years to repay. A student who needs to finance the full cost of a university education may never be able to repay. Americans owe $1.6 trillion in student debt, large enough to destabilize the economy if all students refused—or for some reason were unable—to repay. Other high-income countries do have better access to quality education. Yet their social mobility is only marginally better than in the US.

We can end this.

The crash in 2008 was destructive. But we now have more debt than in 2007, real median wages to repay them are stuck at 1980s levels, and central bank interest rates and balance sheets are nowhere near pre-crisis levels. The COVID-19 pandemic has further increased public debts, and a prolonged economic crash would be far worse than that of 2008.

We can solve this.

Are you happy at work? About half of all employees are not satisfied with their jobs, according to a 2017 survey. Their biggest complaint? Not enough respect.

We can help end this.

We've long expected wonders from the future. But now we're looking at a great wave of unemployment thanks to displacement by artificial intelligence (AI) and robots, and extraordinary damage from climate change.

We can take advantage of the first and mitigate the second.

How? *Monetism*. This is a term I coined to describe a new economic system grounded in a new way of managing money.

With this new economic system, we shift the emphasis from production (capital) to distribution (money). We align our economic system with current realities. This change goes to the heart of our world.

* * *

Once upon a time and not so long ago, people produced almost nothing. Markets were rare because people had little to sell. Then slowly our current economic system arose: capitalism.

Capitalism brought us progress beyond anyone's ability to foresee. In 1800 you might have imagined a telephone, but not a desktop computer. And such unpredictable changes have continued. But today we have to ask the following: Has traditional capitalism given us a new surprise, leading us past the need for it as it has existed? Could it be that—in this new world—capitalism is imposing unaffordable societal costs and threatening the very economy it built?

Though capitalism arose in a world of scarce capital and labor, we now have abundant capital, and technology is so advanced that the need for labor may dramatically shrink. According to the University of Oxford, AI will place 47% of jobs at risk in the US and 54% in Europe within 20 years.[5] AI won't affect only repetitive manual operations. Your own job may be at stake.[6] Those who think this situation resembles the Industrial Revolution, with new jobs springing up to replace old ones, are simply assuming the future must repeat the past. They are demonstrably wrong. In *The Second Machine Age*, Erik Brynjolfsson and Andrew McAfee show that since 2000, we have witnessed "the great decoupling": The benefits of automation are accruing to the owners of capital, not to workers' wages or employment. Who would then afford the products of automation? This is already happening.

Automation should be a godsend, a liberating opportunity for more leisure, and it still can be. But in the world of capitalism, people gain purchasing power from their jobs. And as people lose jobs or get lower-paying ones, they buy less and suffer.

In turn, companies produce less, more employees lose jobs and consume less, and companies produce even less. Economies enter a tailspin.

So consumption—based on the availability of money—will increasingly drive the level of production. How will capitalism—based on the idea that the more we make, the higher the wages, and the more we buy—cope in a world where poor distribution reduces production?

And AI isn't the only force skewing the distribution. Capitalism itself tends to concentrate wealth and increase inequality. Thomas Piketty published three centuries of data showing inequality has always been increasing, except for a short 45-year period following two world wars and the biggest economic crisis on record.[7] This inequality reduces the spending of most people, for it so happens that people with high incomes and wealth consume (spend) little of what they earn proportionately, while those with lower income consume all or even more.

That's not all. In *The Spirit Level*, Richard Wilkinson and Kate Pickett show how inequality within a country correlates negatively with many measures of well-being—the more inequality, the less well-being—while capitalism's key measure of production, gross domestic product (GDP) per capita, correlates with no measures of well-being at all, at least in high-income countries.[8] Then why are global societies so obsessed by sheer production?

*   *   *

A less unequal income distribution would increase production, that is, economic growth. But what about stimulating smart growth? What we produce and how we produce it? Progress has created enough resources and technology to tackle any issues we may face. Today's problem is that free markets don't necessarily channel them in the best directions at an optimal speed.

For instance, look at climate change. We could easily control it with existing technology, but free markets are just too slow. Yet it is already causing more severe hurricanes, floods, heavy snowfalls, heat waves, droughts, and wildfires.[9]

A common story in most change management courses involves cooking a frog (which I reluctantly repeat given my strict vegetarian diet). If you toss a live frog in a boiling pot of water, it'll leap straight out, but if you put the frog in cool water and slowly warm it up, the frog will actually cook before realizing it should have jumped out.[10]

This parable parallels our collective lack of response to climate change. Like the fabled frog, we are sitting around as the atmosphere warms and sea levels rise. An October 2018 report from the Intergovernmental Panel on Climate Change found that, to avoid damage, we must change the global economy at a rate and extent that has "no documented historic precedent." As Myles Allen, a climate scientist at Oxford put it, "We need to reverse emissions trends and turn the world economy on a dime."[11]

Instead, we've actually been going in the opposite direction.

* * *

In the 1980s, society had an epidemic of the ideology "perfection of free markets." Directing money toward the right projects was increasingly left to unbridled markets.

Elected governments lost control over money creation—that was left to private agreements between banks and borrowers—while globalization bred a race to the bottom for tax rates, as governments vied to attract corporations and wealthy people with low taxes and loopholes. We all hate taxes, but in a very unequal world, if governments can't effectively tax the wealthy, how can they raise the funds to tackle issues like climate change and poverty? The only solution was to increase public debts. That has worked until now, when most countries' debts are deemed unsustainable.

The UK and the US pushed privatization to the extreme, even in health care and education, hoping for lower public expenditure. Instead, they ended up with higher costs and worse outcomes for citizens compared to Europe and Japan, where health and education is largely subsidized and often provided by the government.

The contrast between what society needed—better distribution of resources—and the prevailing ideology of leaving all distribution to the free market, with a mandate to maximize the value of production, led to the obvious. Since the 1980s everything has gotten worse: inequality, GDP growth, and productivity growth. Well-being measures have stagnated or gotten worse.

The problem is systemic and tweaks won't help. Too much has changed from the early days of capitalism. Globalization and AI are here to stay. If we want to turn these forces from threats to opportunities, we must pull back and look at the socio-economic universe we live in. That perspective will show we need an upgrade, and with monetism we can achieve it. We can solve problems that have seemed as permanent as time itself.

But there are obstacles, some of them inside us.

*   *   *

If you were born before 2000, your grandparents lived in a society where they could amuse themselves by attending human zoos. As late as 1958, in the exposition of Brussels we had such zoos where Black and Asian "primitive natives" were displayed for the entertainment of visitors.[12] Go back a bit more than a century and you find slavery was considered normal, like poverty today, accepted for millennia before society realized it might be immoral.

Society is the result of complex processes and interactions, but they boil down to decisions—past and present—taken by billions of people. And the decisions can become entrenched, as custom or "way of life." Society can have habits.

For each of us, habits automate our mental processes. They free the thinking brain from work. Watch piano virtuoso Yuja Wang play "Flight of the Bumblebee" and you may be amazed at how nimbly her fingers control the keys. Much of it is habit, bred of long practice. She has largely automated the process and doesn't have to think about it in the same way you or I would. Habits both help and hinder us. We carry them out unthinkingly, so we may not notice the bad ones.

Society's habits can also be bad. Slavery is one example, and in many US states where it was a habit in the 1800s, it has left a trail of conscious and unconscious racial discrimination to this day. Here's another societal habit: If you lived in Italy before 1981 and had a tough time finding a wife, the law would give you an easy solution. You could rape a woman, even a teenager, and the law would compel you to marry her in repentance. *Il matrimonio riparatore*, they called it. No prison or other penalty—just wedding the woman you raped.

Looking back, it's easy to spot these horrors and wonder how people could have been blind to them. But we know it happens. (Marry-your-rapist laws are actually still on the books in several countries.)

Habits are unavoidable. And we've become habituated to capitalism as it now exists. Yet it has undergone its own gradual shift, from a source of prosperity to one of weather disturbances, social inequalities, and slower prosperity growth. But we are used to it. We're accustomed to its workings and no longer question it, although we have ample proof that the economic theories underpinning unbridled free markets are flawed.

But we're not stuck in habit loops. In humans, a part of the brain is always monitoring which habits are turned on. Suppose you're driving a familiar road, one you can drive almost without thinking about it, and the truck in front of you starts acting unpredictably. Your prefrontal cortex immediately shuts down the autopilot and takes over, paying full attention to the truck. The danger is obvious and imminent, and we break through the habit. Capitalism, persistent poverty, or climate change are unfortunately not obvious, imminent threats, and society does not have a prefrontal cortex. As a society, we are more akin to the frog in heating water.

But we do have a glimpse of hope: Research shows that we can change the most deeply rooted habits. How? By deliberately switching off the old habit and developing an alternative.[13] Society needs a plan B, a habit that remakes today's capitalism.

Fortunately, we have a means right at hand: money.

* * *

Two events in the beginning of my adult life focused my attention on the topic of money.

The first occurred when I got a job straight out of college. I suddenly shifted from having to count every cent to knowing I would likely never have money issues. My dad was a reasonably high earner, but at 46 he suddenly became an unemployed, divorced, single parent. Regaining and keeping a job was harder than he expected, and involuntary unemployment was tough to cope with. The feelings of uselessness and insecurity can easily become depression and anger. As a result, I lived mindful of money.

Luckily, I lived in Italy, where education is more or less free and, thanks to merit-based scholarships, I could graduate from Politecnico di Milano. It's rather unknown abroad but a world-class university in teaching quality. My college education cost in total about €5,000 (about 6,500 USD back in 2009); had I lived in the US, where capitalism has taken over education, I would never have had the courage to take out a six-digit loan to pay for my university expenses. Because of this bit of fortune, I ended up being recruited by one of the best strategy consulting companies in the world, which quickly turned me into a highly sought-after professional in the job market. My freedom from money anxiety was a big relief. It changed the way I thought about life and the way I made day-to-day decisions. I shifted from prioritizing money to making the most of my time. I have de-prioritized my career and prioritized relationships and the writing of this book, both more fulfilling than getting promoted faster.

Freedom from money constraints has also led me to wonder this: Why do so many people have money issues? Why can't we all live more comfortably, without having to worry about money? And what on earth could still induce stress in wealthy people?

I envisioned a society where no one ever had the anxiety of living paycheck to paycheck, where people enjoyed control over their time, where they could fulfill their lives and become better human beings. How was this goal not possible, I thought, in our world of endless goods and services?

Yet millions of families in high-income countries still live in financial insecurity, much worse than my family's. Lack of money haunts their lives and forces unwanted decisions. It breaks up marriages, limits treatment for illness, stunts education, and narrows opportunities. And when economies crash, as they did in 2008, it all gets worse.

The second event that focused my attention on money occurred at college when I learned how society manages money. Thanks to a combined background in economics and the science of operations, I immediately sensed the system was inefficient, perhaps deeply flawed, and for sure prone to crises. I was shocked when I later discovered that most economists and politicians had given little importance to the role of money since the 1980s.

After university, I had the chance to provide strategic advice to banks, large corporate clients, nongovernmental organizations (NGOs), and governments. I ultimately specialized in government transformations and economic development, including the management of economic crises and the future of labor markets. I was fortunate enough to look at society from many different points of view, gaining perspectives from people of the most diverse backgrounds, from subsistence farmers in low-income countries to ministers and CEOs of high-income ones.

The privilege of developing expertise in so many disciplines and industries and the exposure to the perspectives of so many players in society is uncommon, and is limited to those few strategy consultants who serve the public, the private, and the not-for-profit sectors. Most academics specialize in a narrow slice of society and rarely consider multiple disciplines or how theory translates to the lives of real people. If you add my interdisciplinary education and my humble origins, there are probably only a handful of other people in the world who are in the position to propose a realistic alternative to capitalism. I believe I am the first to dedicate years of my life to this end.

And I had to do it, as in my role as a consultant I could only give second-best advice. I was unable to overcome the systemic limitations of our capitalist society, that in real life sounds like this:

> *"We can't fund this project, though it would be useful to society."*
>
> *"This project is beneficial but likely unprofitable."*
>
> *"The returns are too uncertain and lie too far in the future."*
>
> *"This initiative would distort free markets."*
>
> *"This policy would damage a certain industry that provides many jobs."*

With all the progress we have achieved, why can't we fund projects to solve the most critical societal issues?

Our capitalist societies present us with an array of paradoxes and impossible trade-offs. For instance—

1. We have to work full-time for a living even when machines could allow for more voluntary activities.

2. We have to reduce taxes to attract businesses and high-income people to stay in the country, but then we lack the funds to support all other citizens.

3. Central banks raise interest rates to reduce present inflation, but the action leads to lower investments and growth, potentially even increasing inflation in the long term.

4. We need banks to increase credit to grow the economy, but credit leads to debts that cause instability and recessions.

5. We need significant economic growth to ensure economic sustainability, but we live on a finite planet and only have 24 hours a day.

Capitalism has become a cage. And it has armed guards. Unfortunately, when you are in such a cage you cannot tell your mates to escape. You know they will get shot. I am also in the cage of capitalism; we all are. Within the bounds of modern capitalism, I am limited in the professional advice I can give to companies and governments. But with this book, I hope to free all of us from the cage by convincing the guards to hand over the keys: the management of money.

* * *

I call the next phase of capitalism *monetism*.

In 2017, UK prime minister Theresa May justified her refusal to raise nurses' pay because, she said, there is no money tree. She was wrong. We've had a money tree ever since the gold standard fell in 1971.[14] We just haven't understood how to use it. Monetism is a practical recipe for harvesting the money tree.

But what is money if it is no longer tied to gold? Can we just print more and we all become richer, or would that just create inflation? People to this day do not understand money. I will argue that most economists do not fully understand it either, and they certainly did not when the gold standard fell. Unable to cope with inflation, they had to find a way to limit the amount of money that could be issued. Capitalism provided the solution.

The free market would create money. Here's how it works. When a bank grants a loan to a borrower, it creates a deposit in that amount. The click of a button creates a bank loan and a bank deposit. In the words of Mervyn King, "Governments allowed money to be a by-product of credit creation."[15]

The theoretical foundation is the following: If a borrower is willing to take a loan and promises to repay it, they will have to use the money wisely to create value needed to repay both loan and interest. The interest rate is the price of that loan, set by free-market dynamics. The bank is free to set the interest rate, and the borrower is free to accept or reject it. Free markets work well on paper, but they fare quite poorly when faced with the reality of human beings and their cognitive biases.

Banks also have biases. With their overconfidence in good times and risk aversion in bad ones, they cause business cycles and recessions. And while the theory assumes they would lend to productive uses, only 15% of loans go to businesses.[16] The rest? Most go to buy existing assets like real estate, causing the inflation of their prices. Other loans go to people who can only consume on credit—until the wealth concentration machine of capitalism makes them so poor they can't repay these loans.

When borrower defaults reach the point where they cause a crisis, society can't afford to let banks go bust, as they create over 90% of all the money in circulation, and the economy could collapse—really collapse, not just a crisis of a small percentage of GDP. Hence central banks must bail them out.

In summary, the approach that capitalism requires to create and allocate money is riddled with flaws and challenges. Monetism is not a new ideology but a new approach to create and allocate money in a way that high-priority issues are quickly addressed. While the choice of these issues can vary by country and political views, I envision monetism as a pragmatic recipe to—

1. Gradually deploy a universal basic income to end poverty, reduce inequality, and provide security for those whom AI will increasingly displace.

2. Improve people's well-being in an environmentally intelligent way.

3. Confront climate change quickly and minimize the disasters ahead.

4. Have more control over inflation without causing economic recessions, thereby eliminating business cycles and their hardships.

5. End the dependence of capitalism on GDP growth, since it's now unrelated to well-being.

6. Enjoy the full benefits of AI, robots, and super-productivity. As Rutger Bregman asks, Why keep creating jobs if we don't need them or enjoy them?[17]

With monetism, every ordinary person gains more freedom. In fact, we take the helm of our destinies. Thanks to automation and innovation, in the long term we won't have to work most of our lives for a salary unless we want to. People on the lowest economic rungs can feed their families and give them quality health, shelter, and education. We will be free to travel more, start new businesses, write novels, be with our kids. We can buy more goods, services, and experiences, spurring the economy. We can gain more education, realize our capacities, and keep up with changing times. We can be creative with our lives and control our identities. We can minimize regrets on our deathbeds.

Sound utopian? It would have been 50 years ago, but now it's not. And the COVID-19 pandemic has brought us much closer to it.

* * *

As fate would have it, by the time I got to the end of writing this book, the world had changed dramatically. Before COVID-19, the idea of governments creating trillions and giving them away to people and businesses was very controversial, with limited room to maneuver. Yet, after the trillions were printed in the wake of the 2008 crisis, central banks have since printed even more to cope with the pandemic. The money ultimately reached governments that gave it away to people, supported emergency investments in health care, and made other investments for economic recovery. Thus far, this has been the biggest experiment of creating money and using it to redistribute resources in society ever attempted.

But what constitutes a crisis and who should decide? Is climate change not a crisis worthy of printing money? And why does it have to be up to the discretion of central banks or governments to decide when to print money, how much to print, and how to use it? These questions cannot be answered during an emergency, but it would be reckless to keep counting on policymakers' discretion and ability to improvise. Society is out of whack on multiple dimensions and crises will keep coming. In the post-COVID-19 world monetism is not a hypothetical and controversial socio-economic model, but a proposal to put structure and guardrails around today's improvised economic policy.

The socio-economic context that gave birth to capitalism is long gone. Money itself has never been fully understood. Yet, everything we rely on—our job, retirement, children's education, health, and the future of the planet—is linked and dependent on the laws of capitalism and money creation. Both of these laws are outdated.

It is no one's fault. The system is complex and most people only see a piece of the puzzle. But we can change this. Worse crises are beyond the horizon and we can hear them rumbling. Monetism is the way not just to prevent them but also to gain unprecedented control over our lives and enter a new era of well-being.

* * *

I have organized this book as a journey of five steps.

Part one looks at personal well-being and shows that, while money can't guarantee it, too little money makes it very difficult to pursue happiness and life fulfillment. After the grim acknowledgment that most individuals are stuck in economic insecurity, the rest of part one explores the feasibility of a revolutionary proposal: universal basic income (UBI) that puts everyone above a minimum comfort threshold.

Part two looks into money, where it comes from, and why we don't have enough to afford a UBI. It shows that money creation and money management have undergone tremendous changes only in the past century, but it is still far from being optimal, and after the 2008 crisis and COVID-19, the time is ripe for changing money again. But most proposals are diminished or dismissed because they are at odds with free-market capitalism.

Part three, therefore, looks at capitalism—how it emerged, evolved, and became a success in the past, but how it is now the biggest roadblock for a new wave of progress.

In part four I finally present monetism, a new way of managing money that can overcome the threats and realize the opportunities that capitalism has brought to us but is now unable to deliver on. In describing monetism I will answer several questions. What are the societal objectives it should pursue? How should money be managed? What about taxes and inflation? Who will make the many decisions required?

After exploring risks, barriers, and interest groups likely to oppose monetism, part five will provide a roadmap for implementing this new system at a national level, but also at the local and global level.

Without further ado, I wish you happy reading. Should my effort to use clear and pleasing language falter, I apologize in advance. I also apologize to economists, psychologists, environmentalists, politicians, historians, philosophers, and engineers. You may find this book an oversimplification of your fields of study. But a compromise is needed to make this book holistic, multidisciplinary, and broadly accessible. There is no point in writing a book that hopes to transform society if most citizens can't understand it, and my main hope is that the awareness of many will transform into demands that political leaders can't ignore.

And now let's begin with everyone's bottom line.

I.
WELL-BEING

What matters in life? We all face this question, and the answers guide our most fundamental choices. One obvious answer is well-being matters, with its facets like happiness and life fulfillment. Since virtually everyone wants it, society should maximize our chances to achieve it. But what is well-being, really, and what yields it for us? We sense that money may be part of the answer—but only part, and scientific studies bear this out. Let's look more deeply into these important questions and see how well modern society supports people in pursuing their well-being.

Chapter 1

Two Happy Marriages, Seven Satisfying Jobs, and One Fulfilled Life, Please

How important is money for well-being?

In the movie *Crazy Rich Asians*, we see ultra-rich people leading glamorous, exciting lives and yet their well-being doesn't always match their wealth. The matriarch, Eleanor Sung-Young, is a controlling woman with secret satisfactions but little visible joy, and wealthy cousin Astrid Leong-Teo is clearly depressed. Their money gives them everything except the thing people want most. The obvious question is: why?

So let's first delve into well-being. What is it? We all sense the answer, but it's surprisingly hard to pin down analytically.

Researchers identify three components of individual well-being: happiness, life satisfaction, and life fulfillment. But they are not individual components as, say, three large slices can be the components of a pie. Pie pieces have clean boundaries, but here we're dealing with the human mind, and the brain has trillions of interconnections, so the aspects of well-being have overlapping, interwoven borders. Moreover, well-being may have components psychologists have not yet studied. But if we focus on these three—happiness, life satisfaction, and life fulfillment—can we say one is more important than the others? How do we measure them? How do they affect us? Historically, there has been confusion about these issues; I will try to summarize the current consensus and add suggestions of my own.[1]

Happiness tends to relate to positive and negative emotions, experienced day to day. Some researchers call it an *affective component* of well-being, as it is based on affect—that is, the experience of feelings or desires, sometimes expressed visibly, as in smiles.

Life satisfaction is more of a judgment about our life based on criteria that each of us define. Psychologists call it the *cognitive component* of well-being, as it is based on an individual's judgment of what constitutes a satisfactory life. If you have been a lawyer all your life, raised a family, and enjoy professional respect, you may say that your life satisfaction is high.

Life fulfillment describes how meaningful your life has been for you. Hence, if you are that same lawyer but always wanted to be an astrophysicist, you likely feel less life fulfillment. Aristotle talks about this quality and contrasts it with the feeling of being happy. He argues that all good people should aim for a moral and fulfilling life. However, psychologists have researched it less, due partly to difficulties in measuring it and to its greater subjectivity.

All three are important. Happiness is the most obvious aspect of well-being and the most immediate. We see the other two through a rear-view mirror, but they are also basic. (And for those of you who believe in something after death, there is more to life than ongoing positive feelings.) First, life satisfaction affects happiness and researchers have found that happiness correlates with different measures of life satisfaction and vice versa.[2] A sense of life satisfaction makes you happy.

But life fulfillment is arguably more important than life satisfaction. In fact, the latter is loaded with comparisons between one's life and everyone else's. As a result, life satisfaction can become more a question of "How good is my life compared to what society defines as good?" rather than "How meaningful is my life based on who I am, the talents I possess, and what I really want?" The difference is serious—indeed, central to our life decisions. In her memoir, nurse Bronnie Ware writes that the most common regret of dying people is "I wish I'd had the courage to live a life true to myself, not the life others expected of me."[3] I will therefore keep life fulfillment and life satisfaction separate and give more importance to happiness and life fulfillment over life satisfaction.

How do these qualities interact with money in everyday life? Conventional wisdom says that the main ingredients for well-being are a satisfying job and a happy marriage. That's too simple, and we'll look beyond conventional wisdom. But let's start here and try to understand how much of a difference money makes for these two choices: our job and our life partner.[4]

MONEY AND WORK

In college you may have agonized over which major to choose. Philosophy? Engineering? Economics? The decision can be tough because it can affect your choice of career.

And your career choice is fundamental for many reasons. First, we spend a lot of time at work. Consider an average person working 40 hours a week, Monday through Friday. That individual spends 33% of her time at work for those five days, and 50% if we exclude eight hours of sleep a night. If we add time spent preparing for work, including a commute, this percentage rises. Second, a job is the only way most people can earn money. Third, we tend to develop our friendships on the job. Fourth, our work defines how we contribute to society. We are social beings, and we organize and collaborate to achieve goals we could never reach individually. When asked what we *do*, we answer, "I'm a teacher," "I'm a farmer," "I'm a doctor," and in that way describe our role in society and, to some extent, our identity.

Many religions highlight the importance of work as both a responsibility to society and a means to fulfillment. The number of people doing volunteer work also shows our desire to contribute. For instance, Wikipedia would be just another forgotten dot-com without its army of dedicated volunteers. In the United States, about one in four people does some kind of volunteering at least once per year.[5]

Since we devote ourselves to the job for most of the weekdays, it can greatly affect our well-being. One study found that a good job fit adds an average of 1.5 points of life satisfaction on a 10-point scale.[6] As you will see later, that is a much higher boost than getting married, so think twice before staying in a bad job to afford a wedding ring. Bronnie Ware also notes that two of the top five regrets of the terminally ill are job related: having worked too much and not having followed one's passion.[7] In another study, finding meaning in one's work increased motivation and personal fulfillment, and reduced stress.[8] When our work is meaningful, we are fulfilled almost by definition. We're doing what we want, and thus we have a stronger sense of purpose and less stress.

On the other side of the spectrum are the high-stress jobs, with burnout or depression at the far end. In a survey of 9,000 financial workers in cities across the globe, 40%–65% of bankers (depending on the country) felt partially burned out, and between 10% and 20% were totally burned out, after working consistently between 80 and 120 hours a week.[9] Some jobs lead to high levels of depression: Among bus drivers the rate is more than 16% compared to the average of less than 7%.[10]

Given the importance of our jobs in our lives, let us look into how important money is to us when we're 1) choosing a job, 2) leaving it, and 3) deciding to stay in it.

1. **Choosing a job.** The Corporate Executive Board (CEB) runs a quarterly global survey involving tens of thousands of employees. One of its questions is, List the top three drivers of attraction to a job. In both 2016 and 2017, compensation came first, followed by work-life balance and stability. The rank order varied among countries, with people in the UK and Australia, for example, putting work-life balance first, but overall, money was clearly predominant, both in developed markets like the US and Germany and developing ones like China and South Africa.[11] These results have remained pretty stable year after year. We should note that money and even work-life balance are relatively easy to assess before taking employment, but on-the-job factors such as *people management* are harder to ascertain, and applicants are therefore unlikely to consider them in these decisions or mention them in the surveys.

2. **Leaving a job.** The CEB also asks the top three drivers of attrition. Here, number one is future career opportunities, with compensation second, and people management third. The top two are related to money, since "future career opportunities" correlates highly with the future compensation, and basically individuals in the first two categories were saying they'd jump to jobs that paid more. People management is consistent with many studies that find a bad boss is one of the most common deal breakers. Notably, respondents mentioned people management more often in developed markets like the US. It did not make the top three in China, for example, where all three related to money: compensation, development opportunities, and career opportunities.[12]

3. **Staying in a job.** In 2016, the most comprehensive study ranked 35 countries for job satisfaction. Work-life balance proved the factor most correlated to job satisfaction, while compensation scored consistently low.

Intriguingly, Colombia ranked as the top country for job satisfaction, and other developing countries like Mexico, Russia, and Chile did well too.[13] But we see the same pattern in the US. A 2014 survey found that "liking people at work" and "work-life balance" are the most common reasons people want to stay.[14] The American Psychological Association in 2012 found that people stay in their jobs because they "like the work they do" and "the job fits well with other aspects of their lives," while benefits and pay came in only third and fourth.[15] In *The Fifth Risk*, Michael Lewis quotes a longtime civil servant who could have become a lobbyist: "I've never felt the need to go over to the other side and make three times the amount of money. If you like what you do, you just keep doing it."[16]

But we all know people who remain in jobs they loathe. Why don't they leave? Here money reappears, with financial and family responsibilities as the most common reasons to stay in a bad job.[17] As Ware noted, money can keep people in jobs that they don't like and they typically regret it later in life.

As you might expect, available job opportunities also affect the decision to stay in a job. In the European Union, one study found a significant correlation between staying on the job and high unemployment: the fewer opportunities available, the more people hang on to what they have.[18] It's likely true every-where, since most of us need to work to keep a roof over our head.

Later in his life my dad became an uncommon exception to the trap of a bad job. He has been a scrupulous saver all his life, putting every expense greater than 50 cents into an Excel spreadsheet, which he used to maximize savings and keep my mother in check. Money did not bring him happiness, but it did save him from the misery of having to hold on to a horrible job full of corruption. With two children still in school, he quit his job in the midst of the 2008 crisis. It was his last job until he received his retirement ten years later. His savings finally bought him something valuable, though his obsession with money likely contributed to the end of his marriage.

In sum: Our job is very important to our well-being, and, on average, we consider money first when choosing a job. However, the main sources of well-being from work are not related to money, but rather to good work-life balance and liking the work we do. One reason may be that compensation is easy to measure and write into a contract, while job satisfaction is more subjective. We often don't know a job is horrible until we have begun it, and met our boss. But here is where money becomes a trap: Even once we know the job is bad, the security of a salary can make us cling to it, especially when there aren't many other jobs around.

MONEY AND WEDDING BELLS

Who doesn't deem the choice of a partner in life very important? Researchers focus on married individuals, as it's more difficult to otherwise determine whether a partnership was serious enough to include in the sample. I am therefore bound by this limitation, although I am not married but am happily partnered.

Researchers find married men and women overall are not just happier and more social, but, as one global study showed, they also enjoy better health and suffer shallower emotional lows than single or divorced individuals. These results hold true even when accounting for the fact that happier people get married more often than less happy ones. Surprisingly, this is not true in every country: The same study found that marriage actually leads to a decline in happiness in Latin America, the Caribbean, and sub-Saharan Africa.[20]

How much happier are married people? One study found that the difference in happiness between the married (including those who would later divorce) and singles was 0.3 on a scale of 0 to 10 (or about 1/33 of it), much less than the 1.5 point increase from a good job fit.[21] This result feels counterintuitive, and it may stem from the inclusion of dissatisfied individuals who would later divorce.

The book *Singled Out* found that people in a lasting marriage were happier than those who divorced by 0.4 point on a 1 to 4 scale. That's a tenth rather than a 1/33. Moreover, divorced people were 0.3 point less happy than people who never married.[22]

It is not surprising that divorce on average generates a short-term increase in well-being. Just after divorcing, people feel happier, suggesting relief from a bad marriage. However, negative consequences emerge in the longer term, such as higher levels of depression, less life satisfaction, and more health problems.[23] Compared to other losses, people 40 and older feel going through a divorce is more emotionally devastating than losing a job, about equal to experiencing a major illness, and worse than a spouse's death.[24] While researchers partially disagree on the absolute importance of marriage, the one common truth across studies is that we should avoid ending up in an unhappy marriage.

But what role does money play in 1) choosing a life partner, 2) ending up in a divorce, and 3) deciding to stay in a marriage?

1. **Choosing a life partner.** This issue attracts more researchers than does the choice of job. But it is also more complex and harder to fully grasp, as culture, religion, and constantly evolving social norms all intervene. In progressive countries where most women have careers and aspirations as high as men's, the process differs greatly from that in traditional cultures like Swaziland. My Swazi driver was excited when he had saved the 5,000 emalangeni (about $500 back in 2013) he needed to be granted permission by his future wife's parents to marry. While recognizing the variety of results that we may find, let's seek the common traits.

A 1989 study of almost 10,000 people from 37 countries defined four spectra for long-term mate selection, largely independent of one another. The first spectrum is the importance we give to resources and status versus love; we will sacrifice a portion of romantic love if the partner has money, and sacrifice economic stability if love is strong. Men are more likely to do the latter than women, though, of course, they have always had more resources to sacrifice. The second spectrum is emotional stability versus physical attractiveness. Here again people will trade off one for the other, and men are more likely to accept emotional instability if their partner is attractive. You could have guessed that one, couldn't you?

The third spectrum is education and intelligence versus the desire for children and family. These don't seem like opposites in the West, but the survey was conducted worldwide. Men are more willing than women to sacrifice their partner's education and intelligence if their partner wants more children. The fourth spectrum is sociability versus similar religion, another non-Western opposition. Here, men and women don't differ significantly in the extent to which they'll accept a less sociable character if their partner has the same religion.[25]

Most studies on mating give similar results: Money is just one of many aspects we consider.

2. **Ending up in divorce.** Marriage rates halved between 1965 to 2013, and divorce rates doubled.[26] As of the latest available data in 2014, European countries lead in this unfortunate league, and Belgium is first with more than 70% of marriages ending up in divorce. The US is above 50%, while Spain, Portugal, the Czech Republic, and Hungary are all above 60%.[27] Why do marriages fail

and how can we keep more of them together? To what extent does money split people apart?

Again, these are difficult questions. Many studies have analyzed differences in divorce rates based on varied attributes, including money. One found that couples with a combined income of $25,000 to $50,000 were about 35% less likely to get a divorce than couples with a combined income below $25,000. If the household income of the couple exceeded $125,000, this percentage grew to 60%.[28]

In 2009, Jeffrey Dew analyzed the correlation between rate of divorce in the US and debt, assets, and frequency of arguments over money. His study revealed that couples with debt are more likely to divorce, especially if they take on the debt after the marriage. Couples with no assets are much more likely to divorce than couples with assets, and couples arguing over money are much more likely to get divorced, from 30% more likely for wives arguing less than once a month, up to 160% more likely for husbands arguing daily.[29]

Studies on divorce also claim that arguments about money are common and much more difficult to settle than other kinds,[30] and those who believe their partner does not spend money wisely are less happy[31] and 45% more likely to divorce.[32] This is the second strongest predictor after drug/alcohol abuse.[33]

But a high income does not ensure financial agreement. In a survey of more than 80,000 people globally, couples with high annual income (between $250,000 and $500,000) turned out to fight over money more often than couples with low income (less than $20,000).[34]

3. **Staying in a marriage.** What are the secrets behind a good marriage? And if the marriage is deteriorating, what deters couples from divorcing? Does money actually keep people in a marriage?

Several studies have attempted to answer the first question. Some traits are intrinsic to a partner and some arise from the relationship. Among the first kind, the most common are open-mindedness, kindness, selflessness, emotional health, and faithfulness, as well as the ability to communicate and listen well. Among the relationship traits, the most common are friendship with the partner, good chemistry, good spiritual life, dedicating time to the relationship, openness, and mutual respect. Money never comes up in any study on successful marriages, and if asked specifically, it typically ranks among the least important factors.[35]

But, of course, some people stay in marriages that make them unhappy. According to psychiatrist and author Fredric Neuman, money is a big reason. People are unwilling to pay the cost of a divorce and surrender money and the physical house in a settlement. Beyond money, they also mainly fear loneliness and want custody of their children.[36] A UK survey of 2,000 married couples found the same results: Four out of ten of them were not fully satisfied with their marriage, and five of the top ten reasons for not divorcing related to money and financial constraints.[37]

Luckily for my mother, she established an intermarriage relationship with a doctor, hence money was not a limitation and she went through with the divorce. She lost the trust and ultimately the relationship with me and my sister, but from the limited interactions I have had, she is clearly happier than before the divorce. Unfortunately for people without her monetary security, it is much more difficult to choose between a bad marriage and a life of financial struggle.

* * *

To summarize: Money is only one factor we consider when choosing a partner, and it is difficult to understand how much importance we give to it. What is clear, though, is that debts and a lack of money significantly boost the chances of divorce. As with job satisfaction, successful couples cite money as among the least important factors in their happiness, even though it also keeps us stuck in bad marriages.

It seems people need a minimum amount of money to be comfortable. Without it, our well-being declines in our job and marriage and likely many other aspects of our lives. At the same time, money alone won't make us happy with our job or marriage, and it can actually be counterproductive if we give too much importance to it.

As we dive deeper into research that directly ties money and well-being, you should be familiar with the terms in the following box.

Some Basic Terms

Money is the actual means of exchange, the dollars, pesos, or rupees you use to get goods and services.

Income is a periodic stream of money you earn from labor (wages), from investments (profit, rent, or capital gains), or from government transfers.

Income per capita is the average income of the people in one country. (Capita comes from the Latin *caput*, or head.)

It's closely linked to the concept *of* **GDP per capita**, which is the monetary value of all finished goods and services produced in a country, divided by its total number of people.

Wealth is the value of everything a person owns, including cash, physical assets like real estate, financial assets like stocks, and anything else with money value.

MONEY AND WELL-BEING GLOBALLY

There are many versions of the following chart, showing happiness and life satisfaction on the vertical and income on the horizontal, and they all look the same. For any definition of these, the chart reveals well-being in low-income countries is on average significantly worse than in high-income ones, but the relationship seems to fade within the high-income countries, and after about $17,000 of GDP per capita, a flat line seems to fit the distribution better. In other words, the low-income countries vary a great deal in well-being, but since they all have roughly the same GDP per capita, other factors likely account for it. The high-income countries vary much more in GDP per capita but have roughly the same well-being. Hence, authors Carol Graham and Stefano Pettinato found no correlation between income and life satisfaction when analyzing the low- and high-income countries as separate groups.[38]

But some researchers see a relationship between well-being and income if you use a logarithmic relationship[39] rather than a linear one.[40] This would mean that countries' well-being does correlate with income, but not as strongly as in a linear relation. That is, you'd have to increase income by a lot in order to increase well-being by a little. These findings, though, are statistically significant only for low-income countries,[41] while in high-income countries the variance—how far the data spreads out from the average value[42]—is so great that the relation between well-being and money could be just about anything.[43]

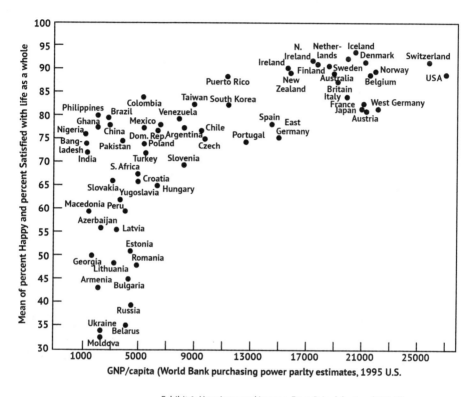

Exhibit 1: Happiness and income. From R. Inglehart and H-D. Klingemann, "Genes, Culture, and Happiness," MIT Press, 2000

The comparison across countries has many limitations, though. Contrary to popular belief, the limitations don't stem from cultural differences (the determinants of happiness are actually quite consistent across cultures[44]) but from the difficulty of isolating income as a cause. For instance, countries with higher income per capita also have more freedom and democracy, and less corruption, which some researchers have found to be as important or more important than income.[45] Religiosity also seems a key factor: Religious Latin American countries report higher happiness and life satisfaction than one would expect from their income per capita, while nonreligious, ex-communist nations show the opposite.[46]

To overcome the confounding issues, researchers looked for the determinants of well-being in different individuals within countries. The findings confirm that people with a higher income have greater well-being than those with lower income, though the correlation is much weaker for happiness than for life satisfaction.[47]

Why? Again, happiness is more linked to emotions while life satisfaction involves a cognitive assessment, a judgment, and people consider low income a sign of failure and dissatisfaction.[48] Happiness correlates more with non-income factors like freedom in deciding how to spend time.[49]

One famous study confirming these findings is that of Daniel Kahneman and Angus Deaton who in 2010 found that happiness ceases to rise after $75,000 of income, while life satisfaction continues to grow with the logarithm of income—that is, slowly.[50] Though the $75,000 threshold pertains to the US and would be different in other countries, their paper created a broad consensus that beyond a certain level, income does not make us any happier.

I happen to be writing this chapter while in Costa Rica, one of the countries with low income per capita but high happiness. Its government actively pursues well-being as one of its goals. Its life expectancy and happiness exceed those of the US.[51] When I asked locals about their secret, the most common answer was their ability to appreciate what life brings to them, instead of comparing it with some expectation of a successful life. While these responses are only anecdotal, the outlook happens to be in line with most religions and life philosophies, and it could help explain why faith correlates with happiness.

Psychologists have also begun presenting scientific evidence that the absence of expectations is indeed a secret of happiness. Daniel Gilbert describes *synthetic happiness*, the ability to make ourselves happy, as a supplement to *real happiness*, caused by outside events, and he argues that both are equally good. But even though our brains can help us synthesize happiness, we can switch off this ability in many ways, like setting high expectations.[52] For instance, if you're going to Bali expecting long white beaches and clear water, you will be unhappy with substandard beaches and waves, and likely unable to appreciate the vibe of Ubud, the sunsets over temples, the rice fields, or a surfing lesson.

So overall the picture seems to be—

1. Within a country, money is positively correlated with life satisfaction, but above a certain level of income, it has no correlation and does not affect happiness.

2. Across countries, considering low- and high-income countries as separate groups, happiness does not correlate with average income per capita, while life satisfaction correlates only among low-income countries.[53]

The last way of analyzing the data is by shifting from point-in-time analysis to evolution over time, referred as *longitudinal analysis*. What happens as countries and individuals get richer over the years?

Taking a country lens, we find the famous quandary known as the *Easterlin Paradox*: As high-income nations get richer, their happiness doesn't increase.[54] Scholars challenged the Easterlin Paradox at first, but the consensus has shifted toward recognizing it and offering the following explanations for it.

1. **Inequality.** Betsey Stevenson and Justin Wolfers highlight growing inequality as a possible cause.[55] Nations may get richer, but the bottom of the income pyramid does not. The rise in happiness of those getting richer is fully offset by the decrease in happiness in low-income people. Or depending on the country, the rich getting richer are not getting any happier, and the poor not getting richer are also not getting any happier. Richard Wilkinson and Kate Pickett reached a similar conclusion, showing that inequality affects an array of metrics related to well-being while GDP per capita does not.[56]

2. **Income differences.** Some researchers have claimed that relative income explains well-being better than absolute income.[57] It's not how rich you are, but how rich you are compared to others. In fact, this variable can fully explain the changes in individual well-being linked to income, making absolute income insignificant.[58]

For example, imagine we are measuring whether having a newer model smartphone makes you more satisfied. The answer is likely yes. But what if we also measured whether having a better model than most people makes you more satisfied, and vice versa? If this latter measure correlates more with smartphone satisfaction, it won't really matter if yet better smartphones are designed. People's satisfaction from having a newer smartphone comes more from the fact that others do not have it rather than from the actual powers of the new device. Now, I do not know whether this is true for smartphones, but relative differences in income seem to explain differences in happiness and life satisfaction better than the growth of absolute income. The widening gap between low- and high-income people could explain stagnant or falling well-being even when average income is growing.

3. **Adaptation to income increments.** Once people can pay for the necessities, they adapt to further increases in income.[59] In other words, if people above a certain income level get a rise in income, they adjust their lives to it and feel they need it. A Gallup survey in the US asked people, "What is the smallest amount of money a family of four needs to get along in this community?" The results showed that the average perceived minimum income grew in time as much as the average real income (income adjusted for inflation). If you are making $60,000 a year, you believe you can live just fine by owning a house and a car. As your income grows, you upgrade your car and move closer to your workplace. Initially, you thoroughly enjoy waking up later and feeling the higher acceleration of your car, but wait long enough, and that becomes the new normal. Now the thought of commuting and driving a cheaper car feels like a sad life. So as people receive higher income, they get used to it.

Research in Germany and Switzerland has found similar results.[60] One study suggested that people fully adapt once income covers their basic needs. The researchers first showed full adaptation among German homeowners but not for German renters. They then showed full adaptation after five years from an increase in income among people of rich European countries, though not for people in low-income European countries. Finally, surprisingly, they demonstrated how in high-income countries, GDP per capita in 1960 predicted 2005 happiness better than 2005 GDP per capita. This result shows that changes in GDP over those 45 years have been irrelevant for happiness. Overall, it seems that above a certain level of income, people get used to further increases, while below that level, they don't.

LIFE FULFILLMENT

Up until now we have not talked about life fulfillment. Only one study has tackled this head-on: a 2016 investigation by the medical device and pharmaceutical company Abbott. It surveyed nearly two million people, asking what made them feel fulfilled and how would they rate their life on a scale of 1 to 100. The results indicate that life fulfillment is not much related to income. Among the 10 countries highest in life fulfillment, Germany is the only high-income one. The other nine are middle or low income, with China and Costa Rica taking the top two spots. The US ranks below the global average.

The situation is similar at the individual level. Worldwide, the most important feature for a fulfilled life is family (32% of respondents), with *success* far behind in second (12%), and *giving* at third (8%). What are the barriers? Money was the biggest (44%), followed by time (33%), and work (20%). These are what people believed to be important in general. But in the assessments of their *own* life fulfillment, the highest scores were linked to people valuing family and spirituality. It's interesting to note that the lowest life fulfillment scores came from the people who cited *success* as their main determinant for living a full life.[61]

These insights seem well aligned to what major religions have been saying all along: Love for money is a hindrance to the pursuit of life fulfillment, although the good use of money can help (see the shaded box on money and religion). Here again, as with happiness and life satisfaction, we see money (or the lack thereof) as more a limitation to life fulfillment than a driver of it. And though you'd think people would deem success, often linked to money, as part of a fulfilled life, it's actually the opposite—at least in the only major study we have. Emphasizing success is not successful.

Money and Religion

While I understand the skepticism of the emancipated Western world toward old writings, religious figures have seriously pondered well-being and life fulfillment. Though I am no religion expert, the similarity among the four global religions with the most followers is striking.

Christianity: Jesus Christ is the most known religious figure in the West; most Christians remember his famous quote about money: "It is easier for a camel to go through the eye of a needle than for a rich man to enter the kingdom of God."[62] Most interpretations suggest that it is the love for material things that prevents people from doing good, and thus they become unworthy of heaven. Elsewhere, Jesus praises the good use of money, like that of the Samaritan who cared for the person beaten by robbers.[63]

Buddhism: I have a favorite quote from the current Dalai Lama. A journalist asked him what surprised him the most about humanity, and he said, "Man surprised me most about humanity. Because he sacrifices his health in order to make money. Then he sacrifices money to recuperate his health. And then he is so anxious about the future that he does not enjoy the present; the result being that he does not live in the present or the future; he lives as if he is never going to die, and then dies having never really lived."

If we go back 2,500 years, Siddhartha Gautama starts life as a prince and

continued

only after abandoning his riches and experiencing the poverty around him does he start his quest for spiritual peace. This quest ultimately leads him to become the Buddha after he finalizes a meditation technique that brings him, and many after him, to enlightenment. Money plays no role in achieving life fulfillment, but Buddha is also aware of the importance of money for human stability and welfare, and recognizes different types of *good happiness* derived from wealth: the happiness of ownership, the happiness of not being in debt, the happiness of earning wealth without engaging in harmful activities, and the happiness of sharing wealth. Buddha also mentions the harmful side of wealth: its temptation for people to pursue insatiable desires, to constantly crave more without achieving the feeling of satisfaction.[64]

Islam: We find similar ideas in the Qur'an: "The example of those who spend their wealth in the way of Allah (i.e., spend their wealth on good deeds like helping the poor) is like a seed [of grain] which grows seven spikes; in each spike is a hundred grains. And Allah multiplies [His reward] for whom He wills. And Allah is all-Encompassing and Knowing."[65] And: "Never will you attain righteousness unless you spend (in Allah's Cause—i.e., helping the needy) from that which you love. And whatever you spend—indeed, Allah is Knowing of it."[66]

Hinduism: While the views on wealth are mostly unwritten, in Hinduism it is important to earn wealth by honest means, to share it, and to avoid becoming greedy.

IN SUMMARY

The upcoming chart summarizes what researches found when examining the people of different countries. Regarding the relation between individual well-being (happiness, life satisfaction, life fulfillment) and money, the most important points to keep in mind are:

1. Money can limit well-being if people can't satisfy basic needs.

2. Beyond a certain point, money does not matter anymore for happiness, but can only appeal to the ego and increase the life satisfaction from having more than one's peers.

3. Life fulfillment is even less related to money, which is a limitation only when totally absent or when considered the main purpose of life.

Well-being

		Happiness	Life satisfaction	Life fulfillment
Point in time	Country level	• High-income countries happier, but beyond 20,000 USD of GDP per capita, relationship ceases to be significant		• Only 1 out of 10 highest fulfilled countries is high income
	Individual level (within countries)	• Higher income irrelevant for happiness beyond a certain level of income	• Higher income leads to higher life satisfaction	• Lack of money limits life fulfillment but those pursuing success as their recipe to life fulfillment report the lowest levels of life fulfillment
Evolution (time series)	Country level	• Only low-income countries the growth of GDP per capita led to higher happiness and life satisfaction. • In high-income countries further increases in GDP per capita are irrelevant to higher happiness and life satisfaction. • High-income countries with higher inequality have lower happiness and life satisfaction.		N/A
	Individual level (within countries)	• Relative income matters more than absolute income. • Full adaptation to higher income levels for people in the high-income brackets, while people in the low-income brackets are happier if their income increases.		N/A

Exhibit 2: Summary of insights on the relation between income and well-being

At the country level, researchers have shown that it is not income that matters most for average well-being, but probably other factors correlated with it, such as freedom, lack of corruption, and friends to count on.[67] While there are likely many more causes than those the researchers have identified, the key point is that even at the country level, increasing income will not automatically improve well-being.

Unfortunately, most governments still assume that individual well-being can be enhanced by boosting per capita GDP. While many scholars now seriously question the importance of GDP, the research and especially the adoption of new metrics are taking a long time.

Chapter 2

Gazing Up at the Comfort Threshold

Above and below: Why the view looks so different

Money and well-being have a complex relationship in many ways, but one theme runs throughout: Below a certain level it affects well-being; above that level, it doesn't. And though our world now abounds in extraordinary wealth, most people in both low- and high-income countries are actually below the comfort threshold. Their priorities are different, overall, from those above the threshold. The lack of money shapes their very existence.

THE PYRAMID

Abraham Maslow was known as a *positive psychologist*, because unlike earlier thinkers such as Freud, he focused on well-being rather than mental illness. And if you've given any study to human motivation, you know his famous hierarchy of needs, which you can see below.

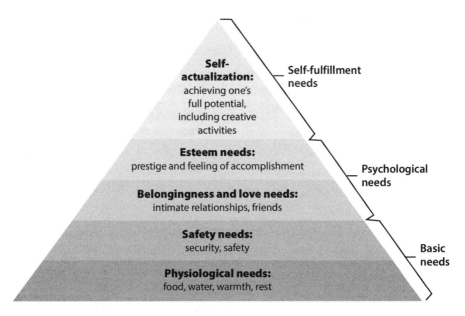

Exhibit 3: Interpretation of Maslow hierarchy theory by Simply Psychology

Most fundamentally, he said, we have physiological needs (such as food, water, air, and health) and safety needs, which include the security of meeting physiological needs in the future. The poor are often battling to meet these basic needs. Next up, Maslow identifies psychological needs, which include the sense of belonging and love from friends and family and, above it, esteem, which refers to recognition in society.

Maslow calls these four tiers *deficiency needs*, and they form the base of a pyramid of prerequisites. If you are deficient at one level, he says, you will lack motivation to satisfy needs above it until you fulfill that lower need. At the same time, once you satisfy a deficiency need, it will cease to motivate you. If you have enough water, for example, you don't seek more. If you feel safe, you don't seek more safety.

At the cap of the pyramid lies the self-fulfillment or *growth needs*. They're a little different. They don't vanish once fulfilled, since we don't pursue them out of deficiency in the first place.[1] He described self-fulfillment in these terms: *"What a man can be, he must be. This need we may call* self-actualization. . . . *It refers to the desire for self-fulfillment, namely, to the tendency for him to become actualized in what he is potentially . . . to become everything that one is capable of becoming."*[2]

STATE 1 AND STATE 2

I have used Maslow's framework to look at what we desire and why, and though there are a lot of good things about it, I want to change it as we go forward. Every human being has a unique character and personality. I don't think we can say that self-fulfillment always comes before or after esteem and belonging. In fact, there are artists in cheap lofts without security about physiological needs, who are nonetheless fulfilling themselves. And is self-fulfillment alone the highest state one can aim for? In his later work, Maslow did recognize a *sub-need* of self-fulfillment called *transcendence need*, which is about helping others reach self-fulfillment.[3]

Bottom line: As we move forward, I will consider a simplified and more universal version of Maslow's theory. I condense his layers into two states.

People in State 1 struggle to meet basic needs or lack security about meeting them in the future. They are in a *survival state*, and they likely pursue money to satisfy basic needs today and tomorrow. With rare exceptions,[4] we do need money to meet physiological needs. We also need it for safety. Our security about meeting future physiological needs depends on our ability to gain money in the future, or possession of enough savings today.

People in State 2 can easily meet their basic needs and are comfortable about doing so in the future, because of their savings or other means (such as government safety nets, family and friends, confidence in their own abilities, etc.). People in State 2 can focus on happiness and life fulfillment, which Maslow suggests are linked to family, friends, love, self-esteem, recognition, and self-actualization. I call it the *life fulfillment state*, not because people in this state have fulfilled their potential but because they have a chance to. Basically, the boundary between these two states is like the surface of the sea. Below it you have to swim; above it you can fly.

Of course, the real border between these states is blurred, with many gaps. Some people can live in both states at once or can swing between them based on whether it is sunny or cloudy outside. But let's keep this as a general framework to think about our society.

State 1: We have to pursue money to secure long-term access to basic needs.

State 2: We could pursue happiness and life fulfillment, each in our own way.

And the latter is really a pursuit, as most people have to figure out first what a fulfilling life would look like for them. We have Maslow, scientists and psychologists, religions, and you can mention more, but we should consider any external influence no more than guidance. We are uniquely different from one another. We do react similarly to the events of life, but the recipe for happiness and life fulfillment depends on our starting position, our character, our mind patterns, and our soul if you believe in it. We are in a pursuit, which will likely continue for life.

THE MONEY MATRIX

Take a look at the following matrix. It has four quadrants, created by splitting people along two dimensions. The vertical split separates people with the means to live comfortably (State 2) from those without (State 1). The horizontal split separates people who mainly pursue either money (above) or life fulfillment (below). This split is very rough, of course; people can move around and most people are probably somewhere near the horizontal line. Few would say they only pursue money, but you'd probably agree that most people deem it very important and then perhaps at some point ask themselves what to do with their lives. If you are not convinced, ask yourself, How many times a month do you think about money versus how to live a fulfilling life?

The people in the bottom two quadrants will have fewer regrets to tell researchers like Bronnie Ware on their deathbeds. In the bottom left corner, you have the ones I call *Monks*, people who pursue life fulfillment even though they lack security about meeting basic needs (now or in the future). In the bottom right corner are the *Explorers*, people who can meet these needs and pursue life fulfillment, seeing money as a means to achieve it, if important at all. They are Explorers since they have embarked on a true journey.

If everyone was a Monk or an Explorer, we would live in a rather happy society. Unfortunately, most people are in the top two quadrants. On the left are the Concerned Parents, people in State 1 whose main objective, understandably, is money. Like parents concerned for the future of their children, they worry about having the money to meet crucial needs now and in the future, for themselves and their families.

In the top right quadrant are the Squirrels. You've seen cartoons where a squirrel endlessly hoards nuts and acorns. In a similar way, some people are just chronic accumulators of money. The more they make, the more they feel they need. These people seem locked into the pursuit of money, even if money won't make them any happier or more fulfilled.

MONEY AVAILABILITY

	Low security to meet basic needs (survival state)	Can comfortably meet basic needs (life fulfillment state)
MONEY	**CONCERNED PARENTS** People pursuing money to achieve long-term security in meeting basic needs.	**SQUIRRELS** People mistaking means for ends, failing to shift away from money as the object of pursuit.
LIFE FULFILMENT	People pursuing well-being even if they lack money to provide security over meeting basic needs. **MONKS**	People seeing money only as a means to achieve happiness & life fulfillment. **EXPLORERS**

*(vertical axis label: **MAIN OBJECT OF PURSUIT**)*

Exhibit 4: Segmentation of people based on money availability, and object of pursuit

What makes someone a Squirrel? Why do Squirrels continue seeking more and more, even when they already have so much they don't even have time to spend it? While I believe much of this is due to cognitive biases that may unconsciously lead us astray, I will not dwell on this topic, as it goes beyond the scope of this book.

Squirrels are a minority, even in high-income countries like the United States. And it is not up to society or governments to sort out their lives. They have the opportunity to pursue happiness and life fulfillment. My priority and the purpose of this book is mostly to help those who don't. What is relevant for us is knowing that Squirrels exist, and society should ensure that the will to accumulate for some does not disrupt society for others.

THE WORLD OF CONCERNED PARENTS

Who has enough time to dedicate oneself to the pursuit of life fulfillment over financial security? State 1 is in some sense a subjective concept, but hard facts should convince you that too many people are in it and struggling to get to State 2. We'll look at high-income countries, since we have more data about them; if most of their residents are in State 1, most of the rest of the planet is too.

Let us start with poverty. Countries in the Organization for Economic Cooperation and Development (OECD) are the most developed in the world, and the OECD defines poverty based on income. As of November 2020, OECD reported the impoverished made up between 5% and 27% of their populations. In most OECD countries the figure is between 10% and 20%. Italy is at 14%, and the US at 18%.[5] We are talking about nations with the greatest prosperity in history and yet more than almost one in five people are fighting to obtain the fundamentals. If we were to look globally and take an income threshold slightly higher than the $1.90 a day of extreme poverty, almost half of the world is poor, living on less than $5.50 a day.[6]

What about the peace of mind from being able to comfortably meet physiological needs in the future? Or better yet, assume you were to lose your job. Would you be in a condition to comfortably meet basic needs in the future? Unfortunately, statistics are hard to come by, since we lack a common definition of "comfortably meeting basic needs should you become jobless." It would depend on many factors, but four are probably the most important: 1) the average accumulated wealth, 2) the time needed to find another job, 3) government safety nets, and 4) subjective expectations for the future. Let's start with the average accumulated wealth, where we have easily comparable data across countries.

Credit Suisse publishes global wealth data every year. I refer to 2019 data, before COVID-19 affected people's wealth. By 2019, more than a decade of growth has occurred after the 2008–09 recession and the stock market is at its highest ever; if anything, the 2019 picture looks rosier than it really is. The following chart represents the percentage of people who have total wealth, including the value of their house, below $10K and $100K, two of the thresholds that Credit Suisse reports.

At a global level, 57% of adults have less than $10,000, and 89% have less than $100,000. Even in North America and Europe, the percentage of people with less than $100,000 (including house value) is around 60% and 70%, respectively, and it is above 90% in every other region of the world.

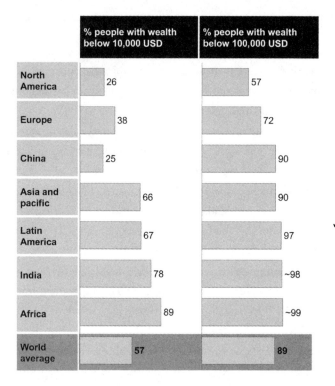

Exhibit 5: Share of population with total wealth (financial and nonfinancial) below 10,000 USD and 100,000 USD based on Credit Suisse global wealth databook 2019

It is not immediately easy to determine whether the $100,000 is a lot or a little, especially because wealth is something you accumulate over a lifetime. To a retiring US citizen, $100,000 may look like very little but quite a lot for a young European whose retirement is managed through public pensions. Nonetheless, when you consider that the value of housing is included in the $100,000, it is clear that this level of wealth is likely insufficient to allow people to sleep well at night if they lost their job. At any point in adulthood, you need a house to live in, ideally without forcing you to commute too far to work. And if you live in one of the main cities in North America or Europe, $100,000 is unlikely to get you a house. It may get you a mortgage at a bank to buy a house, but once you lose your job and cannot repay the installment loans, the bank will take your house away.

And if one is forced to sell their home to buy food or health insurance, that would not really feel like living above the comfort threshold, would it? If we strike out the value of the house, then the situation looks much worse.

A 2017 report from Bankrate found that about 60% of Americans lack enough savings to cover an unexpected expense of $500.[7] Another study by Bloomberg and New America concluded that a surprise expense of even $10 would cause 28% of respondents to worry.[8] That's less than the price of a movie ticket.

Such figures come at a time when conventional statistics suggest widespread prosperity. For instance, in November 2018, with the US unemployment rate the lowest in 49 years, a survey by the Center for Financial Services Innovation found that 47% of people spent as much or more than they earned, 36% couldn't pay all their bills on time, and 30% had more debt than they could handle. In addition, 16%—about one out of six Americans—had delayed seeking medical care because of debt.[9] The US Fed found similar figures in its 2018 well-being surveys, with 41% of Americans struggling to meet an unexpected $400 expense.[10]

We are talking about the biggest economy in the world and one of the wealthiest in income per capita. And the situations are only marginally better in Europe. In 2019, one in three people could not afford unexpected expenses in the EU.[11] If we consider wealth as the only source of security in case one lost their source of income, most of the world is stuck in State 1.

What about the other factors that could bring security: employability, government safety nets, and future expectations? Luckily, if we lose our job, we can still count on the economy yielding new job opportunities quickly, and the government providing unemployment benefits first and social assistance after (at least in most advanced economies). But this is only partly reassuring, given 1) our economy has proven very unstable; 2) youth unemployment is rising in many countries and AI is threatening to take even more jobs; 3) many new emerging jobs require new skills that people may not have the time, money, or even the confidence to learn; and 4) governments seem to be exhausting their ability to support the population, under the weight of high taxes and a large public debt. Proposals to cut social welfare programs such as the Affordable Care Act (Obamacare) are common in the US, while in Europe many crisis countries implemented austerity policies that harmed low-income people. Given these trends, the expectation for the future is far from reassuring.

The global financial crisis of 2008 brought widespread unemployment, especially among youth, and increasing poverty rates.[12] It also brought thousands to the desperation of taking their lives. Suicide rates in 2009 rose everywhere, increasing by up to 5% in some European countries and up to 7.5% in some US states.[13] Governments had to dig deep into their pockets to sustain people and the economy, but limited by their finances, some also took unpopular measures like cutting funds to social welfare programs.

Take a blender and put in low wealth, an unstable economy, automation, and government austerity. Mix together and you create insecurity. The COVID-19 pandemic has caused this situation to emerge again in 2020—and to accentuate its worst aspects.

Today in high-income countries, most people wonder whether they will keep their job (or find one), whether they can provide a good education and happy youth to their children, and whether they will afford a decent retirement when they get old. This is our reality.

If most people are in State 1, needing money and hoping for one of the few well-paid jobs able to secure a comfortable future for themselves and their families, how many will also find a way to live a fulfilling life?

People in State 2 can deal with their issues individually and have the comfort to pursue fulfillment, but for those in State 1 it's a different story. Each of us can work to move toward State 2, but the gains of some often mean the losses for others, and society should create the conditions to move *all* people above the comfort threshold. These conditions should be in place in a matter of years, not decades or centuries.

We have the resources and the technology to do this. We can ensure that every human comfortably meets basic needs. We can shift them up, but we just haven't managed to yet.

This book will not dwell on improving the aspects of our society that can make growth 0.X% higher or reduce poverty by 0.X%. Plenty of books and researchers are looking at the margins. This book is a quest to answer the question, Could we be missing out on the opportunity to leapfrog toward a society where everyone can shift to State 2?

Chapter 3

Universal Basic Income: Too Good to Be True?

*The evidence shows it works, yet right now
massive taxes would have to pay for it*

Can we solve this problem directly by raising the floor for everyone? By giving everyone a basic income, money every month in the bank account, to guarantee minimum security?

Observers have debated this proposal for decades and some have piloted and implemented it under the name *universal basic income* (UBI). A UBI program is a direct transfer of money to every citizen—wealthy and poor, employed and unemployed—in an amount that covers basic needs. It thereby guarantees everyone an equal right to health, shelter, food, and education.[1] These transfers are unconditional, meaning there are no restrictions on the use of the money and no requirements to get it other than being a living adult citizen. UBI would be a very direct way to ensure that all people reach State 2.

In fact, I defined the comfort threshold, State 2, not as a specific level of income or wealth, but rather as a condition in which people feel they can comfortably meet basic needs in the future, in line with Maslow's definition of safety needs. A UBI program gives everyone long-term security. It ensures they can cover their basic expenses and they can do so without having to work continuously in a paid job or possess accumulated wealth.

Two scholars trace the idea of UBI all the way back to St. Ambrose (c. 340–397 AD).[2] More recently, people of widely different backgrounds and political views have proposed UBI programs, including Martin Luther King Jr. and Bernie Sanders, in addition to Milton Friedman, the Adam Smith Institute, CEOs Elon Musk, Richard Branson, Mark Zuckerberg, Facebook's lesser known co-founder Chris Hughes (who launched the Economic Security Project centered on UBI), and many others. In high-income countries, UBI gained momentum in the early '70s when Republican US president Nixon tried to pass the program in Congress, and again after the 2008 crash with new pilots emerging in several high-income countries and in 2019 with Andrew Yang making it the centerpiece of his US presidential election campaign.

Yet almost no country has had the courage to actually implement this transformational program nationwide. Why?

ARGUMENTS FOR AND AGAINST UBI

Let's look at both sides of this debate and try to understand whether UBI is desirable and feasible.

The anti-UBI side, including both liberals and conservatives, makes these objections against it:

1. It would lead many people to stop working, impairing the ability of employers to hire employees. Too few workers would be an economic and social disaster.

2. Without work, people would lose a source of life fulfillment.

3. Recipients would spend the money unwisely, surfing and getting high all day.

4. Recipients would be free riding on those still working.

5. It would be unaffordable without confiscatory taxes on the wealthy.

UBI proponents, on the other hand, challenge each of these criticisms on the basis of morality and the real-world evidence.

Pilots of UBI programs abound in both low- and high-income countries.

However, most are limited in duration and scope, and only Alaska and Iran currently give income to all citizens for an unlimited time. In Alaska the amount varies depending on the return of its sovereign wealth fund, but it's typically below $2,000 per person per year. That's far from covering basic needs. Iran launched the only nationwide program that comes close to providing enough for basic needs. The amount was 29% of median household income at the start of the program ($1.50 a day per household, which in US prices would be $16,389.64 a year).[3] All other pilots in low-income countries have a narrow scope and typically offer low amounts.

Nonetheless, they all yield good insights into whether the objections to UBI are well-founded.

Objection 1: It would lead many people to stop working. The evidence says the opposite is true. In *Utopia for Realists,* Rutger Bregman does a comprehensive analysis of most previous UBI experiments and reports an "unmitigated success," noting some cases of statistical error and even forged data in attempts to cast doubt on a program that actually undermines the ability of capitalists to get cheap labor.[4] In *Basic Income,* Philippe Van Parijs and Yannick Vanderborght ran a similar analysis of past UBI experiments and reached similar conclusions.[5] Ioana Marinescu, an economist from the University of Chicago, assessed all programs in the US and Canada and concluded, "Our fear that people will quit their jobs *en masse* if provided with cash for free is false and misguided."[6]

Negative income tax (NIT) programs,[6] often designed to be economically equivalent to UBI, show similar results. The recent and broadly advertised experiment of UBI in Finland—focused on unemployed people and substituting a small portion of their unemployment benefits with a generous transfer of 560 euros per month[7]—showed a slight increase in the hours worked compared to a control group.[8]

In a few cases, pilot programs with significant transfers[8] have seen a noticeable reduction in average working hours. But the explanation is either external factors—such as the economic recession in Iran due to sanctions—or reasonable alternatives to work, such as extending education, caring for an elder or a newborn, or early retirement often linked to health conditions. There is a clear difference between people exiting the labor market permanently, which most policymakers rightly fear, and reducing the number of days they work per year. The latter is desirable in many circumstances. We will see how automation will continuously change the nature of work. Adult training will be a necessity and UBI pilots have increased the number of people going back to school. One UBI recipient in the Finnish experiment said that she "is less anxious because she no longer has to worry over calls from the job center offering a job she can't accept because she is caring for her elderly parents."[9] This woman has not left the labor market: She is actively caring for two people. Some UBI recipients spend more time looking for a better job fit and, as such, their average working hours decrease. They aren't exiting the labor market but trying to find a more satisfying job for the long term. Studies on lottery winners such as Win for Life in Belgium have added further evidence that people receiving free money do not just stop working, and only in a few understandable circumstances do they reduce their working hours.[10]

Pilot UBI programs in low-income countries also support the view that people keep working. Those who receive free money often work more rather than less. They increase their earnings, their assets, and their savings, and they spend money wisely on health and education for their kids. The cash gives them enough security to avoid striving for basic needs in inefficient ways.[11]

When I was in Swaziland assessing smallholder farming practices, I found that more than 40% of these farmers who planted maize for subsistence—often in patches of land too dry to grow it—ended up with less maize than they could have bought with the cost of inputs.[12] And that's not counting the time spent farming or trying to steal maize from commercial farmers or chasing animals as they fled fires in the cane fields. These are all examples of time poorly spent in the desperation of getting food. In UBI pilots, recipients avoid these types of waste and invest their time in starting small businesses—like producing bricks or baking bread—that lead to more value for them and society.[13] Programs have operated in villages in Kenya, Uganda, Namibia, India, and many other places. According to the Overseas Development Institute, most low-income countries now run unconditional cash-transfer pilots.[14] The amount per month is typically near the threshold of poverty set by those countries, around $10–$40, obviously a pittance compared to needs in a developed economy. Yet the positive impact of such small amounts of free cash is an eye-opener.

Objection 2: Without work, people would lose a source of life fulfillment. This argument is empty and often comes from labor unions. Their existence depends on people working, so it's understandable that they'd oppose a program that lets people live in dignity without working or working less. But the claim is self-contradictory. If people find life fulfillment through paid work, they will want to keep working even after receiving UBI. If a pursuit yields life fulfillment, you will do it even for free, as so many volunteers do.

Unfortunately, many of our current occupations provide negative life fulfillment. People often resent their jobs, but need them to access life requirements. As Rutger Bregman wrote for the World Economic Forum:

> In a 2013 survey of 12,000 professionals by the *Harvard Business Review*, half said they felt their job had no "meaning and significance" and an equal number were unable to relate to their company's mission, while another poll among 230,000 employees in 142 countries showed that only 13% of workers actually like their job. A recent poll among Brits revealed that as many as 37% think they have a job that is utterly useless. They have what anthropologist David Graeber refers to as "bullshit jobs."[15]

Another problem with this criticism is that even those few pilots showing a decrease in employment only showed recipients were working less or taking temporarily leave. People weren't leaving the workforce, but working two to four fewer weeks a year.[16] The rare cases of people leaving the labor markets, temporarily or through early retirement, required conscious choice given their circumstances. The woman caring for her elderly parents in the Finnish experiment made a conscious choice. It is hard to claim that such a free choice reduces her life fulfillment.

Objection 3: Recipients would spend the money unwisely, surfing and getting high all day. The old aristocracy and clerics have proffered a version of this disrespectful argument for centuries without evidence, which instead supports the exact opposite: People use basic income money wisely.[17] Yet these critics have been terrified by the idea that people could have leisure time, break the law, rebel against them, and even refuse to work for them. This last aspect is the most interesting one, and it opens a moral and philosophical question about freedom and free riding.

Objection 4: Recipients would be free riding on those still working. Critics holding this view often mention this as a limitation of freedom on the part of those working. UBI supporters and notable economists have a different view of who is a free rider. Some observe that the wealth of nations today is only possible thanks to the technological progress achieved by our previous generations. Since no one alive today could have accomplished much without previous progress, it is fair that everyone alive today receives a share of this common inheritance.[18] Universal basic income would represent such a share. According to this view, we are all free riders on our previous generations, and it would be unjust if the only beneficiaries are those directly leveraging those technologies in their businesses. Many economists consider rent-seeking—*extracting profits* without creating value in the process, a term originally coined for landlords collecting rents—a form of free riding. And as I will explain later, our socio-economic model includes a concept of *risk-free returns* that allows people with accumulated wealth to get money without doing anything at all. Is this not free riding?

And what about freedom? In a world where most people can meet only basic needs with their paid employment, are we not somehow slaves of employers? If employers needed employees as much as employees needed a job, the situation would be balanced. But people will do almost anything to feed their families while employers rarely become as desperate. One of the biggest justifications for labor unions is to level this imbalance. But what if jobs become too scarce? We may not need much human labor if automation replaces most occupations; in *The Rise of the Robots,* Martin Ford argues that it will happen soon. He also suggests UBI to replace the lost purchasing power. Artificial intelligence is not simply new technologies; it is new, automated employees.[19] Without UBI, all past technological progress would increasingly benefit just the few who can run their businesses with robots.

But let's not confuse friends with foes. Automation is a friend that, if combined with UBI, can free everyone. People can choose whether to engage in paid work, what type of work, and for how long, rather than having to take what's available to meet basic needs. As we've seen, job fitness correlates with job satisfaction more strongly than salary does, provided bills are paid. And with UBI, people can take more time to find the job that fits their skills and passions.

Robots can also make our lives better and longer, since they will surpass humans on a vast array of tasks. Self-driving cars and trucks could prevent thousands of deaths in car accidents. In health care, some 98,000 people die every year from medical errors in the US, many more than car accidents, AIDS, or breast cancer.[20] Artificial intelligence can reduce these mistakes in many areas.[21]

For this reason, I am very skeptical of proposals such as taxing robots (advanced by some) or inhibiting automation in any way. Why slow down progress? Why make people waste time and energy on tasks machines can do better?

Objection 5: It would be unaffordable without confiscatory taxes on the wealthy. The last charge against the UBI involves funding. Even if society could afford to produce more goods with fewer workers, we'd still need to find funding for a UBI. This is the obstacle that has prevented any country except Iran from fully implementing UBI. Iran and Alaska are singular cases, since both are rich in oil and can fund a UBI program, though, as I've explained, only a partial UBI in Alaska.[22] In Iran it's relatively larger but only because the cost of living is much lower than in any high-income country. What about the rest of the world?

UBI supporters claim a UBI program set at the country's poverty line would be affordable and could even pay for itself in high-income countries. The program is affordable if it is implemented as an NIT, where people receive the full UBI transfer if their income is below the poverty threshold, but only a portion (or nothing) if it is higher. Researchers at the University of Michigan ran such a simulation of the US for the year 2004.[23] Their analysis conservatively assumes an average reduction in earned income of 12.5% due to people working less, despite the limited evidence that they would. Depending on the minimum guaranteed income (75%–133% of the poverty line) and the rate of phasing out benefits for higher income levels, the cost varied between $112 billion and $635 billion (1%–5% of US GDP at the time). With the threshold at the US poverty line and benefits phased out for income higher than double the poverty line, the cost would be $219 billion, or 1.6% of US GDP. That's not cheap but it's affordable, especially considering that some current government programs, but not all, could be substituted by the NIT.

Bregman is even more aggressive. According to him, UBI paid to everyone would pay for itself. His view is certainly correct considering pilots in low-income countries, where people worked more if they received UBI, while in high-income countries one would have to make a few optimistic assumptions, such as that UBI would sufficiently increase overall spending and entrepreneurial activity. With them, we would see additional growth that could repay the UBI program in the long term. The Roosevelt Institute modeled the impact of UBI on the economy, and under some assumptions one could claim that UBI could repay itself with higher growth.[24]

Van Parijs and Vanderborght are more cautious and propose a partial basic income—one not enough to meet basic needs—which we can fund through certain taxes, including a tax on financial transactions or carbon dioxide emissions, or simply an increase in sales taxes.[25]

While my views overall align with the average supporter of UBI, they differ on two grounds: its affordability and its impact on employment.

WHO PAYS FOR UBI?

In today's economic system, a full UBI program would be hard to afford unless we raised significant taxes from the better off. While UBI could substitute for some but not all of current social transfers, and it could avoid the government-borne costs of means testing, these savings won't be enough. And even assuming that entrepreneurship and greater spending will increase economic growth and thus government revenues in the long term, we'd still need funding for it now, years before these benefits materialize. Since most governments are under continued pressure to reduce their high deficits and public debts, where will the new money come from?

An NIT program would be more affordable, but the cost of 1%–5% of GDP will have to come from somewhere, likely high-income and wealthy people. This is exactly the claim of UBI critics: UBI is only affordable by taxing the well-off.

Many support higher taxes on the wealthy. The International Monetary Fund (IMF) has suggested that a higher tax on the top 1% and potentially on wealth would have no negative impact on economic growth.[26] The IMF has also suggested that inequality actually decreases overall consumption[27] and, hence, a moderate redistribution would increase the potential for economic growth—a conclusion the OECD has also reached[28] and Nobel laureate Joseph Stiglitz has long asserted.[29] *The Economist* too has suggested increases in taxes,[30] given the rising inequality, public debts, and the consequences on economic growth.

I include myself among the supporters of higher taxes on the wealthy (at least when considering the limits of our current economic system), but as we'll see in the next section, it's hard to collect these taxes in a global economy.

Compared to UBI, the cheaper NIT program would also have a different overall meaning, and that's important. The NIT is a negative tax—a transfer to low-earning people at the end of the month or week, rather than a payment up front. The government could obviate this problem by anticipating the transfer needs and balancing any mismatch, but people's perception would still not be the same. Negative income tax is a help for those who cannot make it, while

UBI is the recognition that we live in a society where everyone has the right to have minimal basic needs taken care of.

And that brings me to my second divergence from typical UBI supporters: In spite of pilot results, I believe a UBI program will lead people to work less, and that's ultimately desirable. It is a feature, not a fault, of UBI.

UBI WOULD INCREASE OUR FREE TIME

There is a difference between a short-term pilot and a long-term policy. In short-term pilots, it is obvious that UBI will not significantly reduce working hours, let alone participation in the labor market. Pilot recipients won't risk losing jobs they might not get back when the pilot ends. Hence, pilots on short-term UBI programs can't yield sound evidence that people would keep working if they had a true UBI, one unlimited in time.

Of the longer pilot programs, Alaska's partial UBI transfers $2,000 or so annually, which can hardly cover basic needs. The same is true for the Cherokees who receive up to $8,000 a year as dividends from the casino run by their community. The pilot in Iran actually provides UBI, but it has only been active since 2011 and the study on its impact on labor force participation was done in 2012.[31] What is the likelihood of an Iranian citizen quitting work after a year in which their government has been giving every household $1.50 a day? Would you trust your own government enough to quit working? We hear about huge public debts every day. How can we trust governments' ability to give free money for life?

The studies on lottery winners are more promising. Some lotteries provide a monthly income for life rather than a lump sum, similar to a generous UBI and recipients keep working. Yet, they are the few lucky ones in a society where everyone needs to work. They feel much greater social pressure to work than people would in a society where everyone is receiving some free money.

Depending on the transfer amount, in the long term, UBI will certainly reduce the number of hours that individuals are willing to work over their lifetime. We may never have enough evidence to know for sure up front, but after 10 or 20 years of UBI transfers, more people will gain the confidence to work less or even quit altogether. Maybe they will take early retirement or shift to part-time or do voluntary work and spend more time with the family. That would significantly reduce the labor supply. But wait a second! Why would working less than 40 hours a week be a problem? It should be an objective. As automation increasingly does our work, UBI would let us take advantage of this unprecedented opportunity to do unpaid activities, be that leisure or social-useful work.

Automation-driven unemployment may not be immediately upon us, but it will surely come when we can build robots with the same capacities as humans. And that's just a matter of time. As we will discuss throughout the book, this future is already partly upon us. Since 2000, automation has become more labor-displacing than in the past.[32] Of course, people have been willing to accept lower salaries given the alternative of no income, and employment rates haven't materially decreased. But some employees are already forced into *in-work poverty:* They work full-time but their wages don't allow them to escape poverty.[33]

The researchers studying the Iranian UBI had similar thoughts: "But does the reduction in labor supply, if it occurs, represent a real loss of value to the economy? We doubt that many would consider an agricultural worker forced to work with hazardous pesticides without proper equipment quitting his or her job after receiving a cash transfer a bad outcome."[34]

With UBI, people would abandon the worst occupations first, and employers would indeed have to pay higher salaries or automate these horrible jobs. That's one huge benefit of a UBI program. It will ensure better working conditions and more free time to pursue happiness and life fulfillment (the whole point of life beyond the comfort threshold), which this book is hoping to enable.

And there is a multitude of positive side effects. For instance, UBI could speed up the arrival of *teal organizations*, which Frederic Laloux describes as organizations of largely independent teams that break new ground in self-management, wholeness, and evolutionary purpose, and promise greater job satisfaction, among other benefits.[35] Since people like working in them more, and these organizations even seem more productive, more people could just refuse to work in obsolete hierarchical and purely profit-driven companies.

A gradual introduction of a UBI program will be a core component of mon-etism, and I will come back to it often in the rest of the book. But I want to conclude here with a more philosophical argument on the morality of the UBI, or any program guaranteeing access to basic needs.

August 2016, Botswana—As nine hunters of the San tribe were returning to their families to cook meat from a successful hunt, gunfire from a police helicopter forced them to abandon their dead prey and run for their lives. These tribesmen were "arrested, stripped naked, beaten and then detained for several days for poaching in a nature reserve."[36]

For the good of society, governments assign land to varied uses and to private players. In Botswana, the government deemed a game reserve the best use of land, with one area where wealthy individuals could shoot animals for fun and another where mining companies could extract diamonds. While I'll refrain from judging any of these allocations themselves, I want to point out a hole in the morality of this situation: Society has limited these hunter–gatherers' freedom to life in a basic state of nature, so it must at least maintain their universal right to survive, and a UBI program represents such a right.

If you are not yet convinced about the merit of UBI, try to answer this question: Imagine you will be reborn on Earth 100 years from now and have no control whether you'll be a rich kid with access to education or a poor kid illegally hunting impalas for food. You can decide right now to buy insurance that guarantees you UBI and lets you survive without being chased by lions or police. Would you agree to some higher taxes to buy this insurance? For those believing in reincarnation, this question is not just a thought experiment.

Nonetheless, the main question remains unanswered: How do we sustainably fund a UBI program? Is it realistic to think that we can tax the wealthy? Or do we have to find another solution?

Chapter 4

Funding UBI in a Globalized and Unequal World: Piketty's Dilemma

The limitations and unreliability of taxes

UBI critics have a fair point: If we want to fund a UBI or even an NIT program, we would need to raise taxes. That's the way things work in our society. When there are issues that the private sector does not fix on its own, governments can raise taxes to solve them. As long as governments tackle the right issues, people would be willing to pay taxes. That's the theory. But does this work in practice?

The people below the comfort threshold are those we are trying to move above it. Taxing them would not be useful. We are therefore left with those above the comfort threshold. Can we convince them to accept higher taxes? And how should we tax this group, given some still have much more than others? And what about tax avoidance (loopholes) and tax evasion (illegalities)? Can we really rely on taxes to fund a UBI program that aims to bring everyone above the comfort threshold?

PIKETTY'S WORK ON INEQUALITY

In *Capital in the Twenty-First Century*, author and economist Thomas Piketty presented three centuries of data on income and wealth distribution mainly across eight countries. The results were unequivocal: Within any of these countries, income and wealth have always been concentrating, except for the period between World War I and 1980. Piketty observed that wealth has always grown faster than the economy itself, except during that period, which saw a massive destruction of wealth and far loftier taxes on the highest earners.

If society had begun with a rather equal distribution of wealth, high returns would not create wealth concentration, because those high returns would go to everyone in similar proportions. But wealth has always been concentrated since we've had statistics, indeed, since we've had history books. The ability of existing wealth to generate additional income without any work creates this perpetual accumulation. Therefore, Piketty's core thesis is that when the return on wealth (the income generated by wealth as a percentage of the value of wealth, such as 5% per year) is higher than the economic growth rate of a country (how much additional income is generated in a country, such as 3% per year), wealth tends to concentrate continuously.[1]

Even though the value society generates in one year is growing, year after year, the share going to wealth gets bigger and that going to labor shrinks. According to Piketty, this is true after accounting for taxes that reduce the value captured by wealth. This process has been reversed only through wars, economic crises, or political revolutions that confiscate most wealth, such as the French Revolution.

Piketty also shows that the future average return on wealth will likely continue to be higher than the economic growth rate. As a result, a capitalist economy will *by its very nature* breed high inequality—leading to a world in which inherited wealth plays a greater and greater role.

While there are some criticisms of Piketty's analysis, including a lack of identification of root causes such as why the return on wealth is always higher than economic growth (a topic we'll come back to), his main insight is valuable and clear: In the past three centuries, wealth and income have almost always flowed more and more to the top, and we are nowhere near solving this problem. We have actually reached inequality levels similar to those in Europe before World War I.[2]

SHOULD WE WORRY ABOUT INEQUALITY?

Is inequality an issue, though? One could argue that as long as everyone gets better, we shouldn't worry about it. Suppose everyone rises above the comfort threshold and can pursue life fulfillment. Who cares if some get much more than others in monetary terms? In truth, there are studies showing that inequality by itself makes a community less connected and causes other issues such as higher crime rates, more school dropouts, and lower life expectancy.[3] But those studies can't really assess a situation where everyone is above the comfort threshold, as no country can claim that achievement. The view that I take in this book—my opinion, given that we cannot have empirical evidence—is that inequality is a problem that governments should solve, to the extent that it prevents people below the comfort threshold from rising and staying safely above it.[4] And this is happening.

We can debate for decades on the right way to measure wealth concentration and whether it is right that the richest 1% own between 20% and 35% of wealth in any given country. But the big picture is clear: If existing wealth captures an increasing share of yearly income, it is likely that an increasing share of people is getting worse off and falling even further away from the comfort threshold.

Research seems to confirm this hypothesis. According to the McKinsey Global Institute, around a quarter of citizens in the G7 countries have seen declining after-tax inflation-adjusted incomes, mostly affecting those people employed in middle-wage jobs. And if it was not for taxes and transfers, we would have a lot more poverty. In France, for example, poverty rates would be almost 40% without taxes and transfers, while they stand below 10% with them.[5] But forget poverty; most people are still not above the comfort threshold and some are sinking instead of surfacing. It's only thanks to taxes and social transfers that we've contained the share of people getting poorer, and this fact is in strong support of Piketty's solution to his dilemma: a progressive tax on wealth, to compensate for the tendency to concentrate it.[6]

A progressive tax means that the tax rate increases as the tax object does. For example, people with higher incomes pay a higher tax rate. The same would be true for people with more wealth—that is, assets of all kinds. If you have three mansions, millions in your bank account, and several financial assets, your tax rate on wealth will be higher than those owning just two apartments and a few hundred thousand in savings, and most people with limited wealth—let's say a house and some savings—would pay no taxes on it at all.

THE PROBLEM WITH TAXES

With such a tax, the government could redistribute wealth to the rest of the population. An efficient way would be through a UBI program. But is this approach feasible? Piketty himself observed that since money and people can freely circulate among countries, any country enacting such a tax would risk an outflow of money, people, and companies to other locations.[7]

The case was different in the 1950s and 1960s. If you think taxes are high today, consider that in 1960 the US tax rate for those with yearly incomes above $400,000 was 91%.[8] In the rest of the developed world, taxes on the highest income brackets were also in the 55%–90% range until the 1980s.[9] Economies at that time were growing briskly without wealth concentration. Yet high taxes on the wealthy may be off the table in a global economy. Indeed, moving wealth has become much easier with electronic money, and the practice is widespread. An estimated 10% of global wealth is parked in tax havens, half of which belongs to people with $50 million or more, or the richest 0.01%.[10]

Even without considering tax havens, international competition to attract companies and talents have caused tax rates to fall year after year. The Trump administration is only the most recent among 17 of the G20 countries to cut corporate tax rates since the mid-1990s.[11] Christine Lagarde, head of the IMF at the time, was rightly concerned that this behavior could trigger a "race to the bottom" and keep governments from collecting the funds they need for public services.[12]

Piketty's suggestion was for a global progressive tax on wealth—one where people are taxed based on all the wealth they possess, financial and physical, irrespective of where they move their financial wealth. Those who have a yacht in the Caribbean, three houses in the US, and financial wealth across multiple countries would incur a tax rate based on all these possessions. Piketty himself suggests that we would need an international agreement on global taxation, which he deems utopic.[13] Piketty's global tax on global wealth, collected by some undefined global authority and then somehow redistributed to countries, is indeed highly unlikely in the foreseeable future. Yet we can achieve less ambitious but still useful versions of it, and, as Piketty himself suggests, we *should* pursue these.

The most workable wealth tax is one on physical assets that cannot cross borders, and many countries already use it. Taxing real estate and land of value above a certain threshold (perhaps excluding one house per household) would both redistribute money and give people reason not to own second houses that they leave empty and land they keep idle.[14] In fact, people owning multiple houses and land would have to rent them out or use them to generate returns in order to cover wealth taxes. In a world with finite physical resources, those who own them should have the motivation to use or sell them, rather than letting them sit there.

One implication of this tax is that the prices of these physical assets may decrease. As we will see throughout this book, lowered prices of land and houses would help the majority of the people who pay rent and limit the rent-seeking behaviors of landlords. As Winston Churchill famously said, "Roads are made, streets are made, services are improved, electric light turns night into day, water is brought from reservoirs a hundred miles off in the mountains—and all the while the landlord sits still."[15]

Beyond taxing physical wealth, we should not rule out some international collaboration on taxation. The world is intensely globalized and, except for the unfortunate momentary drift of the US under Trump, international collaboration has been increasing. The Agreements of Montreal (banning ozone-depleting substances) and Paris (limiting global warming) are just two examples. Another is the decline of bank secrecy, which had been a way for many countries to attract unlawful money and offered wealthy people a safe haven for hiding their wealth from tax authorities.

While not easy, there are ways to raise more money through taxes from people with high wealth. For the EU, Piketty estimates that a tax on wealth of up to 2%, depending on wealth level, would yield about 2% of GDP per year.[16] It could fund a partial UBI if implemented as a negative income tax (NIT). Governments could raise tax rates in the future if automation takes more jobs and wealth grows even more concentrated, thus funding a more generous UBI.

WE CANNOT HOPE FOR HIGHER TAXES TO BE A SILVER BULLET

While higher taxation of the wealthy is indeed an economic solution to both inequality and a good step toward funding a UBI program, its political feasibility makes this solution unreliable, in my opinion. We just cannot consider taxing the wealthy the silver bullet that will fix all society's problems, or even fund a UBI program. We need a plan A, while pursuing higher taxes as a plan B. There are several reasons why.

First: Everyone hates taxes. You don't get elected by advocating higher taxes. Even assuming a Bernie Sanders–type politician became president, wealthy people would always find a way to avoid taxes. The creativity of tax accountants will always outrun that of policymakers. An example: In 2014 in the US alone, $3.2 billion of tax deductions were granted to over 3,000 wealthy taxpayers as they donated land for conservation purposes. Donald Trump was one of these and much of the land in question was land around his own property that would secure higher privacy and a higher evaluation for this property.[17]

Second: Even assuming society manages to tax some of the wealth or raise the top income tax rates to around the level of the 1950s, wealthy people will find a way to reverse those policies. Their money will still have influence and that will affect politicians who will ultimately find a scheme to turn off progressive wealth taxes. We will see in upcoming chapters that the economic theory that became mainstream in the 1980s and led to slashing taxes was not born out of independent debate among scholars. For example, Nobel laureate Paul Krugman assessed the effective tax rate of the top 400 earners in the US. His findings? Thanks to political negotiations, the tax rate on capital gains was lowered to 15%, hence the richest people in the US paid less than 20% in income tax, a rate lower than that paid by Americans who earn their income through hard labor. More recently, Emmanuel Macron was elected president with the promise of making tax cuts a priority. First, he reversed most taxes on wealth and then proposed to reduce income taxes, which had earlier led several wealthy French businesspeople to leave the country to avoid them.[18] If France, the symbol of égalité, *fraternité, liberté* is cutting taxes, is there really a hope for taxes to be the source of a UBI program?

Third and perhaps most importantly, the money we collect in taxes will be barely enough to sustain the continuously increasing need for government spending. In OECD countries for which we have data, yearly government spending has risen from 29% of GDP in 1970 to 43% in 2010. To fund these expenses, governments should have raised the tax rates, but as we have seen, they have done the opposite. This explains why in the G20, public debts increased from the low of 27% of GDP in 1973 to 40% after the two oil shocks to 64% before the 2008 financial crash, all the way to over 90% in 2016.[19] The COVID-19 crisis will further increase public debts.

There are massive spending gaps right now and more coming in the future. As we will see throughout the book, governments are often the only players that can pick up the tab and pay. For instance, they are the only ones that can pursue many infrastructure projects. And many social needs are becoming more expensive, such as environmental cleanup, basic research, better quality of public education, the increased costs of an aging population, costs to reskill the labor force as automation changes the nature of jobs, and many more. At the same time, financial and economic crises take tolls on governments and we are in an economic system offering about one crisis per decade.

In a nutshell, governments will need an ever-increasing amount of money, yet taxing the wealthy is difficult and hard to sustain. But where else can governments turn? If they cannot significantly increase taxes on the wealthy, where will they get the money?

This is a serious issue, not just to *go forward* and fund a UBI, but even to *not fall backward* and maintain the services like public health and education that most people enjoy. Privatization of these services has fared poorly in the US, which faces the highest health care and education costs among the high-income countries, with poor average outcomes. For example, according to the World Health Organization (WHO), life expectancy in the US is one year less than in Costa Rica or Chile, and half a year less than in Cuba.[20] The high cost of healthcare has a domino effect: Because people can't afford to see a doctor, they may go to work sick; they may miss out on early diagnoses; they might forgo life-saving treatments; or they could even go bankrupt trying to pay medical bills—and endanger their family's welfare.

To better grasp the nature and scale of these issues, we need to address how our capitalist socio-economic system works. Piketty, Bregman, and many others have shed light on important issues, built the case for change, and proposed transformational solutions. But if I were running a government, I would still try to answer the same old question: How can I get the necessary money in a sustainable way?

Given this is the practical question that governments have to answer, let us start our journey into understanding capitalism from its inseparable companion.

II.

MONEY

We use money every day in person to buy groceries and movie tickets, and online to pay for subscriptions like Netflix and shift money across accounts. But what is money? Where does it come from? Most people don't know and the answers are surprising to them. More broadly, how does the overall supply of money matter to all of us and how do we regulate it? We hear of central banks and control of interest rates all the time, and they too have important aspects most people don't realize. Some say money is for us like water is for fish. A fish depends on water but doesn't know how it comes into existence. It doesn't understand how evaporation and winds and rains and rivers renew its mineral properties. Or how its chemistry allows for a continuous creation and destruction of water molecules when oxygen and hydrogen meet or part. Money holds similar mysteries for us.

Chapter 5

The Tennis Game of Money

A history of changing money theories

Where does money come from? We deal with it every day, yet if you can't answer this question, don't be ashamed. In one 2017 survey, 85% of the members of the British Parliament couldn't either.[1] Money is so embedded in our day-to-day life that we take it as a given. There is money, we see it all the time, and we'd rather have more than less. But its nature is hard to discern. It helps to consider a brief history of this intriguing item.

THE BIRTH OF MONEY

Travel to the last absolute monarchy in Africa, Swaziland, and you take a voyage back in time. The king assigns land to chiefs, who assign a plot to every male Swazi once he is old enough to set up a family and farm the food they need. A father would pay the dowry for his bride in the prevailing form of wealth: cows. But with epidemic after epidemic, most Swazis grew tired of having their wealth wiped out. They needed a better way to hold and trade their wealth.

Money has always had three functions—1) it makes exchanges easier, 2) it's better at storing wealth, and 3) it's numerical, so it naturally quantifies value.

With money, we don't need to trade chickens for cherries, nor do we need to keep tabs on who owes what to whom, increasingly difficult as communities give way to cities.[2] And we can afford to build savings in a form that doesn't perish. In the search for the right object to function as money, we went through salt, rocks, cowry shells, and ultimately settled with metal coins, banknotes, and more recently electronic digits. But the evolution of money was neither painless nor linear, and I will argue it wasn't conscious or strategic either. It was and it still is rather messy.

THE VOLLEY BETWEEN *REAL* AND *INCENTIVE* MONEY

It was one of those decisions that you don't make on the spur of the moment. The kind of decision that keeps you up at night. For the president of the United States, this was a decision that would dramatically change the world in unpredictable ways, as he was about to open a Pandora's box.

In August 1971, President Nixon announced this momentous decision: "I have directed Secretary [John B.] Connally to suspend temporarily the convertibility of the dollar into gold." Nixon knew the issue was more complex than most people would understand, but he kept his comments brief. He explained a key consequence of this decision in this way: "If you want to buy a foreign car or take a trip abroad, market conditions may cause your dollars to buy slightly less."[3]

But the full consequences went much deeper than most economists understood at the time. To this day, that decision gives us both massive issues and massive opportunities.

Nixon's act was only one stroke—neither first nor last—of an endless tennis game, played by two historical opponents. On one side are those who think of money as a symbol of *real* resources. As such, we must limit it to match those finite resources. Hence, if we tie the value of money to gold, we restrict the amount of it in society. I call this view *the side of constraint*.

Opposing it are those who see money as an incentive to take an action, to produce goods and services. Proponents of this view say we shouldn't tie the value of money to physical assets, and its amount should be as high as needed to get people to produce the most for society. I call this view *the side of incentives*.

The best argument on the side of constraint is that, if money is not tied to a physical resource, it will have no credibility and hence lose value. Its purchasing power will decrease due to inflation. The best argument of the side of incentives is that, since an economy continuously grows, constraining the amount of money would just limit our chances to increase prosperity.

This game has not been played on a sunny tennis court with an umpire. Global wars and economic crises have so far determined the points of this contest. One hope of this book is to influence the next stroke of this money game, and to do it painlessly. But first let us see how the game has played out so far and why it matters to us today.

The contest has taken place in many countries separately, ultimately converging in one big global tennis game. I believe an instructive example at the country level is that of Germany.

WEIMAR GERMANY—WORLD WAR I

The side of constraint was serving the ball toward the end of the 19th century. Money was firmly tied to gold at a fixed value. Then World War I erupted and the German government borrowed a significant amount of money to finance it. The government simply did not have enough gold to pay all the people who needed to be convinced to go to war. The Germans figured they'd beat France quickly, as they had in the Franco-Prussian War of 1870–71, and use France's gold to repay the debts.[4]

As you may know, this plan went awry. The war went on and on, and by the end of it, interest on the debt was four times Germany's total revenue in 1913. With no gold, the German government couldn't raise taxes and toward the end of World War I it resorted to printing money to finance its expenses. Paper money was the only way to finance the activities that Germany needed to run its daily life and an ongoing war. With this decision, the ball was now back to the side of the incentives. Money was the incentive for people to go to war and Germany printed as much as it needed.

But war is a highly unproductive activity, especially when you lose. The credibility and value of Germany's Deutsche Mark (DM) started to weaken in 1919, but the catastrophe occurred between 1921 and 1923. France and Belgium believed Germany could in fact afford war repayments and invaded the Ruhr region, Germany's most productive region. The Weimar Republic reacted by supporting a strike among the workers: No one in the Ruhr was to cooperate with the invaders.[5] But a much lower production combined with an ongoing need for goods and services is a recipe for the disaster called inflation. When goods and services become scarcer, prices normally rise. It's the law of supply and demand. In this case, the Weimar Republic now had to import the coal that the Ruhr had stopped producing and had to pay striking workers to ensure their cooperation.

The solution for the Weimer Republic was to set money printers at full speed. The flood of cash shattered the already weak credibility of the currency, sending the price of goods skyrocketing and making Germany's currency worthless. In 1913, the total currency in Germany was 6 billion DM. By November 1923, you needed a thousand times that amount—6,000 billion DM—to buy a loaf of bread in Berlin.[6]

The field was ready for the ball to volley back to the side of constraint. In November 1923, the DM was pegged to the US dollar and to gold. The policy of passive resistance in the Ruhr and the payments to striking workers stopped and Germany was granted a renegotiation of war payments. At this point, the ratio of gold to paper money did not have to be one-to-one. According to the banking act in the reparation plans of 1924, Germany had to keep an amount of its gold equal to 40% of the value of its notes.

THE LOVE FOR GOLD AND THE GREAT DEPRESSION

But the ball did not stay there long. The world at the time was obsessed with gold. The United States owned most of it and France and England wanted to increase their holdings. The only way to do so in a peaceful way was to run a surplus by increasing exports. Commonly, nations boost their exports by devaluing their currency, making their goods cheaper for other countries, which then buy more. But Germany couldn't do so, since it had pegged the mark to gold. Therefore, it required a reduction in local prices: deflation. Unfortunately, the US was reducing local prices too, and the whole world fell into the spiral of deflation by 1929.

A deflation spiral is dangerous for two primary reasons: It makes public debts impossible to repay—as with negative inflation, the real value of previous debts increases—and it curbs companies' abilities to make profits, and thus reduces production and breeds widespread unemployment. Between 1929 and 1932, Germany slashed the amount of money circulating (from now on referred to as *money supply*) by about 30% in an attempt to cut prices, and prices responded to this policy. Yearly inflation went negative by as much as 11% in 1932. But the real value[1] of production also fell. Unemployment rose as high as 28% in the same year. This was a major lesson, which John Maynard Keynes reminded society: The money supply has to grow to sustain a growing economy.

The supply of money and the size of the economy are tied together with a rope, like two climbers going up a mountain. You can't have one going down and one up at the same time. Soon, the tension in the rope forces the two climbers to move in the same direction. It is the same with the economy. And while it is true that the same money can pass hands multiple times in a day—and if it moves faster it yields more exchanges with the same amount—the speed of circulation cannot increase indefinitely and, in fact, its variation is relatively contained.[7]

Many people blame the length of the Great Depression of 1929 on the failure of central banks to create more money, a decision linked to the belief that the money supply required a strict relation to the gold supply. In the midst of the crisis, most countries realized they had to break this tie, as it was causing unnecessary rigidity, similar to the post-2009 crisis austerity rules in Europe. When in 1933–34 Franklin Roosevelt decided to shift the value of gold from $20 to $35 per ounce, he made many more dollars available for the economy and gave the economy its most significant monetary stimulus. And it worked, not only in the immediate aftermath, but also for the next four decades in which we had far more gold than the equivalent value in dollars, and we could keep increasing the money supply while holding the peg with gold.

The ball was again flying toward the side of incentives, and a well-known player used every last bit of this money flexibility.

HITLER AT THE PRINTING PRESS—WORLD WAR II

Adolf Hitler did not know what he was doing. He historically gave very little importance to economics, whose priority he had to revisit when he became chancellor. He started printing money and a similar form of money called IOUs

---

1   Real value is the *nominal* value of production (that is, at the current price tag) discounted by the inflation rate. Real values are much more illuminating. If you make one loaf of bread and sell it for $10, your value of production is $10. If because of inflation next year you sell the same loaf of bread for $15, the nominal value of production is $15, but the real value of production is still $10. Inflation makes the nominal value seem greater.

(similar to short-term government bonds but printed on paper so they could be exchanged by people as if they were money) and used it to finance social spending, as well as rearmament. The Nazis' social welfare, which included 8,000 day-nurseries, holiday homes, food for large families, old-age insurance, and much more,[8] was one reason people supported Hitler throughout his craziness.

We can summarize his economic policies in one paragraph:

If people can produce, let's give them the incentive to produce and the social security to do so. And since the rest of the world is taking advantage of Germany, we have to build the strongest army and be independent from foreign imports. It will be Germany first, Germany on its own.

Unfortunately for the world, the first part of this policy was highly successful, enabling Hitler to afford the second part: Germany first. Unemployment was basically extinct by 1938. The level of production rose almost 10% per year, and wages increased as well.

After 1939, we all know what happened.

POST-WWII MONETARY ORDER

The horror of World War II was so intense that all countries were predisposed to prevent such an event from ever happening again. One of the root causes was the 1929 economic collapse, which was linked to a flawed international monetary system. But the world had not yet realized that tying money with gold was a problem, and after most countries had broken the tie during WWII, they were now eager to create some sort of order. The gold standard had always been attractive in a world with international trade. Different countries were using different types of money, and distrust of foreign governments' abilities to manage money hindered international trade.

But gold is gold everywhere; government policy can't change its chemistry. The gold standard was the solution to mistrust of monetary policies of other countries. Nations had long held a monetary system with the value of money of different countries (*currencies* from now on) pegged to the value of gold. During times of instability, like wars or economic crises, nations often dropped the gold standard, but typically reinstated it afterward in this ongoing tennis game.

And toward the end of WWII, the ball was about to go back toward the side of constraint.

In 1944, delegates from 44 allied nations spent three weeks at a hotel in

Bretton Woods, New Hampshire, where they negotiated a new global monetary order. It was a system in which the US ensured the convertibility of gold and the US dollar at a set rate. All other countries were to maintain their exchange rate to the dollar within a 1% range, and participants set up the International Monetary Fund (IMF) to give temporary aid to countries unable to meet their obligations. One of the key ideas was that no country should have to impose the kind of hardship on its people that could get politicians from extremist parties elected. Based on the value of gold chosen, the US had enough gold to support the belief that it could back any number of US dollars.

The constraint on money was therefore quite loose in 1944. You can think of this passage as a high lob, with the ball taking a lot of time to cross the net and enter the side of constraint. But ultimately, it did. As decades passed and economies grew, the hidden constraint surfaced and the money supply exceeded the ability of the US to back all the dollars in circulation with gold.

Furthermore, the US was printing dollars to fund foreign aid first and the Vietnam War after,[9] neither of which produced any good or service for the US. Inflation rose. In parallel, the world now depended less on US exports than after World War II, when most other advanced economies were in shambles. Nations started to need other currencies to trade with each other. There were just too many US dollars in the world and countries started asking for gold, weakening the ability of the US to further expand the money supply.

We were fully back to the side of constraint at this point. But rather than forcing unnecessary hardship on people to maintain the exchange rate between gold and the dollar, Nixon simply slammed the ball back to the side of incentives. With his announcement in August 1971, the gold standard fell. Currencies were now free to float against each other and money lost any intrinsic value. *Fiat money* is the term to describe such money. Its value depends on the willingness of all players in society—consumers, producers, governments—to accept the money as payment. Nixon avoided putting hardship on the public, but he compromised the credibility of the currency, which did not help in the fight against inflation.

GOOD RIDDANCE

Sometimes you still hear people say that we should go back to the gold standard. But I have yet to hear any well-informed and logical argument to support this. Given we are in societies with growing populations, growing accumulation of

wealth, and growing economic activity, the amount of money to enable all this
also has to grow. Not by the speed at which people find and dig gold from the
mines, but at the rate that the economy needs, which depends on many factors
but not on gold mining.

The only alternative to growth without more money is for the price of goods
and services to fall so we can buy more with the same amount of money. But
this is one reason the 1929 crisis happened.[10]

This passage from *The End of Alchemy* by Mervyn King, former governor
of the Bank of England, well conveys the need to increase the supply of money
and the "barbarous" consequences of hewing to the gold standard:

> The commitment to gold was seen as a battle between bankers
> and financial interests, on the one hand, and the working peo-
> ple, on the other hand. Never was this expressed so forcefully as
> by William Jennings Bryan, the three-time losing Democratic
> presidential candidate who concluded his speech to the party
> convention in 1896 with the words "you shall not crucify man-
> kind upon a cross of gold."
>
> Keynes's famous description of gold as "a barbarous relic"
> was apposite. What was especially "barbarous" was the decision
> in the 1920s to impose substantial deflation on economies in
> order to go back to the gold standard at the same parities as
> existed before the First World War.[11]

The need to increase the money supply has been the ultimate driver for
abandoning the gold standard, first during the Great Depression and then definitely with Nixon. The reason is obvious: If we want growth, why should we be
held back by the amount of a rare physical asset, whose availability has nothing
to do with our capacity to produce?

Tying the money supply to any multiple of the amount of gold created a
massive limitation. The success between 1944 and 1971 was only due to the
decision to set the price of gold high enough that the US had much more gold
than the corresponding value of US dollars. The tie was loose, and the government could increase US dollars as the economy needed them. That was
no longer true by 1971, and Nixon finally put an end to the nonsense of the
gold standard.

What is money today, then?

REDEFINING MONEY

Gold has nothing to do with it anymore and it is not even a form of payment. If you went around town and tried to pay with gold, people would think that you had either robbed a bank or were trying to fool them with fake gold.

The decoupling of money from any physical asset has made money increasingly immaterial. Its value arises from our acceptance of it as a form of payment, our belief that everyone will accept it in exchange for goods and services we need. But this is just an intrinsic property of money. When gold was money, its value rested on exactly the same belief. If you imagine a world where everyone disliked a shiny yellow metal and couldn't imagine a use for it, gold would have not only ceased to be money but also would have been worthless. Today, as in the past, money is whatever we all routinely accept as payment, and as long as people will exchange goods and services for, let's say, dollars, dollars are money.

Those defending the gold standard are probably quite confused by the evolution of money. Banknotes used to be just a claim for a certain amount of gold. They were the symbol of a credit or debit, depending on your point of view. Now there is no more gold. But we still have notes—dollar bills and pound notes. What exactly are they claims for? Perhaps my definition of money will answer this:

> **Money:** the human convention that allows people offering goods, services, time, and energy to receive a recognition for what they are offering—a form of "thank you"—and to accumulate that recognition to claim something in return in the future. Since material resources are finite while we want to generate infinite reciprocal recognition, fiat money is one of the best inventions of humanity.

While I certainly don't want to imply that money is the only way to give recognition, it is the most universally accepted form of it. The confusion over the concept of money derives from anchoring on what money used to be: a physical object. That idea was stupid enough to lead people to risk their lives in the quest of gold. It was stupid enough to make people kill each other in wars for gold.

The ignorance of humanity in taking such a rare object as the predominant means of payment has led to centuries of wars and zero-sum games in which you and your neighbor cannot both have enough gold at the same time. The world was trapped in a curse in which only few could benefit at the same time, while the rest could only hope for the fall of the few.

Luckily, today no credible economist and only a few politicians propose a return to a system that ties the money supply to a limited physical resource. We don't seriously debate the nature of money, but rather how best to manage its creation and allocation.

And this was the task at hand for those economists who had the ears of politicians and central bankers when the gold standard fell.

THE LAST SHOT OF THE GAME

Given the major shift in the nature of money, one would think that the last shot of the tennis game of money required a deep rethink of our monetary system. Instead of a reconsideration, however, money fell victim to the usual forces—short-termism and inertia—and we focused only on fixing the imminent threat of inflation with tweaks to the system already in place. Inflation in the US grew in the range of 6%–14% per year between 1973 and 1980, taking the center stage of most economic and political debates. Historically, inflation and unemployment had been inversely correlated. If one rises, the other falls. But in that period, both were rising, in what was called *stagflation*, although a double-digit inflation rate raised more concerns among economists than a single-digit unemployment rate. Economists were therefore focused on debating what was driving inflation, the main concern at the time.

Milton Friedman, an influential economist at that time, advanced an economic theory that people and markets were able to form accurate expectations for the future and behave accordingly in rational ways. The expectation of high inflation was therefore a self-fulfilling prophecy, as people would then ask for higher salaries and companies would raise prices to keep up with inflation. The only solution would be for the central banks to slash inflation, whatever the costs. Inflation was the imminent threat, and Friedman's theories and narrative convinced central bankers and politicians to tighten the money supply and slash inflation at all costs.

But how would money creation and management work, now that the gold standard had fallen? This was not really debated in depth. In summary, it continued pretty much in the same way as before the gold standard with only minor variations. No major rethink. And who was creating the most money at that time? Banks!

Privately owned commercial banks (*commercial banks* from now on) had been creating the majority of money since they started issuing banknotes. They created far more paper notes than they had gold in what is called *fractional reserve banking*, and they kept creating new notes whenever they gave loans. The monetary economist Allyn Young estimated back in 1924 that 85% of money in the US came from bank loans.[12] This did not change with the fall of the gold standard, although the Monetary Control Act of 1980 gave the Federal Reserve of the United States (the US central bank, the *Fed* from now on) more control over the ratios between banks' reserves and how much money they could create.[13]

The Fed had achieved statutory independence from the US Treasury back in 1951, although US presidents still maintained a significant influence on the Fed's monetary policy favoring employment over low inflation.

Government printing of money had been long dismissed as inflationary, although central banks routinely purchased government bonds to second the wishes of the presidents and prime ministers, thus keeping interest rates on government debts low. Year after year, governments could get more loans from central banks in the form of bonds, with interest rates often lower than inflation, a solution not much different than printing money. It is not an exaggeration to say that the monetary system post-gold standard was the same as before except for central banks, which really became independent from governments and focused on inflation.

The US was in the midst of the Cold War and free-market capitalism was at war with government-planned communism. It was indeed capitalism that implicitly took the last shot at the money ball. At the peak of society's love for the free markets, at the peak of the belief in the perfect rationality of market agents (i.e., people and companies), and at the peak of the fight against government involvement in the economy, we left most of money creation and management in the hands of free markets.

What does that mean? It means that commercial banks create money whenever an individual, company, or government wants a loan and is willing to pay an interest rate high enough to convince a bank to issue the loan and take the risk. The bank would therefore create money in the form of electronic deposits. Money springs into being from loans. It is part and parcel of credit.

And this was pretty much the end of the history of money (or at least every-one thought so until 2008). The tennis game ended with a draw. Money was no longer constrained by gold, but still limited through banks' lending policies and central banks' unwillingness to accommodate politicians' desires.

What happened in the 1980s after this change? Paul Volcker, the head of the Fed, defeated inflation. This act caused an economic recession, but his-tory tells of a short-term pain that slew the inflation monster and ensured the credibility of a fiat currency.

Central banks around the world—some sooner, some later—started pri-oritizing low inflation and emulated a monetary system similar to that of the US. And as for inflation, the system was an extreme success in keeping infla-tion low, which made money and monetary policies boring subjects. Mission accomplished by the heroes of the 1980s. Economists focused on other topics.

But wait. Not so fast. . . .

The financial crisis of 2008, protracted weak or even negative inflation (as in too low rather than too high), and the need to keep the economy alive dur-ing the COVID-19 pandemic reopened the Pandora's box of money. Could this eventually be the time to sit down and rethink the monetary system? And could the future of money enable funding a UBI program?

Chapter 6

How Money and Banks Work Today

How money springs out of nowhere, and why its creation
was tied to banks' credit

The next two chapters will require your full attention. We have looked at the history of money but only at a very superficial level. To keep going we need to get into the weeds, and I bet most of you will be puzzled by what we'll find.

We first need to understand how money and banks work today and the rationale behind keeping it that way (this chapter) and then x-ray this resulting monetary system to find any flaws that could open the door to a new way of managing money that could fund UBI (next chapter).

HOW CAN COMMERCIAL BANKS CREATE MONEY?

A bank, in the simplest terms, is a company in the business of storing people's wealth, providing deposits to make and receive payments, and deciding how much people and companies can borrow and at what prices. Banks were never designed to create money. The understanding that a growing economy needed a bigger money supply arose in the 20th century, while banking has been around for millennia and modern banking, depending on its definition, started between the 12th and 18th centuries. It just so happened that when the gold standard fell, banks were creating most money through their lending activities and we therefore built a monetary system around it.

Whether you know how a bank works or not, you might still be surprised that almost all money is created when banks issue loans. When a person gets a loan approved, a bank officer taps the keyboard and a deposit account arises—money out of thin air, or "fairy dust," as one economist called it after he actually went into a bank to see the process with his own eyes.[1] We can be more precise: Banks create deposits, not money, though borrowers use these deposits as money.

That money circulates in the world and may wind up in your paycheck, where it is, of course, not a loan. Because you deal with this non-loan money all the time, the fact that most money comes from loans may be a surprise to you.

The power of banks to manufacture money is nothing new. In fact, it lies at the heart of banking. Since their very early days, banks could already create money in the form of banknotes. They had some gold or silver, but international trade wasn't a thing, so even most borrowers would get bank notes to trade locally rather than physical metals. In fact, as these notes became generally accepted for payments, they acquired the same value as the corresponding amount of metal. It makes sense. If you can turn a paper note for 10 ounces of gold into 10 actual ounces of gold, the note is worth as much as the gold.

By issuing new notes, banks created money that people could spend or save, and if they simply printed money without the gold to back it up, no one could tell the difference. No one really knew if the amount of paper circulating was more or less than the amount of gold in banks. And no one cared, as long as they could use banknotes to buy what they needed and convert them into gold at will.

But if they doubted it, or some winds of war made an internationally recognized form of payment look attractive, they'd all rush back asking for their gold, in a *bank run*. Bank runs were, in fact, common, and since any commercial bank could print banknotes, the whole concept of money was in for a roller-coaster ride. One red flag was the discount at which the banknotes traded.[2] If a banknote was supposedly worth 10 ounces of gold, but people traded it at 2 ounces, it meant they assumed they only had a 20% chance of getting the 10 ounces.

Undoubtedly, many bankers made a lot of money at the time by just cashing in gold and printing paper. Before a bank would really run out of gold and declare bankruptcy, you can rest assured that some bank owners would have stashed some getaway gold under their mattress (or in another bank). Many of today's conspiracy theories on money are based on how old banks worked, which was indeed messy and unfair.

The instability of this system led governments to establish a monopoly over the issuance of banknotes, reducing the instability and the opportunistic behavior of bankers. Today, in every country, central banks are the only players allowed to print banknotes.

But the key role of commercial banks to create money has all but disappeared. If anything, it has increased with the move toward a cashless society. Over 90% of all the money supply comes from bank loans.[3] The ultimate source of your salary and your company's revenue is a debt of someone else. And every time you or someone pays off a loan, matter meets antimatter, money vanishes, and the money supply shrinks by that amount. Economists deemed this approach the most effective way to ensure that money creation gave people incentives to use money effectively and not just create inflation. And there is some sound logic behind this reasoning.

If you are not an economist, you might be surprised. Doesn't the central bank have a monopoly over money creation? Why can commercial banks create money through credit-debt agreements? And why can they create money with a few taps of the keyboard while I have to work all my life to gain a salary just to get by?

To make sure we avoid the common conspiracy theories, we need to better understand money and the current banking system.

THE RELATIONSHIP BETWEEN MONEY AND REAL STUFF

To understand and evaluate the logic of tying money with banks' credit, one needs to understand the tie between money and the real stuff that people and companies buy and sell. And to understand this tie we need to break down *stuff* into some more precise language. Terms such as goods and services, resources, technology, salary, income, capital, and wealth are not clear to most people, and some terms are even debated among economists; so, I will state one view and stick with it for the rest of the book.

Goods and services are what we as people demand to satisfy different needs and wants for our lives. They include a fantastic variety: pizza, apps, housecleaning, Christmas trees, and so on.

Resources and technology are terms I will often use as an umbrella term to include anything that is needed to produce a good or deliver a service. *Resources* are the physical components, which are typically somewhat limited: water, minerals, people, and so forth. *Technology* represents the knowledge to make the most of resources, be it embedded into a machine or into an organization model. I use resources and technology instead of *factors of production*, which is more often used in economics but less practical to be repeated in day-to-day life.[4] But the concept is the same: Resources and technology, or the four factors of production—land, labor, capital, and entrepreneurship—are what is needed to produce goods and services.

Salary, or wages, is an amount of money people receive in exchange for their work. It is the incentive that gets people to give up their free time for work.

Income is the overall amount of money that people receive from different sources, typically salary, returns on wealth (could be dividends or selling assets such as a house at a higher price than the original cost), and transfers to/from the government. This definition holds at the individual level but also at the national level, where we can define gross national income (GNI) as the sum of all income generated by the citizens. A related concept is the more well-known GDP, the value of production of goods and services of a country in one year.[5] We will come back to GDP; for now, let's just observe that a high GDP means that the nation's constituents are producing goods and services of a relatively high total value.

Wealth is anything that has a monetary value. The value can come from the income that the wealth can generate in the future, or the monetary value that anyone is willing to pay in exchange for the possession. Farm land or a company are valuable for the income they are expected to generate in the future, while a 1985 bottle of Dom Perignon is worth whatever a person is willing to buy it for. A good such as wine is also part of one's wealth until it is consumed, and this is how I convince my partner to let me stock up my cellar. Wealth at a country or global level tends to grow continuously, because each year we produce things that we do not consume: housing, infrastructure, companies' assets, art, and so on. As long as there are no wars or other devastating events, wealth keeps increasing.

Given we live in capitalism, what is capital? And what is the relationship between money and this stuff?

Contrary to common usage, capital and money are not the same thing. In fact, money is not even part of capital, at least in the sense capital had back when capitalism was conceived. The association of capital with money (or financial assets) probably stems from the use that Karl Marx made of capital. Throughout this book, I will use capital with the meaning that Adam Smith had in mind, that which many economists hold to this day: "*That part of a man's stock which he expects to afford him revenue.*" In plain English, it's any tangible asset that one can use to produce goods and services in the future. Think of a tractor to plow a farm or the robots building cars today, but also commercial buildings and residential houses, although they can only produce rent.[1]

This usage of the term differs from Thomas Piketty's. He treats capital and wealth as if they are identical. For his purposes, this choice may be better, since he wanted to show that the return on wealth concentrates it. But I will have to distinguish wealth, capital, and money.

Money is part of wealth, and it is the portion of financial wealth that is not invested in any asset but just kept in its liquid form: Cash or a deposit account at a bank. We keep liquidity mainly for three reasons: to buy things, to save and buy things in the future, or because we don't know where to better invest it. This is true for individuals, companies, banks, and governments. The rest of financial wealth includes shares, bonds, and other types of financial assets.[2] Economists often refer to money as *liquidity* due to our ability to swap it for almost anything else: a good, a service, bonds, stocks, land, capital, anything.

Here is where the concept of money gets complex. Money is both part of wealth, and what defines the value of all other components of wealth—including bonds and stocks—and all goods and services, through the free exchange of any of these for money. It's a loop. And managing money is therefore complex. If we had a very simple economy with a fixed population that only has one need satisfied by eating three apples a day, it would be quite easy to define an optimal amount of money and where the money should go: the production of a precise number of apples. But in a permanently growing economy, with a growing population with changing needs and growing accumulated wealth, managing money is complex.

To further complicate the situation, money needs to be created and allocated

---

1 If one thinks of banking, then money is capital for banks, as it provides a lending service in returns for interests, but let us focus on the real economy for now.

2 When we think of global wealth, bonds and credits are compensated by debts and net global wealth would not include them, but part of our individual wealth is any loans we have given or investments we have made in companies and governments.

before real people and companies actually put it to use. In fact, resources don't always come ready to use from nature. We have to extract (and possibly refine) minerals. We must convince human beings to work and educate or train them. We have to produce energy and distribute it where it is needed. We need to develop knowledge, communicate it, and, when needed, convert it into technologies and capital to produce goods and deliver services. Without money up front, we'd face the classic chicken-and-egg problem, as we wouldn't be able to persuade people to develop resources and turn them into goods and services. We always need an up-front investment to get all the resources together and start producing or delivering something, as most suppliers only get compensated after they have produced and sold.

Money represents that up-front incentive needed. It can transform the value of a certain product X that people will develop later, into an incentive that a company can distribute today to produce that very product X.

The laws that regulate the creation and allocation of money need to allow for people and companies to do at least three things: 1) to have the incentive to produce stuff that society needs that is of increasing value every year, where up-front investments are typically required, 2) to have enough money to exchange any previously accumulated wealth, which also grows year after year, and 3) to allow people to save as much money in liquid form as they desire, which fluctuates depending on saving preferences but also tends to grow with the size of the economy and the aging of the population.

All of this needs to happen without creating much inflation.

The questions that we as a society have implicitly tried to solve are these: Who manages money and how?

IF SOCIETY WERE A FAMILY

I am going to introduce an ongoing metaphor for our socio-economic system so it feels more familiar. Imagine our society is like a family. Let us say mom is the central bank and dad is the government.[6] The firstborn represents the system of commercial banks, and you, me, and the rest of the siblings are citizens. Who should manage money and how?

Besides people keeping tabs with each other, the predominant form of money throughout history, only three options have been tried at a national level, often co-existing. The first: governments mining metals and turning them into money. The second: banks creating banknotes or electronic deposits. The third: government printing money or money equivalents.

Back to our metaphor. Most of history has been like a motherless family (central banks weren't around), with the father sending all the children out to look for gold to turn into coins, and the firstborn (the bank) printing banknotes. But the children needed more money than they could find gold and the first-born was immature and greedy in creating and distributing banknotes. The family funds were very unstable and mistrust grew in the family, oftentimes ending in feuds (bank runs, hyperinflation). The family needed a mother, and societies found her when they created central banks.

I have mentioned central banks a few times. What are they? Central banks (or federal reserves or monetary authorities) have a monopoly on the creation of the national currency. For each currency, there is at most one central bank that decides monetary policy, and this is why in countries using the euro, some people complain about the loss of monetary sovereignty: their national central banks can no longer control the monetary policy of their own country and instead, the European Central Bank (ECB) decides it. This is equivalent to hav-ing the grandmother manage money for all the children and grandchildren. Some in-laws are likely to be unhappy.

At their birth, central banks were dependent on the government and through them, government could print as much money as they wanted. In the family metaphor, the family was very patriarchal. And as long as central banks depended on the government, money was often mismanaged, printed to finance wars and other nonproductive activities, and the result was inflation. Individuals still rule democratic governments and they have their own goals and short-term political pressures. When governments controlled monetary policy, they had a magic wand to build consensus: print money and give it to people through dif-ferent kinds of subsidies, or perhaps create jobs in the public sector to ensure full employment. One result was often lower productivity, higher inflation, and economic instability. It was the equivalent of a father loving his children to the point of wasting money on pampering and spoiling them, ultimately proving bad for their character.

Internationally, governments still fully own most central banks with few exceptions.[7] Whatever the shareholding mechanism, there are always strong mechanisms to guarantee the independence of central banks from their share-holders, protecting from both political pressure and private interests. This independence includes funding. It is in fact central banks that pay dividends to governments, and not government paying the salaries of central banks' employees.[8] And even when private shareholders own the central bank, most of the dividends go to the government.[9]

The central bank can also decide the *monetary policy*, a set of decisions aimed at making the right money supply available for the economy to function well. Functioning well means having enough money for economic activities to flourish, but not so much money that it destabilizes the economy with inflation. Even though the mandates of different central banks can put more or less emphasis on price stability, all central banks have the same tools and they use them similarly. They all try to *increase* the amount of money when the economy is *slow* (high unemployment and low growth), and *reduce* the amount of money when the economy is running *too fast* (low unemployment and increasing inflation). When central banks increase the amount of money, we say they're adopting an *expansionary monetary policy*; when they limit the money, they are pursuing *contractionary policies*.

While an expansionary policy can be reasonable to sustain economic growth and the growth of wealth, why would we ever want a contractionary monetary policy? The answer goes back to the risks of inflation, but also involves the fact that central banks don't have rigid control over the money supply. They can only exercise influence over commercial banks, which have the direct responsibility of creating money through credit when borrowers demand loans.

Commercial banks cannot issue their own notes, but they can continuously multiply deposits with no real limit, much beyond what the theory of fractional reserve banking suggests.

Suppose a commercial bank has $10,000. Assuming a common reserve requirement ratio of 10%, the bank can create loans for up to $100,000. This common textbook description is not accurate. The bank can borrow reserves from other banks or the central banks directly and lend even more, creating even more deposits. As the book *Modernising Money* shows, the fact that central banks are also the lenders of last resort means that a bank can create loans of even more than $100,000 and ask the central bank for a loan that would, in turn, create new reserves.[10] As long as commercial banks hold sufficient reserves, the central bank would print any money to meet any demand of depositors asking to convert their deposits in printed notes.

In summary, we stopped governments from creating money because they were too frugal, and we stopped tying money to gold because there was too little of it. But we have not looked for new options and just kept the only option that we did not consider a failure: commercial banks' creating money when giving loans, with some controls from an independent central bank. Is there any rationale to this or did we just not bother to think about different options?

WHY BANKS?

We need to be very clear that commercial banks can only create deposits, which are tied to loans. If a bank gives a loan to someone who is then incapable of paying it back, the bank does lose money. If you get a loan and the bank creates a deposit, when you use the money and withdraw cash (or send a transfer to someone else), your bank needs to come up with that money. And if you do not repay your loan, the banks will have lost the money. Because of this, banks do not just create as much money as people ask, but only do so if they think they will get the money bank, and they will charge interest on the loan for the risk they take on non-repayment. Banks' main tasks are in fact those of assessing the risk of people and companies asking for loans and deciding whether to lend and at what interest rate. With multiple banks doing this, we have a market with millions of people incentivized to *sell* loans and therefore create money for those who can repay it with sufficient interest for the banks to make a profit.

And how can people or companies repay money that they initially do not have? The answer is simple: Invest money into something that will yield more money in the future. The rationale for having banks take care of money creation is that it's the way that maximizes the value generated by that money, with *value* defined as whatever price people are willing to pay. If more money comes in than goes out, there is value creation that can repay banks' interests. This is the way capitalism works, and given we are in a capitalist society, money management has simply followed the theory of capitalism.

But as much as some economists wanted to believe markets are perfectly rational and self-regulating, we've already had a long history of banks' opportunism, greed, and extravagance, and therefore we gave central banks some control over what the banking system does.

HOLDING THE REINS

With private banks creating most of the money, it was evident that central banks had to have a firmer hold of the reins. Many regulations have been introduced throughout history to enable this and an important one was to separate banks that create money from banks that invest money. Imagine, as an owner of a bank, you can create deposits out of thin air and use that money to buy and sell companies, stocks, bonds, and so on. You basically have the power to swing those prices and to take ownership of companies. The power to speculate or to even influence economic decisions would be huge.

Regulations that are more central to money management are those that influence the value of loans banks can give. Without going into technicalities, it is important to understand that central banks operate their monetary policies by influencing interest rates at which commercial banks can get money,[11] which indirectly leads to changes in the value of loans they grant to their customers.

You can think of interest rates as the price of borrowing money. From the law of supply and demand, the higher the price, the lower the demand, and vice versa. So by moving interest rates up and down, central banks influence the demand for loans and subsequently the value of loans in the system and, finally, the money supply. If I lost you, here is an easy example.

Imagine the juiciest apples growing on a tree 10 miles from home. You want to run there to eat the apples, but you don't have enough energy to cover the distance. You also don't have any food. In fact, you would need to eat 10 apples in order to run 10 miles. However, when you make it to the tree, you can consume 10 apples to replenish your energy to run home and bring back 15 apples in your backpack. You love running and really want these apples, but you can't get started because you don't have the apples needed to make the first leg. Luckily for you, your neighbor has apples and can loan you the 10 apples you need. In return, he wants his apples back and an additional 6 apples for his efforts. Your neighbor is behaving like a bank, lending to you and charging interest. Your math is good enough to see that if you can only bring 15 back but must pay the 10 apples you received plus 6 for interest, you will lose on the deal, so you don't take it. If the interest rate was lower, let's say 3 apples and you really liked running, you would run 20 miles and overall gain 2 apples, so you'd take the loan. Your neighbor earns 3 apples and you earn 2 apples. You liked earning your apples, so once a week you take a loan and make the run. If the interest rate were even lower, let's say 1 apple, you might take the loan every day, run 20 miles a day, get very fit, and make 4 apples a day.

As you see, the lower the interest rate, the more money borrowed: zero in the first case, 10 apples a week in the second case, 10 apples a day in the third case.

It's useful to emphasize that no central bank makes the decision as to whether you want to run for the apples. It involves just the runner and the neighbor—essentially, the borrower and the commercial bank. Central banks only try to determine the interest rates at which commercial banks can receive loans (from the central bank or from other commercial banks).

When central banks want to boost the amount of money circulating in the economy, they cut interest rates. As these loans grow cheaper, commercial banks can either 1) reduce their own interest rates, which will attract more people seeking more loans, or 2) keep the interest rates high, and, with the higher margin, lend to riskier borrowers.[12] Since a higher loan volume means higher returns for commercial banks, cheaper lending to banks leads them to give out more loans, hence increasing the money supply.

When central banks want to shrink the money supply, they just have to raise interest rates. But here the trouble starts. As the money supply grows, people typically repay loans (interest rates are low and they can often get new loans to repay previous ones). But when the money supply shrinks, people and companies often can't repay (due to higher interest rates and more difficulty in getting new loans). Lack of repayment is called *default*, which leads people into desperate situations and companies into bankruptcy.

This is what happened in the 2008 financial crash.

Chapter 7

The Unsolved Money Puzzle

The gap between theory and reality and the
failure of the banking system

When the US economy crashed in 2008, Federal Reserve officials held urgent meetings to decide on a course of action. The minutes of these meetings became public in 2014, and they were "one of the most detailed portrayals of the fear and confusion that reigned in the autumn of 2008. . . .. The US Federal Reserve struggled to comprehend the danger facing the global economy,"[1] according to the *Financial Times*. Janet Yellen, who was a member of the Federal Open Market Committee (FOMC[2]) but had not yet become chair, said of its response, "We are desperately trying to power a bicycle uphill rather than pressing an accelerator on a high-powered sports car."[3]

The Fed had seen trouble coming, but it hardly grasped all the consequences when they hit and it yearned for stronger tools to contain them.

We've seen how we got to the monetary system we have today. But given the shock of 2008, we need to ask: Have we solved the money puzzle yet? Or was the modern monetary system a key component of that crash?

I will describe three broken pieces of a money puzzle we never really solved: 1) commercial banks have tools to make the money supply grow or shrink, but they lack the right goals; 2) central banks lack both sufficient tools and the right goals; and 3) in the end, it's all debt out there. Everywhere.

COMMERCIAL BANKS: CREATING MONEY FOR SHAREHOLDER VALUE

As we've seen, loans create virtually all money in existence today. A banker taps on a keyboard and creates a deposit and there are dollars where none existed before. If we want to grow the economy, we also have to grow the money supply so our credit and debt will also keep growing, at least in the long term. We have to ask: Is that a good idea? Should commercial banks be creating over 90% of our money?

Mervyn King, who should know, says the power of these banks is "the most serious fault line in the management of money in our societies today."[4]

Why?

We rely on commercial banks to bring the right amount of money into the economy and channel it to productive uses. These are fundamental functions. But commercial banks have their own goal and they're clear about it. They want to earn profits, to *maximize shareholder value*. They take actions in their own self-interest, which often doesn't align with the intent of central banks or with the ultimate goal of increasing real economic growth and well-being for the people.

I'll discuss three ways commercial banks regularly fail: 1) they create too much or too little money, leading to booms and busts; 2) they funnel resources to socially damaging activities; and 3) they inflate land and house prices instead of stimulating production.

All three destabilize the financial system, our economy, and society overall.

1. THE BEST OF TIMES, THEN THE WORST OF TIMES

Here is a fundamental question that affects everyone's life: What determines how much money banks feed into the economy?

The answer isn't regulations or reserve ratios, nor is it central banks' interest rates, according to the research of Josh Ryan-Collins and co-authors. The answer is confidence and fear.[5] When banks feel upbeat about economic conditions, they freely give loans. When they grow anxious, they withhold them.

And these psychological states are subject to inborn biases.

Consider: Every year, the World Economic Forum ranks risks to nations and industries, based on surveys of hundreds of well-informed people in universities, corporations, and NGOs. In 2007, the year the H5N1 bird flu peaked, these individuals ranked pandemics 4th out of 24 risks. In 2013, with no head-lines about epidemics, the pandemics category dropped to 20th. Then Ebola struck and in 2015, pandemics rose to 2nd place. Two years later, when things had calmed down, it fell to 11th.[6]

There were booms and busts in ranking pandemics. Confidence and fear.

Risk-ranking illustrates the recency bias. In making decisions, we attach more importance to recent events than older ones, though it often makes little sense. For instance, right after seeing an auto accident, we drive more carefully. In performance reviews, bosses base judgments more on the work of the last few months than of the whole year. In one three-decade study in Georgia, sales of insurance rose after floods, but fell back to normal after three years.[7]

We're all subject to this tendency. Suppose you have $1,000 and a friend asks you for a loan. How would you respond if another friend had just repaid you a $1,000 loan with an additional $300 of interest? Would your answer change if this other friend had instead said he couldn't repay the loan at all?

In the first case, you'd presumably be quite willing to lend. You might even give more if you could, because you'd just made a profit on a similar deal. In the second case, you might be reluctant to lend even for 50% interest. You'd just been burned. But if that second case had occurred six years ago, it wouldn't have the same effect.

Bankers are vulnerable too. If the economy is thriving and people are repaying their loans, bankers feel confident and lend freely to maximize the banks' profits and their own bonuses. They may cut their interest rate to win a loan over a competing bank, so overall interest rates tend to drop, moving closer to their cost of funding. Bankers may even take foolhardy risks, as many did before 2008. But if the economy is faltering, defaults occur and bankers grow wary of giving any loans, even at much higher interest rates.

Unfortunately, this is the opposite of what we need.

The recency bias creates cycles. We repeatedly experience a rapid growth of the money supply (faster than what people care to save or can use to produce), leading to price bubbles and inflation, followed by a crash, an excessive shrink-age of the money supply, and economic agony.

Before 2008 the urge to maximize profits caused banks to take excessive risks, and they lost more money than the banking sector ever made in its his-tory.[8] Indeed, several studies have shown that the more *shareholder-oriented* a bank was going into 2008, the worse it performed.[9]

The Financial Crisis of 2008

1. Interest rates were low and the economy was thriving, so banks shoveled out a massive volume of loans, especially on collateralized real estate.

2. The rise in housing prices made real estate look even safer, leading to more and easier-to-obtain housing loans. They became available to people who in normal times would not have qualified for such loans, as well as speculators who could buy multiple houses and resell them for higher prices. As a result, more buyers poured into the real estate market.

3. Demand for homes swiftly exceeded supply, and housing prices rose further in a classic bubble. Banks assumed prices would just keep rising and saw little reason to deny a mortgage: If a borrower defaulted, they could repossess a house that had appreciated in the meantime. The *ninja mortgage*—no income, no job, no assets—became a symbol of banks' exuberance.

4. In order to make even more money, banks deployed financial wizardry to repackage these loans and sell them to non-banks, creating a loophole in banking regulations that allowed banks to give out even more loans.

5. Seeing excess growth of money supply and inflation, central banks raised interest rates, thus increasing mortgage payments.

6. Some people could not afford to repay the loans and banks started to repossess and auction the houses to recoup their money.

7. The bubble burst. With all these houses being sold, supply now exceeded demand, house prices plunged, and banks could not recover their money.

8. Several large financial institutions were close to default and were all bailed out except Lehman Brothers, which declared bankruptcy in September 2008.

9. Lack of confidence from banks, companies, and households led to the biggest global economic recession since 1929. People halted spending, companies halted investments, and banks reduced credit.

10. Even if central banks were quick (some more than others) to reduce interest rates, commercial banks remained afraid of lending, so the money supply stayed low and the impact of the crisis persisted for the following decade.

The ultimate irony lies in the lack of accountability. When imprudent risks lead banks to bankruptcy, the economy often can't afford it. Our whole economy is based on banking credit, and the default of a bank would destroy all money—the deposits—created by the bank, as well as people's savings, and lead to a chain of defaults of people, companies, and possibly other banks. Complex financial instruments tying banks and other financial institutions together made the risk of a systemic failure even higher. Hence, the government had to step in to prevent calamity. The 2008 financial crisis is one of the many economic downturns and recessions linked to the banking system.

Estimates of the cost of the 2008 financial crisis vary wildly, but the order of magnitude is about one full year of GDP for the US.[10] To make it more tangible, if you live in the US, the financial crash stole about one year of income from the *average you*. The miscalculation of risk is the result of incompetence that might attract sympathy if you and I didn't have to pay the price. Some foresaw this result. In the movie based on real events, *The Big Short*, one of the protagonists believed that banks knew governments would cover their losses and keep them afloat. In this case, bankers did consider the risk, but counted on average citizens to pay for the luxurious lifestyles their reckless actions gave them. The banks were gambling with your money and you didn't know it.

In summary, business cycles are not a physical law. They are in large part a consequence of giving commercial banks the power to define the money supply.

2. WHERE DOES THE MONEY GO? FUNDING SOCIALLY DAMAGING ACTIVITIES

Let's now consider a different situation. You still have an extra $1,000 and two people ask you to lend it to them. One is a long-standing friend who has always repaid loans of much more than $1,000. The other has never even asked for a loan and you two barely know each other. There is no question about whom you'll lend to.

Now, would you change your mind if I told you that your first friend wants that money to invest in an oil company, while the second wants to invest in a solar energy company? You might, but a bank would not. A bank doesn't care how the money it creates affects society. It cares about profit, which is linked to the risk-adjusted interest rate its borrowers pay. An oil company is almost riskless, at least in the short term, while a solar energy company is not, and it was prohibitively risky when solar panels were first invented.

This has been a major complaint in the aftermath of the 2008 financial crises, when central banks relied solely on the banking system to restart the economy. The bankers, in turn, gave cheap loans to oil companies but little to renewables. The ECB, for example, purchased corporate bonds of oil and gas companies and car makers. Unsurprisingly, an array of NGOs demanded that this policy stop.[11] True champions of free markets should also oppose such a practice, since it gives some companies an unfair advantage over others, distorting competition.

But the problem is much broader than just preferentially funding companies that contribute to pollution. Banks create money with no consideration of the social implications. A bank approaches funding a hospital, a school, or a company producing golden toothbrushes in exactly the same way. It decides whether to create and assign money purely on the potential for profit. As a result, it typically leaves the funding of societally useful projects to NGOs or to the government, if they can collect charity donations or taxes to afford it. As we discussed in Chapter 4, today they may not always be able to.

3. WHERE DOES THE MONEY GO?
THE LURE OF THE UNPRODUCTIVE

Let's change the situation once again. You still have two friends asking for your $1,000. One agrees that if he does not repay, you become the owner of a vintage bicycle that he is buying with your $1,000. Your other friend is not going to buy a physical asset but needs the money to enroll in a cooking course, as he wants to become a baker. These friends are equally close to you, and if you want to minimize the chance of losing money, you lend to the friend buying the bicycle. If he fails to repay, you can sell the bike and get most of your money back.

Banks act the same way and this behavior defeats the whole purpose of tying money to credit. The idea was for credit to lead to a productive activity that generates value in itself, like the cooking class. But if banks prefer to create money for the purchase of existing physical assets, there is zero value creation by definition. A bicycle just gets a new owner.

Consider buying a house. With enough loans to home buyers, house prices go up, as they did before 2008. Economist Laurie Macfarlane observes that in these cases "the total productive capacity of the economy is unchanged because nothing new has been produced: It merely constitutes an increase in the value of the land underneath. We have known since the days of Adam Smith that land is not a source of wealth but of economic rent—a means of extracting wealth from others."[12]

Instead of value, the banks create inflation. Adair Turner, former head of the UK Financial Stability Board and former chair of the Institute for New Economic Thinking, explains—

> The vast majority of bank lending in advanced economies does not support new business investment but instead funds either increased consumption or the purchase of already existing assets, in particular real estate and the urban land on which it sits. As a result, unless tightly constrained by public policy, banks make economies unstable. Newly created credit increases purchasing power. But if urban real estate is in scarce supply (which it is in many cases), the result is not new investment but asset price increases, which induce yet more credit demand and yet more credit supply. Credit to finance investment in non-real estate accounts for no more than 14% of the UK total, and the same broad pattern is found across the advanced economies and increasingly in emerging ones.[13]

He describes how the proportion of bank credit going to real estate has risen dramatically,[14] swelling its price while starving investments that the economy needs to grow. It should not be surprising that housing has witnessed the highest average returns, as well as the most stable, since 1870. Its 7% yearly return exceeds even stock market investments.[15] We should also start calling the returns on housing by their real name: inflation. An increase in the price of a house is by definition its inflation.[16]

Now, rent or mortgage payments—one of the largest expenditures for a household—has a typical weight in the Consumer Price Index[17] of around 15%.[18] The Index is the best measure of inflation as it affects the average person's consumption. If the annual inflation for housing is 7%, every year it alone contributes one percentage point of inflation (7% times 15%).[19] In 2017 in the US, 81% of core inflation growth was housing.[20] And that's just the direct impact. Companies and especially small businesses pay rent that, at least in part, is passed on to consumers through increased prices. As such, housing contributes more than half of the typical 2% inflation target, in large part because banks are providing massive credit for the purchase of houses.

If you consider low- or middle-income households living in cities, their expenditure on housing is much higher than the average 15%, and can even reach 50%. For these people, an annual 7% increase in the price of housing means that their total cost of living increases by at least 3.5% per year, for some even higher than 5%, considering the price of housing in many cities grows faster than average. I invite you to go into the labor statistics of your country and look for the last year that wages for low- and middle-income families rose more than 3% a year.

Maybe the most definite proof of banks' inadequacy to allocate the money supply comes from a recent IMF paper that finds that when banks' credit shrinks, productivity decreases—with less IT-uptake, innovation, exporting, and adoption of superior management practices—but when credit expands, there is very limited impact on productivity.[21]

In summary, the first issue of our monetary system is the overreliance on private institutions that understandably aim at maximizing profits, even to the extent of unfairly wagering with taxpayers' money. They end up 1) creating too much or too little money, 2) not channeling it to socially useful though less profitable activities, and 3) inflating land and house prices instead of stimulating productive activities. That's how they destabilize the financial system and our economy. This is the opposite of what we need. It is between naïve and reckless to think that commercial banks could be the main transmission channel for a central bank's monetary policies.

Let's take a look at the second major problem.

CENTRAL BANKS: COMFORTABLY CONFINED TO THE KITCHEN?

Central banks are incredibly influential in our society. I have not cast central banks as the mother of society lightly. Unfortunately, while women in most OECD countries have obtained their full emancipation and are fiercely fighting for gender equality, central banks have barely stepped out of the kitchen, or more precisely, they have been recently captured and relegated there. Central banks in all developed countries used to have a vast role in society. Most were created under the condition that they would fund government expenses. Many played a significant role in economic development by supporting sector development, be it the financial sector (US and UK) or industrial sectors (Japan, France, Italy).[22] All this power vanished. The powerful tool of creating and allocating money, that magic wand that allowed governments to shape the socio-economic fabric of society—and often used it to build political consensus—has been turned into a wooden spoon to stir the stew.

Unlike women, central banks have shown no will to fight for a larger role in society. On the contrary, they are uncomfortable with greater expectations on them. Let's see what's going on here.

INFLATION, INFLATION, INFLATION

In the modern age, most central banks have sought goals such as holding prices stable (inflation control) and promoting financial stability (avoiding *systemic risks* like over-lending in good times, with results such as bank runs and recessions).[23] In terms of monetary policy, central banks generally have a dual mandate of controlling inflation and unemployment. But from the 1980s on, many central banks emphasized low, stable inflation.

The ECB is near one extreme. It states, "The primary objective of the ECB's monetary policy is to maintain price stability,"[24] with an inflation target close to 2%. The Federal Reserve sets forth two aims: "To foster economic conditions that achieve both stable prices and maximum sustainable employment."[25] Yet it had trouble shifting its focus from inflation even as the events of 2008 were unfolding. The transcript of the June 2008 FOMC meeting shows 468 mentions of "inflation" and 35 of "systemic risks/crises." At the September 16 meeting, which actually occurred a day after Lehman Brothers failed, there were 129 mentions of "inflation" and just four of "system risks/crises."[26]

The emphasis on inflation comes straight out of the Milton Friedman view that the free markets can take care of economic growth and employment, while central banks need only ensure that prices don't change too much.

The independence of central banks from governments protected them from answering to a head of state, but with their narrow mandate on inflation, how well do they answer to the public? The best gauge is citizens' overall well-being and if their mandate is aligned with it, we could at least be sure we were all rowing in the same direction. Unfortunately, the focus on limiting inflation can worsen general well-being.

Central banks used to run their monetary policies according to the Phillips curve, devised by A.W. Phillips in 1958. Unlike most economists, he led an adventurous early life, working in an Australian mine at 16, running an outback

movie theater, hunting crocodiles, and enduring a three-and-a-half-year intern-
ment by the Japanese in World War II. His curve basically described a seesaw
between inflation and unemployment. Remember this concept of the Phillips
curve as it will come back later. As inflation rose, unemployment tended to
drop, and as inflation fell, unemployment tended to rise.

Most central banks and economists have been increasingly questioning the
tightness of this relationship and have made several tweaks, but there is clearly
some correlation between the two. In a nutshell, targeting inflation can cost
jobs. Moreover, research shows that a 1% increase in inflation affects well-being
much less than a 1% increase in unemployment.[27] If the price of milk and
chicken goes up by 1%, it causes less suffering than if the jobless pool does.
This is particularly painful for the most vulnerable groups, like youth and disadvantaged or discriminated groups. Martin Sandbu highlighted this unfortunate
consequence of considering that an economy that is overshooting its potential
is as dangerous as one that is undershooting it.[28] Vulnerable groups lose jobs in
a downturn while a moderate inflation has limited consequences. A mandate
focused on keeping a low inflation rate turns the eyes of central bankers in the
wrong direction, leading to decisions that may reduce well-being.

Why the bias toward keeping inflation low? Why keep the central bank in
the kitchen when it could achieve much more? The answer involves a misunder-
standing of inflation, as well as genuine problems linked to high inflation rates.
Let's look at the latter first.

Many countries have lived through periods of *illusory growth*, with incomes
rising but prices rising faster. People may think they are getting richer, but their
higher paychecks buy less and they are actually poorer. In these cases, due to a
combination of factors, suppliers lack the time, ability, or motivation to increase
their capacity and opt to keep raising prices. For instance, if a baker is used to
selling 20 cakes a day and suddenly sees ongoing demand for 40, she could hire
more employees and buy more ingredients. But raising prices is faster, easier,
and less risky.

In the extreme, when suppliers come to expect high inflation and start
raising their prices to stay ahead of it, we see the phenomenon known as hyperinflation, with prices doubling as fast as every week (Weimar 1921–23) or every
day (Zimbabwe 2008–09). If you go to Zimbabwe, you'll find people selling
the currency they used during that time. They have notes worth 100 trillion
(100,000,000,000,000) Zimbabwean dollars issued in the span of two years.

All money stored in Zimbabwe kept becoming worthless every week, and at one point the 100 trillion-dollar note would hardly buy a bus ticket. By the end of 2008, the nation's inflation had hit an annualized rate of 800 billion trillion percent.[29] As I write, Venezuela is in similar straits. As grocery shelves emptied and citizens fled the nation, inflation reached 24,600% on May 31, 2018,[30] and by October, the IMF estimated it would reach 1,370,000% by the end of that year.[31] All such countries have failed to increase the supply of goods and services, and to incentivize investments and in a panic, they resorted to printing money to fight off rebellion.

Such cases elicit awe and are catastrophic both for the economy and citizens' well-being. They are the kind of experiences that countries involved tag with #NotToBeRepeated. And indeed, even without getting to hyperinflation, high inflation, say above 10% per year, is problematic. People get used to it and start expecting it; therefore they negotiate higher wages and companies increase prices. This was Milton Friedman's argument in the 1980s, which convinced everyone to just kill inflation at all costs. But we wound up too frightened of inflation, a phenomenon that we have yet to fully understand.

Let's look at what really breeds inflation. Most people think the cause is printing money, but this is not necessarily true. You are unconvinced? Look at the recent massive money-printing operations led by developed nations with well-functioning central banks.

Japan has had low or negative inflation for two decades, and the rate has remained low even after printing trillions of new yen under Abenomics since 2012. In 2017 the Bank of Japan's ownership of government bonds came to exceed 40% of the total.[32] Such operation requires the Bank of Japan to print trillions of yen to buy government bonds. What was the impact on inflation? Very limited. What matters is not when money is printed—after all, a central bank could create it and simply hold it—but when it reaches the economy through spending or investments. In Japan, the government had already spent money it did not have by borrowing it, and banks and citizens were asking low interest rates, so Japan could borrow a lot. The Bank of Japan's purchase of government bonds had the effect of ensuring that previous government spending was affordable. And that led to a continuous growth in savings, infrastructure improvements, and low unemployment. Most importantly for the purposes of this book, inflation is still low despite the biggest per capita money printing operation in history. *Printing money does not automatically lead to inflation*, despite the conventional wisdom.

The European Union and ECB's massive quantitative easing (QE) program post-2008 crisis provide another example. QE refers to the creation of money by central banks and the purchase of different types of assets as the channel to inject that money in the economy. Even though the ECB had been buying government bonds at the pace of trillions of euros per year, nations have not increased their spending because of the austerity rules of the European Union. The money of the central banks went into the pockets of previous holders of government bonds, who happened to be mostly people with enough wealth that more money didn't really change their buying patterns. As a result, overall spending increased little. The other main transmission channel from central banks to the real economy is commercial banks gaining more reserves and giving out more loans to productive investments. This also did not happen, unfortunately, at least in the immediate aftermath of the crisis. As of March 2021, excess reserves parked at the ECB by banks in the eurozone surpassed 3 trillion euros.[33]

The quantity of money does not inherently change its value. This idea is a legacy of the gold standard, when paper money was just a substitute for gold. Suppose there were 100 units of gold in the national treasury and you printed 100 dollars representing this supply. Each would be worth one unit of gold. But if you printed 200 dollars, each would be worth half a unit. Money lost value as you manufactured more of it.

But today money itself, not gold, is the unit and things are different. As economist Richard Vague said in his review of 47 nations, most since 1960, "More often than not high inflation does not follow rapid money supply growth, and in contrast to this, high inflation has occurred frequently when it has not been preceded by rapid money supply growth."[34]

Remember: We need a continuous increase in the money supply to enable economic growth. Inflation doesn't come from the money supply itself, but from the price of goods. And that depends on the balance of supply and demand. In other words, inflation happens only when people (and companies, and governments) increase demand (spend more on goods and services as opposed to higher savings), and when companies like the bakery either don't have enough time to increase supply (though sudden spikes of demand are rare) or they just take advantage of the greater demand to boost prices instead of investing to increase supply.

That is, inflation is behavioral.

If people preferred holding money in savings instead of consuming, more money would end up in these higher savings, with no impact on inflation. If companies preferred investing rather than increasing prices, we would actually see more real growth instead of higher inflation.[35]

Of course, if money is printed too fast and for too long, and ends up rapidly increasing spending, it would cause inflation. When companies don't have time to increase supply, inflation is the natural reaction. But every year the money supply grows and this is a prerequisite for economies to grow.

TAMING INFLATION WITH A HAMMER

Policy could affect the behaviors causing inflation. With the right incentives we can get people to save more, companies to invest more, and so on. But here is the problem. When governments and central banks split their mandate, they restrict their ability to individually pursue their portion of the mandate.

Governments are responsible for enabling economic growth and inclusive well-being, but they have limited tools. They can't print and allocate money, nor influence how much banks lend. They can try to raise taxes and re-allocate the tax revenues, but they also have to consider companies and financial wealth escaping abroad. Raising taxes can also decrease people's spending or investing, which can actually reduce economic growth. Governments could waste less, one might say, but that is a separate, longer discussion and this could only work to a certain extent.

Central banks are responsible for inflation, but their sole conventional tool is interest rates, which can limit inflation but only at the expense of real economic growth. In fact, when central banks increase interest rates, consumers (people and companies) end up paying more for their loans, leaving them with less money to buy things.[36] This higher cost of funding also leads companies to trim back their own investments, as it cancels out any investment with returns close to the now higher cost of funds. This can explain Richard Vague's finding: If the money supply does not grow, it is likely that companies are investing less, ultimately falling behind consumer demands; and being unable to meet these demands, they end up increasing prices.

In the bakery example, the cake buyers have less money, so the bakery's sales slow. The baker will therefore not increase prices, thus limiting inflation, but at the same time, she will also limit additional investments. When demand was growing, the baker might have thought about extending her shopfront, but now the loan to fund that expansion costs more *and* she's selling fewer cakes. Most likely she'll scrap the idea of expanding. The workers who would have done the construction will never get the job and the extra money from it, and we lose an opportunity to grow the economy. Therefore, increasing interest rates is bound to reduce both consumption and investments.

Since society pursues economic growth, while we may want to cool off consumption, it never makes sense to reduce investments. Inflation itself is caused by insufficient supply—too many people are willing to buy at current prices, so prices rise—yet to increase the supply we need greater investments, which cheaper loans can incentivize. Raising interest rates is a hammer that pounds everything down: inflation, investments, growth, and consequently employment and well-being. Yet it is the only conventional tool we have equipped central banks with.

There is a rational justification to use interest rates, but it is reminiscent of long-gone circumstances. When all people are working full-time, the theory goes, companies compete for scarce labor, wages increase, and companies are forced to raise prices to remain profitable. In this situation, of course, one must reduce investments and only pursue the most value-adding ones, and interest rates would be an adequate tool. This theoretical argument does not hold in light of current trends. Since the 1980s, one could argue we never really were at full employment, and for sure wage growth has not caused inflation but rather lagged it. In fact, companies' profits have been significantly increasing as a share of GDP.[37] Whether it is market concentration, failure of antitrust or weak unions, increasing automation opportunities, or globalization, the emerging outcome is that companies have been able to charge higher prices without having to pay higher wages. Trying to curb investment, employment, and wages for the sake of reducing inflation in the current context seems illogical to say the least. Companies raising prices in the 21st century is not a reaction to a higher cost of labor.

And the issues with raising interest rates do not stop here.

When central banks raise interest rates, they make government debt more expensive. Governments find it harder to increase public debt, limiting their ability to support citizens (you), who suffer from cuts in education, health, infrastructure maintenance, and other forms of basic support. When you face any of these problems, our monetary system is at least one of the root causes.

WHAT HAMMERS CAN'T DO

Reliance on interest rates has at least two more significant downsides.

First, interest rates are slow to reach the economy. After central banks change interest rates, banks and consumers may need months to alter their lending and spending behavior.[38] This delay compels central banks to act in advance and limit the money supply before inflation actually reaches the goal.[39] The result? Investing becomes more expensive, right when people could afford more or better products and companies need investment to provide those products. At the point when we especially want the bakery owner to expand or shift to higher quality products like gluten-free bread, we make it tougher for her. Central banks should always enable economies by increasing supply and quality,[40] shifting the demand-supply balance to a higher level of real production.[41] But instead, they must intervene beforehand to shrink the money supply.

Second, higher interest rates can't stimulate spending. Central banks have actually been successful at limiting inflation for the past 30 years, though at the expense of potential growth. Their failure lies not in keeping inflation low but in avoiding recessions or at least enabling fast recoveries. In the 2008 financial crisis, central banks were quick to bring interest rates down almost to 0%, but it was already too late. Even more worrisome, in the EU, even 10 years of interest rates of 0% did not kick-start consumption or lead to inflation. The reason? Have you ever tried to remove a screw with a hammer? It is difficult. And while cutting interest rates works well to increase investments, consumption remains screwed down.

Consumption still mostly depends on people's income and savings and to a lesser extent on consumer loans. When central banks cut interest rates, the main path to greater consumer demand has three stages:

1. Convincing companies to take loans to invest and hire more people

2. Hiring unemployed people and/or increasing the salary and confidence of people already employed

3. Getting consumers to buy more

And if demand isn't growing, what company would take out more loans to increase its spending at Stage 1, even if interest rates are low? Companies always ask if there is a market to make a profit. If people are buying less, prospects look worse. It becomes more difficult to have such a market. In Europe between 2007 and 2009, corporate investments fell by €200 billion, and most companies that later increased investments only did so due to higher consumer demand or the anticipation of it.[42]

What are the alternative channels to increase demand? One involves the value of your nation's currency. When you lower interest rates, you may reduce its value compared to foreign currencies. For instance, a unit of your currency that had been worth 1.25 euros may now be worth only 1.10. Foreigners would find your country's goods—iron, say—cheaper and import more. As a result, foreign demand might kick in Stage 1 of the growth cycle. However, that would only happen if other countries' central banks kept interest rates as high as they were, an unlikely event in a global crisis. Moreover, currency devaluations may increase the price of imports, since other nations' goods are now relatively more expensive. Countries that are net importers (their imports are of higher value than their exports) could see the beginning of a slippery slope.

A second channel is loans to people to stimulate their spending more directly, but this approach simply anticipates future consumption. The future will inevitably arrive and people will have to repay those debts, reducing their consumption at some future time.

And I challenge any honest, financially savvy person to contend that taking out loans to finance consumption is good financial practice. Consumption does not give people the means to repay loans and interest, which can only come from other sources of income or from a reduction of future consumption. Funding consumption with loans typically traps people in a cycle of debt that becomes increasingly harder to repay. Yet consumer debt was an important component fueling the economy until 2007, at least in the US, where debt-to-income ratio for the bottom 95% of the population grew from about 80% to almost 160% between 1989 and 2007.[43]

What about unconventional tools? Here it is not fully clear what central banks can or cannot do (with the possible exception of the ECB, which has more sharply proscribed boundaries, though gray areas persist). Central banks have mostly used the unconventional tool of *quantitative easing*, in various forms. Quantitative easing is not substantially different from interest rates. Its strategies are not new. In simple terms, quantitative easing differs from conventional monetary policies in that 1) it can affect different types of interest rates, and 2) it can channel the money more selectively.[44] Typically, governments end up paying lower interest on new loans and could get more of them. Unless austerity policies are in place, governments can foster people's spending by cutting taxes, providing more subsidies, and increasing direct consumption and investments. All of these approaches help fight off recessions, but we are still talking about interest-bearing loans. At some point any new loan has to be repaid. Spurring consumption with cuts in the interest rate will only defer the problem of low overall demand to a later time.

So central banks seem to have their hands tied. They can limit inflation but at the expense of economic growth, and when in a recession, they can't quickly boost consumption and get the economy back on a sustainable track. They can only make credit cheaper, buying some time and pushing the problem further in the future. The question remains about whether central banks can create and use different unconventional tools. In most countries they definitely can, but why would they? Central bankers do not face pressure from citizens, yet they have to respond to lawyers if they overstep their mandate. They prefer a conservative approach, one that still guarantees long-term convergence to their inflation targets, rather than experimenting with untested tools, until things get bad enough that they are forced to. The unemployed citizens falling into poverty and potential suicide are just too far away for most central bankers to hear their despair and even when some do, they often lack the authority to do anything about it. In the minds of central bankers, there is an elected government to attend to such people.

To summarize, this second problem is actually one of governance. Both governments and central banks have specific mandates to pursue, independently of each other, but neither has all the tools to do so.

But why have we equipped central banks with just the tool of changing interest rates? Why do we let commercial banks create business cycles, and withhold from central banks the proper tools to manage them?

In a family, mom and dad are peers, with complementary (if not interchangeable) roles, and by collaborating with each other, they leverage each other's strengths. That's one reason why we'd rather grow up in a family with mom and dad under the same roof than in two separate houses.

IT'S ALL DEBT OUT THERE, EVERYWHERE

The very nature of our modern money is the third and perhaps the biggest problem of our monetary system. Our dependence on commercial banks and our practice of managing inflation through interest rates are actually born out of this third problem.

The argument went, people seeking money would create value with it. As society gained more and more value, we'd all benefit. This is the classic view of loans: You borrow money and put it to work. For instance, you open a dry-cleaning shop in a new business district and earn enough to repay the loan plus interest and make a profit. This is still the view of most economists today.

Beyond its inaccuracy—since most banking credit goes not to value-creating activities but real estate purchases—money infusion is only one side of the coin, and for every loan there is also a debt. To bolster the money supply, we have to increase debt in the system. And there is a lot of it out there. Back in 1929, Allyn Young was writing, "There is, in fact, so much confusion respecting the real nature of credit that we shall do well to observe that credit is in fact a very simple thing. Credit is merely the other side of debt! In a borrowing transaction what appears to the lender as a credit, appears to the borrower as a debt. Much confusion would be avoided if, in discussing monetary problems, we should use the word 'debt' in place of 'credit.' The real facts discussed would be unchanged. But the mode of discussion would necessarily steer us clear of a number of dangerous fallacies."[45]

Should we have so much debt?

LOST IN THE DEBT HOLE

In the mid-20th century, General Motors was the richest company on Earth, a byword for success and smart management. In 2009, it still had almost 100,000 US workers, with more than 60 models sold by 6,240 dealers. Yet it was teetering. Sales had fallen throughout 2008 and after the September crash, credit tightened and wary consumers bought far fewer vehicles. That autumn GM's debts were $170 billion against $110 billion of total assets.[46] Things got worse. In the first quarter of 2009 its production dropped 40% and GM posted a huge loss of $6 billion. By May it was burning through $113 million a day.[47] When the company filed for bankruptcy on June 1, it owed $173 billion and had assets of $82 billion.[48] Debt had swallowed it.

In a company, excess debt increases vulnerability.[49] Debt-to-assets, debt-to-equity are examples of metrics Wall Street analysts use to gauge the riskiness of corporations. The higher the ratios, the bigger the red flag, since if its revenue drops, it may have trouble repaying the interest on its debts. Like GM, it could wind up at the mercy of creditors.

Private individuals and governments face a similar hazard. Society has its own ratios. For instance, if a government's debt-to-GDP ratio is 50%, that means its debt would take half a year's GDP to pay off. So, the higher a nation's debt-to-GDP ratio, the more time it would need to pay its debts. As a result, it might seek to collect more taxes, just as a company facing big debts might want to raise its revenues.

We can also look more broadly, not just at public debt-to-GDP, but also at public and private (households and corporate) debt-to-GDP. Let's call it the overall-debt-to-GDP ratio. One study examined the last 140 years and—unsurprisingly—found that high overall-debt-to-GDP is a strong predictor of financial crisis.[50] Now, one could argue that we could still grow credit and the economy while reducing the overall-debt-to-GDP ratio. We'd do it by increasing the denominator—GDP—fast enough. Think ½ to ⅖ to ⅜ and so on. This argument has not found empirical support at a global level, at least in recent years: Credit and debt has been growing faster than nominal demand or GDP in most economies.[51] Credit has to grow not only to allow the exchange of more newly produced goods and services—GDP—but also exchanges of existing wealth, which is much bigger than GDP. And in any case, even a stable high debt-to-GDP ratio would not shield us from the instability of debt itself.

THE SAND CASTLE AND THE WAVES

Debt can cause instability in many ways,[52] but I want to highlight one not sufficiently appreciated: the need for banks to constantly revolve a massive amount of debt.

All debt is, in theory, flexible. A loan has a repayment schedule, at the end of which banks[53] (and borrowers) can decide whether to renew the loan or not. Global debt (private and public) soared above $230 trillion in 2017 and was on its way toward $280 trillion by the end of 2020,[54] more than three times global GDP, and commercial banks must continually renew or withdraw this credit.[55] Think about a skilled juggler who keeps many balls in the air. That is more or less what banks have to do, and they drop some balls. Sometimes too many.

Since we live in a world whose economy still needs growth, you can compare our socio-economic system with a group of workers (banks and companies) building an ever-bigger tower (goods and services) with sand (debt). Meanwhile, ocean waves (repayments or defaults) keep washing lots of sand from under the building and the workers have to quickly replenish that sand, lest the tower falls. And if strong waves start pounding the base too quickly (multiple big defaults or just unrenewed loans), the tower will fall. That's what happened in 1929 and 2008. That's why an economy based on debt is less stable.

And since we need that money to sustain not just economic growth but all exchanges of existing wealth as well, a system based exclusively on credit is even more dangerous. In fact, while GDP is a measure of a flow, wealth is a stock. Backing the value of wealth (e.g., your house) with credit is equivalent to funding long-term investments with short-term instruments, a financial practice considered high-risk and important to avoid. This is, unfortunately, what society overall is doing today. If we add existing wealth to our metaphor, we should add heavy rocks on top of the sand tower, which makes it even more likely that it will topple.

But the risk of debt is even higher if we consider the trend in inequality that Piketty highlighted. The sand is still being washed away and there are heavy rocks on top of the tower, but most wealth is getting concentrated on one side. The tower ends up with all the rocks on one side and the higher it grows, the greater its slant and the more its center of gravity shifts outward.

If borrowers could foresee the future and ask only for loans they could repay, we'd have fewer issues with a debt-based economy. This hypothetical but unrealistic ability is actually a key assumption at the base of free-market capitalism. But this is clearly not the case, and when we combine a debt-based economy with the tendency to concentrate wealth, we create a tower that periodically falls.

In 2007, we reached a historically high overall-debt-to-GDP ratio and allocated too much of the huge pile of debt to people who could not repay it. The economy crashed in 2008 with defaults on credit, followed by a reduction of the money supply and of the value of wealth. As a result, people lost confidence and bought less. Many corporations, large and small, saw revenues tumble and went bankrupt. Many people were suddenly out of work; the US was shedding over 800,000 jobs a month in the depths of the crisis.[56] Some governments quickly stepped in to save banks and jump-start a recovery with higher public spending, as the US did. The stimulus package that Obama launched in early 2009 included $800 billion of additional spending on infrastructure, as well as social security initiatives. The crisis in the US stopped earlier than elsewhere, but public debt exploded and has not gone down since.

The governments that did not launch stimulus packages for fear of swelling public debt fared much worse. Germany spearheaded the effort to cut debt in the eurozone with its austerity policies and it was rightly blamed for the low economic growth and unemployment in the euro area over the 10 years follow-ing the crash. For instance, some austerity measures cut funds to social housing, education, and health care, increasing unemployment. Keynes explained in 1936 that austerity can only make a financial crisis worse and, while some of Keynes's views have gone out of fashion, no one has ever proposed another recipe to stop economic recessions. When the economy crashes we desperately need someone to increase spending and investments. In fact, even in normal economic times, we always need to increase spending and investments. We require money, which in today's system means more credit and more debt. But suppose society needs more money but can't afford more debt. What then?

At today's level of inequality and debts, this is not a hypothetical question.

WHO CAN AFFORD MORE DEBT?

Debt is one thing if it gets repaid on time, quite another if it gets revolved. Prolonged debt can cause a borrower havoc from interest payments.

Governments tend to be affected by this syndrome. Italy shows the conse-quences: It has actually had a budget surplus before interests for most of the last decade, at the cost of flat or negative growth. Yet its public debt kept growing and as of February 2018 was 132% of GDP, the highest rate in the eurozone after ailing Greece.[57] And this debt has continued rising because of interest payments, amounting to about 5% of GDP. Those payments could have gone to government services, reduced taxation, and growth, but they wound up as interest paid to those creditors lending money to governments. Most developed countries are in a situation similar to Italy's, though less serious.

Others have found ways to dribble this seemingly inescapable debt-trap. For instance, Japan has had a debt-to-GDP ratio above 200% for several years and no longer provides a scenario of full repayment, yet it pays close to 0% interest. But Japan is in a special situation, as a large chunk of its government bonds are owned by its central bank that tries to keep interests on government debts extremely low. The Japan government barely pays any interest and it can just keep revolving the public debt indefinitely. Germany (60% of GDP as of 2018[58]) also pays limited interest and is reducing its debts but it is constantly financing its spending with trade surpluses—that is, with money paid by countries running trade deficits. More precisely, given citizens and companies abroad buy more goods and services from German companies than what they sell, Germany is producing for the rest of the world and its government can tax employees and companies for that production that goes abroad. Since the world is a closed system, though, the surplus of Germany requires a deficit of some other country, so not everyone can follow Germany's example.

Unless governments follow the example of Japan, their public debts could grow to the point that high interest repayments may put pressure to lower public investments or to increase taxes. And most high-income countries are indeed going in Japan's direction. Forced by the combination of the 2008 crisis and the 2020 COVID-19 crisis, the central banks of most high-income countries have accumulated a sizable share of government debts thus keeping interest rates very low and making large government debts more affordable. But if we leave aside this unconventional and still controversial behavior of central banks—which will be central to my arguments for a shift to monetism, which I will present beginning with Chapter 12—governments, especially those without their own currency, could not afford much more debts before being swallowed by interest payments. And if governments can't afford more debt, who can? Can it be private companies?

Adair Turner showed that when governments do not increase their debts, the private sector compensates and keeps the money supply growing.[59] But the same question applies here: Can companies continue to afford it?

They could handle more debts, but only if they invest and generate future profits to repay both debt and interest. And profits don't flow automatically from a business plan. They come from people buying a company's offerings at prices higher than costs. In a weak economy with low consumption, as after an economic crisis, companies refrain from taking more debt to invest in projects that at the time seem unlikely to pay for themselves. After a crisis, corporate executives are no less risk-averse than bankers. Firms selling to the richest customers might still borrow, as the very wealthy can always afford consumption, but these companies are a tiny segment. Their investments, spending, and the spending of their employees can't sustain a whole economy. And we definitely don't want to reach a point where most people work to make golden toothbrushes for the wealthy.

So, while banks are lending less because of poor prospects and human biases, companies themselves are seeking fewer loans. Both sides are hunkering down.

And if governments were out of the picture, there is only one societal player left: the mass of consumers. Us.

But can we afford to further indebt ourselves to lift a sagging economy? In most high-income countries, a small percentage of the population, say 10%, owns 40%–80% of the wealth. In the US, one of the least equal nations, the tilt is dramatic. In 2016 the top 1% of families controlled 38.6% of all wealth and the top 10%, 77.1%, according to the Federal Reserve.[60] These ten-percenters can consume even during recession and take debt only to invest or speculate on existing assets. Their taking more debt would not increase consumption, since their propensity to consume is much lower than the rest of the population's. Their earnings are so great that they can save much of their income.[61]

What about everyone else? Some 20%–50% of the population is middle class and owns most of the remaining wealth. These individuals commonly have a mortgage to pay and are often savvy enough to understand that consuming on credit would launch them into a vicious cycle of increasing poverty. The rest of the people, the majority, possess almost no wealth. They rely on a salary to cover expenses, most likely have rent or a mortgage that they struggle to pay, and may have other loans on depreciating assets like cars, bikes, and electric appliances. Many people in both the latter groups[62] are already in debt beyond what is sustainable or desirable, and clearly should not go deeper into debt to restart the economy. The average US household in 2017 owed $137,063 in debt, against an average annual income of $59,039.[63] All major OECD countries are in a similar boat. In 2019, household debt was 88% of net disposable income in Italy, 95% in Germany, 105% in Spain, 107% in Japan, 122% in France, 142% in the UK, 181% in Canada, and 217% in Australia. In other words, a recovery built on more consumer debt would be a brief glow, gone before you feel the heat.

So, how can people already so indebted afford to lift us out of recessions or stimulate any additional sustainable growth?

Here is the shocking truth about debt: It will never be repaid. Not government debt. Not corporate debt. They will just be revolved and increased indefinitely and if this was not the case, it would be a disaster. The only debt that will be repaid is household debt, since old people can't get long-term debts because banks know they will die. If people lived forever as governments do, and many companies could in theory, they would also have an ever-increasing debt. This is the only way to increase the money supply in a system where money, credit, and debt are tied at the hip. As long as we live in a debt-based society, we should all stop seeing debt as something that will be repaid but rather something that will be continuously refinanced. If anything, we should discourage household debts and promote companies and government debts, given these never need to be repaid.

WALKING THROUGH WALLS

If debt equals credit and credit creates money, a society with a lot of debt must also be one with enough money to climb out of a recession and sustain the investments and consumption needed to grow. If this response isn't occurring, it must mean society can't tap into that money. Theoretically, it may seem impossible. Money is *liquid*—it's easily available—and economists will tell you that there is a lot of it out there. And they are right. Savings in the recession have been among the highest in recent history.[64]

Where is the money, then? Someone must be sitting on piles of cash that are neither invested nor spent, in what is commonly called a *savings glut*. A savings glut is a breeder of low growth. This problem again traces back to inequality, since the wealthy have by far the most money to stockpile. So, this money becomes not working muscle but a kind of fat, lying in bank accounts or invested in unproductive assets. Meanwhile, others can't pay for everyday needs.

The solution is to make that money productive again. But how?

We might do it by getting the government to increase its investments in infrastructure like highways and offer more government bonds (i.e., get more indebted), which the people with extra cash could buy. But unless central banks keep the interest rates low, excessive government debt would just postpone the problem.

We might also do it by taxing those unproductive savings, but that would require getting our hands on the money that millionaires or global companies are hoarding and hiding in tax havens. Some of it is visible but kept overseas where tax authorities can't touch it. According to a report from Moody's, the three largest tech companies alone were sitting on $464 billion in such cash at the end of 2016.[65] That's over half of Obama's five-year stimulus package after the 2008 financial crisis. In December 2017, legislation greatly lowered their taxes on it and spurred many companies to bring billions back. But this fact highlights the problem. Companies will bring money home only if they pay light taxes.

Taxing wealth itself could work, if it were feasible. In the 2015 Peterson Institute convention on income inequality, one of the presenters showed that if we taxed only 1% of the wealth in the EU and shifted it to people at the bottom of the wealth distribution, their higher marginal propensity to consume— that is, their greater share of extra income that would be spent—would have increased demand by about €200 billion (about 215 billion USD), enough to close the output gap (a different way to say that we could reach the production potential of the economy).[66]

And this policy could even increase growth while reducing the money supply. In fact, if we redistribute money toward those with debts, they could use part of it to repay their debts and part to buy more goods and services. We would increase growth by speeding the circulation of money, instead of letting it sit idle in deep bank accounts.

But we need to be realistic about the difference between theory and practice. According to the *tunnel effect* of physics, you can theoretically walk through a solid wall and come out on the other side. Yet the chance of it happening in real life is about the size of an infinitesimal in calculus, and unless you are drunk or highly distracted you are not going to throw your body again and again against a wall. Nothing is wrong with the theories of economists and the proposals to solve everything by taxing wealth, but given our discussion in Chapter 4, this road cannot be our only escape.

In a world where wealth gets reasonably distributed, whether through free markets or taxation, the idea of constantly growing the money supply through debt might have succeeded. This is not our capitalistic society. The combination of a debt-based monetary system and open-border capitalism with increasing inequality is intrinsically unstable and unsustainable, a tower of sand.

IS IT ALL A PLOT?

These problems are fodder for conspiracy theorists. For a conspiracy theory to spread, it must be simple enough for unsophisticated people with a medium to low level of education to understand. Our socio-economic and monetary systems are complex, so all related conspiracy theories are simplistic and severely flawed. In this case, the theorists would like you to view wealth (or the money supply, which they often confuse with each other) as a pie and banks as parasites devouring it, because *they create money from nothing and require payment as interest in return* (interest being a piece of the pie). With enough time, the parasites will gobble up the whole pie.

This vision is flawed for at least two reasons. One, the wealth (or the money supply) is not a finite pie, but is constantly growing. As long as banks take less interest than the value of new wealth (or money) created, they don't shrink the pie but actually expand it. The bakery owner borrows to expand her shop, and makes enough money to repay the loan and more. Two, parasites are systems apart from the host that subtract nutrition from it. What they take, you lose. But banks are tightly integrated into society. For instance, their interest rates become salaries of employees and profits of shareholders, who will consume and invest back in the economy.

The conspiracy theorists, unsurprisingly, get it all wrong in complaining about the basic functioning of banking. This is not to say that banks do not have an unfair advantage; they do, as long as our economy depends on them. But they gain this unfair advantage not because they can create money—deposits, to be precise—but because they are the only ones that can. The economy would shrink to a nutshell without them. That is what creates our dependency on banks, and that is one feature of society that this book attempts to change.

Even though conspiracy theorists are creating massive damage to society by spreading fear, anger, and distrust, we need to educate them and we also need to unwillingly give some credit when they are onto something. And in fact, one of their claims is—shockingly—not excessively wrong.

We, along with our governments, *are* in the hands of banks. In Italy, the last government of Silvio Berlusconi, which I'll refrain from judging, but which was democratically elected, was overthrown in 2011 and replaced by a non-elected technocratic government. The reason? Creditors like banks had lost confidence in the Italian government's ability to repay its bonds and started to sell them. Interest rates on Italian bonds rose, eventually exceeding 7%. A level that high was impossible for Italy to pay back and those high interest rates forced countries like Ireland and Portugal to seek bailouts from the EU. When a country depends on credit, it depends on creditors. The new technocratic government led by economist Mario Monti—who had never held elective office—had one main goal: to reassure creditors that the government could repay debts. His policies massively tilted toward gaining market confidence, at the expense of growth and social support to citizens. *The Economist* described his recipe as "winning more plaudits from the markets than the public."[67] This is not democracy. It's *creditocracy.*

Might bankers abuse their power in other ways? Sure. For instance, the scandal over the London Interbank Offered Rate (LIBOR) went to the heart of the banking system. The LIBOR influences the interest rate that people worldwide pay on loans or receive from savings. Around 2010, it was the benchmark for payments on some $800 trillion worth of financial instruments,[68] or about 10 times global GDP. No one can imagine such a sum. So, by nudging the rate a tiny bit upward, cheating banks could make millions. A cartel of six top banks did exactly that, siphoning money from countless borrowers.[69] The banks were embezzling from their customers.

The stakes are too high, and as much as I despise the attitude of conspiracy theorists, in this case they have only slightly exaggerated. Their slogan that "the whole population has been enslaved by banks" is extreme and provocative, but close to being technically correct, given that *debt bondage* is defined as a practice similar to slavery by the United Nations.[70] And our dependence on banks and credit does not come from some law of nature, but from the human decision to tie money to credit.

A PAINFUL MESS

While it is unclear whether the root cause of the 2008 crisis was the inequality created by capitalism or the banking and monetary system or both, money creation is central to current issues. Tying money to credit makes our economy too reliant on banks and on debt, which wealth concentration makes it difficult to repay. The crisis of 2008 was followed by the longest recoveries, and also the most unequal.

The statistics sometimes say one thing while people see another. For instance, when analysts measure growth solely by average GDP per capita, they miss the fact that the recovery has benefited a narrow slice of the population. It's worth stressing that average is misleading. It ignores distribution. If 99 people have nothing and the 100th has $10 million, the average person in the group has $100,000. This "statistic" implies widespread wealth where there is almost total destitution. In the US, the focus on an average hides the fact that 95% of the income growth after the 2008 crisis has gone to the top 1%.[71]

That's a key reason so many people are dissatisfied with the status quo. They are rightly concerned. We now have more debt than ever, while central banks and governments—who saved the day in 2008 but imposed significant hardships on people—now have higher public debts and less room to maneuver interest rates. Are we ever going to make it out of the COVID-19 economic recession?

And if you think the solution is classic prudence, spending less and saving more, the reality is, in our system that would doom us all. The titles of some news articles describe the paradox:

Saving More and Cutting Debt Might Sound Like a Good Plan to Deal with the Recession. But If Everyone Does That, It'll Only Make Matters Worse.[72]

People Weren't Supposed to Be Saving This Much Money—And Now It's a Big Problem.[73]

As we've seen, if everyone were saving and repaying debts, economies would flatline. Saving wouldn't increase bank lending rates, since banks can already lend as much as they want. Money would grow scarce and consumption would drop. Companies would close, destroying more money, purchasing power, and production.

An IMF paper estimates that an increase in the US propensity to save from 5% to 6% of annual income would reduce private-sector demand by 3% of GDP.[74]

This is quite an issue, since we are now urging everyone to save more for retirement. The ratio of retired people to workers will keep rising in the near future, so current taxes may not be enough and it might seem like a good idea for everyone to save more. But how do we do that without causing an economic catastrophe?

Redistribution would work. Some people are just saving too much, and if multimillionaires and billionaires started spending much of their savings or paying higher taxes, that could also help. But we can't rely on them to do it. The more wealth gets concentrated, the more we need those without wealth to get into debt, thus increasing the money supply and sustaining the economy. And debt keeps growing.

If we suggest citizens save more or repay debts it would lead to an economic collapse. Surely I am not the only one who thinks this situation is a little outrageous. What kind of monetary system have we put in place? This is a mess. A mess one should expect from a system that was neither designed nor thought through.

We still haven't solved money. People suffer the negative consequences of this fact even if very few of them realize the root cause. Given no institution is adequately challenging the way we manage money, many are taking matters in their own hands and proposing alternatives to our flawed monetary system.

In the next section we will assess proposals that could become transformational and see if any of them solve our original question: How can we sustainably get as many people as possible above the comfort threshold?

Chapter 8

Time for Permanent Money?

Cryptocurrencies are a walk in the past—
decoupling money from credit could be the future

You may find the unsolved money puzzle shocking. How can money, as entrenched in our daily life as water, be so poorly managed and understood? And how come no one is doing anything to change that?

The quick answer is that most economists turned their attention away from money after the 1980s, assuming the banking system supported by an independent central bank focused on price stability would solve the money puzzle. Since this innovation seemed to tame inflation, money became an uninteresting topic and research into it wouldn't get you published in a top journal. In fact, if an economist was to question the consensus on the management of money, others would look at them with suspicion.[1]

Most economists failed to even contemplate the possibility of a crisis such as the Great Recession of 2008–09. But this situation has recently started to change. Skeptics are now questioning the independence of central banks, and new forms of money are emerging, as are alternative monetary theories. Let's assess these and see if any can help with our goal: How can we rapidly but sustainably get as many people as possible above the comfort threshold?

I will go through four categories of proposals for changing money that could be transformational: cryptocurrencies, company currencies, community or complementary currencies, and injections of permanent money.

CRYPTOCURRENCIES

I have bad news for fans of cryptos: Their potential ranks, in my view, at various levels of poor. The impetus for cryptocurrencies came from mistrust in central institutions. The idea was to have a decentralized system in which anyone could "mine" digital coins and use them as a "currency of the people." So, one of the traits of cryptocurrencies is that once you mine them, they're yours. They are not attached to a credit-debt contract. In this sense, they are a form of *permanent money*. That's an advantage of these new currencies. Unfortunately, it's the only one.

Bitcoin is the most famous of them and it's nothing more than a piece of software that a technology can recognize. Anyone with a certain piece of hardware can *mine* bitcoins by solving algorithms. A technology called *blockchain* enables exchange of these bitcoins by validating the payer's ownership of bitcoins, thus sidestepping our standard pipeline for digital payments, the banking system.

The value of a bitcoin was initially very low, but as people liked the idea behind it, they started buying them and the law of supply and demand kicked in. By December 17, 2017, a single bitcoin was worth $19,782, enough to buy a new car. By January 14, 2019, a bitcoin was worth $3,677. Its value had declined by 81%. Post-COVID-19 a bitcoin was worth more than $60,000, as people looked with suspicion to the biggest money printing in history by central banks and saw the limited supply of bitcoin as a guarantee of value. As companies such as Tesla started accepting payments in some cryptocurrencies, these further increased in value. We don't yet know the nadir for bitcoins.

These currencies are just too volatile. One core objective for a currency is to provide stable purchasing power over time. Cryptocurrencies are not currencies, but speculative assets, like gold, except that gold has industrial and ornamental applications. Cryptocurrencies are merely digital ons and offs. Nothing more.

And there are the many other problems associated with them.

The biggest is the very reason bitcoin was created: lack of a central authority. In August 2018, the website CoinMarketCap listed 1,818 different cryptocurrencies.[2] We're seeing a version of the 1800s Wild West, when banks could create their own currencies. Those currencies often became worthless and ignited bank runs. That is why central banks arose in the first place.

Most crypto fans like the idea of a decentralized system but don't realize that the current monetary system is already highly decentralized, arguably too much, because we leave too much to credit–debt agreements between banks and borrowers. We've seen that independent central banks—not governments—print money and even then, just a tiny portion of it. Commercial banks create the vast majority of money, but they do it in response to free-market demand for loans. As Ann Pettifor puts it, "Involvement of the public in decisions about the allocation of money is what happens when individuals apply to banks for loans, which, if granted, play a role in increasing the money supply."[3]

And while the money supply currently grows through people demanding loans and promising their repayment by creating value, cryptocurrencies spring into being from people running software. There is no value creation, no equality, and no meritocracy at all here. If this money were distributed equally to anyone, it could fund a UBI program, but only a central authority can give all people a digital account and credit them with a digital UBI. A decentralized system running UBI is utopian. And inflation would still be an issue that only central authorities can manage.

Moreover, the creators of bitcoin have placed an upper limit on the number of them: 21 million. People are mining new bitcoins in the cyber world every ten minutes—it's like finding gold—but the ceiling is set.[4] How different are cryptocurrencies from the gold standard? Cryptocurrencies are a walk into the past, not a peek into the future.

While it's possible that some of the most widespread cryptocurrencies like bitcoin will become an investment asset like gold, such evolution would be a sign of the distrust in any system and in institutions, and potentially of the size of the black economy.[5] There is no rational way to store wealth in cryptocurrencies than in gold in a digital form. Its price is more stable, central banks will likely continue to buy gold, and we actually need gold in the real economy. On the other hand—in my opinion—as soon as the roller coaster of cryptocurrencies' values start affecting economic stability or lead to more suicides than citizens and lawmakers can tolerate, these cryptocurrencies may as well be banned and their value plummet toward zero. The true and useful innovation of cryptocurrency lies not in the actual currency but in the digital exchange without banks' intermediation. Indeed, there is no technological limitation that forces electronic payment through the banking system and, in fact, central banks have taken notice.

CENTRAL BANKS DIGITAL CURRENCIES (CBDC)

A cryptocurrency issued by a central bank would likely be a digital currency, with no need of blockchain to settle payments.[6] This idea is increasingly discussed and to be investigated further "seriously, carefully, and creatively," according to Christine Lagarde.[7]

But CBDC would be less disruptive than one would think. Such a system may indeed put an end to banks' fees for exchanging money, an important innovation but not disruptive. It could lead most citizens to prefer a deposit that is not a bank deposit, like any digital wallet or a very basic digital account with the central bank. Again, an innovation but not disruptive for society or, in my view, for banks.

The reserve bank of Australia would differ, and mentioned the risks on the stability of the financial system as a key argument for not creating its own cryptocurrency.[8] A report of the Bank of International Settlements seems to come to a similar conclusion and could be summarized as "there could be benefits but at the risk of destabilizing the banking system."[9]

Their fear is linked to the fact that more than 90% of our money supply is just banks' money. Imagine everyone asking for their money because they prefer having a central bank's cryptocurrency in a digital wallet on their phone. Banks don't have that kind of money. It could cause a run on the bank.

I think this assessment is shortsighted. Indeed, a run on banks may occur, but central banks could still create as much of the new digital currency as needed and lend it to the bank that is facing a bank run. Central banks are lenders of last resort and they would likely continue to be during the creation of a central bank digital currency.

Of course, we are talking about a new banking system. There are a few more changes needed. But let's not be lazy with innovation, especially on something as important and as currently suboptimal as money creation and management. But the reason why this innovation will not solve the money puzzle is that most creation of new money would still arise from banks and borrowers agreeing to create loans. A loan between one person and another would not create new money, because permanent money would pass from the digital wallet of one to the digital wallet of another. Only the banking system would expand the money supply. Once the loan and money are created, the bank money could be moved to a digital wallet and force the central bank to create the digital currency, which is a form of permanent money. But this is the same thing that happens when people ask for cash today.

There is one significant innovation that could come from CBDC, which is the end of "Too Big to Fail." In fact, should a bank go bust, all monies that were moved in digital wallets would no longer be connected to the deposits of the failing bank, and would not disappear. The systemic effect of banks' bankruptcies would be much smaller. We could afford not to bail out banks and as a consequence we would likely see more prudent banks. This is the biggest innovation from CBDC. Not a small benefit indeed. But we would not solve our baseline concern of getting everyone above the comfort threshold.

Unless central banks were allowed to create money and give it to people, which would require a significant change in their mandate and policy tools, all new money creation would still be linked to commercial banks' loans. Maybe economies would grow faster by avoiding some financial crisis, but it would still be up to governments to tax excessive concentration of wealth and redistribute it as UBI. The Piketty dilemma would remain unsolved. Changing the nature of money is insufficient. Something else would need to change. Let us look at the other possible monetary reforms.

COMPANY CURRENCIES

What if a corporation created its own money, even if not crypto?

Money management would still be decentralized and independent from central banks, with all the problems I've described, but at least it would have the backing of a company offering goods and services. We already have many examples on a small scale. You use them often. Any reward card, such as airline miles, credit card points, and ice cream cards ("buy 10 get 1 free"), is actually a company currency. These are new currencies. They let you buy just one kind of product, but they are new currencies nonetheless. Airlines can print more miles by doubling the miles you gain on certain routes for example, or offering free miles to employees as a perk. Different companies are linking these systems, so I can convert my airline miles into American Express points with which I can buy Amazon vouchers, with which I can buy anything I want.

Why do you think Amazon has not issued its own coins, though? The company has probably thought about it. The problem is that an Amazon coin would be hugely successful and governments would not approve it. Amazon and Alibaba are the only corporations that could actually back their money with most of what we require. They don't own hospitals or education centers yet, but they could in the future. Amazon or Alibaba could offer a currency that is more credible than a government-backed one: They are global and they can offer many goods and services that governments cannot. But governments will rightly—in my opinion—prevent them from issuing a currency. That's because they could basically substitute for the state and as much as you may like Jeff Bezos or Jack Ma, most democratic countries still want to elect their heads.

When Facebook announced its intention to create Libra, its own company currency, it did raise a sense of discomfort among several regulators; they weren't concerned about companies issuing vouchers or a bunch of start-ups creating cryptocurrencies. The impact of these monies on a national scale is completely negligible. But when someone with billions of users, more citizens than any government can count, proposes to issue a currency, regulators and central bankers have to take notice.

While Facebook is not Amazon or Alibaba and cannot back its own money with goods and services, its size is sufficient to cause concern. And the concern of regulators has in fact led to a significant reduction of the scope of Facebook's Libra. What you will need to look out for to understand whether Libra will be a concern for the stability of the global monetary system is whether Facebook starts creating money; the more they start giving loans and offering Libra as incentives to users or employees, the more Facebook will be setting up a parallel monetary system.

Having said this, I acknowledge that I may not be forward-looking enough. Maybe the solution to money is indeed to fully liberalize creation and encourage competition among different currencies. The companies or people who do better at it will succeed, while other currencies will disappear. We could have a virtual wallet with euros, dollars, bitcoins, Amazon coins, Facebook's Libra, airline miles—a real variety. However, monetary policies and the markets are already too complicated and I don't think adding more variables will bring us more stability and sustainability. Free markets have benefits but their perfection is oversold.

COMMUNITY CURRENCIES

Local community currencies, also known as complementary currencies, are becoming promising. The Sardex in Sardinia is a famous example, but there are many more around the world, including the WIR franc in Switzerland, the Bangla Pesa in Kenya, the Mumbuca in Brazil, and many more. The Sardex is a parallel currency, pegged to the euro that companies and consumers in Sardinia use. Companies can have a negative balance of Sardex—a debt—as long as they spend within the Sardex circuit, keeping the balance of Sardex in the system constant.[10] Since people are both producers and consumers within the Sardex circuit, the system ensures that lack of money won't limit the demand of consumers or companies' investments.

This is very powerful. Remember that money is an incentive. People do things to get it. With a community currency, for example, one could send his or her child to childcare and pay in credit and, in the meantime, he or she might work on a farm and provide the very food bought by the childcare center, gaining credits for it from the center, thus closing the balance. Value-creating activities benefit the community and, if money is the limitation, allowing it to run negative is all it takes to give people time to create value and earn the money to close the balance. Running negative is equivalent to providing credit to consumers and companies, without the costs and bureaucratic processes that banks employ. A scheme like the Sardex solves the chicken-and-egg problem of development for free, as there is no interest on negative balances. The assumption behind it is that we don't need banking activity to understand who will repay and who will not. We assume that given the social ties and reputation effects in a community, everyone will repay sooner or later, and the absence of interest makes this repayment much more likely.

The Sardex model is not the only one. One could create an actual currency—paper, digital, or crypto—that people accept only within a certain community, in parallel to the national currency. One rationale for community currencies is that a central monetary authority can only have one monetary policy, and it may not be the best for an individual community. The euro is an example: ECB monetary policy is optimal for only a few of the members, while for most it is either too loose (Germany) or too tight (Italy).

Community currency is a successful system to make monetary policy more precise and granular and to provide interest-free, bureaucracy-free liquidity. In fact, in most cases, community or complementary currencies have increased the sales of companies that adopt them.[11]

But they only work within close communities. If you could exchange the currency externally, the Sardex might not hold its peg to the euro. Nonetheless, in many communities, a local currency can solve the problem of a loss of monetary sovereignty that the euro area is experiencing. If Italy or Greece needed a different monetary policy from the rest of Europe, and most monetary experts including myself think they do, a national currency that people use for local exchanges could help. While impact assessment is still in its infancy, since this approach seems to increase economic activity locally, it might do the same at the state level.[12]

A problem with these currencies is that if chronic inequality exists within the community, the balance may never be settled. A few would build up unlimited credit while others have unlimited deficits. For example, if most labor becomes automated in the distant future, a local currency would run into the same issue as national currencies: Too many people would lack a salary to close their negative balance. At the end of the day, these currencies are still based on credit and debt, which works only as long as debtors can repay creditors.

Moreover, the bigger the community, the greater the problem. It's hard to develop large imbalances in a small community, while if the community gets bigger, maybe as big as a country, then inequalities can increase and the old problem of excessive wealth and debt accumulating would affect community currencies in the same way that it affects the official currencies and the banking system managing them.[13]

Nonetheless, local currencies are an ingenious reaction to the failure of a central monetary system to meet the needs of a local community. The increase in economic activity after their creation is a clear sign of this.

Could local currencies fund a UBI program? Depending on the design of the currency, they could, and the city of Maricà in Brazil is doing exactly this: It funds a UBI program with a newly created currency pegged to the Brazilian Reais that recipients can use for local purchases. The program has offered small transfers to each citizen for years and is now in the process of expanding it with more generous transfer, not to all citizens but to those with income below a certain threshold, some 52,000 citizens or about a third of the city population. The cash will be transferred with no condition and not in the form of loans.[14] The sustainability of this program will be based on the ability of the Banco Mumbuca and the municipality to manage inflation and the currency value compared to the Reais, but such a program is an inspiration for what could be possible if we rethink the role of money. Could we use the same approach and inject permanent money to fund UBI at a national scale?

INJECTIONS OF PERMANENT MONEY

I define *permanent money* as any money that is permanently into the economic system, does not originate from a credit–debt agreement, and does not carry an interest rate, whatever the nature of such money (physical, digital, or crypto). When people talk about *helicopter money* and *monetary finance*, these are examples of permanent money, because once a central bank creates and distributes it, it is permanently in the system. Tossing money from a helicopter is just a metaphor used by Milton Friedman to make a point, and people use it now to refer at the central bank printing money and giving it away in some form. Monetary finance is a specific use of permanent money to close public debts. I will use *permanent money* from now on, but I may use *helicopter money* when referring to others' proposals. In the following box I try to explain the differences between today's money and permanent money for those less familiar with the idea of helicopter money.

Permanent vs. Banks' Money

From the perspective of a user of money buying fruit at the market or paying online for deliveries, there is no difference between permanent or banks' money. If the world has 5% or 90% of the total money supply being permanent or banks' money, you wouldn't see any practical difference. It's like if you are writing on a whiteboard with a marker: You can still write and read whether the marker is permanent or not.

But from an economy perspective, it's very different whether most money is created and destroyed by banks when they give a loan or whether it is created by central banks and given for free to someone in society. To use another analogy, banks' money is like painting your house with paint that washes off in the rain; when you repay the loan, the money (paint) vanishes. On the other hand, central banks creating and giving money away is like painting your house with something permanent.

When central banks create money to buy assets during quantitative

continued

easing, it is actually not very dissimilar to banks' money: They can always sell the assets and the money will vanish again. Your house is painted, but at any point in time, outside your control, someone can show up and remove the paint on your façade.

That's why it's important to understand that money is only permanent if it is given away, gifted, better if by the only entity that can produce a country currency: the central bank. Remember that banks can only create deposits, which can vanish if a bank goes bankrupt.

As we will discuss, it is useful to have some money that is non-permanent. Sometimes the washable marker is what you want. Another analogy, if you are dyeing your hair, you'll go with permanent dye if it's a tried and tested color you know you like, but you'll most likely want washable dye if you are using blue or green. Similarly, in society there are some experiments that require money to be created through loans, but there are also long-established assets (e.g., houses) and supply chains (e.g., companies fulfilling basic needs) and safety nets (e.g., retirement savings) that will always be needed and require a certain amount of permanent money to enable exchanges.

Gold was permanent because it had the physical property of being permanent. You can melt it and bend it, but you can't make it disappear. Since the gold standard fell, money has become mostly non-permanent and tied to bank loans. But this is not a law of physics. In theory, money could still be made permanent, but it would need to be created and gifted by central banks, rather than being created and loaned by banks.

Community currencies could also be permanent money depending on the rules: the Sardex would not be permanent money (as it is a negative balance that needs to be closed with a repayment and would therefore disappear), but the Mumbuca is distributed as permanent money.

Injecting permanent money means that instead of arising from credit–debt agreements that need to be settled, the central bank (or any other issuer for that matter) creates permanent money—physically or electronically—and gives it to recipients without ever asking for it back. And instead of disappearing when a loan is repaid or a bank goes bankrupt, permanent money continues to exist.

The resurgence of this idea among mainstream economists is linked to the concepts of *secular stagnation*. Conventional economics holds that central banks can lower interest rates until people and companies take more loans, thus stimulating enough investments and demand to achieve full employment. But in many places interest rates have hit zero, yet the economy remained far from its potential.[15] Some central banks have started imposing negative interest rates—fees to hold banks' money—to spur banks to make loans instead of keeping money deposited at the central bank. This tactic has its own issues and limitations, though.[16]

My explanation for secular stagnation was in the previous chapter: Society needs more money but can't afford more debt, and the very wealthy can afford more debt but do not need it. If loans and, therefore, interest rates can no longer bring the economy back to adequate levels of spending and investments, we need an alternative.

Fiscal deficits—as in governments spending more than they collect in taxes—with increasing public debts have been the standard answer. Larry Summers showed that without an increase in public debts, the interest rates necessary to achieve full employment would have been well below zero: about negative 7%.[17] Given the hesitance of politicians to further increase public debts, many economists and research institutes have started suggesting the injections of permanent money.

Economists suggest two main ways to inject permanent money: closing government budget shortfalls or giving it straight to the people. The main problem with either isn't technical. With modern technology, especially in high-income countries, the central bank could easily open an account for every citizen, who could access it online. The problem isn't accounting either. Today, if central banks create money and give it away, they would count it as a loss on their balance sheet and the government would have to repay the loss. But that's just bad accounting, and I will later show it can easily be fixed.

The problem with permanent money is purely political. Most economists agree that once you open the tap of permanent money, it would be difficult to close it. People will demand more of it and pressure governments to issue in excess, thus re-creating the inflationary tendencies of the past. We've also seen dictators abusing this power right up to the present day. But the fear of an event that might happen in a distant and different future because of one that happened in a remote and different past (or in the hands of incompetent dictators) should not close the lid on an idea that can change society for the better. If we find a way to inject permanent money without generating inflation, we may have just found a way to finance a UBI program and perhaps even more than that.

What are economists proposing that entails an injection of permanent money? And has any large country done this in recent history? Let's look into it.

ONE-TIME HELICOPTER MONEY TO FIGHT CRISIS

Adair Turner is one of the most vocal supporters of using helicopter money. He rightly points out that if the problem is insufficient consumption, we have a solution: Give people money. The rationale is simple. If companies are producing goods that people need but can't afford, why leave the goods unsold and people's needs unmet, and make companies cut production and employment? No one benefits. Just give people money to buy these goods. That is aligned with the view of money as an incentive, and Turner says that at this moment in history, the incentive is not strong enough to make companies increase production levels to their potential. We need more money to increase spending and motivate companies to invest more.

But Turner suggests using permanent money to increase demand only when all else fails. The political risks of losing control of the tap would be significant, and therefore we'd have to make it clear to the public that any operations with permanent money were exceptional.[18]

Willem H. Buiter, global chief economist of Citigroup and a former professor of macroeconomics, offers a similar view: "When the State can issue unbacked, irredeemable fiat money or base money with a zero nominal interest rate . . . there always exists a combined monetary and fiscal policy action that boosts private demand—in principle without limit. . . . Deflation, inflation below target, 'lowflation,' 'subflation' and the deficient demand-driven version of secular stagnation are therefore unnecessary. They are policy choices."[19]

Institutions including the McKinsey Global Institute (MGI)[20] and Positive Money[21] have suggested that the ECB and the BoE use helicopter money to spur demand in the aftermath of the 2008 crash.

In the EU, the ECB mandate actually forbids direct financing of governments, and a form of permanent money would have had to go straight into people's pockets, the solution proposed by the campaign QE4people.[22] Liberals often prefer this alternative because it is independent from government decisions and highly democratic. But it is also unprecedented and, hence, we are not technically or operationally ready for it. If the ECB decided to distribute money to everyone, it would need months if not years to set up the policies and infrastructure before the launch.

Ben Bernanke, former head of the Fed, has a similar opinion. We should prepare now, he says, so central banks have this tool in their arsenal.[23] Unfortunately the COVID-19 pandemic hit and central banks were not ready yet.

Bernanke was also of the opinion we should use permanent money only in exceptional situations, when conventional tools fail. Like Turner, he views the use of permanent money as complex, and potentially a limit to the independence of central banks.

These limited-use proposals would help economies emerge faster from crises, but they couldn't fund an ongoing program like a UBI. If a government financed a continuous UBI by increasing its debts, it would soon be unaffordable. Furthermore, a debt-funded UBI could increase spending but also inflation. Without a different system to manage inflation, central banks would just tighten the money supply with higher interest rates. Those rates could lead governments to default on their debts.

JAPAN

As mentioned in the previous chapter, Japan exemplifies a solution, or better, a work-around to the problem of public debt sustainability. Since 2002, Ben Bernanke has been suggesting Japan use helicopter money to fight deflation.[24] Japan seemed to ignore the idea, but deficit government spending has continued or even increased and the Bank of Japan started buying government bonds at virtually no interest. While this is not permanent money, it is very close to it. If a bank renews a debt continuously at 0% interest, the situation is, economically at least, equivalent to permanent money. The borrower has the money but suffers no penalty for continuously revolving the loan and thus can hold it forever—or at least until the bank renews it at higher interest. While Japan has denied it will issue permanent government bonds—that is, bonds that have unlimited life, which would clearly be permanent money—many believe Japan is using helicopter money in a politically acceptable way. It's a more complex mechanism with a different name.

Has the solution worked in Japan?

Inflation is still low and lower than any institutions desire. Economic growth is not high but that's also due to a declining population. On a per capita basis, Japan has grown more than many European countries. As a comparison, using the World Bank GDP per capita inflation adjusted, Italy GDP per capita was 7% less in 2019 than in 2007 while Japan's was 8% higher. The US did better at 12%, but even France and Spain grew less than Japan on a per capita basis over the same period.[25]

Besides the fact that I am Italian, I picked Italy to compare with Japan as it has similar demographics: an aging and declining population and both countries share a similar attitude toward household debt.

Japanese people are fiscally very conservative. They don't like personal debt and they have a high propensity to save. While economists would see this behavior as catastrophic, in fact it is making the Japanese much more secure. Because the private sector borrows and spends so little, the government is borrowing and spending to compensate, and it thereby ensures an increase in the money supply and real growth. Confronted with insufficient private investments, the Japanese government faced a choice. It could either 1) invest and spend directly, employing people and increasing their savings, or 2) face a socio-economic collapse by halting government deficit spending. They chose the first.

If one looks only at long-term growth potential as the objective of a society, then a collapse might have forced a restructuring of the economy, more private sector innovation, and ultimately even higher growth. But this is both wishful thinking and a political choice; forcing a collapse for uncertain but potentially higher long-term growth is not necessarily better than creating a more inclusive and stable society that grows a bit slower.

Italy was forced to collapse by the European treaties, and the collapse did not lead to the restructure of anything; instead, it brought populists to the government. The Japan way was the Italian way before adopting the euro, which is the reason many Italians are skeptical about the eurozone fiscal austerity rules, and consequently of the euro overall.

Furthermore, if Japan gave money to the people directly instead of spending it by the government, one would think that the private sector would have grown more to serve the higher spending power, rather than being the government directing resources in the economy. Japan's version of permanent money is interesting because it's an ongoing policy, not a one-time money drop. Japan's government annually runs a large deficit—at least by European standards—and the central bank increasingly funds it. How it is used is less relevant and up for political and economic debate. What if this deficit was used to fund UBI instead of increasing government discretionary expenditures year after year? It could lift all people above the comfort threshold forever, and maybe even get to faster growth with more private sector activity.[26]

Many suggest the Japan way can work only in Japan due to their high propensity to save. I will challenge this view throughout the book and show that as long as companies or governments take out more loans and invest them, savings will grow by the same amount.[27] Households may have a different propensity to consume, but savings are not only households' savings, and the more investments and government deficits, the more the income becomes available to either save or consume. Therefore, high savings is more likely a consequence of high investments and high deficits than an enabling feature. And in fact, similarly to Japan, Italy also had among the highest saving rates and they have started to decline as austerity policies were gradually introduced.

But as for inflation staying low, I can believe the argument that this might be a Japanese phenomenon. Anyone who's been to Japan knows that its culture is very different from the rest of the world's. They consider tipping offensive, one sign of a culture that deeply values fairness over profit. Companies, especially small businesses, could be less prone to charge as much as customers can pay, and instead charge (on average) what they think is fair. If you have been to Japan, this description will resonate with you, but it will look merely anecdotal to economists and seem a failure to the typical businessperson. Yet the Japanese government's massive spending has increased employment and people's savings but not prices, and statistics prove it.

Could the world use Japan's scheme, then, and use a continuous injection of permanent money to fund UBI and other important investments? A universal basic income can bring people above the comfort threshold, but we also have many other societal challenges. We urgently need to bring climate change under control. Germany needs better infrastructure, as does the rest of the European Union, the United States, and many other countries.[28] The US must improve its education and health costs and outcomes.[29] Japan needs to care for its aging population while at least maintaining the same overall production, and it can only do so through higher productivity per person, with automation being an important enabler. Could the central banks of these countries just print the money and direct it with some mechanisms toward solving such issues?

CHINA

China developed through a strategy that would require a much longer discussion than I can afford here, but in summary, China has shown the fastest growth rates ever seen for a large developing country and sustained them for decades. We know that for a country to produce more, it needs to create more money, and while there were some minor foreign investments into China, most of the money to fuel growth was domestic. Where did China get that money? You should know the answer by now: commercial banks. Except that in China, all major banks are state-owned.

China's adoption of capitalism in the form of the market mechanisms and some private property rights has been a necessary condition to its growth, but it would have been insufficient without the massive loans that state-owned banks created. And given that both commercial banks and the central bank are government-owned and not fully independent, this is another case of government-led money creation that has spurred faster growth. Today, Chinese banks are allowed to issue permanent bonds: bonds that never need to be repaid. The Chinese central banks can buy them to provide liquidity—money—to banks in need. This is another way to inject permanent money *in disguise*.

GIVING MONEY CREATION BACK TO THE PUBLIC

Quantitative easing operations in the US and Europe post-2008 crisis and then during COVID-19 were a big step toward Japan's monetary strategy. Central banks' holding of public debts rose to levels similar to Japan's, giving much more room to governments to raise more debt and spend more. The Pandora's box has been opened again and many have taken notice, proposing that the power of creating money be taken away from banks, at least in part, in favor of the public, represented by the government.

Martin Wolf, economic commentator for the *Financial Times*, urged radical reforms to put money creation in public hands.[30] A similar appeal came from Robert Skidelsky in his book *Money and Governments: A Challenge to Mainstream Economics*.[31] Advocacy group Positive Money in the UK and EU has long been advocating that ECB money creation be put to use to fight societal challenges rather than go to banks or fossil fuel companies.

Yanis Varoufakis, the former minister of finance of Greece, challenges the very idea of having an independent central bank and proposes that the government issue money, either directly or as what he calls *fiscal money*.[32] Here is his argument: If a government can't raise taxes or issue more public debt, the only source of funding becomes the central bank, which also becomes responsible for the fiscal policy of a country. But there is no democracy if people have no choice over central bank officials.

This argument is also solid, but Greece is not the best brand for these ideas. While the European Union has imposed measures too harsh on the Greek people—no other country in contemporary history has lost over a quarter of its GDP in peacetime—Greece earned a lot of its own troubles. It ran an average trade deficit of 5% of GDP between 1980 and 2014, and only in 2013 reached a trade surplus, after heavy pressure from its creditors to reform the economy. Forget about the money for a second: For almost 35 years Greece had been consuming goods and services produced by other countries without giving back any goods and services it produced. That's like asking your neighbor to cut your lawn every day, promising to return the favor in some distant future. When you become old and can barely walk, your neighbor is rightly annoyed that you cheated him. In this, globalization is very just: If you want to access the world's goods and services through imports, you have to give something back through exports.[33] Greece had not done so for 35 years and the market rightly punished it.

Nonetheless, Greece lost some sovereignty by being in the eurozone. If it had its own currency, it would almost certainly have devalued it. With a weaker currency, Greek people could have afforded fewer imports and foreign countries would have enjoyed very cheap olive oil, feta, and vacations on the Greek islands. Less money would have gone out and more would have come in. Without the euro, Greece would sooner or later have paid back its neighbors with their goods and services.

It is worth noting that these proposals for putting money back into public control are not new.

In 1936, economist Henry Simons advocated using what he called *actual money* to determine fiscal policy. Later, in 1946, the Fed chairman said that taxes for revenues were obsolete, because the US government could finally print dollars, which had just become the reserve currency.[34] He was actually wrong, given the dollar's peg to gold, but that peg no longer exists today. Soon after, in 1948, Milton Friedman also proposed that central banks create money to manage government deficits and remove money when the government ran surpluses. But the most ambitious proposal that strikes at the core of banking came even earlier.

Eighty years ago, in the aftermath of the Great Depression of 1929, Irving Fisher, one of the leading economists at the time, wrote, "The chief direct cause of the depression was the one-third reduction of the money stock between 1929 and 1933." And "The only sure and rapid recovery is through monetary means." He blamed the banks for this and was one of the most vocal supporters of what is known as the Chicago Plan, based on a 100% reserve banking.[35] With the constraint of 100% reserve, banks cannot give loans by simply creating a deposit with a keyboard. They lend only what they actually possess. All money would have to be permanent and issued by a central institution, which in Fisher's time was under the control of the government. This idea goes far beyond any others for permanent money, since it would completely end the banks' power to create money. The advocacy group Positive Money and Mary Mellor, author of *Debt or Democracy*, are now putting forth similar proposals.[36]

Fisher died in 1947, but not before writing to President Truman urging "a law which will sever the tie that now binds bank loans to the volume of checkbook money." In plain English, he asked for a way to inject money into society without creating debt. A recent IMF paper revisited the Chicago Plan and supported the benefits that Fisher claimed in 1936: better management of business cycles, the elimination of bank runs, and the reduction of both public and private debt.[37]

But after Fisher's death, the world went in the opposite direction and we have become a world trapped in public and private debt, unable to avoid or manage the business cycle.

Plans like Fisher's would allow the government to fund UBI and many other socially useful projects, since the government or the central bank would have to continuously create money to enable economic growth. Taxes would become a tool to reduce excess in the money supply, but we wouldn't need them to fund the government, as it would just create all the money it needs. Taxes could become a way to manage inflation or to provide incentives and deterrents in society.

You can imagine that banks were not happy with Fisher's proposal, nor were those who wanted the government to take a minimal role in the economy. In fact, excess power in governments often causes corruption and opens the road to dictatorships. For this reason, I still believe we need independent central banks, albeit with a very different mandate. At the same time, I am strongly in favor of permanent money, while limiting the power of commercial banks to create credit.

MODERN MONETARY THEORY

Modern Monetary Theory (MMT) tries to put into an economic theory what many have proposed: Put the public more in control of the power of money creation. MMT's main proposition is governments that can issue currency through the central bank have no real limits to their deficit spending, because the central bank can always print money to repay those debts. The real limit to government spending would be inflation and not the size of the public debt. The word *debt* is actually inappropriate, proponents say, because a debt from the currency issuer is financial wealth for the rest of the private sector.[38]

The central bank can (and will, in their view) support government deficits by printing any money the government owes. This form of permanent money continuously circulates in the economy and gets saved, expanded through bank loans, and spread generally. And if the government is spending money well, maybe on important projects or programs that fix market failures, we shouldn't worry at all about government spending. If inflation was to occur, only then should governments raise taxes, thus reducing private wealth that would in turn reduce consumption below inflationary levels. Among their proposals is often a job guarantee at the minimum wage, which would serve a purpose similar to UBI—bring all people above the comfort threshold.

Before claiming or celebrating a great breakthrough, though, we should understand the criticisms of using permanent money, and how a change in money creation and allocation would affect the broader socio-economic fabric of capitalism. In fact, even though MMT is well-grounded in standard economic theory, most economists strongly contest the idea of running government deficits funded with central banks' money to fund a job-guarantee scheme, deeming it a useless and outdated application of Keynesian economic theories.[39] And this is happening at a time when most economists do think that governments should spend more. The level of critique to MMT by economists that are at the same time strong supporters of huge fiscal spending to restart economies have always puzzled me. *What are the critics saying? Why is permanent money considered the devil in the economic community?*

One weak argument against permanent money holds that it would be ineffective to increase spending, since most people would just save the additional money. If this claim was true, it would be an even stronger reason to use permanent money. Savings give people security and, in fact, people save more in uncertain times.

But at least three criticisms of permanent money deserve more attention. The first is the old inflation bogey: In economists' view, any creation of permanent money will necessarily generate inflation in the long term, with hyperinflation as the ultimate monster. We have already shown that tying money to credit is an important cause of inflation (and instability), since too much credit goes to purchasing real estate. Still, critics could argue that permanent money allocated through governments or given to people would generate even more inflation. The second criticism is that it would weaken central banks' independence, and hence they might yield to democratic demands for more money to be distributed or spent, leading again to inflation. The last is that permanent money is incompatible with the ideal of free-market capitalism. A central bank or a government would decide how much money to create and how to use it. At the minimum, these choices would crowd out private sector investment, considered of higher quality than more wasteful public investments. At worst, the lack of checks and balances—for example, higher interest rates on government deficits when the public debt is too high—would lead to even more wasteful spending and ultimately inflation.

While MMT scholars address the issue of inflation convincingly, they do not recognize the issue of public spending crowding out private investments. Traditional economics explain the process of crowding out completely wrong—unsurprisingly I may add, given they completely neglect money and banking—but they are ultimately right that the more the public spends, the fewer real resources are left for the private to use. (See next box for more details.)

MMT vs. Traditional Economics: Settling the Score on *Crowding Out*

Traditional economics claims there is a limited pool of savings and when governments spend more, they tap into this pool leaving less to fund business investments. Interest rates would go up in a bid for limited savings and the private sector would invest less. These claims are just wrong. There is no such thing as limited savings. When banks create a loan, they create a new deposit—or savings account—that can fund investments.

Instead, MMT is much more on the money. When governments spend more, if you follow the money, two things happen in parallel: 1) the government spends money, which means that private bank accounts of companies and citizens receive money and 2) the government raises funds through taxes or by selling bonds. When raising funds, money goes back to the government and in cases where the government is spending in a deficit (not raising sufficient taxes), a financial asset (a government bond) is created and left in the system, increasing financial wealth. The bond could be used as collateral for bank loans or central banks could buy it, as they have done substantially since 2008; therefore the money supply can also grow from deficit spending. It is clear that there is no limited pool of savings here.

In the case of spending and taxing, the money supply and private wealth are unchanged, while in the case of deficit spending, the money supply is either unchanged or increased by the banking system and private wealth is increased by the value of the bond. If one were to print money to fund government spending, the impact would be equivalent to deficit spending, with the bond purchased by the central bank.

Nonetheless, the crowding out may still happen, in which case private wealth may take a hit if the private investments would have generated a higher value than the public spending. In fact, whenever the public spends, it blocks real resources. If a government pays your salary, you are busy and cannot work for someone else. Real resources are limited and higher government spending increases the competition for them, which may ultimately raise their prices. And resources are very diverse. Even with economies not at full employment, if everyone is hiring doctors and data scientists, their prices (wages) increase immediately. You can't convert the unemployed into doctors right away. The same is true for natural resources. If a government starts investing in projects using cobalt, electric vehicle manufacturers would face higher costs for raw materials. And if the price of resources increases, prices of goods are likely to follow and the central bank may jack up interest rates sooner, increasing the cost of funding for businesses and limiting their investments.

On the other hand, if the public spends on resources that no one wants by hiring unemployed people, for example, the impact on private investments is minimal. Companies may have to pay a bit more than the minimum wage to convince folks to shift to a private-sector job. And if public spending generates demand for companies working below capacity, it could even crowd in more private investments.

In summary, when the public spends more, it competes with the private on a limited pool of real resources. But the crowding-out effect, if it happens, has nothing to do with less savings and little to do with higher interest rates. As an independent referee of this debate, MMT wins for the explanatory accuracy of what happens when the public spends, but traditional economics rightly raises the possibility of crowding out (although with the usual excessive dose of inevitability that comes from the insistence in working with deterministic theoretical models). The more important question that I will address in the next chapter is whether free-market private allocation of resources is the perfect holy grail we are made to believe it is.

I hope this book will generate arguments in favor of bringing money theories back to the center stage of economics. But to change society, we need more than MMT. Convincing citizens and policymakers that society should continuously inject permanent money to fund UBI (or a job guarantee, as MMT proponents would want) and any other societal priorities will require 1) strong evidence that the markets are failing big, not only in creating and allocating credit, and that leaving *all* allocation decisions to free-market dynamics is *less* efficient rather than more, 2) an alternative or complementary way to allocate money and therefore resources, one that will not lead to governments' waste and inflation, and 3) a new and convincing approach to better manage inflation.

Points 2 and 3 will be part of my proposal for monetism. But before getting there we need to x-ray benefits and limitations of the markets. It is time we get to know capitalism in depth. So far, we've looked at society and history from the point of view of money. We've recognized a few issues that trace back to tying money to credit, a process linked to the ideology of free-market capitalism. We have spoken of how capitalism concentrates wealth, which could be the root cause of the instability of our economy in the first place. And we've looked at the use of permanent money, which could be a debt-free solution to finance UBI, society-beneficial projects, and increase aggregate demand when the economy needs it, but which also clashes with free-market capitalism.

Let us then open the door and meet capitalism.

III.

CAPITALISM

The hands of capitalism have devised the modern monetary system. It's time to zoom in on this powerful craftsman. What is capitalism? Why should free-market capitalism mold money management? As we'll see, the basic axioms of capitalism don't hold up to even brief examination and, more importantly, we have moved beyond them. For centuries, production was the key to economic prosperity, but now distribution has become the weakest link. We can make far more than we can buy. We could shift production toward more useful goals. And we could produce more sustainably. The real problem isn't how much we produce, but what and how. We can solve this problem, accelerate our economies, and enjoy the bounty that automation promises us when people have more spending power. But we need to shift the focus from more production to better distribution.

Chapter 9

Divorce Without Alimony: The Love Story of Capitalism and Government

Their former marriage and uneasy separation

Think of Usain Bolt being beaten for the first time at the 100 meters, or Michael Phelps losing in an Olympic final, or news that your favorite celebrity takes drugs. You'd still probably respect them. In this story, capitalism is a highly important figure that made a mistake by tying money with credit. Despite this, capitalism is still quite the name about town. Tying credit with money was a screw-up, but it doesn't change more than 200 years of progress that capitalism brought us.

However, the screw-up was a big one and it is important to ask questions. Did Usain Bolt or Michael Phelps just have a bad day? Do they need to adapt their styles or are their careers ending? And if I keep idolizing the addicted celebrity, will my children see my adoration as consent to such behavior? We need to understand whether the days of capitalism are over, if there is a better alternative, and what consequences we face if we persist in an economic system that no longer improves our lives.

MEETING CAPITALISM

People have written enough books on capitalism to fill a library and its definition can vary greatly. I'll keep this section brief and focus on what matters most to our discussion in this book.

Adam Smith provided theoretical and moral foundations for capitalism in *The Wealth of Nations* (1776). A country's wealth, he said, is the value of what it can produce. The more it produces, the more it satisfies its citizens' needs. Capital— physical goods that can optimize the production of goods and services—is what allows people to organize, specialize, and increase the productivity of limited resources. By boosting production, the wealth of nations increases.

You need more than capital, of course. Physical goods don't manufacture goods and services on their own. You need a process and the main pillar of capitalism is the ideology of free markets. By giving people the freedom to pursue their self-interest, it holds, sellers will compete to best satisfy the needs of consumers. That is, they'll vie to offer the best goods at the lowest price. Those who do well will gain the reward of profit. At the same time, consumers gain higher quality goods at lower and lower prices, and they therefore buy more. As an example, think of how computers have improved, fallen in price, and spread over the past decades.

Sellers will start businesses wherever they see an opportunity for profit, and they'll compete until the price drops so far that profits vanish, unless even better solutions emerge to solve consumer needs. A business not making money is a powerful sign that people no longer need its good or service, or that someone is providing better value for the money. The failure of such businesses can be a sign of *creative destruction*: Innovation in another sphere that creates better products and services, and where those businesses that don't or can't adapt become obsolete. Think of how digital cameras killed the film processing business. Kodak is just one of the many companies that wound up in bankruptcy by failing to adjust.

In theory, the free market works its magic by what is known as perfect competition. That is, rational suppliers provide rational consumers with exactly what they need at the lowest possible price. Here lies the moral justification of capitalism: It is the best solution to satisfy ever-growing human needs.

Of course, few actual markets work that way. Nobel laureate Daniel McFadden calls markets "rough, murky, tumultuous places where commodity attributes shift, supply is uncertain, prices are volatile, and information is imperfect."[1]

The division of profit between the owners of capital and labor is also a matter of freedom. It occurs in wage negotiations. As employees become more valuable and harder to find, their wages increase. If they're less capable of generating value for companies and easily interchangeable, the opposite happens. As a result, people seek to acquire the scarce skills that yield higher wages, which in turn are only possible because these employees and their abilities generate even more value for the company and ultimately for society.

As the world developed, capital morphed and included the concept of money. The so-called *capital markets*—often called Wall Street in the US— would channel capital (savings) to the suppliers deemed most likely to grow more valuable in the future. It's similar with banks, although banks can create new deposits and expand the money supply while the stock markets can't.

Continuous innovation would fulfill the unlimited needs of human beings, thanks to the unlimited drive of profit. And this permanent growth will ensure the profits to remunerate Wall Street and repay banks' loans with interest but also pay salaries so that citizens can afford an ever-growing level of consumption.

Neither painless nor stable, capitalism has nonetheless delivered extraordinary progress for over 200 years. But the trend arguably reversed in the late 1970s. Since then, the past 40 years have witnessed slower average growth rates, increased inequality, more frequent economic downturns, and a stalemate in levels of well-being in most high-income countries.

What happened? The reversal occurred just after proponents of capitalism demanded its full emancipation from governments. In the aftermath of the 1929 crisis and World War II, the father of modern economics, John Maynard Keynes, built a consensus around the idea that governments should have a pivotal role in fixing the imperfections of the free markets. Thirty-five years of inclusive growth followed (inclusive as in everyone benefited), and US GDP increased nearly fivefold from the 1940s to the 1970s. But things changed when free-market capitalists demanded the government take a minimal role.

Let's take a look at this despised government.

INTRODUCING THE GOVERNMENT

What are governments? Why do we need them?

We haven't always had them, but societies have always had some form of leadership even before civilization emerged. At the very basis, the reasons are that 1) human progress to this day depends on effective collaboration, but 2) there are multiple opportunities for individualistic self-interest sabotage that could ultimately bring down tribes, cities, countries, and societies in general. Evolutionary theory and game theory have long shown the coexistence of the two, and governments were formed to ensure we harness the opportunities of higher forms of collaboration. Governments can therefore write laws to limit sabotage and raise taxes to pursue large collaboration opportunities that groups of people or companies could not pursue. Think of large infrastructure projects, supporting the poor, or defending the population from invaders. The goals among governments vary and are not always written, but in the developed world they typically include welfare and well-being, respect for freedom and individual rights, and helping citizens live comfortable lives with respect for one another.

Since citizens pay for governments through taxes, my view is that the goal of governments must be enabling the collective well-being of these citizens, with the only limit being the insurance of sustainability for future generations. I say "enabling," as a government can't just give its citizens well-being. Every person needs to figure out his or her recipe for happiness, life satisfaction, and life fulfillment, but some preconditions make that pursuit much easier and more successful. I believe governments should strive to provide these preconditions to everyone. They should be directly responsible for shaping society so that all people can achieve the comfort threshold and shift from State 1 to State 2.

Let's forget for a second that we call it *government*. On these pages, I describe the government as a pretty nice character that defends human rights and seeks to improve citizens' well-being. It may make mistakes, but its official role and actions would put it among the good characters of a novel. So why is it that so many of us despise the government?

Society's view of the government has changed throughout history, based on how much the government was improving society or just taking advantage of it. How did this bad reputation arise?

GOVERNMENT MEETS CAPITALISM

The early encounters between government and capitalism were harsh. You could safely say that governments locked capitalism in a basement with almost no food or water. One of capitalism's main pillars is private ownership of property, a key precondition to motivate owners to invest in improving their property.

Imagine you found a land rich in valuable minerals. Would you spend the time and money to build a mine if you thought that, once you'd extracted the minerals, government officials might stroll in and seize them?[2]

The same was true for agriculture. In the past, governments were kingdoms and empires and they owned most of the land. In the feudal Middle Ages, nobles owned the land and assigned some to peasants to use, but the rights to access land were far from secure. Even today, Swaziland assigns about half of its land in this form, which according to the IMF is an important limitation to improving agricultural yields.[3]

Most countries today grant and protect private property rights, since countries going the opposite direction have learned painful lessons. When Zimbabwe, upon gaining independence, confiscated the farmlands of white people, the new owners didn't know how to effectively raise crops on them. The country shifted from being one of Africa's growing stars to one that relied on the World Food Program to feed its people. Between 2000 and 2009, agricultural revenues dropped by €12 billion and as revenues fall, government tax revenues do too. And the *smart* idea of just printing money did nothing to compensate for the huge losses of production. The skills were just not there anymore, and local banks are now advising farmers to give consulting contracts to the white farmers who had their land confiscated.[4]

Venezuela's government is setting the nation back centuries in terms of poverty, infant mortality, and homicides; you can add as many metrics as you like. Its economy was projected to shrink by half in the five years ending in 2018. The government did it by a mix of expropriating land and businesses—such as oil companies, utilities, and telecommunications firms—while limiting the freedom of businesses to set prices and transforming Venezuela into one of the most corrupt countries on Earth. The hyperinflation from printing giant waves of money made the headlines, but the root cause is the rejection of the most basic principles of markets.[5] Capitalism is locked in the basement in Venezuela.

Aside from such disasters that are mostly reminiscent of exploitative forms of government, modern governments and capitalism have enjoyed some sunny days together. By granting and protecting private property rights, governments have sealed win-win agreements that put both capitalism and government in business. Private owners have become more willing to invest in the production of goods and services in the pursuit of profits. Investments require funding, making banks happy since they can give more loans and make more profits.

Investments also lead to technological improvements, as well as increases in real production levels and in paid labor. In turn, consumption increases and governments have more prosperity they can tax. And in turn, both governments and companies can invest even more. This is how the magic cycle of economic growth starts; it's how capitalism and government can be best friends.

The history of economic development from nearly every low- to middle- to high-income country includes a significant strategic role for governments in creating and channeling money (and credit) to businesses in strategic economic sectors. For example, South Korea is one of few large countries that most recently caught up and even surpassed the living standards of some Western societies. The relationship between capitalism and the government has gone much beyond friendship, to the extent that people often use the term *state capitalism*. After the Korean War in the 1950s, the South Korean government invested US foreign aid in education, infrastructure, and communication. When Park Chung-hee took power through a military coup in 1961, he had the right environment for economic growth,[6] even though he lacked natural resources and land per capita was scarce. In response, he nationalized commercial banks and created special-purpose banks that gave cheap loans for development purposes, as well as guarantees for foreign loans. These development banks provided 73% of the loans in 1964. In the 1960s, investments rose almost 30% per year and real GDP almost 9% per year.[7] Because the nation lacked technology and resources, its trade balance was highly negative in those years, so it shifted to export-oriented heavy industry in the 1970s, and attracted foreign investments. China has applied a similar strategy for its development and achieved an even faster development than South Korea.

How could government and capitalism have such a great relationship in some countries? The answer is the same as in real-life relationships: communication and compromise.

While private property rights are a win-win, free unregulated markets are not necessarily so. Many supporters of capitalism want the perfection of free market to be a dogma and that means a global free market, with free trade between countries, including free financial flows, without any central coordination and limited regulations. The free choice of individuals would ultimately lead suppliers to satisfy demand and foreign competition would spur efficiency and innovation. In the long run, each country would focus and specialize on the goods they were best at, and everyone would benefit. We cannot pretend that companies in the Philippines make better cars than those in Germany, and Germany can't pretend to have beaches like those in the Philippines—or Greece or Palma de Majorca, which is basically a German community now.

While the theory may seem persuasive, the path to this long-term ideal may not be a straight line and officials in many East Asian countries have been more pragmatic, keeping a strategic role for the government. On the other hand, these governments left most operations to the private sector, often with the exception of banking, education, and health care that needed a faster and more inclusive push than what private initiative would have led to. Think about it. In a poor country, what profit opportunities are there to start with? Creating money through loans and funding strategic public and private investments accelerated their economic development.[8]

Capitalism and government are still married in these countries, but we cannot say the same where capitalism was much more demanding: the US and the UK, and to a lesser extent many other high-income countries.

There once was love between government and capitalism, even in the US. Franklin Roosevelt's solution to the 1929 crisis was to start a deal by which the government intervened to solve free-market downswings. Keynes gave theoretical underpinning to this approach, claiming that as long as governments maintained a certain level of total spending, the free markets would work their magic in providing the goods and employing workers.

In the meantime, to finance the world wars, every high-income country raised tax rates significantly, and given the high inequality of societies at the time, the wealthy paid the highest income and inheritance tax rates. As Piketty documented, the top rates went from basically 0% to 40%–80% in 1920 to between 70% and 98% in the 1950s, with the US and UK imposing the highest rates.[9] While countries wasted these funds in the war, the tax rates remained high and progressive for long after the war ended, giving governments more funds for public services like education, health, and investments in infrastructure and research.

Economists invented the concept of the GDP in the 1930s and it quickly became an important metric for capitalism. If continuously increasing the value of production makes everyone better off, economists felt we needed a way to measure it.

Back in the 1950s, it definitely worked. In most countries, as GDP rose and unemployment fell, metrics of people's well-being improved. Life expectancy in the last two centuries has doubled in many countries. Illiteracy, homicide, and suicide rates have declined, as have poverty, hunger, teenage pregnancy, smoking, wars, child mortality, and much else. GDP and economic growth looked like the silver bullet that benefited both free markets and citizens, and consequently the government. In those days, President Kennedy called economic growth "a rising tide that lifts all boats."

While inequality was remarkably better in the 1960s than a century earlier, it was still prevalent. In 1962, a revealing book put the increasing affluence of the US in perspective, and President Kennedy was among the readers.[10] In *The Other America*, Michael Harrington depicted the living conditions of the 50 million people who still lived in poverty in the US. The book was a huge success and the government took on the task of eradicating poverty in the US. President Johnson increased various benefits and the approach partly and temporarily succeeded. This was arguably the height of the relationship.

Then things changed.

In the early 1970s, the neoliberal ideas of Milton Friedman and Fredrick Hayek became increasingly influential. They held that government involvement was intrinsically inefficient and we should leave every aspect of economic activity to the free markets. They both knew that market failures occurred and both proposed that the government give cash to people to ensure minimum living standards.[11] There was no contradiction between this idea and free markets; indeed, they felt it would accelerate free markets. The markets would still be free to operate, but the government would replace some welfare programs with a transfer of cash that people could use as they wished. It was like a tough discussion between parents: "I know you are trying hard to help, but your efforts are just wasting money, so give the kids to me and I'll take better care of them, for less."

After three years of pilots, Nixon proposed a UBI program that passed the House but failed in the Senate. Nixon himself ended up abandoning the program, influenced by an 1834 report of the Royal Commission of England that depicted the results of a UBI pilot in Speenhamland as catastrophic.[12] Though this pilot had lasted for 40 years, the report determined that "weeds increase in the fields, and vices in the population."[13] The conclusions in that report were forged, as later reexamination found, but the chance to win the fight against poverty had passed.[14]

At the same time, in fact, the US government had significant issues outside its borders, both economic and political. But political issues may have been the real deal breaker in the relationship between government and capitalism, and their comfortable coexistence was in for a shake-up. There was a new opponent in town, ready to take down capitalism and give governments a much bigger role.

GOVERNMENTS MEET COMMUNISM

If Adam Smith is the father of capitalism, Karl Marx is the father of its most known alternative. Marx directed his harshest criticism to the division of society between those who owned the limited capital, which he used as a synonym for wealth, and those who had to work for a salary. Since most wealth was in the form of land, private ownership of capital would lead to intrinsic inequalities, with a minority of the population benefiting from the toil of the working class. The foundations of communism are instead shared ownership of property and of the means of production, an economy planned by the government, and the principle that we are all equal and we should all equally benefit from the available wealth.

As World War II was ending, Russia and the US had played the biggest roles in defeating the Nazis and they had the highest say in crafting the post-war world order. But the ideological differences between communist Russia and most of the rest of the developed nations led Russia to stay out of the Bretton Woods agreements. And the ideological conflict soon became known as the Cold War. Russia and the US started supporting foreign political leaders in those countries' disputes, fighting the Cold War by proxy on someone else's land. The long struggle was harsh and reached its peak with the Cuban missile crisis and the Vietnam War. While the US lost the Vietnam War, it was the Soviet Union that ultimately fell.

The ideology of communism simply didn't work. The incentive of private property rights is much more powerful than being forced to work for the public sector, and the attempt to plan every single aspect of an economy to the number of shoes needed in a certain province was just an impossible feat. There is not a single case in history of a communist economy attaining the prosperity and living standards of high-income countries. Most strikingly, we see the difference between communist North Korea, still playing Cold War games while its people starve, and capitalist South Korea, viewing its delirious neighbor on smartphones and curved TV screens. China, communist in name but not in practice, has followed an economic model like that of South Korea, although much more authoritarian from a political point of view. It was only after abandoning its communist economic ideologies that China managed to kick-start economic development.

Even though the communist economic ideology ultimately fell, it may have been enough of a flirt to lead capitalism and government to a permanent separation.

THE NEOLIBERAL DIVORCE WITHOUT ALIMONY

Neoliberal ideas were already brewing in the aftermath of World War II, but the hero in town was Keynes. The brilliant, witty economist blessed a wedding between government and capitalism. The narrative of the day was, as long as the government can maintain a high overall demand, the economy will tend to full employment, and that will realize production potential. The problem with this view was that in our economic system, a high overall demand also encourages sellers to take advantage of that demand and hike prices. As a consequence, rising demand leads to higher inflation. The more we buy, the more we pay. Economists considered this pain worth tolerating to ensure full employment, as long as we could control the rate of inflation. And they believed we could.

In the 1970s, this understanding foundered before the phenomenon of *stagflation*. Both inflation and unemployment were steeply increasing. What was causing the inflation if many are unemployed? Such problems strain relationships and that's what happened here. Exponents of neoliberal capitalism blamed the government for excessive unproductive spending. Keynesian theories supporting higher government spending looked flawed, Keynes was no longer alive to explain why stagflation was possible (see next box for my take on stagflation, a phenomenon that changed capitalism forever), and Milton Friedman and Fredrick Hayek had an alternative that seemed much more appealing to both politicians and businesses.

Revisiting Stagflation and
Why It's Relevant for Africa

Stagflation refers to a combination of high unemployment and high inflation that many economies experienced in the 1970s. Keynesian theories held that only when most people were employed and negotiated for higher wages we could have inflation. The combination of inflation and unemployment was at odds with this theory and opened the door to neoliberalism. Yet, had neoliberalism been in place in the 1970s, the US would have likely seen even higher unemployment—perhaps riots. Here is why.

Unemployment can be explained by the combination of 1) increasing productivity, which allowed companies to produce the same with fewer employees, and 2) a demographic boom that added workers. In this situation, it is difficult to create enough jobs to absorb the growing labor force quickly enough. Many emerging markets, particularly in Africa, are in this dangerous situation. In the long term, a demographic boom leads to more growth and possibly with jobs for everyone, but unemployment can rise in the short and medium term.

But how can high unemployment co-exist with high inflation?

Milton Friedman blamed central banks creating money and lending it to governments to pursue full employment, as Keynes's theories recommended. According to Friedman, prices could not increase unless the money supply did.

Friedman rightly spotted a major flaw in the link between unemployment and inflation,[15] but he was inaccurate on what caused stagflation and how to manage it. In fact, employment in the US, thanks to the pursuit of full employment, increased from 78.7 million people in 1970 to 99.3 million in 1980,[16] a job creation of 2.1 million jobs per year. This result was never repeated in any following decade, not even after the 2008 recession.[17] Unemployment—which in any case was well below 8% except in 1975— arose mainly from the Baby Boom. And if inflation of 6%–14% was the price to pay to avoid a higher unemployment, it might have been worth it. If I were a leader of an African country today, I would sign on immediately to a scenario of 10% inflation and 8% unemployment.

Meanwhile, how much inflation in the US was caused by debt-fueled government spending?

The US was bleeding cash to finance the Vietnam War, an incredibly unproductive use of resources. Growing competition in the automotive industry from Japan and Germany led to the first trade deficit for the US, which meant the dollar was less in demand internationally and would tend to depreciate. Two Gulf crises created supply shocks and boosted the

continued

price of energy. And since the cost of energy becomes part of the cost of many other goods, these crises led to higher prices overall. Many economists have suggested that these supply shocks were the main cause of the 1970s inflation.[18]

The fall of the gold standard and people's uncertainty over the Fed's ability (and commitment) to maintaining the value of the currency also added inflationary pressure, as Milton Friedman himself pointed out.

In summary, the 1970s may well have been the most difficult decade in recent US history and while printing money and government spending may have enabled inflation, stagflation was mostly due to demographics, the waste of resources in wars, and higher oil prices. If austerity policies had been in place, it's hard to know what could have happened to the US.

In the midst of the Cold War, anything that smacked of communism easily became fodder for political propaganda. Hayek in particular worried about the strong role of government. In *The Road to Serfdom* he claimed that any government intervention is a limitation to freedom and a step toward a dictatorship, and he sowed his ideas on fertile soil. According to Sonja Amadae, the US government was working hard to show the superiority of liberal democracy, in a world where some Western intellectuals and societies admired socialist planning.[19] Reducing the government's role in the economy quickly became a winning horse for politicians, and Ronald Reagan rode it to the Oval Office. Milton Friedman became the new hero and free-market neoliberal policies quickly replaced Keynesian ones. The neoliberal agenda included increased competition through deregulation and free trade, a smaller role for the state, privatization, and limitations on the ability of the government to run fiscal deficits.[20] You only have to look at the neoliberal fingerprints all over EU austerity policies to know where they came from.

But before neoliberal capitalism reached the EU, Margaret Thatcher implemented it in the UK. The rise of neoliberalism marked the divorce between capitalism and government, but if we consider Hayek and Friedman as the judges settling the divorce, they both required alimony in the form of a UBI program (or a negative income tax in the case of Friedman), which neoliberal capitalism never provided.

It promised more meritocracy and equal opportunities instead: the American dream. The greater freedom to operate in a deregulated but competitive market would result in more innovation and economic growth, which in turn would trickle down to increase the prosperity for those who worked hard for it.

How did that go?

THE (UN)EXPECTED FAILURE

Initially, it seemed promising. The US and the UK had a higher average growth than their European counterparts. But their higher growth mostly came from faster population growth. We weren't seeing greater productivity leading to higher GDP per capita. Furthermore, anything that becomes privatized increases GDP by accounting convention, further inflating GDP figures.[21] And ultimately the world realized that there is much more to prosperity than average GDP growth.

Average well-being has not improved in the US or the UK in the last 40 years,[22] and this trend holds true even if we don't consider the 2008 crash.

Joseph Stiglitz looked deep into this issue and here is what he found: The inflation-adjusted median income for an American male worker has decreased 47% from 1969 to 2009. Inequality has continuously risen, with over a fifth of income going to the top 1% (11.3% went to the top 0.1% in 2012). The wealth is even more concentrated, and 35% of US wealth belongs to the top 1%. These levels of inequality are comparable to those before 1929 and the Great Depression.[23] The average was growing, but most people weren't benefiting.

The RAND corporation analysis has framed the same issue differently: If wages had kept growing with productivity growth as they had until 1970, the median wage in the US that today stands at around 50,000 USD would be between 92,000 and 102,000 USD.[24]

Why did growth become so disproportionate with neoliberal capitalism?

We are back with Piketty's framework. The period of the two world wars saw great wealth destruction, as well as high taxes to fund the conflict. Afterward, an unprecedented growth rate exceeded the after-tax return on capital, keeping the distribution of wealth rather constant.[25]

But neoliberalism increased the after-tax returns on capital by slashing taxes and by making it easier for financial wealth to seek out higher returns globally. Compared to the late 1970s, tax rates in the US have decreased for income, corporate profits, and capital gains.[26]

Unfortunately, growth did not increase as promised. In the 1960s, real growth in the US averaged over 4% a year (and about 3% on a per capita basis).

Growth fell to about 3% in the 1970s (and 2% on a per capita basis), a period marked by two oil crises and the Vietnam War. But then when politicians introduced the neoliberal recipe, growth remained the same in the 1980s and 1990s, and ultimately fell to less than 2% (and less than 1% on a per capita basis) in the 2000s and did not materially recover in the last decade.[27]

At the same time, globalization restricted labor income from spreading wealth among the masses. Median wages (adjusted for inflation) in high-income countries have stagnated or decreased in part because the supply of labor has exploded globally. According to Nobel laureate Robert Solow, this swelling of the labor supply has weakened the position of workers versus employers.[28]

Employers can now easily pick the country with the most favorable labor laws and cheapest workers. They outsource some unskilled jobs while they automate others. The reduction in labor union participation, from 24% of private sector US workers in 1973 to 6.6% in 2012,[29] further weakened workers' power in negotiating for better wages.

The new, global demand for labor also explains why highly skilled workers have significantly increased their income. The top global talents and the lowest-paid workers do benefit from globalization, but everyone in the middle is losing out.

And if all this was not enough, the technological revolution has enabled high-tech companies to capture an increasing share of the economy. That would not be a problem per se, except that most of these companies don't need many employees to function. The OECD has, in fact, found that the increasing profits of new tech companies are the main source of stagnating median wages[30] leading to inequality.

The combination of neoliberal capitalism, the technological revolution, and globalization has led to inequality levels unseen in the last century, and many people have fallen short of the comfort threshold. It should come as no surprise that in most cases well-being metrics are worse in the neoliberal UK and US than other high-income countries.

Unfortunately, the rest of Europe soon joined in. In the 1980s the share of income going to the top 1% in the rest of Europe was still decreasing,[31] a continuation of the post-war trend. But then, following the neoliberal script of slashing taxes and deregulating the economy, inequality started to increase everywhere, especially in the UK. Piketty showed that there is perfect inverse correlation between the decrease in the tax rates brought by neoliberalism and the rise in top earners' share of the national income. The transfer to the top 1% in Europe and Japan was only 2%–3% of national income, while it was about 10%–15% in the UK and US.[32] Neoliberalism caused the rise in inequality.

And as low-income people grew poorer, national consumption could only increase through higher debts. According to IMF, household-debt-to-GDP ratios increased gradually, from 35% in 1980 to about 65% in 2016.[33]

The promise that the rising tide of growth would lift all boats did not materialize. And after four decades of increasing inequality and loans to repay previous loans, the neoliberal castle fell in 2008, as badly as in 1929.

Governments and central banks had to save the day again, and they prevented the catastrophe of 1929 everywhere but Greece.

In the 1930s and the 1970s, we saw major changes to tackle the root cause of the problem. But after the 2008 crash, no such changes occurred. Some constraints on finance have been put in place. Governments and central banks implicitly (and exceptionally) re-embraced Keynesian policies to fight recessions, some sooner, some later. But these are just patches that may no longer work in the next crash. Neoliberal capitalism is still in place.

And as I've mentioned, it is the neoliberal scorn for any central coordination that led to the tie between money and credit. It is this ideology that prevents us from creating permanent money and using it to fund a UBI program or fight broadly recognized problems like climate change. The fathers of neoliberalism did not want market failures to proliferate unregulated, but they were neither the politicians making the laws nor the lobbies influencing them.

The version of neoliberal capitalism we wound up with is failing, but even more worryingly, its defenders are preventing society from trying any solution inconsistent with it. Some people are rightly questioning whether neoliberal capitalism has any practical value or if it's one more flawed ideology, just like communism.[34]

THE RISKS OF INERTIA

In understandable disorientation, protest votes have brought extremism and incompetence to power, in those very economies most overexposed to the risks of debt and most militarily active. Protectionism is rising. And the weapons industry is again growing the economy. *Is this situation much different than 1939? Was historian Walter Scheidel right when he claimed that only violence is The Great Leveler?*[35]

If you think these concerns are exaggerated, consider Branko Milanovic's analysis of the link between inequality and wars. He shows that when domestic inequality is so high that the local demand can't sustain high returns on capital, the wealthy must look abroad to further enrich themselves.[36] In plain English, the wealthy own most companies (40% of stocks are owned by the top 1%, 44% by the next 9%[37]). When the middle class and the poor have no more money to buy their products, the wealthy lobby governments to make sure they can invest and get higher yields from other countries, and invade them if their investments are at risk. According to Milanovic and other historians, this is the most plausible justification for World War I, as well as for colonialism.[38] And in 2017 the IMF wrote, "In 2007, about 80 percent of the fixed income index ($15.8 trillion) yielded over 4 percent . . . this proportion has now shrunk to less than 5 percent ($1.8 trillion). In the United States, this dearth of higher-yielding securities combined with the portfolio rebalancing effects of QE has resulted in a search for yield . . . the search for yield has also led to greater capital flows and more borrowing by low-income countries."[39]

This search for yield is what led to previous foreign wars, and while we can hope that today it would be unacceptable, I would not want to be in a country that is defaulting on debts owned by people and a government in nations with a highly active military. Inequality is not just a threat to social cohesion within countries: It's also a threat to peace between nations.

Chapter 10

Flaws in the Core: Cognitive Biases and Broken Promises

Why neoliberal capitalism might work—for a different species on a faraway planet

T hese poor outcomes of neoliberal capitalism are clear evidence of its failure. But while looking at outcomes is the right way to evaluate any strategy, it's also important to understand the weak links. Perhaps if we just patch up neoliberal capitalism, we won't need to change much else. Let's dig deeper into neoliberal capitalism.

BIASES AND SELF-INTEREST DEFEAT PERFECT COMPETITION

The moral and social justification for neoliberal capitalism is grounded on the theory that the freedom of people and companies to organize, negotiate, and exchange resources would lead to organizations that best meet the changing needs of people. Free markets, with no or very limited outside interventions, would be the most efficient solution to organize our economies, whether it is banking, education, health care, transport, you name it.

This theory rests on many premises, but two are the most important: 1) people can accurately assign probabilities to future events, such as their ability to repay a loan, their future salaries, whether they will like an electric car, whether they prefer a vacation today or more savings for retirement, the future of tax rates, interest rates, inflation rates, and you can add what you like here; and 2) they behave rationally to maximize their personal utility as a consequence.

Now, the first is clearly unrealistic. People don't have all the information needed and the talent required to build alternative scenarios and give them probabilities. But even if they did, people are notoriously poor at gauging probabilities, and we would be wrong most of the time. Indeed, even economic forecasts are often wrong. Radical uncertainty is more plausible, and alternative theories of "complexity economic" have been recently emerging (more on this in Chapter 18).

Yet, this unrealistic assumption lies at the root of tying money to credit. If borrowers knew their likelihood of success and their future income potential, they would only accept as much credit as they could repay. If banks knew these things, they would only lend that much and only to the counterparts that would repay. But the world is far too complex, and since banks base their statistical analyses on the past, these are, at best, inaccurate. The future is not the past and continues to surprise us. Many mainstream economists seem unable to grasp this concept and keep hunting for universal laws of economics that must lie out there somewhere.

When the financial crash of 2008 hit, Queen Elizabeth asked why no one saw it coming.[1] The answer is simple: that reliance on past information. While statistical evidence based on history is one possible—and valuable—way to understand the future, it cannot be the only way and it will definitely not forecast rare events. We will never see things coming if we don't play ahead of the game and prepare for an uncertain world.

In Mervyn King's words, "A capitalist economy is inherently a monetary economy, which behaves very differently from the textbook description of a market economy. . . . Our inability to anticipate all possible eventualities means that we—households, businesses, banks, central banks and governments—will make judgments that turn out to have been 'mistakes.' Those mistakes are at the heart of any story about financial crisis."

The second assumption about our consequent rationality is also flawed. Though we barely understand the human mind in its entirety, behavioral science has clearly shown that we often do not act rationally.

After rebranding itself as behavioral economics, behavioral science can now count six Nobel Prizes in economics[2] based more or less on this core concept: The brain makes predictable and systematic irrational choices. Laureate Richard Thaler wrote, "If you look at economics textbooks, you will learn that *Homo economicus* can think like Albert Einstein, store as much memory as IBM Big Blue, and exercise the will power of Mahatma Gandhi. Really. But the folks that we know are not like that. Real people have trouble with long division if they do not have a calculator, sometimes forget their spouse's birthday, and have a hangover on New Year's Day."[3] A common critique of behavioral economics is that it focuses too much on deviations from human rationality that do not really matter on average in the big scheme of things. Thaler has the perfect response: "To qualify as Econs, people are required to make unbiased forecasts. That is, the forecast can be wrong, but can't be systematically wrong in a predictable direction."[4] And it is "systematically" that is important here, as one definition of cognitive bias is "a *systematic pattern* of deviation from norm or rationality in judgment."[5]

Among hundreds of cognitive biases that psychologists have identified, two matter especially for us. The first is that we fear losses more than we seek gains of the same proportion: We have a risk aversion bias. The second is that we excessively discount future benefits and losses: We have a present bias.

The combination of these two undermines the main pillar of neoliberal capitalism, and capitalism in general—perfect competition. According to this theory, suppliers would strive to provide the best features to their products and services at the lowest price to win over customers. Instead, suppliers have a common bias and interest in reacting to any increase of purchasing power—so when more people want to buy more—with a riskless strategy: price increase. Because of our cognitive biases, we delay risky investments that may pay off bigger in the long term. This is not to say that companies don't invest in reaction to an increase in demand. Far from it. Rather, they invest less or later than a perfect competition model would imply, because of their risk aversion and present bias. In a 2017 global survey of business executives, 38% of respondents listed risk aversion as the key reason for not investing in all attractive opportunities.[6] And that's just respondents who were aware of the bias and could acknowledge it. Those reduced or delayed investments are enough to allow for inflation and price increases, before we see meaningful increases in supply and quality.

The same is true for the present bias, especially given the pressure that capital markets place on CEOs for big, ongoing profits every quarter. In *Makers and Takers,* Rana Foroohar wrote that in one survey, 80% of CEOs stated they would pass on an investment worth a decade of innovation if it meant they would miss a quarter of earnings results.[7]

If you add to these biases the common interest of suppliers in keeping prices high, perfect competition requires a utopia. Assuming competing companies do not talk to each other—some do—if all suppliers of a certain product keep prices high, they are all better off at the expense of consumers. A price war doesn't benefit any company, only the customers: us.

Different industries behave differently, but in general, companies have a common interest in keeping prices higher than they would under perfect competition. Moreover, we often end up with oligopolies, where few large companies control a market. Coca-Cola and Pepsi are a well-known example. More recently, we see Google and Facebook with online ads. But even when an industry is less concentrated, like smartphones, the common interest of suppliers in making money can ensure that prices stay high enough for most players to enjoy huge profits.

The book *Nudge* describes the example of student loans in the US. Thanks to government guarantees and subsidies, they became a riskless product for banks. Under perfect competition, the price for these loans would end up very close to the cost of funding for banks, but in fact the opposite is true. Banks don't compete on price at all. They just battle for the attention and trust of students.[8]

In my own experience in start-ups, I've seen that once you have an innovative idea, most established market players will only collaborate with you in exchange for exclusivity so they can charge higher prices.

As a consultant, I have often worked on growth strategies for large companies. One of the questions that heads of strategy often ask is, "Is there enough demand to grow supply while avoiding a price war?"

Some examples of strategic management of supply are broadly available. Wikipedia can give you a good explanation of how the Organization of the Petroleum Exporting Countries (OPEC) works to maximize profits for oil-rich countries at the expense of all other countries and consumers, or how the global monopoly over the diamond industry emerged and its high prices for diamonds persist to this day, again at the expense of buyers.

This behavior should not surprise anyone. Any marketing class in business school will teach that the best pricing strategy is to *price as high as customers are willing to pay.* So companies have a duty to increase prices if customers can afford it. Otherwise the executive team is often deemed underperforming, and it tends to get replaced by one that raises prices to take easy profits. This quest for the highest price also leads companies to lose sight of the morality of their price policies. If you look deep enough into pricing algorithms built to maximize profits—and I know first-hand people who developed some of these—you will find discriminatory practices. For example, financial institutions may increase the fees for your current account or your insurance premiums if you are deemed unlikely to shop around for cheaper competitors. This practice may look reasonable for a free-market capitalist, but in practice it leads those with less education to pay higher prices than a digital-savvy college graduate for the same product. And this is without considering AI that can automate these decisions based on past biased information that may discriminate based on gender and race.

Some economists are rightly questioning the hypothesis that free markets offer the lowest possible price to consumers. Adair Turner strongly challenged the belief. Joseph Stiglitz claims America has a huge monopoly problem and writes that "now we know that higher profits can arise from a better way of exploiting consumers, a better way of price discrimination, extracting consumer surplus, the main effect of which is to redistribute income from consumers to our new super-wealthy."[9]

"Exploiting" is exactly the right word, especially when sales managers and advertising companies are trained to leverage different fears and biases in people, leading consumers to make irrational choices without even realizing it.

The IMF has found that growth of price markups over marginal costs have increased by 8% since 2000 in 16 advanced economies.[10] In other words, companies have been able to further increase the margin of what they charge on top of their costs.

The success of Amazon in price wars is the exception confirming the general rule that perfect competition does not exist. Amazon made low prices a key part of its strategy, and never walked back from this, gaining the trust of consumers. Amazon has been a game changer wherever it has competed. Companies are not used to unfettered price competition. When Amazon announced it would enter the healthcare business in the US, the share prices of US healthcare companies fell by some 9% in one day.[11] The share price of retailers reacted similarly when Amazon bought Whole Foods in 2017. The convulsions of price wars shake any sector Amazon enters. We often forget that stock prices are based on the expectation to make future profits for the shareholders. In this case, lower stock prices may be worse for shareholders, but they are a sign that consumers will likely benefit from lower prices.

However, Amazon is a very new phenomenon and it's not big enough to change the way capitalism works today. The fact that inflation is generally positive is proof that capitalism remains very far from perfect competition. While technological progress should make products of the same quality cheaper, a generally positive inflation signals the opposite. We had to focus central banks on limiting inflation to tame suppliers' thirst for higher prices, and we limited growth in the process.

Our cognitive biases and the common interest of suppliers in keeping prices high make perfect competition a dream, and that's a big glitch in capitalism. The price mechanism is broken, perfect competition works only in a utopia, and the invisible hand of free markets can't succeed. Inflation should be called "capitalism tax." Proponents of neoliberal capitalism were rightly concerned with inflation, but instead of trying to influence these behaviors with incentives they went for cutting the money supply when things get out of whack.

If we add the inflation linked to suppliers' opportunism and risk aversion, to the inflation from real estate due to receipt of excessive credit (from Chapter 7), to the inflation due to the decline in investments when central banks increase interest rates to combat inflation (also from Chapter 7), we can pretty much say that the cause of inflation is capitalism and the decision to tie money to credit.

However, I do not want to imply that, despite the absence of perfect competition, we should dismantle capitalism. I want to make it explicit that this book does not advocate destroying what capitalism has given us. It has utterly transformed the world in the last four centuries and bestowed benefits too numerous to list.

But we are moving beyond capitalism, and its rigidity supported by a flawed pseudoscience economic theory that is locking society into a cage. Mariana Mazzucato highlights how we have a discourse problem: We discuss policymaking assuming perfect competition as the natural state, with some deviations to tackle.[12] If instead we start by considering competition and the free markets as intrinsically imperfect and biased, we acknowledge the problem and we'll seek a socio-economic system that corrects these imperfections, or at least manages the consequences.

If imperfect competition leads to unfair high returns while harming economic growth (for example by delaying or avoiding useful investments), we have a major issue that governing institutions must understand and tackle. It is not surprising that in this context the returns on wealth are higher than the growth rate, and wealth keeps concentrating, as Piketty described.

And imperfect competition is the root of all recessions. In the next exhibit you can see the two intersecting cycles of growth and recessions. As long as companies increase investments and raise salaries, people buy more and the growth cycle continues. It's only when companies increase their profits through lower salaries or higher prices that the cycle of growth shifts. Overall spending drops and we enter a recession. Central banks raise interest rates, consumption drops further, and investments fall as a consequence.

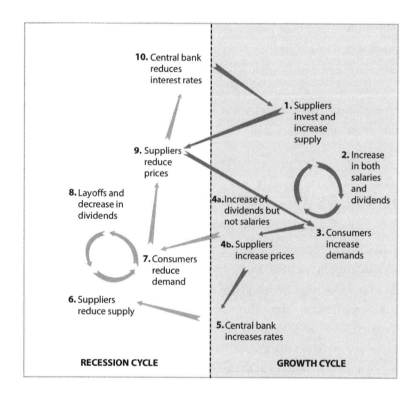

Exhibit 6: Intersecting cycles of growth and recession

We've had more than a century of business cycles where growth and recessions alternated.

Capitalism is hurting itself with its own principles. Companies raise prices as people can afford more, even if that affordability comes through increasing household debts that banks arc eager to fuel. At the same time, productivity gains, automation, and the globalized supply of labor are limiting wages, and making debts difficult to repay and further consumption unaffordable. These are the twin causes of recession cycles.

In light of this major flaw, did neoliberalism actually keep any of its promises?

BROKEN PROMISES IN THE WORLD OF IMPERFECT COMPETITION

Neoliberal capitalism did not become mainstream just because Keynesian economics could not manage inflation. Its proponents sold it to the world with an array of promises, including growth and well-being, but also the full benefits of capitalism, which would include 1) freedom and protection of property rights, 2) meritocracy and equal opportunities, 3) efficient resource allocation, and 4) innovation.

Growth has not been inclusive and well-being has not improved, but what about the other promises?

1. FREEDOM AND PRIVATE PROPERTY RIGHTS—FOR THE WEALTHY

A basic foundation of capitalism is people's free choice in spending their time and money, using their property, and pursuing the education and profession they want. These freedoms are not just the foundations of capitalism but also benefits on their own. I challenge anyone to argue against them as fundamental rights.

At the same time, we know that anarchy—lack of government and laws—is only a superficial, illusory freedom, since it leads to the law of the jungle. Some gain the power to restrict the freedom of others. If free market is more like anarchy, we are pursuing freedom in the wrong way.

The inequality of income and wealth limits the freedom of people who have less. Individual purchasing decisions in fact drive the allocation of resources, and those who can buy more have more weight. The allocation of resources also determines the professions that the market requires and hence what people need to do to earn money. The book *Dollarocracy* highlights how inequality leads to diminishing the value of democracy.[13] What is the value of an equal right to vote, if what matters most is where we funnel our resources, and an ever-smaller group of wealthy people can strongly affect this funneling with limited influence from the elected government? The neoliberal version of capitalism would give democratic government, which is the expression of the public will, as small a role as possible. Instead of a monarch with full powers, we would have an elected government with very little power, with most power in the hands of markets. And who rules in the markets? Those with the wealth to allocate resources.

But this view is even worse if we acknowledge that the wealthy strongly influence even the little power left over in government. Larry Bartels found that US senators are five to six times more likely to respond to interests of the rich than those of the middle class, and there is no evidence that the views of low-income constituents have any effect on their senators' votes.[14] In *The Great Escape*, Nobel laureate Angus Deaton also raises this concern:

> There is a danger that the rapid growth of top incomes can become self-reinforcing through the political access that money can bring. Rules are not set in the public interest but in the interest of the rich. . . . The countries in the OECD that have seen the largest increase of income at the very top are the countries that have seen the largest cuts in taxes on top income.[15] . . . If Democracy becomes plutocracy, those who are not rich are effectively disenfranchised. . . . The very wealthy have little need for state-provided education or health care; they have every reason to support cuts in Medicare and to fight any increases in taxes.[16]

Are you surprised that Donald Trump proposed and passed a tax reform expected to slash $1.5 trillion a year of taxes,[17] mostly benefiting the rich, and has proposed a 2019 budget that cuts Medicare, Medicaid,[18] and subsidies for student loans?[19] I am not. But I am sad because those low-income people who were manipulated into voting for him are the ones the Trump administration hit the hardest.

Let me make it clear: This issue is not a partisan one but a structural defect in the combination of capitalism and democracy. The greater the inequality, the more the democracy becomes a mere veil over the interests of the wealthy.

In *Global Inequality*, Branko Milanovic collects several studies showing that US members of Congress are much more concerned with issues affecting rich rather than poor constituents. This fact holds true whether the government is Democratic or Republican. Branko concludes that

> Whether the poor or the middle class care a lot or not at all about a given issue has no influence on legislators. . . . The rich spend billions on funding political campaigns and, like oil and pharmaceutical industries, in lobbying; as a result, the policies that are in their interests are implemented. In a positive feedback loop, pro-rich policies further increase the income of the rich, which in turn makes the rich practically the only people able to make significant donations to politicians, and thus the only ones who get a hearing from politicians. The political importance of each individual becomes equivalent to his or her income level, and instead of a one-person one-vote system, we approach a system of one-dollar one-vote. . . . A plutocracy is thus born.[20]

And since governments are more and more dependent on credit to fund their ballooning debts, the influence of private creditors, mostly the wealthy again, is even higher.

"Dollarocracy" is an adequate word for this system, as the 1% with the most wealth and access to credit can steer public policy and limit the freedom of the other 99%. The freedom to pass wealth down through generations can perpetuate these imbalances forever, and this is why Branko echoes one of Piketty's proposals: a high inheritance tax.[21]

But capitalism limits freedom in still other ways. Perhaps the most important limitation is the need to have a job to satisfy basic needs. While understandable in the past, when employment opportunities prevailed and collective work lifted us from widespread poverty, it is less comprehensible today. Good jobs are lacking and will become scarcer as productivity increases. Salaries have stagnated or even decreased and the competition for investments between countries has forced governments to increase employers' flexibility in dealing with employees. Elizabeth Anderson and James Livingston rightly argue whether we have real liberty or are really all just slaves of employers, at least to some extent.[22] The rise of "in-work poverty," people employed full-time but with such low wages that they fall below the poverty line, reinforces the risk of "forced employment."

Still, working full-time to be poor is still better than not working and dying in the cold on a park bench.

And arguably, we really have defensible property rights only if society fairly manages the tool to assert them: money. But if too many people can't get enough money and must go into debt and even sell their property to meet basic needs, it is questionable that they enjoy true property rights.

Even so, if we had equal opportunity, we could at least defend capitalism on meritocratic grounds. Right?

2. MERITOCRACY AND EQUAL OPPORTUNITIES—FOR SOME

Through greater privatization neoliberal capitalism could shift more activities to a for-profit basis, and profit is the reward for those who spend time, energy, and thoughts to offer something buyers desire. Consumers make free decisions and society remunerates producers and sellers who best satisfy them. Successful companies remunerate their workers, and the more they create value, the more and the longer they can pay their employees. In a different way, workers who are skilled at working together and contributing to their companies' bottom lines receive more money to buy more goods and services.

And the more sources of finance develop, the less you need money in advance to thrive in the economy. Suppose you want to be an entrepreneur and you have a good idea. Free markets have enabled the rise of business angels, incubators, and venture capitalists who can give you money in exchange for part ownership of your start-up. If your company has ambitious growth plans, you can get loans from banks or you can list your company on a stock exchange. In case you fail, certain laws limit your responsibility and make an entrepreneurial career less risky.

It all sounds wonderful. Unfortunately, our system is also limiting meritocracy and equal opportunities, and inequality is still to blame. Oxfam denounced the fact that 74% of billionaires owe their wealth to rents and not to producing something useful to society.[23] The book *Twilight of the Elites: America After Meritocracy* shows how equality of opportunity is a myth, unless we can all get quality education (among other aspects of human development). Access to this career booster is certainly not equal in the US, due both to high tuition and the cost of living during the college years.[24]

Globalization also halted the rise in workers' salaries while companies' profits increased. So it broke the meritocratic chain that was meant to allow workers to benefit from their contribution to companies' profits, and to buy more goods and services.

Under this lens, it is not surprising that the US and UK—the most neoliberal countries—rank among the lowest in social mobility among the high-income nations. In a country with perfect equality of opportunity, the correlation of parents' and children's incomes would be zero, meaning there is no predictable correlation between what a parent earns and what their child will earn because everyone starts out with the same opportunities. Of course this is rare. In the US, for example, the correlation is 0.5, meaning that parents' income is responsible for about 50% of what a child will earn. Only the remaining 50% is dependent on other variables unrelated to parents' income, such as luck, grit, demographics, and so on. Indeed, the rate in the US is the highest—the least socially mobile—among all OECD nations.[25]

The chances of jumping between two opposite poles is quite low. Only 6% of children born into low-income families become high earners,[26] a fact that effectively shatters the American dream of equal opportunity. The book *The Spirit Level* and the OECD have shown that the least equal countries have less social mobility. Miles Corak demonstrates a strong correlation between income inequality and similarities across intergenerational earning, with the US, UK, and Italy having both the highest inequality and least social mobility.[27] The strata are increasingly harder to cross. If you are of a racial minority or a woman, it all gets even harder.

3. EFFICIENT RESOURCE ALLOCATION—REALLY?

Neoliberal exponents also argued that if we tied all money to interest-bearing credit, we might make the most of limited resources. People need to repay more than they borrow, so they have to make good use of what they have. The drive for profit combined with competition also reduces the room for waste, as companies that are more efficient shoulder the less efficient ones out of the market. Governments, not subject to for-profit pressure, can only get money to allocate resources if they can convince people and companies to pay taxes or to lend them money, keeping governments' resource allocation limited and under a tight leash.

That's the theory. What's the reality?

Again, there's a disconnect. The concentration of wealth arguably breeds inefficient resource allocation. There is increasing evidence that giving small amounts of free money to poor people leads to wise expenditures on education, health, and investments, and not on alcohol and tobacco, as most people incorrectly believe. On the other hand, wealthy people spend money in ways that are more questionable. Even assuming they don't waste it on harmful activities (and the high cocaine content of London sewage waters tells a different story), you need a damn good argument to convince anyone that we use resources better in producing luxury goods than in providing food, health, education, and shelter for everyone. Here are a few findings from a report of the United Nations: In 1998 the world spent $400 billion on narcotic drugs and $780 billion on the military. In contrast, an additional $6 billion could have given universal access to education to people in all developing countries, and an additional $13 billion could have given the same people universal access to basic health and nutrition.[28] We can debate the figures, but the order of magnitude is striking, and the situation has not changed in the last 20 years. Universal education would have cost $22 billion a year in 2015 according to UNESCO.[29]

Idle and Underutilized Resources

Two more problems add to this misallotment. First, many resources lie idle while people still have unmet basic needs. Pick any need you want. You'll find unemployed people and available technology to increase supply of goods and services and fill that need. For instance, many nations need better infrastructure and construction companies often have extra capacity, but government funding constraints keep these resources idle.

This is why a local currency like the Sardex boosted the GDP of Sardinia. These currencies give people more money so they could produce and consume more instead of leaving resources unused. This is also why when a crisis hits, central bankers throw neoliberal theories out the window and lend money to governments to mobilize idle resources.

The biggest gaps in my opinion are in early childhood education and elderly care. The unemployed could be trained as caregivers for the elderly or for children, achieving both social and economic benefits. In the EU, only 34% of children below 3 years old have access to center-based childcare, leaving an opportunity to employ about 4 million people who are instead unemployed. And such investment would have more financial returns than any other education investment, given most brain development happens in the first years of life.[30]

A similar issue to idle resources is having valuable resources underutilized, the biggest example being women. In most countries the mix of tradition and human biases lead to women being underpaid and overlooked for promotions. Just closing the entrepreneurship gap between men and women would increase global GDP by up to 5 trillion, or 6% of today's GDP.[31] If women were to achieve the same roles as men, GDP could be $28 trillion higher at a global level by 2025.[32] That's 26% of GDP in 2025, not a minor inefficiency.

Environmental Damage

The second issue might be even more critical. Any damage to the environment, including climate change, is a direct consequence of resource misallocation.

For those who don't believe that we humans have caused climate change, 97% of scientists studying the topic believe that we have and that the evidence discredits the few skeptics. The remaining 3% have ties with the oil or coal industry and hence are not independent researchers.[33] The reason why human-led climate change is not as accepted as the science would justify is that oil and gas companies have fabulous wealth still buried in the ground and if we shift to renewables too soon, most of it would become worthless. These companies fund public relations agencies, lobbies, and politicians to undermine the scientific conclusions about the future of climate. So politically there is still a debate, but it's vacuous, since we know the answer. I will get back to climate change, as this is a defining and existential challenge of our century.

What is the free market doing to solve this challenge? Well, first of all we should remind ourselves that free markets caused the problem in the first place. Climate change, or any damage to the environment, is an "externality," or side effect, of economic growth.

We have the technology today to produce 100% of our energy needs through clean energy, but due to short-term economic considerations, the shift is not happening fast enough. Coal and gasoline are overheating our planet, but they are still cheaper than many clean alternatives. The laws of free markets are blind and present-bound.

Almost all new technologies follow the same course. In the early stages they are very expensive, but they get cheaper as companies grow more efficient at producing them. The Boston Consulting Group first described the concept of *experience curves*: Every time the cumulative production doubles, the cost of each unit decreases by a rather constant percentage. So it's very shortsighted to compare the costs of a mature technology like coal power with those of an emerging one like solar. The latter has only begun to climb the experience curve and could become much cheaper in the long term. But this is another limitation of free markets.

Many governments that could solve these issues lack the funds to provide incentives to turn our economies to clean energy. But thanks to those that could and did invest in renewables, mostly through subsidized energy prices, companies started mass production of solar panels and plants, which in turn led to a 90% cost reduction over 10 years.[34] As I write, we stand 178 years after the discovery of the photovoltaic effect, 134 years after the creation of the first solar cell, and 64 years after silicon solar cells hit the market.[35] Why did solar energy finally become as cheap or cheaper than fossil fuels only in 2017? Because significant research only began in the energy crises of the 1970s. Until then, governments paid no attention to the topic and the free market was splashing around in oil.

And even today, when people propose initiatives like future bans in the sale of non-electric cars, you have individuals like the president of the German Automotive Association saying that such "drastic proposals have nothing to do with a market economy and pave the way to a planned ecologic economy." Well, maybe a planned ecologic economy is part of the solution, because free markets do nothing to guarantee that we will react in time to save our planet from catastrophe.

The free-market solution to climate change is to impose a carbon tax (or even better, create a market to trade pollution allowances) so that the price mechanism would reflect the cost of the environment. This is definitely better than not doing anything, but is it enough when we face a problem scientists say will cause extraordinary havoc? At the same time political opposition is still strong enough to keep these taxes or carbon prices ridiculously low. The real costs of climate change and other environmental damage could be huge, and it would even be wrong to put a number on it since people's lives are at stake. As such, it may well require the higher ecologic planning despised by those who favor neoliberal capitalism.

We are hardly living in a society that uses resources efficiently: We are rushing to produce more luxury goods and weapons instead of providing universal access to basic education and health, cleaning up our planet, and curbing climate change. With neoliberalism, we allocate resources to maximize the profit coming in from those who have money to pay. There is neither a physical law nor any evidence that shows this allocation is efficient, when measured against societal outcomes. Some of this allocation makes activities useless and even hazardous to us all.

4. INNOVATION—TO SOME EXTENT

The drive for profit and free-market competition has fostered constant innovation. And innovation has been a key to our progress, creating new technologies that better met our needs, gave us new powers (such as handheld communication), and slashed the cost of goods and services. It has been a spectacular success. The last few centuries have seen the greatest progress in history, not just economically but socially as well. If you are not convinced, or just want to see all the details, there are plenty of sources available.[36] But with our bias toward emphasizing the negative and the media's focus on bad news, many people think that the world has grown worse. While that may be true for some countries and in specific ways—like access to basic needs in the US—if we look across outcomes and take a global view, the world has definitely become a much better place, even in the past 40 years. This promise was fulfilled.

But is neoliberal capitalism the best recipe for maximizing innovation?

Already today, we see many cases where neoliberal capitalism frustrates our ability to fully tap the innovation potential.

Bias Toward Short Term

As we've seen, people—investors—have a bias toward the short term. They will invest in projects with lower risk-adjusted returns if those returns materialize sooner. As a consequence, they focus too much on the short term (except for a few like Warren Buffett). People working for funds, investment banks, and to lesser extent sovereign funds have quarterly objectives based on profit. They therefore prefer investing in companies that seem to promise short-term returns. Companies also evaluate their top managers based on the value of their company on the stock market, which depends on investor decisions to sell or buy. Companies also end up preferring short-term returns, which unfortunately often leads them to sacrifice long-term investments with uncertain but potentially large returns. Governments undertake some of these investments, while others are lost opportunities for society.

In this light, who would invest in a project that required 50 years to pay back, or any project that lost money but provided great social value? Who would research a technology that could enormously increase productivity, but would not profit the company creating it? Only governments and NGOs, which collect money from us, and very few billionaires like Richard Branson and Bill Gates who could not care less about profit anymore and focus only on innovation and social impact. Thanks to the good they do, the enormous wealth they accumulated helps humanity rather than sitting somewhere in shorter-term investments to simply grow further, which is where many other billionaires put their money.

But the only reliable source of these long-term uncertain investments—which could be so helpful to stop climate change—is governments. However, a global tax system remains far-fetched for now, and we cannot expect government taxation to be a reliable source of important long-term innovation projects. Many of these opportunities are obviously lost. Since 1980 US Federal spending on education, infrastructure, and scientific research has fallen from about 2.5% of GDP to 1.5% of GDP,[37] and this is a direct consequence of the neoliberal ideology.

Unaffordable Innovation

Inequality also limits innovation. Many inventions are in fact improvements in the quality of products, but if their prices also increase, many people won't be able to afford them. As a result, the potential for innovation declines as many new and helpful upgrades lack viable markets to sell into. If you are an entrepreneur, you've probably faced situations in which your idea was too expensive for most people yet not "luxurious" enough for the very high end. If you have a retail business, you are probably very familiar with this phenomenon as well, as you see sales volume being higher for cheap low-quality products than less affordable but higher quality ones.

You might argue that if everyone got the high-quality high-price product, we'd be wasting resources. On the contrary, the poor end up wasting resources because they are poor. They will buy the cheap light bulb that burns out quickly and consumes more electricity. Or kitchen utensils with shorter life spans. Considering the life-cycle cost, these bulbs are more expensive and wasteful than the more expensive neon or LED lights. And the harm to the impoverished can be far worse, for they tend to eat cheap, low-quality food, and as a result may spend a fortune in health-care bills and even die of problems related to obesity and high cholesterol.

Many earthquakes afflict the center of Italy, but do you think people have money to build quake-proof buildings? Even when the government has provided funds for reconstruction, the buildings often collapsed in later earthquakes.[38]

Why? In fact, governments also prefer low price to high quality, and sometimes even over safety. In late 2017, the Australian government set a fixed reimbursement price for bioprosthetic heart valves required in cardiac surgery. The price matched that of the lowest bidder, but compared to higher quality alternatives backed by clinical evidence, the device subjected patients to an increased length of hospitalization and a significantly higher need for a pacemaker, in a second procedure. Sadly, most hospitals chose to use the low-quality option fully funded by the government, as they didn't want to pay more for a better device. Even worse, for the same heart valves in mid-2020 the Dutch government decided not to reimburse any noninvasive heart surgery to substitute heart valves unless open-heart procedures are high risks. Basically if you are a young patient in the Netherlands with aortic stenosis and need a valve replacement, the public hospitals will cut you open and keep you in the hospital for a week instead of using a more expensive medical device to deploy the aortic valve through a small hole in your leg and send you home the day after with a minuscule scar.

The fact that most people and even governments cannot afford the quality products that innovation bestows is bad per se and it's a disincentive to invest in more innovation. Of course, the luxury market is different. We see the inequality in people purchasing $300 bottles of water or buying tea in a 7-star hotel for $200. Most economists do not care where production goes, though. If I can make more money with 1,000 golden toothbrushes rather than 1,000 bottles of medicine, hooray for the golden toothbrushes!

Alarmingly, we were already heading in this direction before the 2008 crisis, at least according to analysts at Citigroup. A report back in 2005 claimed that the US, UK, and Canada were becoming "plutonomies": economies powered by the wealthy. The authors suggested that their clients divest from companies serving the shrinking middle class and focus on those catering to the luxury segments. And in fact, the "plutonomy stock basket" they suggested had outperformed the market by an average of 6.8% annually, an enormous amount, in the previous 20 years.[39]

Here is how Martin Ford describes this horrible "golden toothbrush scenario":

> The most frightening long-term scenario of all might be if the global economic system eventually manages to adapt to the new reality. In a perverse process of creative destruction, the mass-market industries that currently power our economy would be replaced by new industries producing high-value products and services geared exclusively toward a super-wealthy elite. The vast majority of humanity would effectively be disenfranchised. Economic mobility would become non-existent. The plutocracy would shut itself away in gated communities or in elite cities, perhaps guarded by autonomous military robots and drones.[40]

Only If It Doesn't Kill Jobs

The last limitation to innovation is the need to employ the full population to allow their consumption. That is foundational to capitalism and it seems obvious and good to most. If you don't earn, you can't buy. While this is a great incentive for people to contribute to society, what happens when there just aren't enough jobs? If we pursue—as we should—as much automation as possible, many people will ultimately lose or reduce their earnings and won't be able to afford the product of highly automated businesses, which will in turn have less of an incentive to innovate. Of course, they can still make golden toothbrushes for those who own the robots, but since almost no one wants this "plutonomy," governments commonly act to limit innovation.

For example, a proposal to tax robots has gained some traction and renowned supporters like Bill Gates. And trapped in the cage of capitalism, even a Nobel laureate of the caliber of Robert Shiller endorsed the productivity-killing proposal of taxing robots.[41] South Korea has scaled back some incentive on automation,[42] which had led the country to become the largest adopter of industrial robots.

But why would we want to limit automation? Why force people to spend time on activities that they don't want, just to get a salary? If they gained life fulfillment from those activities, they might do them for free or much less. If we reach this absurd point, why not just give people free money and the time to pursue well-being, while robots do most of the hard work?

Brilliant economists proposing to limit automation are a symbol of the confusion within the darkness of the cage of capitalism, with intelligent people contradicting one another and themselves, in a show of genius turned mad. Why on earth would we stop machines that are more accurate than humans from doing the hard and heavy work instead of us? It is only because in capitalism we need jobs to pay salaries to afford life.

And the issue goes beyond automation. In capitalism creative destruction is a value, as old companies with obsolete goods and services or business models disappear in favor of better ones. But if creative destruction becomes economic destruction, reducing jobs and spending, we enter a vicious cycle with no precedent. We can easily imagine a world in which the telecom industry disappears, when high-tech companies give everyone free internet access and have an interest in doing so because of ads sales. The banking industry could shrink significantly if we shifted to a society where everyone has more savings and doesn't need as much loans. Payment services are already available with free apps, and deposits could stay safe in accounts in central banks or even on one's phone.

But governments are hardly ready to cope with the resulting high rates of unemployment, and without sound alternatives to give people purchasing power, they retreat to protecting incumbent industries and companies from innovation and competition, killing the spirit of free-market capitalism. Is it then the fault of government or capitalism? Should the government allow a massive crisis to make the point that free markets aren't working?

IN SUMMARY

Neoliberal capitalism has clearly failed across the spectrum and it is suboptimal to achieve any of its stated promises. It is arguable whether it was ever a success. The IMF itself, one of the biggest sponsors of neoliberal reforms, had to admit that "neoliberal policies might have been oversold."[43]

When a strategy fails, normal people reconsider it. The failures of neoliberal capitalism make the case to reevaluate all of its features, including the ban on the use of permanent money. Permanent money is a tool locked away in a box. It could not only sustain the economy at times of crisis, but also help fund a UBI program to enable all people to pursue well-being.

In Chapter 8 we mentioned that the rationale for banning the use of permanent money was the risk of inflation, and the idea that government allocation of money would crowd out private allocation, deemed a better breed. In this chapter we saw that neoliberal capitalism is still causing inflation, and its resource allocation is all but efficient. I am not saying that the government is more efficient than the private sector. It is most often the opposite. But free markets have done even worse than any modern government would in sending resources to better destinations—that is, to education, healthcare, infrastructure, renewables, and social protection.

Yet we can't overcome a habit—almost an addiction—like that of capitalism without a sound alternative. Would going back to pre-neoliberal capitalism be good enough?

Chapter 11

It's a New World: Production Now Depends on Distribution

We could produce more and better if only people could afford it

Most countries deployed Keynesian remedies to the 2008 crash, and central banks bought government bonds, in a soft form of monetary finance reminiscent of war times. Countries in the European Union that stuck with a neoliberal policy of government austerity did much worse, to the point that the Council of Europe has even declared these policies in Greece a breach of human rights.[1] Consequently, more economists started wondering whether neoliberal capitalism was oversold.

In the previous discussion on stagflation, I explained that the shift to neoliberal theories was not really justified and their introduction coincided with the continuous worsening of multiple social and economic outcomes, especially for the least well-off.

Today one could say we live in a society where Keynesian and neoliberal views are on equal footing, at least in most countries, including the US. But this is not good enough. Taking the perspective of citizens, Keynesian theories saved many from unemployment and poverty over and over, and only had the fault of not being able to manage inflation in the 1970s. Neoliberal theories tamed inflation but also gave us inequality, slower growth, exploding debts, financial crises, higher poverty, and unnecessary hardship on the population. There is little reason for putting them on equal footing to Keynesian theories and the reaction to COVID-19, even in Europe, looks like a stronger embrace of Keynesian capitalism. But many still fear that as soon as the COVID-19 crisis is over, governments would go back to unreasonable and flawed policies of running budget surpluses, which always end up affecting those most vulnerable.

A systematic shift back to Keynesian theories would indeed be a welcomed step in the right direction and a more natural starting point for an evolution toward monetism. But we should ask ourselves this: Is it enough to go back to pre-neoliberal capitalism? Or is our world changed so much as to make capitalism obsolete? I argue that 21st-century societies—in high-income countries at least—have outgrown capitalism and are ready for the next step.

In fact, Keynes did not really have a different solution to the problem of inflation from what we are using these days. And fixing capitalism by walking 70 years into the past would mean we have learned nothing.

Moreover, Keynes lived in a different world to the one we live in today. We have to adapt to the real environment, as Keynes would have himself. Economists' love for simple theoretical laws, at times supported with scant evidence from past data, unfortunately limits their ability to plan for the future. New important trends are already changing the fabrics of societies, and just as any business would, society needs a good forward-looking strategy to prepare to the changing context.

And strategy is my full-time job, which is why with this book I step into a turf that has been too long left to academic economists, attempting to find laws of economics and get their name into the history of the discipline. Societies and economies are not like our physical world with immutable laws. They are messy and continuously changing, more like the weather and the climate. And while it's important to understand their dynamics, it is at least equally important to have strategies in place to react to the continuous changes and unpredictable uncertainty.

A DIFFERENT WORLD

I do not want to suggest that economic growth should be the purpose of 21st-century societies, but one of the arguments to consider capitalism obsolete and put it behind us is that it is no longer adequate even to achieve its own objective.

In the next chapter I will look at what monetism should aim for, but here I will make my case for why capitalism will remain unable to achieve the growth potential of our economies.

Economists have been debating what drives economic growth. Is it the investments to supply goods and services (from now on, "supply") that pays workers a salary to afford the consumption? Or is it the demand for goods and services (from now on, "demand") that convinces companies to invest, hire, and pay salaries? This debate is an important one for our purposes. If economies grow "pushed" by an increase in supply, then we can only focus on increasing the supply as much as possible, which involves making our resources more productive. Capital and technology is what allows us to produce more with less, and therefore a society centered on making the most of the limited capital is pretty much all that matters.

If instead the economies are "pulled" by the demand of customers, and only when consumers buy do companies mobilize to produce and become more productive, then the focus has to shift to ensuring there is sufficient demand for companies to make the most of resources that would otherwise be left idle, including workers. Neoliberal capitalism—and capitalism in general—works well on the assumption that supply drives the economy. Just focus on helping companies become more productive and all will be good. Keynes thought overall demand mattered at least as much.

My view on what drives growth? It depends. But in most advanced countries we are permanently entering a time in which we could produce more than we have purchasing power to afford, a situation called by many economists "secular stagnation."

In the 1800s, as all countries were underdeveloped, supporters of a supply-driven economy were generally right. People and companies got loans or raised equity to produce things, and as they hired people and paid salaries, they created their own demand, since employees received a salary and bought goods and services with it.

This is also the time-sequence that money follows: First a company asks for a loan, and banks create the money in the form of a deposit. This deposit is at this point a savings in the companies' bank account that is rapidly spent and transformed into an investment. The initial deposit becomes revenues of suppliers and salaries of workers, again a form of savings.[2]

Investments to increase the physical capital provide society with better technologies that increase productivity and the production potential of the economy.

Inflation is typically higher in the early stages of development, so people are less prone to keep money in liquid form. In fact, inflation can strip their money of value quickly, so they would rationally invest it or consume more straightaway.

As capitalism was first emerging, every country stood at this stage of underdevelopment. Back then, society was so poor that it's hard to imagine it. In 1800, average life expectancy worldwide was less than 30 years, and half of all human beings died before adulthood.[3] Most human beings tilled the soil. Corporations as we know them didn't exist. Travel was costly and arduous—the word derives from "travail"—and communication was as slow as travel itself. And capital? The world had little of it, and every bit of additional capital could generate life-improving goods. And that world had a huge need for labor. In fact, almost everything was labor-intensive. We had to make the best use of the limited capital and motivate people to give up subsistence farming and work instead. In 1803 economist Jean-Baptiste Say proposed that supply pulls the economy, and as long as we can increase supply, demand will grow in tandem. Capitalism was a good solution, and it fulfilled many of its promises of freedom, better opportunities, more efficient resource allocation, and more innovation.

But is that still the case today, given all the knowledge, technology, capital, and labor available today? Is supply—investments—still the driving force of economic growth?

INEQUALITY-INDUCED SECULAR STAGNATION

Secular stagnation is a term economists use to describe an economy that grows very little, neither because we can no longer increase our productivity nor because resources are becoming scarcer, but simply because there is not enough demand to justify a higher value of production. Resources are therefore left idle—especially people, who are left jobless.

This theory reemerged again after the 2008 crisis and most researchers and institutions have indeed pointed out as the main causes the following: rising inequality, the consequent excessive debts, and an aging population that requires higher savings. This goes back to the discussion of the *saving glut*, with less money recirculating through the economy in the form of demand of goods and services. Growing debts from governments and households helped compensate the lack of demand for a bit, but now there is so much debt that no one can afford more, even with interest rates at the 0% lower bound.

There is an emerging consensus on some version of this phenomenon among economists and institutions, including the IMF,[4] the OECD,[5] the Economic Policy Institute,[6] The Brooking Institutions,[7] and the list goes on.

Two considerations are even more important.

The first—when there is a lack of demand, we not only lose production in one year but we also delay our ability to produce more and better, our productivity. This is limiting our progress.

A report from the McKinsey Global Institute found that half of the loss of productivity compared to the beginning of this century was due to the post-2008 lack of demand and uncertainty. And by asking business executives directly, the authors found that roughly half of the companies that had grown their investments were doing so only in reaction to an increase in demand.[8]

Notable economists like Antonio Fatás and Larry Summers have highlighted that in economic slowdowns, companies reduce R&D expenses, an important source of innovation.[9] The Boston Consulting Group showed that the sales in machinery, industrial and IT automation, that enable productivity growth in their clients, drop significantly during economic slowdowns.[10] And after the 2008 crash, the IMF forecast a level of production potential that was 15% lower than before the crisis, showing a permanent effect.[11] Fed chair Janet Yellen also supported the idea that overall demand pulls the economy. In 2016 she coined the term *high-pressure economy* to describe one in which higher demand and protracted low unemployment lead to a faster growth of the production potential.[12] And by 2019 her hypothesis seems to have been right. The US reached the lowest level of unemployment since 1969 fueled by the post-2008 stimulus, yet inflation was still low. In fact, wages of the poorest had finally started to rise;[13] people who were previously discouraged and outside of statistics started looking for a job,[14] companies started investing more in training their own people, given it was more difficult to find alternatives; and some even reduced hiring requirements and trained less-skilled people on the job.[15] These events can grow the production potential of an economy.

Overall, we see that in this period it is a lack of demand, especially after an economic crisis, that limits production, productivity, and progress.

My second consideration is that all trends fueling low demand and recession are either unavoidable demographic shifts or intrinsic to capitalism, and therefore we cannot just consider them a temporary "shock." The trends include—

1. Population aging, leading to an increased need for saving for old age, a permanent trend unless we allow our governments to be unprepared for epidemics or allow free markets to make health care unaffordable to most.

2. The shift from a growing to a declining population, also a permanent trend in high-income countries that will extend globally. Global population is expected to plateau and start declining in the second half of this century.

3. The dependence of our economy on debt causing its instability is intrinsic to capitalism and the tie between debt and credit. Any other way of creating and allocating money would be outside the market mechanism.

4. The inequality in wealth and income is also intrinsic to capitalism as Piketty showed, and taxes—which capitalism tolerates—are insufficient to bring inequality under control.

5. Automation, globalization, weak labor unions, and unequal access to quality education are often considered the root causes of income inequality. And aside for automation, all the others are intrinsic to the ideology of the "perfection of free markets."

These trends were not present in the early 1800s, nor in 1950. We are just in a different world. Since overall demand now pulls production in high-income countries, we face a big problem: Capitalism does nothing to ensure a distribution of purchasing power that increases overall demand, or even maintains it. As Nick Hanauer, creator of the campaign for a $15 US minimum wage, put it, "In a capitalist system, rising inequality creates a death spiral of falling demand that ultimately takes everyone down."[16]

And more changes await on the horizon.

AUTOMATION AND ARTIFICIAL INTELLIGENCE

In May 2016, a Chinese government official told the *South China Morning Post* that one factory "reduced employee strength from 110,000 to 50,000 thanks to the introduction of robots."[17] Such news is—and will be—more and more common. According to the University of Oxford, artificial intelligence (AI) will replace as much as 47% of jobs in the US and 54% in Europe, within 20 years.[18] The McKinsey Global Institute claims that the technology we have today could replace an average of 49% of working activities,[19] and while the adoption and diffusion of AI technologies will take some time, by 2030 its impact might be 3–5 times larger than today.[20] And in *The Rise of the Robots*, Martin Ford shows how AI will not just affect low-skilled jobs. AI is a form of intelligence, of professional competence. It could take your job.[21]

Many economists and institutions are not concerned. After all, whenever there is automation there is higher productivity, which means higher incomes that will generate more demand and jobs. We've done it before. Back in 1800, about 60% of the population in France and Italy worked in agriculture. The Netherlands employed 40% in this field and England 30%. Today all these countries employ less than 5% in agriculture.[22] Nonetheless, we are not very far from full employment. Innovation has provided an array of new jobs.

But can we really reemploy half of the population in the 21st century?

Other people and economists think it's different this time, and innovation and higher incomes won't guarantee a job for everyone. I agree, and here's why.

In the report "Jobs Lost, Jobs Gained," the McKinsey Global Institute found that there could be enough new jobs to offset the jobs lost due to automation, but over 60% of those new jobs are based on the assumption that rising incomes around the world will translate into increased demand for goods and services. The remaining 40% of new jobs are linked to an increase in public and private investments, especially in elder care, infrastructure, and energy transitions.[23]

But we have just discussed that rising incomes are concentrated and don't become new demand and new jobs, and government budgets are insufficient. And even assuming that new demand will generate new investments and supply, it is likely that it will be increasingly automated and not reemploy as many people as we expect.

If you think of smartphones for example, they came out of nowhere, enabled by emerging information and communication technologies (ICT) and are now an over $400 billion market, or 0.5% of global GDP. But if you generously estimate that 2.5 million people work in the smartphone value chain,[24] you are still talking about only 0.05% of the global working age population.[25] And these 2.5 million employees are not necessarily new ones, as smartphones reduced the production of normal phones, cheap cameras, GPS devices, and anything you can do with smartphones. Overall, they may have even reduced employment.

And AI had nothing to do with it. That's another important point that is often missed. The issue of limited employment opportunities is not one in a faraway future where intelligent machines will replace humans. It has been happening already before we even bring AI into the picture.

Eight million people in the US work in retail sales or as cashiers,[26] jobs that a giant like Amazon has been making redundant through online sales. This is a change in business model that just requires fewer people and has nothing to do with AI. AI is now making Amazon services better and could ultimately lead to fully automated grocery stores, but the reduction of jobs in physical stores has already started.

And even high-skilled jobs are already at risk thanks to these alternative business models. Think of IKEA, that through the modularity and standardization of their products requires fewer engineers and designers. Canadian start-up Vention has adopted a similar model to manufacturing of industrial machinery. Designers can now design on Vention software, pick from a vast array of standard components, and when done, there is no need for engineers to validate the projects. It's all in the software. Again, no AI needed but automation nonetheless. Vention did not even exist when I started writing this book in 2014 and by 2020 it is reshaping the world of industrial manufacturing. Many more start-ups are emerging and revolutionizing sector by sector, often with less need for labor.

These new business models are enabled by the third industrial revolution, the one starting in the 1990s with ICT and the internet. AI is considered a new general-purpose technology that will power the fourth industrial revolution, but the impact of ICT and the internet is already one of a lower need for labor. In fact, a shrinking amount of value generated in the economy is captured by labor as opposed to shareholders and wealth-owners.

THIS TIME REALLY IS DIFFERENT

This phenomenon is recent but it has already started, and was called by authors Erik Brynjolfsson and Andrew McAfee *The Great Decoupling*. Since 2000 automation has unmoored production from job creation and wages. Productivity has continued growing, but employment and median wages have grown much less or not at all, depending on the country.[27] Other economists have confirmed that automation has become more labor-replacing than labor-complementing.[28] This is THE argument for why this time is different. While the steam engine and electricity made work simpler and allowed more workers to participate and be more productive, ICT already started making work more complex and reducing the need for labor. AI will knock this trend out of the stadium and automate all the simple tasks that the first two industrial revolutions have created.

Most economists studying AI and income inequality expect AI to increase inequality. The benefits from higher productivity through AI will be concentrated among the shareholders of few companies winning in the AI race, and their highly skilled workers. There are few topics regarding the future where you can witness so much consensus among economists as the fact that AI adoption will increase inequality.[29]

Kai-Fu Lee, one of the world's most renowned experts on AI, describes this risk best, explaining that the AI revolution would have major implications within one generation, given AI products are just algorithms that are "infinitely replicable and instantly distributable," and between a developed venture capital industry and the Chinese government and entrepreneurs doubling down on AI deployment, AI will be everywhere very soon.[30] As many other technologists, Kai-Fu does raise the alarm that the invisible hand of free markets won't be able to intervene. In his words—

> Make no mistake: this is not the normal churn of capitalism's creative destruction, a process that has previously helped lead to a new equilibrium of more jobs, higher wages, and a better quality of life for all. The free market is supposed to be self-correcting, but these self-corrective mechanisms break down in an economy driven by AI. Low-cost labor provides no edge over machines, and data-driven monopolies are forever self-reinforcing.[31]

It's hard to resist the evidence that the markets will not automatically provide enough jobs and wages to afford the very production that sophisticated companies and machines could deliver. And for those countries with a growing population, the impact on unemployment will be even higher, and unemployment can bring down societies, even the most advanced and modern.

In reaction to Brexit and the election of Donald Trump as US president, Oxford professors Carl Benedikt Frey and Michael Osborne published a study that, they say, "suggests that automation has been the real cause of voters' concern.

The prime victims of recent technological change want anything but the status quo. The populist rebellion in America, Europe, and elsewhere, has many causes, but workers losing out to technology is seemingly the main reason."[32]

Some voters are stressed and upset because they see their salaries reduced. They need money to pay their bills, and it can only come from wages. That's how capitalism works. Faced with the threat of losing their only source of prosperity, they're open to politicians who promise change, any kind of change.

CAPITALISM IS NOW OBSOLETE

The picture portrayed in this chapter is a complete flip of neoliberal assumptions and a deep crack into capitalism itself. Weak demand is now a cause of unemployment and underemployment, and it can even reduce the pace of innovation and productivity. The production potential increases more slowly because of lack of overall demand, a situation the use of permanent money could easily solve.

If Janet Yellen had pursued a high-pressure economy without using permanent money, she would have had no choice but to allow even more credit creation and potentially shift inflation above the stated target of 2%. And this seems to be the course of action that her successor as Fed chair, Jerome Powell, is taking. But this strategy would still not guarantee that money flows to those who need it and would spend it. Enormous injections of credit after the 2008 crisis made fat cows obese. By 2017, according to Oxfam, 82% of new wealth creation went to the top 1%. The portion going to the billionaires alone could have ended global extreme poverty seven times over.[33]

Capitalism is simply not built for distribution. It is built for production, although an excessively unequal distribution of buying power now limits even production, capitalism's main goal.

We no longer live in a world where capital is rare, or where a massive need for labor ensures that employees get a stable and meaningful share of money. And the forces fueling inequality and secular stagnation have started to bite. The limit on our economic progress today and in the future will be the purchasing power that keeps production humming and innovators inventing new products and business models.

When we have a new need, or a new solution to better satisfy a need, it's not hard for a company to find the money to buy the capital—the machinery and technology within it. And unemployed or low-paid, overqualified people will jump at the opportunity. Take the reaction to COVID-19. In a heartbeat the demand for face masks and ventilators was fulfilled by the market. The creation, testing, and approval of vaccines also happened very fast, also thanks to governments funding some of the research and most importantly guaranteeing demand at scale for the vaccines. If money is available, companies will produce.

Modern Monetary Theory (MMT) proponents, and Keynes before them, are quite correct to "call bullshit" on the received wisdom that there is limited capital that is tied to our savings and allow limited investments. They point to the ability of central banks to print money and finance the government that can invest and by doing so paying companies and people who increase their savings.[34] More fundamentally in my opinion is the important role of banks that continuously expand credit and therefore allow investments and savings to increase. People think of savings as opposed to spending, and it's true for a household. But in the economy, savings are the results of someone taking out more loans to invest. Investment growth is possible not because people save more, but because more loans are pumped into the economy that turns them into income and savings (and indeed the government is the biggest borrower, as MMT proponents emphasize).[35] But only if citizens can afford to buy will companies see a chance for profit, invest, and demand more loans.

Both capital and labor are abundant today. But we underutilize both because we have created a limit by tying money to credit and letting the free market channel most wealth and income to the few. Purchasing power, and the resulting weak demand, has become the weak link of economic growth. Distribution now holds the reins on production. And if a well-distributed purchasing power is the driver for 21st-century economic growth, capitalism is already obsolete.

Capitalism's side effect of high inequality thus has become a limit to production. The market for wages is already broken, with real wages stagnating or decreasing and people facing in-work poverty. The market for goods and services is also broken, with built-in biases and common interests delaying investments in favor of price increases. The market for money is also broken, as discussed at length in Chapter 7, on the money puzzle.

Government regulation and redistribution have helped in the past, but they have reached their limits. Imposing minimum salaries or limiting layoffs is suboptimal in a global economy, since companies can set up shop in a different country. The same is true for redistributing wealth through higher taxes, as Piketty proposed. And public debts are too high according to both citizens and politicians. Central banks have already started acting and have been printing money, but capitalism left them with no tools to do anything other than lend that money to banks and governments, limiting the fall when economies collapse and kicking the can down the road to the future.

LEGO metaphors always help: Capitalism has already built all LEGO pieces we need. We have different colors, shapes, and sizes. We now need to focus on how to use the pieces to build something great. More LEGO blocks will just make our creation clumsy and ultimately collapse from its own weight. But instead of allowing architects and designers to shape our creation, capitalism doesn't allow any adult in the room. It throws more blocks in it, sees the stronger kid taking all the blocks from the other crying kids, and doesn't allow anyone to intervene.

Governments can only tax and raise debts by paying interest to the wealthy. Central banks can only make loans cheaper to banks and governments. Everything else is left to the markets, basically to those who have money or can get cheap loans.

Within these limitations our society is doomed to continually endure deep crises and longer recoveries. I greatly appreciate the proposals to improve capitalism (such as *Re-Imagining capitalism*[36]) and to reduce the cronyism that defends the established incumbents (such as *A capitalism for the People*[37]), exemplified by many of the policies of Donald Trump, as highlighted by Nobel laureate Angus Deaton.[38] But reforms will not be enough, and I have not even mentioned the time pressure that catastrophic climate change has put on our economy (more in the next chapter).

Capitalism may have been a winning strategy around 1800 and on into the early and mid-1900s, but this strategy only succeeded because of the circumstances of the times. The world has since changed, and capitalism has become an old and outdated approach constricting us more and more. So now, 21st-century societies—at least in high-income countries—have outgrown capitalism. In the same way that growing humans need bigger clothes and plants need repotting, societies need to evolve their socio-economic system. And we now need an alternative that can better distribute buying power. And the instrument that most directly distributes buying power is not capital. It's money.

IT'S TIME FOR SOMETHING NEW

We need monetism, a system where we create some money permanently and direct it to achieve the societal goals, independently of free-market credit creation or of the ability of government to tax citizens.

We need a system that caters to the complexity of human societies in a context of uncertainty and continuous change, not one that seeks a theoretical long-term equilibrium in a dream world where omniscient human beings make only rational choices. The idea that an invisible hand that needs no steering could give us the best society was appealing, but it was not much more than wishful thinking.

And we need a system that allows everyone to rise above the comfort threshold.

A shift to monetism is much easier said than done, and here are some important questions: What should these societal objectives be? Who can define them? Are they universal or do they vary by culture and historical period? And how can we tame the enemy that is the inflation monster?

IV.
MONETISM

As a person can exist in Stage 1 or Stage 2, society can too. When individuals are financially comfortable enough to enter Stage 2, they shouldn't continue as they have, but rather should reassess their goals and pursue life fulfillment. Society has entered Stage 2 in high-income nations, and it's time to change socio-economic priorities and focus on everyone's opportunity for fulfillment. Monetism is the way forward, the natural heir to capitalism, but what should its specific objectives be? How exactly will monetism work? And what are the risks to mitigate?

Chapter 12

Stepping Back: What Should Monetism Accomplish?

Setting forth the right goals and measuring success

My experience in Swaziland gave me the intuition that something was seriously off in Western societies and I chose to focus more on those instead of low-income ones. The gap between reality and what I knew was possible seemed bigger in Western societies, which are often the role models that developing countries follow anyway.

While working on my MBA at INSEAD, I took a course called Management of Decision Making. Professor Neil Bearden was great at making the key messages stick and he made sure I incorporated this one: Whenever you are making any decision or, really, doing anything in life, ask yourself, "What is the fundamental objective?" It may sound obvious, and indeed it's the first step to defining any type of strategy, be that for a government, private company, or one's life. Yet we too often forget to ask this simple question and end up getting it wrong. Consequently, this question often haunts us in a mid-life crisis, and it is now haunting us at a societal level in our mid-development crisis.

So, as we embark on shaping monetism, let's not make the common mistake of building a system that solves for the wrong objectives.

While the only reasonable and moral purpose of society is the well-being of current and future generations, strategy and policy require qualities we can measure. Otherwise, we are forging ahead blind. And measuring well-being is quite difficult and subjective.

It is therefore understandable that society sought easy-to-quantify proxies of well-being, especially GDP and the rate of unemployment. These numbers seem solid and relevant, and we can use them to make comparisons, set targets, and gauge our progress. The problem is that GDP is no longer a good proxy—it has no correlation with well-being in high-income countries—and neither of these two guarantees that future generations will have the same opportunities we do.

Isn't it time we looked at swapping these metrics for something more appropriate?

THE GDP ILLUSION

Simon Kuznets delivered a major warning when he conceived modern GDP: Do not use it as a metric for well-being. In a 1968 address at the University of Kansas, Senator Robert F. Kennedy put it this way:

> Too much and too long we seem to have surrendered community excellence and community values to the mere accumulation of material things. Our gross national product, if we should judge America by that, counts air pollution and cigarette advertising, and ambulances to clear our highways of carnage. It counts special locks for our door . . . but it does not capture the beauty of our poetry or the strength of our marriages.[1]

All sorts of bad practices bulk up the GDP figure. Among the legal ones, weapons and tobacco are the most obvious. Junk food leads to obesity and disease, both of which increase GDP. Food waste is estimated at $160 billion per year in the US[2] and €143 billion per year in the EU,[3] and that also increases GDP. Moreover, government agencies estimate illegal practices and add them to GDP. Narcotic drugs and prostitution contribute to this figure. The shadow economy overall does too.[4] Crime requires services like protection, lawyers, and large penitentiary and security industries, which further boost GDP. The US has a high GDP per capita partly because its people are the least healthy of the high-income countries and require the most healthcare, which in turn is the most expensive and least effective among high-income countries.[5] The GDP is a net that captures both fish and ocean junk.

At the same time, GDP omits everything that is not purchased at a price. An invisible hand pushes everything toward commercialization, from do-it-yourself activities to cleaning and even sex. If you are a stay-at-home parent, your GDP contribution is zero, but if you hire a nanny and you take a job that can pay for the nanny, the GDP grows both for the nanny and for your work. In the process, the government taxes both of you. The real production is marginally better; you might be better educated than your children's nanny and can generate more value with your time, but you might later regret not having spent enough time with your kids.

Piketty highlighted another issue: GDP measures government public services only by the value of employee salaries.[6] It excludes profit and the cost of the infrastructure used, though it does include them with private hospitals and universities.[7] That means any country privatizing public services will see an artificial boost in GDP, which makes GDP an even poorer measure of production.[8]

The Economist rightly calls GDP an "increasingly poor measure of prosperity . . . not even a reliable gauge of production."[9] If you Google "what is wrong with GDP," you may need more than your yearly vacation to finish reading the search results, especially if you are in the US where vacations are short. Obviously, we can't have much vacation if we are to maximize GDP.

It should not be surprising that rising GDP lost any correlation with well-being. In some instances, high GDP growth has even reduced happiness due to the instability that came with growth, something known as the Paradox of Unhappy Growth.[10]

One of the most interesting statistical analyses appeared in *The Spirit Level: Why Equality Is Better for Everyone*. The authors compared GDP per capita with about 20 metrics related to well-being and found no relation between GDP and any of the well-being metrics in countries with more than $15,000 of GDP per capita. Income inequality, on the other hand, did correlate with most of these metrics. That is, the less equal the country, the less the well-being of its people. This finding held internationally across every wealth class: Even the richest people in more equal societies had higher well-being than the richest people in unequal countries.[11]

GDP, and economic growth more generally, are clearly bad guideposts for policymaking. At a minimum, we should be able to distinguish good growth from bad growth, or even deduct bad growth as a cost to society rather than just adding everything up. If we want to include the production of cigarettes, then shouldn't we subtract their health costs rather than adding them on top? But distinguishing good from bad would raise difficult questions in many cases. Moreover, if we attempted it, we'd no longer be measuring total production. And this is exactly the point. The fact that GDP is not good at measuring production is rather unimportant. The point is that we cannot continue with a blind pursuit of production, however well we measure it.

Production gained relevance after the 1929 crisis and GDP itself made its way into international measurements in 1944. Countries were fighting yet another war and GDP was a measure of what a country could produce and, in case of need, convert into weapons and an army. That was the main concern, in a world of war and manufacturing.[12] The higher the GDP, the greater the economic power. And the legacy continues to this day. The choice of countries included in the G20 is still mostly about GDP, not the number of inhabitants or their well-being.

When we consider inequality, GDP is even more misleading. In recent history the GDP of the US has grown faster than that of France, but the average income of the bottom 99% of people has grown more in France.[13] What's the point of looking at overall GDP growth when so much goes to the top 1%, people already above the comfort threshold, while those people who could actually benefit from more income stand still or regress?

In a democratic society, what is the point of relying on overall GDP or even average GDP per capita? If we are attached to GDP because of its measurability and the importance of measuring sheer production, let's at least focus on the GDP of the bottom 99% or even better, the median GDP per capita.[14] If either of these became the main measure we study, communicate, and hold governments accountable for, inequality would automatically gain importance.

WHAT'S THE POINT OF GROWTH?

I believe it's time to question the importance we give to economic growth itself. As Kate Raworth concluded in *Doughnut Economics*, society should become agnostic about it.[15]

We need to realize that the focus on GDP growth is only a legacy of traditional capitalism, which would collapse without it. But in designing monetism, we could aim to design a system that can function with or without growth.

It is therefore useful to understand why capitalism needs growth. Keep in mind that growth might be a means to an end, but in high-income countries we already saw how growth or average incomes are no longer linked to most well-being metrics. In designing monetism we have the opportunity to lose capitalism's constraint of having to grow and only pursue the growth that is conducive to well-being.

It is useful to be aware of what imprisons capitalism in an endless pursuit for growth so that we can avoid falling in the same trap when designing monetism. There are four main forces that make capitalism dependent on growth.

1. **Inequality: Without growth, capitalism excessively concentrates wealth to the point of implosion.** According to Piketty, this was Karl Marx's mistake. He forgot that growth can partly compensate for the tendency of capital to concentrate without limits. Remove growth and Marx was right, but with enough growth compared to after-tax returns on capital, wealth can actually stop concentrating.[16]

But if growth is much lower than the return on capital, wealth increasingly concentrates until high levels cause a shock that forces wealth redistribution.[17] This shock results from the tension between the wealthy fighting for higher returns while the rest of the population can't afford the consumption that would enable such returns. In the past, this tension has exploded in a quest for yields abroad, leading to colonialism and war (possibly a cause of World War I[18]), or in a financial crisis like those in 1929 and 2008, with people unable to repay their debts, or in revolutions and civil wars, as in 18th-century France or the Arab Spring. According to Piketty's forecast, with after-tax returns on capital of 5% and real growth at only 1%, the long-term equilibrium of wealth distribution would look like this: over 50% of wealth accumulated by the top 1%, the following 9% grasping almost 40% of the wealth, and the bottom 90% having to live on only 10% of wealth.[19] Before reaching such high levels of inequality, another shock would occur. To avoid this concentration of wealth and the consequent shocks, capitalism definitely needs a higher growth rate.

2. **Debts: Without growth, capitalism leads to unsustainable debts.** Governments don't really have to repay debts, because, as discussed, they can just repay old bonds by issuing bigger new bonds and this process will continue forever, with ever-bigger debts in absolute terms.[20] But because of interest

payments, we need growth for governments to be able to sustain the public debt. Public debts have risen constantly for most countries, as they've had to invest in the pursuit of economic growth, as well as social progress. Investments in social impact may not generate money in the future, and even investments in economic growth can yield less than the interest rate on the public debt.

The only way to repay these interests, without resorting to printing money, is through taxes and here comes the need for growth: The greater the growth, the more tax revenues a government can collect, and the easier it is to service the public debt. Taxes at the same time limit economic growth, as they leave people with less money to spend.[21] You can see the fiscal trap: We need growth to service the public debt, but if we collect more taxes to do it, we kill the growth we need—unless, of course, we tax the wealthy, who would keep consuming roughly the same even if they were taxed more.[22]

The need for growth is even more important to repay private debt and indeed borrowers, especially households, need not only to repay interest but also the value of the loan. Tying money to credit means that money is just an anticipation of future earnings, a claim on the value created in the future by that money itself. If you extend this to the overall economy and money supply, for people to repay their debts, they need to create more value than the value of their loans and the interest they need to repay. That's impossible without growth. Without growth, and with credit and money tied at the hip, it will be impossible to repay private debts, especially if governments are repaying public debts in parallel. It is a reinforcing cycle: Repaying debts requires growth and growth requires an increase in overall debts.

3. **Retirement: Without growth, capitalism would make people's retirement unsustainable**. When we built our retirement systems, we had growing populations, in which the ratio of working people to non-working people was high. Since then, many high-income countries have seen a decline in population growth—it's even negative in some countries—while life expectancy continues to increase and young people pursue their educations longer. As a result, increasingly fewer people are working and paying taxes to provide for a growing number of inactive people. This is the case in most pension systems where the government pays retirement benefits to previous generations by taxing the current working population.

People in retirement, as well as those who are in school or unemployed, have needs whose satisfaction depends on the working population producing more goods and services. Growth in population or productivity is essential to maintain this system. The Danish government's video "Do It for Your Mom" was emblematic of efforts to spur population growth. Many other countries are trying both to delay retirement and to increase births. Not as many countries are opening doors to the migrants who boost a nation's number of younger, working individuals, but that complexity exceeds the scope of this book. Even though we have strong need for people to provide for the elderly and youngsters, we somehow fail to employ the ones who are available.

Here we see something else that is not functioning well. We don't need the population to grow if we can't even employ the people we have, right? And we have barely started to bring AI into the picture, which could ultimately provide machines to work for the elderly. We're not short of people looking for jobs; we're short of the taxes that governments can collect to pay for retirement. Those taxes depend on a growing economy, which is a prerequisite for the sustainability of our retirement model. There is an alternative, which is for people to save more during their lifetimes and hence need a lower retirement transfer from governments. But if everyone saves more, they consume less. And since consumption is now the main driver of economic growth, less consumption means lower income, lower savings. Again, another reinforcing cycle is we need growth to sustain the expanding elder population in retirement, but through taxes or higher savings we starve that growth.

4. **Unemployment: Without growth, capitalism would see an increasing unemployment rate.** Our system is great at creating new products, services, and productive systems. Even the most unproductive country increases its year-over-year productivity. In the absence of wars and political or environmental catastrophes, people and companies get better at producing more with the same inputs. No growth—constant GDP—would lead to a constant increase in unemployment, since every year we'd need fewer people to produce what we produced the previous year. Since salaries are the main means for most people to obtain goods and services, no growth leads to an increasing number of people who cannot consume, which will ultimately lead to a recession, if not a revolution. While governments can partially fix this situation by transferring money to the unemployed or hiring more public servants, they can only sustain the system until taxes are too high or their public debt is unsustainable, which would happen rather quickly without growth.

But on this note, is it society that needs full employment, or is it capitalism?

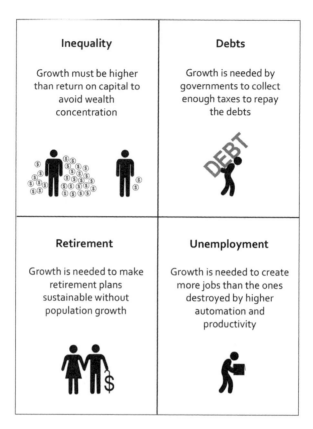

Exhibit 7: Four reasons for why capitalism needs growth

EMPLOYMENT: MORE OR LESS?

Studies on the Ju/'hoansi tribe in Namibia have shown that adults spend a couple of hours a day foraging and the rest of the time in leisure. We clearly do not have enough land to live by hunting and gathering food, and few people would want to. But is it reasonable that a primitive tribe works 14 hours a week and we, with all our progress, struggle to work less than 40? Something, somewhere, clearly went wrong.

One would think that as productivity grows, people would have to work less. But this is not happening. While yearly hours per worker have decreased over the last 40 years, more women have entered the labor force and they have increased the share of people employed in OECD countries.[23]

But in a system aimed at maximizing production, this should not come as a surprise. A country reaches its maximum GDP through full employment, leaving them just enough time to spend their earnings. In the ideal situation, workers would shop online while sitting on the toilet, throw the purchase away upon delivery, and continue buying more stuff. The pursuit of growth and full employment go together. Capitalism is demanding all of our time and it has been quite successful at it.

In 1930, Keynes predicted that people in our day would work just 15 hours a week, forcing employers to pay the same overall for fewer hours. Keynes's idea of full employment made sense from a moral perspective. Everyone would still work, but for much less time per week and per life. But Keynes did not foresee that automation, a global supply of labor, and weaker labor unions would reduce employees' purchasing power. Maybe he expected democratic pressures would force governments to legislate longer weekends or earlier retirement. Well, this didn't happen. Governments are also stuck in a global competition to get residents employed and collect their taxes and we got stuck in this society where people beg for a full-time job that just covers their costs of living.

Capitalism linked employment and purchasing power and, given this tie-in, there is no question that full employment is an important objective. A world in which we can automate most jobs is not far off, but this is a challenge for a capitalist society, not an opportunity. Even if automation substitutes for many workers and frees up their time, policymakers under capitalism may try to invent new problems and new needs so people can get a salary. But again, does society need full employment or does capitalism?

If full-time work gave people life fulfillment, there would be no need to force employment on them. The argument that it does is shallow, as we've seen, and I have recently experienced this myself. For some convoluted COVID-related reasons and bureaucracy, I was forced to take unpaid leave while my transfer to Switzerland was being processed. One month in, I restarted working for free because I love my job and have kept working for free for more than six months. If all of us had a fulfilling job and enough money to thrive, wage employment would become superfluous. Rutger Bregman proposes another theory for society's need for full employment: The rich have always feared riots and misconduct from uneducated masses with a lot of spare time and they also happen to want these masses to work for them. As a consequence, the wealthy aristocracy often sank UBI proposals that made work a choice rather than a necessity. Societal outcomes support Bregman's theory: The well-being of most people in wealthy countries has not increased, yet the top 1% disproportionately enjoy the benefits of others' labor. Maximizing GDP has so far benefited the wealthy, while great numbers of people are stuck begging for a job or locked into one that barely (if at all) covers the bills.

But do the wealthy have a point? No one benefits from riots and revolutions and maybe there are risks if people have more free time on their hands.

As I was working in Saudi Arabia, one important concern was the massive population of youths finishing their studies at a time with limited job opportunities and ISIS in full recruiting mode. With no chance of finding a way to meet basic needs, jobless people of any country and religion could be drawn to criminal activities.

But the danger for society comes from people's desperation and unhappiness, not from their spare time. The threat lies in tying employment to purchasing power and livelihood in a system that no longer needs full employment. UBI pilot programs have in fact reduced crime rates by reducing the travails of poverty. The danger lies not in people having free time, but in having free time *and* no means to sustain their livelihood or have a decent life. Take the well-known Somali pirates as an example: They resorted to crime to fight off industrial fishing vessels that disrupted their fishermen livelihoods. The cause of their criminal activities was the lack of fish, their food, not spare time or some innate pirate nature.

Unemployment in a capitalist economy is indeed dangerous, as the drop in living standards would make the jobless unhappy and angry, and they'd have a lot of time to direct their anger into menacing activities. At the same time, when people would give an arm and a leg to have a job, whatever the conditions, they become less happy with their jobs. With work and purchasing power scarce, money may take on even more importance in choosing a life partner, which in turn leads to more divorces and less happiness.

This shows it is capitalism, and not society, that is incompatible with low employment. Society could do very well in a system in which we used most of our time in voluntary activities that fulfilled our passions.

Should we then try to maximize well-being while minimizing paid employment? In 100 years we could probably run society with many robots and unpaid volunteers. Maybe we will never reach this stage and the idea is utopian, but what if we manage to get to even 50% of people working for pleasure instead of subsistence? Every step in this direction is a step toward letting people freely pursue the activities that fulfill them.

For the time being, though, we are still far from this situation. To start with, an aging population means that fewer workers must support more retired people. The super-productivity from AI is still at least a decade off according to many forecasts. But the biggest reason we are some time away from sending people home for leisure time is that there is plenty of cleanup to do, after the mess that the blind-production machine of capitalism has made of the environment.

CLEANING UP THE ENVIRONMENTAL MESS

Scientists say we are seeing the sixth mass extinction, one whose rate is somewhere between 1,000 and 10,000 times higher than normal. It is comparable to that when an asteroid killed the dinosaurs.[24] We may wipe out 50% of species by 2050,[25] and 99% of species at risk are linked to human activity. We will likely survive, but as species vanish, domino effects occur.[26] If we lose bees, we may lose a good chunk of pollination, and who knows if food will become scarce and we become the next endangered species.

Many complain that any system requiring unlimited growth has a basic problem: Earth's resources are finite. Others argue that we can pursue sustainable growth by increasing the productivity of resources and creating a no-waste circular economy based on recycling. New technologies could prevent the environmental impact of growth. This claim is a major source of hope and I believe it is possible. Furthermore, growth does not mean producing and consuming more. We can grow by increasing the value and quality of what we produce. Through innovation and sustainable practices, we can produce a higher value while using fewer resources. De-growth proponents exaggerate the problems of growth. At the same time, capitalism's blind pursuit of growth had a complete disregard for the environment, with any damage considered just as an *externality*. But the environment is what allows life itself! As long as we consider damage to the environment just an unfortunate side effect of free markets, the technological shift will not happen fast enough.

And we are already late. We only recently started to care about the environment and, by that time, we were consuming resources faster than Earth could replenish them. The Global Footprint Network calculates the annual

Earth Overshoot Day, the date on which we have consumed as many resources as the planet can regenerate in one year. This day has shifted from December all the way back to August 2 in 2017, so in the whole year we used about 1.6 times the resources Earth could replenish in a year.

It is seriously immoral to force our future generations to clean up our mess. Our own elders created this wreckage in the first place, but at least they had the blessing of ignorance. We do not.

Today, people are already suffering and dying from the impact of indiscriminate growth on the environment through pollution, superstorms, rising sea levels, swift and devastating blazes like the Camp Fire, and many other events.

WHY ARE WE NOT ACTING ON THE ENVIRONMENT?

In bodybuilding you typically alternate two phases: bulk and cut. During bulk you just look at building mass and gaining size, while during cut you try to lose the fat. Society has been bulking with indiscriminate growth for centuries, with collateral damage to the environment. Is it time to cut, or are we waiting for a heart attack?

Unlike cardiac arrest, though, harm to the environment does not affect the day-to-day life of society at large. Much of it is subtle. Smoke from indoor cooking stoves is one of the biggest killers (1.6 million people a year), but given it has no enemy and no one to blame, it does not make news and we end up doing little to fix it.[27] The hole in the ozone layer is a good example of the danger from these silent threats. In the 1970s, the depletion of the ozone layer wasn't really affecting anyone. In the 1980s scientists spotted it and warned us of the potential consequences, and by 1989 the world completely banned the use of ozone depleting substances (ODS) in the Montreal Protocol. By 2002 the consumption of ODS reached zero.[28] Yet the ozone layer won't return to pre-1980 levels until 2075.[29] We see danger ahead and we live with the consequences of ignoring it. In the 21st century it is estimated that one of 75 Americans will develop a malignant form of skin cancer. That's over four million people. Likely someone you know, maybe you yourself. In 1935 this probability was only one of 1,500.[30] In Australia the rate will likely be higher.

"Million" is just a word and we are bad at grasping big numbers, so let me give you a better idea of what one million deaths look like. A large US football stadium can hold 100,000 seats. Imagine that huge stadium full of dead people, one per seat. One million deaths are equivalent to 10 of these stadiums full of dead people. That's for a big US stadium. In Europe they would probably fill 15 soccer stadiums.

What about pollution? The WHO estimates 1.7 million deaths per year of children under age five (17 stadiums full of dead children) linked to environmental pollution, with air pollution accounting for almost 600,000 alone.[31] The Lancet Commission found that pollution in general is responsible for about 9 million premature deaths globally in 2015 (that's 90 stadiums), three times more than AIDS, tuberculosis, and malaria combined, or 15 times more than from all wars and violence.[32] Air pollution is the fifth-most common cause of global deaths, with 4.2 million people dying from it per year (42 stadiums), up 25% from 1990. And global warming is increasing air pollution.[33] The total welfare losses from pollution are over $4.6 trillion a year, or 6.2% of global GDP.[34]

These are all silent threats. They do not directly affect our everyday life, so we are not angry with the people who cause them, the way we are about deranged individuals who shoot up schools and movie theaters. What's worse is that each and every one of us is actually aggravating the problem when we eat meat or fish, fly or drive, and heat our houses. We all indirectly contribute, and in response we put our heads in the sand and pretend it isn't happening.[35] "Those stadiums full of dead people can't be my fault."

But whether we acknowledge it or not, there is much environmental damage we will ultimately have to pay for. Kate Raworth lists nine different harms that human activities have caused: land degradation, ocean acidification, ozone layer depletion, air pollution, biodiversity loss, chemical pollution, nitrogen and phosphorus loading, fresh water withdrawals, and, obviously, climate change.[36]

Climate change is now the biggest issue, and ocean acidification stems from it. The scientific community has gone all out in warning us of the potential dangers, as well as the causes.

And though most people acknowledge the issue, it is a silent threat and we don't feel any urgency. A 2014 Gallup survey showed that among a list of 15 threats, US citizens ranked climate change 14th.[37] A May 2018 survey found that only 9% of people placed climate change concerns among the top three issues.[38] With this relaxed attitude, democratic governments have little pressure to act, and if we keep dawdling long enough, we can forget the fresh air, the clear water, and the green pastures.

Bias expert Daniel Kahneman is extremely skeptical that we can cope with climate change. He writes, "We react to threats that are concrete, imminent, and indisputable while climate change is abstract, invisible, and disputed. Climate change requires us to pay a short-term price to mitigate higher but uncertain losses that are in the future. And as long as the issue appears disputed, even if the academy is on one side and some cranks on the other, people will score it as a draw." Meanwhile, economic psychologist Daniel Gilbert says that climate change "has everything going against it. A psychologist could barely dream up a better scenario for paralysis."[39]

Capitalism also reduces our ability to recognize the threat of climate change. According to psychologists, we have a limited capacity for concern about problems: a *finite pool of worry*.[40] As long as capitalism forces people to hold jobs to survive, while automation takes a job away every minute, we will all seek to grab a job while it lasts. As for pursuing well-being, only once we achieve Stage 2—no longer worrying about meeting basic needs in the future—can we fully appreciate the concerns about the environment. The facts, data, and statistics that scientists collect will be more like background noise to our ears.

Do we really have to wait until climate change affects the majority of people before tackling it with as many resources as we can? Every research project and every solar panel installation that we postpone contributes further to the disasters ahead.

Our success in managing the emergency of the ozone layer should not provide you any reassurance. The ban on ODS had a moderately low cost and impact on the economy. Most emissions were linked to 12 large companies and their subsidiaries. George Marshall writes, "You could fit their CEOs around a meeting table and get the issue sorted out."[41] But carbon emissions are central to major economic activities, including energy and agriculture, involving millions of companies in every country in the world. Even though we already possess the technology to seriously reduce carbon emissions, the free market is resisting solutions with much greater force and we need unprecedented public mobilization to get politicians to tackle this issue.

With the 2016 Paris Agreement, we showed that we are not completely blind to this invisible enemy. We've demonstrated the will to tackle climate change, but the promises made were voluntary and unenforceable, and they won't halt the negative consequences of climate change. We need to put our money where our mouth is, and to do that we need 1) goals that recognize our impact on the environment as a serious harm rather than a positive contributor to GDP, and 2) an economic system that channels resources to this end as fast as possible.

If you think we're already doing it, consider this: In 2012, the global investment in renewable energy was $244 billion, while investment in oil and gas exploration and development of new reserves exceeded $1 trillion for the first time.[42] Even worse, the International Energy Association (IEA) raised the alarm that investments in renewable energy had started falling in 2017[43] and were falling even faster than investment in fossil fuels after COVID-19.[44] IMF researchers quantified the direct and indirect subsidies that fossil fuels receive from governments at $5.3 trillion globally.[45] Your taxes end up funding this disaster.

And while today the problem is climate change, tomorrow it will be consequences like desertification. We will need people with the right background to research this field, develop new technologies, and create a deep and evolving environmental industry.

If we acknowledge our brain biases are making us react too late to protect the environment, and we admit the gravity of this threat, we should also recognize that the free markets will not move fast enough to protect us from Hothouse Earth. Environmental sustainability has to be one of the main stated objectives of society, included in constitutions if necessary, and monetism must provide a way to tackle this issue as fast as possible. Failing to do so might really become a real-life version of the fabled frog cooking in a slow-heating pot.

THE COMPASS AND THE STRATEGIC DIRECTIONS

The current socio-economic paradigm holds the following: Society should pursue economic growth and every individual should contribute to it. Forced to earn a living and meet their ever-growing needs, people will offer time and resources to businesses to produce something of increasing value. Governments should protect individual freedom, enable businesses to grow, and support those who can't make it within the limits of their balance sheets. Such society indirectly maximizes the well-being of all its members.

We've seen that the assumption that economic growth is a tide that lifts all boats is old and inaccurate. Most boats are in lakes, unaffected by the ocean's tide.

I propose a more appropriate paradigm for high-income countries: Pursue the well-being of every member while ensuring equal opportunities for future generations.

But if governing institutions use this goal for policymaking, they must know how to measure it and this is a big challenge. Many would argue that well-being is impossible to gauge accurately and any assessment would be subjective and difficult to compare across countries. While there may be merit in such a view, in fact GDP and inflation are equally difficult to measure accurately. More importantly, people overestimate the usefulness of cross-country comparisons. For policymaking, the determinants of well-being and the trends over time are much more important than cross-country comparisons. Knowing what matters for well-being helps set and prioritize policies, and knowing whether well-being is growing helps us understand whether those policies are succeeding.

Some institutions have already opened the way to this approach. The government of Bhutan supplanted GDP with Gross National Happiness, and can already claim success in both happiness[46] and respect for the environment, since Bhutan is the only carbon-negative country.[47] The government of the United Arab Emirates (UAE) established the Ministry of Happiness in 2016.[48] The OECD, with its better life index, has shed some light on the successes of Scandinavian countries, Canada, and Australia.[49] The Boston Consulting Group, in a similar effort, highlighted how 9 of the top 10 countries for well-being are in Western Europe, Singapore being the only exception.[50] The United Nations has also focused more attention on happiness with its World Happiness Report and Index.[51]

I can also be proud of my country for being the first among the G7 to officially adopt a measure of well-being to complement GDP. Starting in 2018, the government of Italy is evaluating its policies along 12 measures of well-being, which include metrics of inequality, absolute poverty, gender equality, crime, carbon emissions, and many others.[52]

Kate Raworth has also done outstanding work in this direction with her visualization of all socio-economic objectives as a doughnut of social and planetary boundaries.

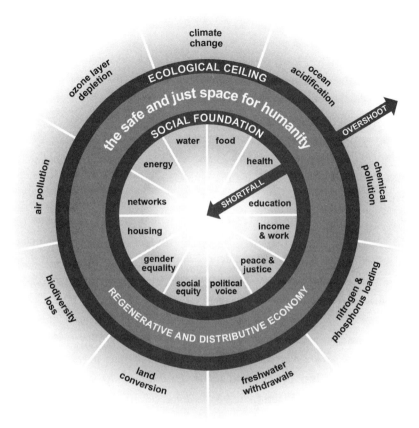

Exhibit 8: Representation of the doughnut by Kate Raworth

The innermost layer of the doughnut is the social foundation we want, and we should avoid shortfall on any of the 12 social foundations that are represented in the doughnut's hole. For these 12 foundations, such as housing and gender equality, society should provide to enable a universal pursuit of well-being. The outer layer is the ecological constraints we must respect, for beyond it lies nine environmental problems like ocean acidification and climate change that we want to avoid.[53]

While I am very much in favor of all these initiatives, we need to do more to understand the determinants of well-being. Sustainability—environmental, economic, or fiscal—is a technical matter, but the determinants of well-being are subjective and may change over time and among different populations. As such, the citizens have to be directly involved to understand what is more or less important.

As such, I propose a survey-based metric that asks people about things that affect the three aspects of well-being: happiness, life satisfaction, and life fulfillment. It would inquire about people's experience with the health and education systems, their feelings of safety and long-term security, and many other important matters. Machine-learning techniques can study the survey results and identify the most critical *pain points* that the government should strive to resolve. We could get results for the whole country, as well as municipalities or population groups, understanding the different determinants of well-being for young and old, males and females, city and rural folks, and many more. And with this valuable information we can prioritize public investments by both topic and geography. For instance, should we put money in more police officers or in transportation? Should we hire more police in region A or B? While such findings can't be the only criteria for making decisions, without them policymakers are performing a theoretical exercise without direct input from the people.

This survey would be a major tool to increase citizens' participation in the political sphere. Just as any good service-oriented company runs surveys to improve customer satisfaction and experience, governments should use them to understand what their citizens need.

Survey-based metrics have some limitations, though, because if a problem does not impact people day to day, they are unlikely to mention it. The sustainability of well-being needs to be left to technical expertise and have its own metrics. For example, we know that on climate change we are on an unsustainable path, although people do not yet feel the issue and would prioritize the topic only when it's too late.

Once we get our bearings pointed toward a sustainable and inclusive well-being, a sound approach needs key principles, strategic directions. These need to take over the role that maximizing GDP and employment has had so far.

I propose four strategic directions: sustainable progress, universal dignity, stability, and time to pursue happiness and fulfillment.

1. **Sustainable progress: Maximize innovation and resource productivity while ensuring equal opportunities for the next generations.**
   Innovation and productivity are the true engines of progress and they

give us a great opportunity to avoid damage to our planet. Capitalism has shown limits on both the pace of progress and innovation, limiting yearly growth and the production potential. Monetism has to increase buying power, as well as direct more resources to research, thus maximizing progress and innovation while preserving the environmental ceiling. As for the metric, we must measure sustainable progress with indexes that look at innovation, resource productivity, and environmental sustainability.

2. **Universal dignity: Guarantee everyone access to basic needs.** This access would provide security to all individuals, who can then pursue happiness and life fulfillment. Capitalism gives limited attention to this strategic goal and even restricts the ability of governments to fulfill it. While equality in wealth distribution is a matter of political debate, and I would agree that a certain level of inequality could foster meritocracy and hence innovation and progress, it is undeniable that the current level of inequality is neither acceptable nor sustainable. Many people lack enough food, health care, education, or shelter, in both mature and in developing economies. Monetism has to make this goal a priority. A synthetic index of access to basic needs would increase the visibility of this issue.

3. **Stability: Avoid disrupting events and enable fast recovery from unavoidable ones.** The disruptions include economic recessions, which we should prevent or limit to months rather than years, but also natural catastrophes including epidemics, which we should mitigate up front and manage appropriately after. Again, capitalism does not focus much on these issues. Its reliance on debt and banks, coupled with income and wealth inequality, leads to cyclical recessions, which its proponents consider a necessary pain. Capitalism is not even sustainable when people save more (or repay their debts) to increase their stability, as a consumption drop would crash the economy. Without savings to obtain basic needs, it should be no surprise that researchers find a correlation between unemployment and suicide attempts, not just in the US,[54] but also in Europe,[55] in Australia,[56] in South East Asia,[57] and in Russia.[58] Other studies have even found a correlation between suicide rates and fiscal austerity policies.[59] It is the stability of people's spending power

that makes society stable. Economic growth is much less important. As for natural catastrophes, capitalism is failing both to prevent them and to provide quick relief. We are commonly in the hands of charity for relief and governments often lack the funds for prevention. Yet more and more disasters are occurring, they're getting worse, and we're doing little to stop foreseeable calamities. Monetism must make addressing these issues a priority.

4. **Time to pursue happiness and life fulfillment: Maximize the time that people can spend in voluntary activities.** Happiness and especially life fulfillment are individual journeys. As a society, we should foster them by giving people the chance to take them. Time is the only limited resource we all have in our lives and one goal of society should be to allow all of us to maximize the time we spend in activities that bring us happiness and life fulfillment. It might also come from the work we do, in case society enables most of us to find a good job fit. In *Utopia for Realists*, Rutger Bregman highlights how people would rather work fewer hours even if they got lower salaries. It's no wonder, since most people do not like their jobs. Capitalism cannot solve this problem, as it requires people to work to get spending power. Very few people have any time to think about what they'd do freely with their lives and about what fulfills them. Most of us are in execution mode, with so many things to do that we postpone thinking about ourselves until a mid-life crisis or retirement—just in time for the regrets to sink in. If we had the luxury of more free time for introspection and for the pursuit of happiness and life fulfillment, we could hope to raise all of humanity to a new level of community and selflessness. Monetism has to make time another priority. A survey-based metric that measures a Time Freedom Index—how much time we dedicate to what we want to do rather than what we have to do—would make this priority more visible. This task would not be especially difficult. In fact, it would not differ much from the American Time Use Survey by the Bureau of Labor Statistics. A metric closer to those we typically see is productivity per hour worked. On this measure, GDP per hour worked would increase even if people could decide to work less. They would be more committed to their work and more effective at it.

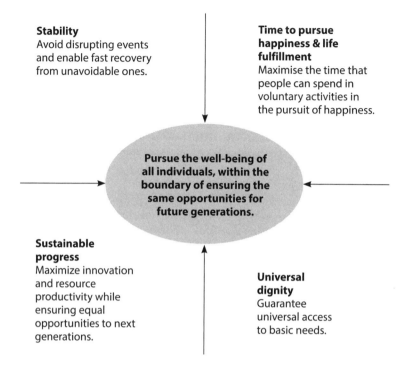

Stability
Avoid disrupting events and enable fast recovery from unavoidable ones.

Time to pursue happiness & life fulfillment
Maximise the time that people can spend in voluntary activities in the pursuit of happiness.

Pursue the well-being of all individuals, within the boundary of ensuring the same opportunities for future generations.

Sustainable progress
Maximize innovation and resource productivity while ensuring equal opportunities to next generations.

Universal dignity
Guarantee universal access to basic needs.

Exhibit 9: Strategic directions to achieve unversal and sustainbale well-being

These strategic directions would not reverse economic growth, as innovations that save people's time would receive more resources from society. For instance, a restaurant cooking at scale for hundreds of people would save time for the hundreds of families that would otherwise have to cook and clean, tasks that most families do not want to perform every day. Meanwhile, curtailing road traffic would receive more attention. Jobs people like would be incentivized while jobs they don't like would be more quickly automated. The economy would still work at its best, but not with the primary objective of creating more GDP and paid employment.

But I want to emphasize the importance of not being constrained by the need for growth and employment when considering economic policy. As long as policymakers believe that a higher economic activity and employment are the only path to higher prosperity and well-being, they will act accordingly. They will slow down automation and protect, or even subsidize, unsustainable and possibly immoral activities. And as long as companies believe that pursuing profit is sufficient to create value for consumers and society, they will not second-guess their practices and will shape their strategies, structures, and processes on a profit-first-and-foremost basis. Only by resetting society's goals and creating a system where everyone can thrive independently on the need for profit or human labor, can we hope that governments' and companies' leaders will make decisions aligned with what citizens would expect of them.

The new objective of pursuing universal and sustainable well-being and these four strategic directions are what I believe society—governments, private companies, and NGOs—should use as the new North Star, and I am confident that most of you would agree that we should be aiming for a sustainable and equal society, pursuing progress while leaving enough time for people to follow their journeys toward happiness and life fulfillment.

* * *

I want to make sure I have not lost those of you who are more grounded in the current economic system and have probably reacted to my indifference toward economic growth by placing monetism into the category of *unrealistic utopian hippie dreams*.

And since I am clearly a supporter of Piketty's argument—without growth, wealth is bound to get more concentrated—how can I not prioritize growth?

I will show in later chapters how monetism can reverse Piketty's equation and achieve both higher growth rates and lower returns on capital, thus increasing prosperity while decreasing inequality.

BRINGING IT ALL TOGETHER

If we look back on the journey of this book thus far, we started by highlighting how our society keeps most people from pursuing well-being; they are too busy meeting basic needs. UBI was a good solution but unaffordable in the short term as it would require some form of global collaboration on taxation or a sustained political will to tax the wealthy. Both of these are not reliable pathways and should be our plan B. We needed a plan A and we found one: permanent money, a tool historically used to finance wars and more generally to fund governments when they had to spend more than they found possible or desirable to collect in taxes. Proponents of neoliberal capitalism have blocked the use of permanent money, citing its tendency to create inflation and give excessive power to inefficient governments. More fundamentally, it would be a recognition that capital is not as limited as we are made to believe and would not deserve such high returns. The alternative in use now, a link between money and credit, has proven problematic as well, since it too creates inflation and it gives excessive power to creditors.

We x-rayed the neoliberal model and found a complete failure. Flaws riddle its assumptions, it has broken all its promises, and its resource allocation proved far from efficient. The world has become more unequal and the economic growth proved nothing more than a short-lived paper fire. While capitalism was a good enough way to escape from underdevelopment, in our developed society it is neither capital nor labor that is limited, but spending power and a mechanism to direct capital and labor to the most useful investments, which is linked to money. It used to be that capital is a limit and money the mere instrument to allocate capital and resources. Now the poor distribution of money is the limit to progress, with citizens either unable to afford what the economy could produce or unwilling to pay higher prices or be taxed to make our economy inclusive and sustainable. We have outgrown an economic system based on capital. We need one based on money.

Matching Keynesian policies with UBI could solve this issue and could also avoid concentrating too much power in the government. As we will see, governments could have no role at all in a UBI program. That's why even the founding fathers of neoliberal capitalism supported this idea.

But this approach still does not solve inflation and it does not address damage to the environment, a new but critical issue. We are at war to reverse climate change and end poverty, and society will keep coming up with challenges, many of which we haven't foreseen, the COVID-19 pandemic a case in point. Central banks have already started printing money and giving it to whomever they are legally allowed to give it to, but in the form of credit. To uphold their mandate, they are venturing into unprecedented money printing but without a framework to do so.

We need to put structure around this money printing and create a versatile model that can quickly channel money to tackle the most pressing issues as they arise. With such a model, the goal of society can cease to be economic growth and full employment, and shift to directly improving the well-being of all people while preserving the planet for future generations.

We now have the compass to point monetism in the right direction and strategic directions that can lead society there. Monetism needs to define how to direct resources to these strategic directions within the constraints we have learned: the old dangers of inflation and excessive power in the hands of governments.

Chapter 13

First Pillar: Harvesting the Money Tree

*Injecting permanent money to pursue universal
and sustainable well-being*

In 2017, UK prime minister Theresa May told nurses who hadn't received a pay raise in eight years, "There isn't a magic money tree that we can shake that suddenly provides for everything that people want."[1] She was wrong. We have had such a money tree ever since the gold standard fell in 1971. It's fiat money, which lets us create as much of it as we want. We just haven't understood the right way to use it.

Terrified of inflation, we took a prudent course, at least on paper: We wouldn't create money unless by doing so we could create goods that required the exchange of that money. From there came the idea that we had to tie money to a credit–debt contract, and allow the deregulated, competitive banking industry to issue it.

History has shown that this approach is ineffective. Beyond lending too much or too little and thus creating business cycles, most credit goes to purchasing existing assets, causing their inflation—exactly what we feared the most.

Earlier we showed that the amount of money out there does not necessarily change its value. This idea is a legacy of the gold standard. Today the supply of money grows continuously but in a form of credit–debt agreements managed by banks.

Can society regain control over the money tree and use it better than banks traditionally have? Historically, the alternative of permanent money—creating money and giving it away for free—has also proven difficult to manage, whether the creation came from governments, private individuals, or commercial banks. Central banks have had some success, but their mandates and dependence on commercial banks has limited their scope of action. Today we do not allow central banks to create money and give it away for free.[2] But we can't deny that a money tree exists, metaphorically speaking (in these days of misinformation and flat Earthers, it's better to state the obvious sometimes), and today the money tree is in the central bank of each country with its own currency.

But who would be the custodian of such a gift? And what is the proper way to use it? If we decided that society could do with more permanent money, who should harvest this money tree and how? Can we just ask the central bank to straight up give away some money for free and limit the amount of money that banks create? And who would get this permanent money?

The core of monetism is about learning to harvest the money tree—use the post-gold-standard ability of modern societies to create money—better than we do today. Let us start by looking at a highly successful system with a complexity similar to that of our societies.

MONEY AND BLOOD

As any med school student will tell you, the human body is a vastly intricate system, with multiple, organized subsystems composed of trillions of cells of different types, organized in structures with organs that perform varied tasks. Each cell is healthy as long as it receives food and oxygen (and does not become infected or grow old), and the human body is extremely good at maintaining its health.

Without us even thinking about it, our lungs fill up with oxygen every second. Red blood cells take the oxygen and deliver it to each cell, which uses the oxygen and gives carbon dioxide and water back to the red blood cells, which the lungs ultimately expel. If a cell is starved of oxygen for a few minutes, it will die. If enough cells don't receive oxygen, organized structures will die. If a vital organ dies, either there is quick intervention (as with a transplant) or the human being dies.

But before dying, the body will put up a serious fight. If we cut ourselves, our body has evolved to create blood clots that stop the bleeding. It happens with no conscious intervention from the brain, as long as the wound is not too big. And when viruses or bacteria attack our body, there are groups of cells ready to fight off the infection and, if struggling, they ask for help and the brain sends more resources by running a fever or producing other chemical substances, or the person will seek a doctor's opinion or a prescription for medicines. Our bodies have effective defenses against most disruptions. Often, unbeknown to our conscious minds, the brain will divert resources to tackle this new priority. But even simple things such as digesting food or walking in cold weather require a diversion of resources—more oxygen and blood to our stomach to digest the meal or a change in metabolism to cope with the cold. It all happens while we ponder which socks to wear. What an incredible machine.

Though society has nothing analogous to a well-functioning brain, is there anything that we could learn from the human body to harvest the money tree? If you think of money as oxygen carried in the blood to different cells, the human body gives us a few insights.

Think of the cells in our heart. They receive oxygen and nutrients so that they can focus 100% of their time on helping the heart fulfill its purpose: the rhythmic contraction of the chambers to pump oxygenated blood to the rest of the body.

Imagine now that these cells had to spend a quarter of their time reaching out into the bloodstream to secure their necessities. They'd obviously be less effective at keeping the heart pumping rhythmically, and it might skip a beat here and there—or worse. Similarly, in our society people have to work to chase their own oxygen. Some get too little and don't contribute to society as much as they might, while others have far more than they need. And while body cells are born with a task already assigned, people must spend time figuring out how they can best contribute to society. Would I be a better teacher, writer, or consultant?

We can fix this situation by opening up society's cardiovascular system and sending money capillaries out to feed every part of it.

HARVESTING THE MONEY TREE: UNIVERSAL BASIC INCOME

The first way to harvest the money tree is by funding a UBI program with permanent money. We can give each citizen a free account at the central bank and every week they would receive a transfer of money that can be spent, saved, or used to repay debts.

While we covered the critiques of UBI earlier, we have not yet described the full array of benefits that UBI could achieve, directly or indirectly. Besides bringing all people above the comfort threshold discussed in Chapter 2—and associated benefits on poverty reduction, health and education outcomes, and well-being—at a societal level, UBI could—

1. **Give people spending power apart from employment**, allowing society to pursue automation at a full clip with no fear of buying slowdowns or depressions that a lower demand for paid labor would otherwise entail.

2. **Multiply other work patterns**, such as entrepreneurship, part-time work, freelance work, and in fact every kind that isn't full-time employment. With their basic needs covered, people can take risks that only wealthy people can comfortably take today, such as starting companies, and then gain the rewards. People will also have smoother transitions between work and retirement, since they can gradually reduce their working hours earlier. Sudden retirement is often a shock and the newly retired have higher death rates.[3]

3. **Improve employee-employer relations.** UBI will give people less need for rigid union regulations, which currently hinder employers in countries like Italy and France, to the point of spurring companies to move to countries with less rigid labor laws. Employers will be freer to hire and fire, thus likely increasing meritocracy and efficiency. Employees can more easily quit and look for better working conditions. At this point we will have a more balanced and well-functioning free labor market.

4. **Bolster productivity.** Employees will be more likely to find jobs that fit their skills and motivations. As their average engagement increases, their productivity and happiness will follow, as many studies on job engagement attest.[4]

5. **Replace some means-tested social schemes** that have high administrative costs and often deter low-income and unemployed people from finding a new job. Most social protection schemes provide

benefits only if people have no jobs or low income. With such schemes in place, people could be worse off by taking a part-time job than remaining unemployed on social transfers. Means testing is also expensive and will grow increasingly so as nontraditional working arrangements such as the gig economy and self-employment become norms. In 2017, several dozen people died in the Grenfell fire in central London, where many social housing recipients lived. Among the many causes, it turns out that the money allocated to check if tenants really had no means to pay rent left insufficient funds to ensure other services, like appropriate fire emergency practices.[5]

6. **Increase freedom in spending**, shifting it from governments and banks to individuals. The government would only have to decide the amount of UBI transfers and not what people use them for, and banks would have less chance to issue loans to desperate people at predatory interest rates.

7. **Eliminate the need to keep dead companies alive.** Today, large employers giving jobs to many can rely on their government to keep them alive to safeguard the jobs. Companies that would go bankrupt if left to market devices are kept alive just to save jobs. Some of these companies can even discount scenarios that would lead to bankruptcy, counting on a government bailout to save jobs, should things go awry. Those days should be history. And the same should be true of companies and industries relying on unsustainable practices: If regulations to curb these practices would send some of these companies bankrupt, so be it. Society doesn't benefit from them; why help them with flawed regulations? To give jobs to people, jobs that damage society at large?

8. **Reduce dependence on the banking industry.** If UBI lets people open a bank account at the central bank, as some economists have long suggested,[6] they will have a risk-free alternative to commercial banks for storing their money. Banks will have to do a much better job of convincing people to deposit their savings, starting with greater transparency in how they lend and invest their money.

9. **Provide an additional incentive for good behavior**, since UBI transfers could be suspended for grave offenses such as crimes or for serious misuse of the income such as for drug addiction.

10. **Allow us all to sleep better at night when we do not give charity to beggars.** I'm never sure if a panhandler really needs money or just wants booze or will be forced to give the money to some pimp waiting nearby. With UBI, we would know that everyone has basic needs covered and if they didn't have UBI, it was because they violated basic norms in one way or another.

Given the many economic and other benefits and its moral justification, a UBI program should be a priority for monetism.

But once we agree on this UBI, we have to make sure we get the program right. In fact, even countries open to the idea of UBI are testing it incorrectly, piloting or proposing programs that lack many of its most important principles. For instance, most are not universal but only for the unemployed or low-income people. These pilots cost governments less than a universal program but encourage some people not to work and breed discontent among those who do and pay taxes to support the unemployed. Populist party M5S in Italy has implemented UBI in name only, a poverty alleviation program with many conditionalities and an incentive profile that disincentivizes part-time work. Other programs or pilots are better designed but are still positioned as social assistance programs with some eligibility criteria rather than a right of citizens.

Let's not confuse the UBI programs that proponents like Rutger Bregman or Philippe Van Parijs have advanced with the pilots making news these days that, while better than nothing, lack vital features and may give a bad name to the whole idea of universal basic income.

HOW MUCH WILL UBI PAY PEOPLE EACH MONTH?

This question could be the subject of long and intricate debate. Pilots rarely give us the right answer. Furthermore, the magic number that they attempt to determine is not a single, static figure but a continuously moving target, part of which is also a matter of politics more than economics. In my view, it should be low where and when societies are close to full employment and higher as societies manage to automate paid jobs away.

My proposal would be to start small and increase the transfers over time. In Alaska and in North Carolina, certain populations have received partial UBI of about $1,000–$2,000 and $4,000–$8,000 a year per individual for the last four decades. We know that at these levels of transfer, there is no impact on the labor supply while many of the benefits have materialized. A sum of $8,000 a year is about $20 a day, more than enough to pay for food. Considering that access to health care and education should be universal—and in most high-income countries it is—this level of UBI would give access to most basic needs. It would still not give people the comfort of a house. Social housing programs are already available in high-income countries and partial UBI should not reduce our commitment to these. But the discomfort of having to live with parents or in social housing will help minimize the number of people who seek an unemployed life.

We should probably stay at this level as long as our economy is not fully reconverted to be environmentally sustainable and automation can't provide most goods and services. Moreover, we still have huge needs for research that could lead to new discoveries and a better understanding of our world—think of nutrition, or cancer, or brain studies. Society will prosper by supporting this research, which remains critically underfunded. Ensuring funding for this research (more on this later) would also create interesting and likely fulfilling jobs.

For the foreseeable future, in my opinion, it is still too early for people to drop back to working 15 hours a week for 20 years of their lives. We'll have to wait a little longer. But that day will come, and we should start reforming our socioeconomic system to allow us to move in that direction.

The transition between partial UBI and full UBI could follow an approach mentioned by Robert Shiller. He advocates a form of livelihood insurance that automatically kicks in once macroeconomic conditions like inequality or unemployment reach a certain level.[7] The key variable wouldn't be income but rather an overall economic index. One metric I would include is the difference between the growth in productivity and the growth in median wages. That difference should be zero, as it was until the late 1970s. UBI transfers could gradually increase until the greater negotiating power of workers reestablished a balanced relationship with employers. If wages started to grow more than productivity, we might have to reduce UBI transfers.

An adaptable UBI could provide the insurance that Robert Shiller advocates while paving the way to a future where we can simply enjoy much more leisure than today. Once partial UBI with permanent money is in place, as robots replace more and more workers, it would be simple to increase the transfer amount. At that point, we might even be able to guarantee an allowance for housing within UBI, and get to full UBI.

Society should not only look forward to that day, but should also anticipate it as much as possible, removing all barriers to productivity and automation. With UBI we should be happy when companies lay off workers. They'd do so because of progress and productivity, and the people without jobs would still have money and could either enjoy more free time or find more socially useful occupations. We should remember that companies release workers when their salary is not justified, which means that they do not create enough value with their time. People are better off devoting the time to something more valuable. Why waste time—again, the only thing that is really limited in life—on efforts that are neither needed nor appreciated?

Labor unions won't go away, but their objectives will shift from protecting full-time employment to demanding fewer hours and better working conditions. From studies on forager tribes, we can estimate that hunter-gatherer ancestors only worked between 2 and 3 hours a day. In modern societies people in standard full-time employment contracts work anywhere between 7 and 9 hours a day, with many employees regularly putting in 12, 16, or even 20 hours a day for 5–6 days a week. It may be useful to consider what societies would look like at the extremes. If everyone worked 16 hours a day, 365 days per year for 45 years of life, it should be clear that no one would have time to consume much and society would collapse. If no one worked, society would collapse as well.

But there is no golden rule that people should work 40 hours a week for 48 weeks per year for 40 years of life. This should change based on the need for human labor compared to the wants of consumers, which highly depends on how much we can automate the provision of goods and services. As much as I love the work I do, I would much rather work for money only 3 days a week, 36 weeks per year for 30 years of life, and dedicate the rest of my time to voluntary activities, hobbies such as writing this book, and leisure time with friends and family. Different people will think differently, but given the opportunity of automation, monetism can give more freedom to people to make these decisions.

And in the long term, if automation is successful, we may even go beyond UBI to Universal High Income (UHI), allowing most people to access the products and services of robots. Who knows? When that day comes, we may give up on prices entirely and give away most things for free, following the biblical suggestion to do good without asking anything in return.

Beyond the amount of UBI transfers, many other details and policies need to be defined. For these, I refer you to the book *Basic Income*, which wonderfully assesses the different options to implement a UBI program and provides a recommended course of action.[8] It addresses questions like these: Should immigrants be entitled to UBI? At what age do payments start? Is the amount the same, independent of age? Can one mortgage UBI transfers? My only disagreement with the authors of that book involves how to fund a UBI program, as they did not understand the opportunity of using permanent money.

HARVESTING THE MONEY TREE: QUICKLY TACKLING SOCIETAL PRIORITIES

The first pillar of monetism is not just a UBI program. Rather, it is also a strategy to harvest the money tree, along the four strategic directions, all aimed at maximizing a universal and sustainable well-being. A UBI program only addresses two strategic directions: providing universal dignity and enabling a future where people can consume while enjoying more leisure time. They're important, but we need more.

If we look again at the human body, we see two more features society can emulate.

First: The most vital parts of the body receive more resources and preferential access in urgent cases. For example, the brain consumes about 20% of our caloric intake. And when people get hypothermia, the blood concentrates around vital organs and away from extremities like fingers and toes. Our body avoids wasting suddenly critical heat, focuses on the essentials, and maximizes our chance of survival.

Second: Our body continuously diverts resources to address priorities as they change. After we eat, more blood goes to the stomach and less to our brain, and we feel like taking a nap. Capitalism is already rather good at creating companies that fulfill needs as they arise. You could compare this feature to blood clotting automatically when we get hurt. The blood composition does the trick automatically. But for serious threats like a disease or a trauma, our brain intervenes and directs resources where they are most needed or makes the decision to see a doctor.

However, society does not deploy fast-track mechanisms to address many urgent situations or prioritize use of resources by need. And even if governments could act as the brains of society, we discussed their limited ability to raise taxes or public debt in a global economy.

We need to find a way to harvest the money tree and give society these two additional features. In the words of economist Ann Pettifor, "If well managed, there need never be a shortage of money for society's most urgent projects."[9]

In an ideal world, the government would be as effective as the human brain and make these decisions. We would just need the government to harvest the money tree whenever needed. In this ideal world there would be less taxation and the government would fund itself mainly from the money tree. Unfortunately, reality is much different. Most nondemocratic governments are plagued with corruption and most democratic governments are plagued with some corruption and political pressure to please voters. Both these situations would likely lead to a wasteful use of the money tree, leading to high inflation. Society has to find a different solution. The one I propose is *conditional transfers*.

CONDITIONAL TRANSFERS

Conditional transfers are typically programs in which money goes directly to members of a disadvantaged population on the condition that they do something in return, typically sending children to school. These cash programs have shown remarkable success in several countries.[10] I am borrowing the term and amplifying the meaning to include any program in which money is given to people, companies, or governments, if they meet certain predetermined conditions.

The first condition involves the use of the money. As with our body, society should guarantee that key organs get all the resources they need and that we promptly tackle any threat with all the resources we can spare. But what are the key organs? What threats deserve this preferential treatment? And what projects can adequately tackle such dangers?

Governments already try to define these threats and provide different forms of subsidies. The European Union, for example, collects monies from all its members and redistributes them in a variety of development funds. If a company in Portugal wanted to launch a green energy project that fit the conditions that an EU fund has established, that company could get the money for it. Many funds are also available for entrepreneurship, either as grants or as 0% loans. Some transfers bolster social security, such as the Youth Employment Initiative of the European Social Fund, which sends money to regions with high youth unemployment rates. These examples are not based on permanent money, but on taxes collected by each country of the European Union. But these funds are an example of a system already in place that ensures a productive use of money. Why not just create permanent money instead of taxing people, which causes them to borrow more, and have the same money created by banks while leaving people in debt?

I will give my hypothesis on which important societal organs and responses to threats could be worth funding through permanent money, guided by society's overall purpose and the strategic directions mentioned earlier. These are just my ideas for high-income countries in the early 2020s. As we will see in Chapter 15 on the governance of monetism, there are multiple options to determine who would actually choose societal priorities.

MONEY FOR HEALTH AND EDUCATION

Two basic organs of society are education and health. People are society's most important resource, so making them better educated and healthier is a precondition to building a better society. In turn, giving everyone access to education and health services fulfills the strategic direction of providing universal dignity—along with the UBI covering food.

But are free education and health care the best solutions? Signing a blank check always encourages waste. Students might indulge and take longer to complete their studies. Doctors might overprescribe drugs and medical tests. The best way might be through merit scholarships for education, or outcome-based grants for hospitals and doctors. Quality education and health may also require better-trained and better-paid teachers and doctors, more of them, or just more research funding. Solutions are likely to be different in different countries. Access to quality education in particular fosters equality of opportunity. Free public education is not enough if the best schools are private and end up attracting students with rich parents. Whether the private or public sector provides these services, equal access to quality education and healthcare should be a priority for our society, and we should redirect whatever resources we need to these, although with strong checks and balances to avoid waste.

In August 2017, I read an article in *La Repubblica*, an Italian newspaper, that dramatically illustrated what can happen without enough funds for good quality healthcare. The author was a woman whose father had collapsed from a heart attack. She called an ambulance and a recorded voice told her to wait on the line. The hospital was just 300 meters away. In the 20 minutes she listened to the recorded voice, her brother ran to the hospital, only to discover they had run out of ambulances. Her father died two minutes before the automatic voice stopped and an actual person asked if there was still a need for an ambulance.[11]

Whether the issue here was funding, disorganization, or simply the operators taking a cigarette break, some problems just need to be solved, and funds are often missing to fix them.

One of my core areas of work is on helping governments understand how to create a *future-proof ecosystem*, given increasing automation. Education systems are all grossly inadequate. For example, to succeed in future labor markets, people will need the ability to continuously learn, adapt, and be able to cope with uncertainty, all skills acquired in the first 1,000 days of life. Childcare and early childhood education in general are the most underfunded areas, albeit showing the biggest returns on investments.[12] Even in Europe and the US, access to childcare for birth through age two is limited. Why? Parents can't afford the costs; returns are too long in the future for governments to prioritize these and, as a consequence, the private sector does not invest. There are millions of potential jobs as early childhood educators who would add incredible value to society and to the economy in the long term, unfilled by lack of funds.

Early childhood in just one example of interventions needed to upgrade the education system. Given the changing nature of work due to AI and increased digitization, many adults will require reskilling services to find a job in a new profession, and an adult reskilling ecosystem is completely missing in most countries.[13]

Ensuring access to quality education and health is equivalent to giving our brain and heart enough energy to think and beat. If we need funds, we cannot compromise with the other government priorities. And we don't have to. I find myself again in strong agreement with Ann Pettifor: "A society based on a sound monetary system could *afford* a free education and health system."[14]

MONEY TO DEVELOP GLOBALLY COMPETITIVE PRODUCTS AND SERVICES

While health and education are very important within a country, in the global society each country has a role relative to others. Each in fact has some competitive advantages, which we can view as their function in the global organism. If you are a heart, your role is clearly to pump blood to the rest of the body. If you are a lung, you should expand and contract to let air in and out.

In a similar way, if you are a country with leading-edge technology and a culture of efficiency, an important role may be to produce the most advanced machinery for the rest of the world. If you are a country with a beautiful landscape, your role may be to welcome tourists. If you are a country with an important culinary inheritance, your role may be to cook for others. This is what led Germany to be a major car manufacturer, the Maldives to be a tourist destination, and Italy to open millions of pizza places and restaurants across the planet.

In a global economy, each country has local resources it can use for global benefit. Of course, countries are not single-purpose entities like the heart, and Italy offers tourism and high-quality cars too. But you get the idea. When a nation sells its specialties, it has an advantage and it gains the export trade that lets it benefit from imports. Therefore, these specialties should also receive the funds they need for the investments, regardless of whether the government or local investors can actually afford the investment. This is the more efficient way to foster progress: specialization on what people, companies, and countries can do better than others.

MONEY TO PREVENT AND MANAGE HAZARDS

Our body shows a remarkable ability to divert resources to tackle diseases and hazards. If society is to fulfill the strategic directions of sustainability and stability, it should again learn from our body. Permanent money should tackle threats to sustainability, such as climate change, and threats to society's stability, including natural catastrophes, epidemics, and financial or economic instability. By avoiding or quickly tackling such issues, we can ensure that our progress continues while minimizing painful disruptions to peoples' lives.

We've talked previously about how funding preservation of the environment can speed up the transition to a sustainable society. Conditional transfers are still the right tool for these investments, which could go to basic research, green infrastructure, clean energy generation projects, forests and oceans protection, and many more programs to reduce carbon emissions or increase carbon capture. Here again, outcome targets in terms of environmental preservations should provide the criteria to both grant funds and assess results.

As for society's stability, the threats come from rare events we cannot always avoid. Conditional transfers of permanent money can target the prevention and relief from 1) natural catastrophes, 2) the prevention and control of epidemics, and 3) the management of banking failures. While there could be other destabilizing events, these are the most relevant ones, considering that UBI should provide universal dignity and hence reduce political instability.[15]

Natural Catastrophes

We can forestall many of them with upgrades in infrastructure, adequate monitoring, and preventive reallocation. For instance, some coastal towns in Alaska are moving away from the sea because of climate change.[16] But in many cases, we don't take such steps due to lack of funds.

In Italy, we have an earthquake every few years that destroys several villages and takes hundreds of lives. Many people then launch fundraising initiatives for the displaced and for reconstruction. The Italian government also makes some funds available. But there are cases like Amatrice. An earthquake struck this small town in 2009, causing light damage, and afterward people fortified a few buildings. Then in 2016 a second earthquake almost demolished the village, including those fortified buildings. Over history, hundreds of thousands of people have died from quakes along the mountainous spine of Italy. Landslides have caused other deaths in the north of Italy. Yet the government has not taken the (extremely expensive) step of securing the areas in the north and building Japanese-style quake-proof buildings in the center. The reason is budget constraints—even though Italy has high unemployment and the expertise to both diagnose risks and build countermeasures. What rational society could leave so many people looking for employment when there is so much work to do to secure our environment? Institutions are slow to react, but in the face of such irrational outcomes, one cannot help being outraged at any additional day that we don't match unemployed people with useful societal projects.

Epidemics

In epidemics, there is no such thing as too much research. The WHO has demanded new antibiotics for the 12 deadliest antibiotic-resistant bacteria, which already cause hundreds of thousands of deaths every year.[17] Ebola and Zika spread panic over pretty much the whole world. Climate change is also hastening the spread of diseases.[18] The COVID-19 crisis gave us an example of this, with most developed countries and many emerging ones directing as many resources as were needed to limit the damage. They funded the resources through higher public debts, but with monetism it could have been funded with permanent money.

Banking Crises

With banking crises, the situation is quite different, though the impact on people's lives is also significant. If a bank were to fail, as I have explained, all the money it created would disappear. The bank deposits people relied on would vanish, they wouldn't be able to pay many debts, and the resulting chain of bankruptcies could bring down the whole economy, with serious consequences for people's lives. Governments or their central banks bail out most banks to avoid their defaults, which beyond the ethical issue actually perpetuates the vicious cycle. As long as banks know that the public has almost unknowingly given them this safety net, they will keep taking excessive risks.

But if we used permanent money, we could just let these imprudent banks go bankrupt, close them down, and have the central bank re-create the money lost in a bank's failure. All clients and depositors of the bank would see their situation unchanged. The central bank would temporarily transfer on its own balance sheet any deposit and loan that the bankrupt bank had given, providing time for companies to establish new loan agreements with other commercial banks. There would be no run on banks; people would know that the central bank would back their deposits. People could even store their money at the central banks in their UBI accounts. The banks' shareholders would obviously lose all their money, but that is the other side of investing: If you take ill-considered risks or mismanage your business, you lose your money.

MONEY TO MAXIMIZE SUSTAINABLE PROGRESS

If we harvest the money tree to ensure free quality healthcare and education, as well as protecting the environment and managing rare events, we almost fulfill the four strategic directions: sustainable progress, universal dignity, stability, and time to pursue happiness and life fulfillment. But we can still do more to maximize progress, which itself can free up more time for people.

By looking at our body in its current form, we have missed the billions of years in which it evolved from primordial organisms. Civilization started only a few thousand years ago and with it our societies have started their own evolution, but it's only a very brief evolution compared to the human body. Society is just starting its evolutionary journey. For the human body, evolution primarily worked through the continual mixing of parental genes, as well as genetic mutations. It was a fairly random process. Now and then natural selection gave some individuals genes that are more useful. Those people gained a survival advantage over others, reproduced more, and passed on that same advantage to their children. Ultimately the more useful genes drove the less useful ones out. To summarize it in a sentence, the body has done a lot of trial and error. How can we maximize the trials and accelerate the evolution and progress of our societies? How can we avoid having to wait centuries or millennia for fundamental social evolutions like leaping from one energy source to the next one, or overcoming cancer?

Research and Development to Increase the Productivity of Limited Resources

A societal concept similar to trial and error is research. Scientists in fact largely proceed through trial and error, experimenting with one hypothesis after another until perhaps they find an answer. Through such research, people can generate new ideas, concepts, and technologies. And free markets then multiply some ideas, like the smartphone or social networks, and kill others, like supersonic travel. To ensure maximum progress, though, the important thing is to maximize that initial trial-and-error stage. Capitalism has helped us greatly by providing people incentives to innovate. As we've seen, however, it also imposed some limitations.

Here too, conditional transfers should come into play. We can fund valuable research projects with permanent money. Again, picking projects and themes requires a technical debate, but the basic guidelines involve focus on increasing the productivity of limited resources: water, land, minerals, energy, and people. It is hardly by chance that the Middle Eastern nations have the best and most efficient desalination plants: They would have no water otherwise. In Japan, with its aging population, the government is paying ⅔ of the cost to develop robotic devices that assist the elderly or their caretakers.[19]

Each country should decide which resources require further investments, with people as the focus. For instance, most countries could expedite automation, and AI is now the most important enabler of the next automation wave.[20]

This would be a key driver of progress, in addition to well-being, since it will give people more time to pursue happiness and life fulfillment.

Funds could be assigned to any research projects that meet the criteria, whether from a private, public, or not-for-profit player. But what is important is that the markets are not the only decision-maker here, or we would miss out on a lot of innovation.

Research and Development to Increase Creative Destruction

In the summer of 2016, I ruined yet another pair of sunglasses. I found a new pair made in titanium, to my surprise, advertised as unbreakable, guaranteed for life, including the lenses. One of my MBA friends reacted with, "What kind of business model is this? Once everyone has bought them, they won't sell anymore." Some of you may spot a flaw in her argument: Most people lose sunglasses, and I have already lost that pair and the following three pairs too. But she identified a key issue: Few companies will sell a product or service that would shrink their own industry. Companies neglect—or intentionally inhibit when they can—any major improvement that would reduce their sales or make them useless. Think of how the smartphone industry has made battery repairs difficult in order to increase phone replacements.

For long-term survival, companies have to ensure that customers regularly buy their products and services at a price that lets them increase, or at least maintain, their profits. Do you think that the private sector will ever create a permanent solution to society's needs and issues? Pick any major need and imagine a scientist claiming tomorrow that he can fulfill it for free, or even better, that he can eradicate it altogether. What would happen to the industry currently based on that need? It would disappear too, right?

This is the original sin of businesses: They will never make themselves expendable. Now, society and each of us immensely desire a need-free world, right? Think of a world with no more diseases, for example. A universal vaccine that keeps you free from any ailment. I can assure you that no pharmaceutical company will ever spend a single cent to research such a vaccine. We all know the recipe for business success: Find a need and fill it. End the need and you end the business. Moreover, even without ending a need, if we could significantly mitigate many issues, numerous industries would shrink or disappear completely.

This is why creative destruction—a key assumption behind the beneficence of capitalism to society—is limited to innovations that yield a profit. If an innovation can't do this, it is unlikely to see the light of day in a capitalist society.

Capitalism pushes companies to go even further. Instead of eliminating issues and needs, companies are creating new ones and solutions to them, keeping more people employed and growing GDP. For example, many people pushed into overeating by marketing campaigns wound up with diabetes, high cholesterol, heart disease, and many other health consequences. In this case, it turned out that the sugar industry was not only avoiding research on the health hazards of their products, but also actively trying to minimize them. For instance, in 2016, *The New York Times* stated—

> The sugar industry paid scientists in the 1960s to play down the link between sugar and heart disease and promote saturated fat as the culprit instead, newly released historical documents show. The internal sugar industry documents, recently discovered by a researcher at the University of California, San Francisco, and published Monday in *JAMA Internal Medicine,* suggest that five decades of research into the role of nutrition and heart disease, including many of today's dietary recommendations, may have been largely shaped by the sugar industry.[21]

To take another example, doctors are key stakeholders of the pharmaceutical industry, and some of them work in for-profit hospitals. How do you think these hospitals and doctors make more money? Option A: By telling patients that their eating habits and sedentary lifestyle have caused the high cholesterol that may kill them and only by changing their habits can they fix their issues? Option B: By prescribing drugs that reduce cholesterol, with several side effects that they downplay or don't even mention? I'll let you guess. Unfortunately, this case is not an exception. Industries like pharmaceutical, food, and energy fulfill important needs, but there is a clear limit to the innovations they can bring.

Here's a further example in which I allow myself some speculation: nutrition. The sister of a close friend of mine was diagnosed with brain cancer. She was a doctor and after refusing a complex operation that could have left her with permanent brain injuries, she took on a vegan diet with one day of fasting per week. After becoming vegetarian myself in 2014, I learned of many studies that heavily criticized the concept of five (or three) meals a day and the consumption of meat altogether. Roy Walford's research has convincingly demonstrated that a low-calorie diet can extend life span by delaying aging and other researchers gathering evidence of health benefits from intermittent fasting and low-calorie diets. In the meantime, the WHO has classified red meat as a Group 2A carcinogen and processed meat as a Group 1 carcinogen, which means that there is enough scientific evidence to state that processed meat is a cause of cancer.[22]

The impact of meat production on the environment is also impressive, especially of beef, which leads to more CO_2 emissions than cars and to a massive use of water, land, and feed that we could use for other purposes. These facts are not well known, as few organizations have focused on these battles. The promotion of a rich meaty diet has led people to think they should eat meat and led some governments to subsidize meat production. Here, scientific evidence already exists and we just need to communicate more.

The same is true to some extent on fasting: Plenty of studies show its benefits,[23] but you can't make a dime by advertising these findings. We'd actually lose a lot of GDP if people started fasting once per week as my friend's sister did. What happened to her? As of January 2019, a decade from her diagnosis, she was stable and her survival had exceeded any statistical expectations. Her theory is that there is an unexplained interference between animal proteins and the process of cellular duplication, given animal proteins are the most similar to human proteins. Could she be right? I have no idea, but this type of question should already have a definitive answer by now.

How can we discover if there are secrets to tapping into free energy, cheap healthcare and prevention, free communication, and other seriously disruptive innovations? More generally, how can we get unbiased, independent answers on important topics like nutrition?

The fact that governments have not acted much on innovations that could wipe out full industries should come as no surprise. How would they reemploy the people from those industries? Monetism fixes this problem, and it lets governments fund these research projects, as well as their communication, without repercussions in the job market.

In fact, a government could set up an independent Creative Destruction Institution with the goal of streamlining established industries through innovations that the free market won't fund. The government can potentially get this money through conditional transfers if they fit the established criteria, and existing institutions like universities can conduct the actual research.

Government-funded research is hardly new or controversial. In *The Entrepreneurial State*, Mariana Mazzucato details how government-funded research led to technologies like the internet, GPS, touch screens, long-life batteries, hard drives, and many others. Most major tech companies today have arisen thanks to government-funded research. Recently, government subsidies to the Dutch company ASM have sustained Moore's Law, which has long accurately predicted the doubling of transistors on a chip every two years or so.[24] COVID-19 mRNA vaccines were also only possible thanks to decades of public research and billions of dollars of public money to develop the vaccines at record time.[25]

Having the government offer a public alternative to the private sector is also not new and it poses a limit to the extent to which the flawed competition in the private sector can damage consumers.

Nobel laureate Joseph Stieglitz has been long advocating a public option on several services,[26] and had we had a public option to produce COVID-19 vaccines that the public had funded, we might have been less at the mercy of private companies maximizing profits in a monopolistic situation instead of maximizing vaccines production as society needed.

If we combine Stieglitz's public option with the success in government-funded research that Mazzucato highlighted, we could see the emergence of a new solution: Governments are funding research in competition with the private sector to deliver existing services at a much lower cost or for free. In the current system, we'd face an economic disaster if this research led to closing entire industries and a fall in GDP, but it would be a sign of great progress with monetism. Unemployed people could still consume through UBI, which might become more than basic as fewer people need to work. The closures of such big companies would mean that a bunch of people were wasting their time in an unnecessary organization, and can now make a better use of their time.

And imagine how life could be better if all recent innovation happened just a few years earlier? More effective cancer treatments could have saved or extended our dear ones' lives. Thanks to the massive public investments to channel private researchers toward a COVID-19 vaccine, there are now hopes that the same technology for those new vaccines could become an effective cure for cancer, almost a vaccine for everything.[27] We could have also seen electric cars exploding decades before Elon Musk took it upon himself to revolutionize the automotive industry with Tesla. Unbiased dietary recommendations could have saved millions from obesity and cardiovascular disease. Much of this could have been realized if we'd incentivized research institutions with the funds to make it possible.

* * *

To summarize, conditional transfers are the second way to inject permanent money into society. They are grants with newly created money (not from taxes and not from bank loans) given to recipients conditioned on using money for—

1) Important societal functions, such as education, health, and the development of sectors in which a country has significant global advantages. This is our body-equivalent to pumping more blood and oxygen to key organs.

2) Tackling critical threats and rare events, such as climate change, natural catastrophes, epidemics, and bank failures. This is our body-equivalent of diverting resources to fight diseases or changing circumstances such as frostbite or heat.

3) Funding research projects to maximize sustainable progress, improving the productivity of limited resources and expanding the scope of creative destruction in the private sector. This is the equivalent of the evolution that our body has undergone throughout millennia.

These conditional transfers, along with a UBI program, would fulfill the four strategic directions to achieve universal, sustainable well-being.

Governments are already funding many of these projects, so permanent money would not have to fully pay for these efforts but rather fill the gap. Moreover, education and healthcare together cost more than 20% of GDP, and it's unrealistic to fund these by printing new money. If we assume that a healthy growth of the money supply is in the order of 10% of GDP per year, any injection of permanent money significantly beyond this amount would likely lead to inflation. In fact, at least two important questions have remained unanswered.

The first: While the body has a well-functioning brain and coordinated organs, society has inefficient and often corrupt governments, as well as selfish, profit-focused private sectors. Who decides which projects receive permanent money? We will address these issues in Chapter 15. While there are multiple options for *who calls the shots*, it will come down to some combination of governments, central banks, and any new independent technical institutions needed to ensure a balance of objective expertise and accountability to the public.

The second: How much can we harvest from the money tree? This question raises the topic of inflation. Although high inflation has been defeated and today the issue in the developed world is too low inflation, starting to harvest the power of central banks to create permanent money may cause new fears of high inflation. If you are a scuba diver using oxygen-enriched air, you know very well that too much oxygen can be lethal. As you dive deeper in the water, the water pressure reduces the volume of oxygen and with one breath you can inhale a lot of oxygen. If you inhale too much, you may get convulsions underwater and likely drown. For this reason, as a trained scuba diver, I am extremely vigilant about depth and I wear a wrist computer to alert me if I am nearing the maximum depth. Society has to do the same. We need to ensure that harvesting the money tree does not reduce the value of money. It would make the incentive of money worthless and the entire system shallow. Remember, this is the whole reason we placed the money tree in the hands of the banking system and tied money with credit. Permanent money needs to be handled with care. As divers can get intoxicated with oxygen if they go too deep, society can get inflation if we aren't careful about injecting permanent money.

The next chapter will describe the second pillar of monetism: handling inflation.

Chapter 14

Second Pillar: Taming the Inflation Monster with Taxes

Inflation management 2.0

Inflation has been a key concern throughout the first part of this book and throughout the last few centuries. Central banks and their employees are the armies constantly monitoring this dangerous creature and often counterattacking. But growth and well-being have been unfortunate casualties in this battle.

Yet, central banks around the world are not as confident of their powers as they might seem, as this honest admission of Janet Yellen's when she headed the Fed: "My colleagues and I may have misjudged the strength of the labor market, the degree to which longer-run inflation expectations are consistent with our inflation objective, *or even the fundamental forces driving inflation* [emphasis added]."[1]

With Pillar One of monetism, we break the spell that binds money and credit by creating and injecting permanent money without requiring a private commercial bank to create loans, credit, and debts. But Pillar One does nothing to tame the inflation monster. While one could make a case that a somewhat higher inflation rate may actually be a good way to redistribute wealth and solve people's indebtedness,[2] since loans would get easier to repay, monetism is a framework that needs to work in the long term and therefore needs to manage inflation, whatever the inflation target.

And inflation is not just a technicality for economists, as anything that happens with inflation affects the lives of everyone. Ultimately, the danger of inflation is the reason society was never successful in creating and distributing permanent money. It's similar to our prehistoric ancestors trying to manage fire. As long as they were not able to manage fires, they wouldn't start any on their own for fear of burning everything down. We have done the same with permanent money. But once we could manage fire, starting our own well-managed fires led to a leap in societal development. Likewise, starting to create and distribute permanent money as described in Pillar One of monetism could lead to an even bigger leap, but we first need to learn to better manage inflation, which is indeed a real danger.

Universal basic income gives money to people who can invest or spend it, but there is no guarantee that supply will increase faster than spending. The same is true for the other conditional transfers. For instance, preventing landslides by securing at-risk mountain areas is just a cost to the government. Giving permanent money to geologists[3] would increase GDP, but it wouldn't produce anything people can buy. The extra money to the geologists would be an additional source of purchasing power and it would chase the same amount of product or services previously available. More spending on the same supply is a major step toward inflation, which occurs when sellers raise prices in response to it.

As for conditional transfers on education, health, and even research, in the long term there are enormous opportunities for a higher production potential. Bright and healthy people discovering new technologies are the essence of economic progress and higher productivity, which can increase supply. But in the short term, higher salaries to teachers or more health expenditures or greater employment of researchers will increase spending for the same products and services. Higher taxes currently compensate for this additional demand, but if we removed taxes and funded some of these expenses with permanent money, demand would grow and inflation could follow.

How do we then solve this historical problem? How do we slay the beast?

THE EASY WAY: SUBSTITUTING DEBT WITH PERMANENT MONEY

There is a simple solution, albeit with some limitations: We limit credit creation. We raise banking reserve requirements and/or interest rates and, as lending declines, we inject permanent money in a compensating amount. So, the overall supply of money doesn't change. It's like reducing the flow from one stream into a lake while increasing it by the same amount from a second stream; the water level stays the same. The only difference is the shift from credit to permanent money, making the economy less exposed to the risk of excessive debt. This proposal is not dissimilar from the proposal of a private debt jubilee funded by central banks such as that of Steve Keen, who explained thoroughly the mechanism and modelled the impact of several economic variables.[4]

Central banks already dampen banks' credit creation to rein in inflation. Yet the standard tools of central banks—interest rates—would not work in a world with a continuous injection of permanent money.

Why not? Suppose a UBI program injects 5% of GDP into the pockets of its citizens. What will people do with the extra money? They have many choices, but at any point in time, most of the money will likely be sitting in some bank account, be it at the central bank or a commercial bank.

So central banks will face a new issue in managing interest rates. Commercial banks will have more permanent money sitting in accounts and given these abundant reserves they won't need to borrow more reserves to issue more loans. As a result, interest rates are likely to be low regardless of any central bank interest targets. It wouldn't matter what interest rates central banks set. Commercial banks would likely have the reserves to lend as much as they wanted to their customers.

This is in fact already the situation after the quantitative easing campaigns that led central banks to create a lot of new money and inject it by purchasing assets.[5] Central banks' money serves as reserves for commercial banks, and now every bank has so many reserves that there is no need to borrow reserves from other banks. Given banks have excess reserves, their price (interest rate) is 0%. No bank would pay more than 0% for something they do not need. In fact, when the Fed wanted to raise interest rates in 2016, it couldn't just use its typical approach; instead of increasing banks' reserve requirements, the Fed resorted to paying interest to commercial banks that parked money at the central bank. By doing so, those banks keep some money out of the economy. These are the same reserves (money) that the Fed had created to buy banks' and governments' financial assets during QE, and now the Fed is paying banks interest for storing this electronic money at the Fed's account. It's like if you are offering to let friends stay in your house, and not only do you not ask for rent, but you also pay them to stay there! They must be very good friends for you to do that!

We'll discuss later how this approach—paying banks to park central banks' money at the central bank—cannot be part of monetism. Why should banks literally get free money from the central bank, in a world where there is no free money for anyone? Banks are the only ones that deserve free money? Really? Why not me and you? Why not governments? Why can't we all get central banks' money and then receive interest if instead of using it we keep it in the central bank's account?

In monetism, reducing banks' credit creation should happen by increasing reserve requirements. As a reminder, commercial banks must keep a certain amount of their reserves at the central bank, based on the volume of their loans, and it's usually around 10%.[6] However, central banks could raise the reserve requirement to 15% or 20%, and the higher the reserve requirements, the fewer loans commercial banks can give without borrowing additional money from other banks or the central bank, at the interest set by the central bank.

Central banks have plenty of room to maneuver from the current 10% reserve requirement to a higher rate, and they would therefore have a tool to limit commercial banks' credit creation, counteracting their freedom from having more permanent money in their deposit accounts. The overall amount of money available would be similar to that in the current system, but the reserves would increase while the money continuously created and destroyed by commercial banks' lending would decline. People and companies would own more permanent money compared to temporary money in the form of credit. With this step, we solve the debt overhang problem afflicting every economy. We can increase money and the economy without further increasing repayment obligations.

Think about it this way: Would you rather have central banks give you $100 for free but make borrowing $100 more expensive, or give you nothing but make it cheaper for you to get a $100 loan? This decision was done for us in the 1980s (cheaper loans), mostly unconsciously, and was never reconsidered.

Here is another way to justify this substitution of debt with permanent money: Our ancestors took loans, invested the money, and generated real wealth with it. Why not recognize their success by substituting debt with permanent money? Why do we keep forcing people to get more bank loans and give real wealth as collateral instead of just recognizing that the wealth exists and create permanent money to back the value of this real wealth? Why not start to substitute all this debt with permanent money, since previous generations have succeeded in creating a lot of real wealth from the loans they received?

Remember the sand tower from Chapter 7, representing debt being continuously revolved by banks and often toppling over? What I am suggesting is to replace a lot of the sand with solid bricks. Sand will still be there. In fact, even with a 100% reserve requirement, banks could still lend as much as they have reserves for, and if they lent it all out, they could still create about 50% of the overall money supply.

Let's assume we would gradually substitute debt with permanent banks' digital currency, until we achieve a 100% reserve requirement.[7] Since global debt is about 300% of global GDP, and high-income countries on average rely on debt even more than developing ones, all high-income countries can go a long way with raising reserve requirements to reduce debt overhang. An estimate of the exact number of years would be a purely theoretical exercise, but we will likely live through a few decades before a UBI equivalent to 5% of GDP of permanent money would lead to a 100% reserve requirement. That should give us time to implement a more sustainable way of managing inflation, which is what I propose in the rest of the chapter.

ISSUES WITH MANAGING INFLATION THROUGH INTEREST RATES

In Chapter 7, we spoke about a few challenges central banks face in managing inflation with interest rates and the banking system as their transmission channel.

First: Delayed response. Central banks can change the interest rate, but this act takes time to affect banks' lending policies, companies' investment policies, and consumer behavior. As a consequence, central banks act preventively. In 2016 and 2017, core inflation in the US was still below target, yet the Fed increased interest rates multiple times.[8] In late 2018, core inflation[9] in the eurozone was still lower than 1% but already many were suggesting an increase in interest rates.

While acting preventively may sound prudent and smart, it is actually suboptimal given the uncertainty of our societies. It's better to have agile, immediately effective tools and act when the problem strikes.

For instance, suppose you are William Tell but in modern times. You stand on a windy prairie, your feet firm on the ground. You turn your head and zoom in on the apple on the head of your son, 300 feet away. You must hit that apple to win freedom for you both. You can choose between your old hunting bow or a modern compound bow. As you instinctively turn to your old, favorite bow, you estimate that it would take four seconds to send an arrow 300 feet, while the newer compound bow would hit the apple in half a second. The wind is strong and is getting gustier. What do you do?

The answer is obvious. The old bow is like a central bank's preemptive strategy. You'd need to shoot ahead of time and yet in four seconds the wind can change and make you wish you aimed a bit further left or right. Since you are too scared to kill your son, you will likely aim too far away and miss the apple. In the same way, central banks are too frightened of high inflation and end up with inflation on average much below their target, which also causes the economy to never achieve full employment and workers have a tougher time negotiating for higher wages, which have in fact stagnated since the 1980s.

On the other hand, the compound bow is an agile strategy, as the arrow hits the target in half a second rather than four, and the wind has three and a half seconds less to change its course. This bow is plainly better and the more unpredictable the winds, the greater the need for it. With inflation, we need a similar tool.

Second: The slowing of economic growth. Interest rates affect both consumption and investments, with a direct impact on investment and a more indirect one on consumption. While the use of interest rates is the cause of this issue, the reason we have so far agreed to sacrifice investments through higher interest rates is more ideological. In fact, many see slowing economic growth as a feature and not a fault of managing inflation through interest rates, but this is based on the ideology of what causes economic fluctuation, unsupported by empirical evidence. Today there is more evidence suggesting that we could progress faster if we managed to avoid economic crises. (See more on this debate in the next text box.) We should therefore aim for a way that manages inflation that does not cause an economic crisis in the process.

Third: The problems with relaunch. Limiting economic growth is even more dangerous given this third shortfall of our current approach: We are unable to relaunch an economy after a crash. As discussed, low interest rates can't directly elevate demand in a sustainable way. Hammers are not good at removing screws.

Fourth: The spray gun effect. The interest rates of central banks affect the whole economy at once. They can't give different stimuli to different areas. For instance, central banks can't spur investments in clean energy, health, and education while limiting demand elsewhere. Their weapon against inflation is just a big spray gun of interest rates, which affects every activity simultaneously. Suppose a plant is part of a large botanical garden, with some sections devoted to cacti, others to tulips, and still others to tropical vegetation. Central banks are the gardeners, but they can only control the weather. They can decide between sun and rain, with different degrees of cloudiness and temperature, but they can't treat different plants differently. So, some plants will suffer.

Earlier we mentioned that the government has more tools to manage inflation but it doesn't use them effectively. We discussed that inflation is largely a behavioral phenomenon, a result of people's behavior in consuming rather than saving and suppliers' in raising prices and underinvesting. The most effective tools to manage behaviors are taxes and subsidies, which central banks cannot use. Only governments can, though they don't do it to manage inflation; that's not their job.

But this approach is not written in stone. It has only been in place (at least to this extreme) for the four decades of neoliberal capitalism with worsening societal outcomes, and therefore we should change it.

Crashing the Economy to Manage Inflation Is Bad 21st-Century Economics

There are conflicting theories on the causes of and remedies for fluctuations in economic growth. The first, which I refer to as *theories of business cycle*, goes like this: There is a natural growth rate based on a stable pace of innovation. Any faster growth is bound to lead to a bust, and the longer the boom, the deeper the recession.

Since inflation indicates that spending is growing faster than the pace at which the economy can increase supply, according to the theory, it makes sense to manage inflation by reducing economic growth in the short term. We just can't grow faster. Therefore, raising interest rates and limiting economic growth at the first sign of inflation is just a way to avoid an otherwise deeper recession. Recessions are inevitable and have no permanent effect on long-term growth, and government intervention to mitigate recessions has no or limited impact.[8]

Larry Summers and Antonio Fatás suggest flaws in this theory, highlighting evidence that economic downturns have ripple effects into the future.[9] They permanently affect the growth of production potential. For instance, companies cut investments in R&D when the economy is weak,[12] thereby slowing technological progress, a key driver of production potential growth.

continued

One alternative theory more in line with Summers's and Fatás's findings is that of Milton Friedman. His *plucking model* of business fluctuations holds that an economy can never exceed its potential, and we can only explain the cyclical nature of growth by our failure to achieve the production potential in those years of slower growth. Unaffordable consumption has nothing to do with the production potential. If an economy was producing a certain value of goods and services, whether consumers can afford them has nothing to do with the potential of the economic machine to produce them.

Studies before[13] and after[14] the 2008 crisis offer evidence supporting Friedman's theory. Fatás has shown how the IMF keeps lowering estimates of the production potential as our economy fails to grow fast enough,[15] a recognition that recessions affect the production potential and/or that we are incapable of estimating the production potential. These estimates should in fact be showing a growing gap that needs more spending, while the IMF estimate of a falling potential supports the opposite: austerity.

And it is not just the IMF: All mainstream economic models lack an approach to modeling a production potential that makes sense.[16] For example, how could Italy have no output gap—the difference between its level of production and the production potential—while having 10% of its workforce unemployed? There sure must be a way to get two million unemployed people to produce something of value, right?

Economists have been revising how to estimate output gaps and now suggest that we have gone far astray from the production potential[17] because we have been unable to keep resources from being idle and innovation to proceed at full speed. Or better, because capitalism keeps diverting policymakers' attention to supply instead of recognizing that demand is the weak link to grow the production potential today (as discussed in Chapter 11).

Despite growing evidence proving we can run Janet Yellen's high-pressure economy (where we stick closer to the production potential and do not limit long-term economic growth with misguided austerity policies), austerity has not died out yet. In Europe in particular, many European countries are assigned unrealistically low output gaps to justify austerity.

If we believe in Friedman's plucking model, in Yellen's high-pressure economy, and in recent economists' proposals to estimate the production potential, our economy over the past decades has performed below potential, and causing economic crises to curb inflation is not the optimal solution. We should find ways to limit inflation without causing crises or slowing progress.

TAMING THE INFLATION MONSTER WITH TAXES

None of us likes taxes. Many feel suffocated by their pressure. Could that despised tool be a gleaming sword that even the inflation monster can't survive?

Pillar Two of monetism is in fact an agile taxation system to manage inflation.

Governments commonly use taxes to raise funds for their many services, but since monetism will make available permanent money for UBI and social priorities currently funded by governments through taxes, governments can refocus taxation on the primary goal of managing inflation.

With taxes we can overcome all the disadvantages of interest rates. Taxes swiftly affect spending—decreasing or increasing it. They leave us less vulnerable to time lags, similar to using a compound bow instead of the old hunting bow. Taxes don't increase the cost of capital for investments, and reducing taxes can quickly relaunch an economy. If interest rates are like a hammer, taxes are like a screwdriver: You change the rotation and you can both screw and unscrew.

And taxes easily discriminate between activities that require different incentives. We could tax fossil fuels, for instance, while not taxing renewables. We could tax home property or even the profit from reselling houses if we fear a housing bubble like the one in 2008. We could tax the profits of pharmaceutical companies if drugs become too expensive, while not taxing profits in industries where lively competition keeps prices low. We could even tax the profits of some drug companies and not others, depending on their behavior. If we think of our economy as a growing plant producing fruits, we can introduce a system that prunes some branches, while letting others grow.

The idea of using taxes to manage inflation is not new, with many economists proposing it at different times in history including Keynes, Abba Lerner,[18] and, more recently, the supporters of MMT such as Stephanie Kelton.[19] I will try to be more specific and propose a new tax system that can best manage inflation.

This new tax system rests on four proposals:

1. Abolish taxes that have a pure fundraising purpose. Keep only taxes that affect behaviors and incentives.

2. Tax a list of unhealthy or unsustainable activities or situations. For example, we should tax tobacco, alcohol, and actions that pollute the environment. More generally, we can justify any tax whose main effect is to limit certain negative behaviors. Going back to Kate Raworth's example, we should tax anything that leads us to overshoot the outer surface of the well-being doughnut.

3. Apply a corporate counter-inflation tax based on companies' profits and investments, with the aim of incentivizing companies to reinvest their extra profits to innovate or scale production rather than pay dividends. This would correct the bias that leads suppliers to prefer price increases over investments or to delay investments longer than they rationally should.

4. Apply an emergency counter-inflation tax as a sales tax to selected goods and services, but only if the overall inflation exceeds a predetermined threshold. We thus remove excess money from the economy. If the inflation does not breach the threshold, we have successfully led a critical mass of suppliers to invest more and earlier while increasing prices less or later, stimulating real growth in the process.

Of this new taxation system, the first point, eliminating or reducing many taxes, is obviously a massive change and would provide relief to the people. It is also a natural outcome of implementing Pillar One, but we can only pursue it together with the rest of the new taxation system. The second point, taxing hazardous activities, is already a common practice and monetism simply highlights its importance and suggests a stronger use. The third and fourth, the company counter-inflation tax and emergency counter-inflation tax, are the real innovations of Pillar Two. The former tries to steer companies' behavior by reshaping the forward growth paths so they find it more sensible to invest in long-term growth than to maximize short-term profit through pricing. The latter is a rapid deployment of a change in tax rates to curb demand, with the key added benefit of not curbing investments and the possibility of a differentiated treatment of different subsets of the economy as needed.

Let's now detail these four proposals, with special focus on the innovative ones: company and emergency counter-inflation taxes.

REDUCTION OF TAXES THAT HAVE A PURE FUNDRAISING PURPOSE

The governments of OECD countries spend 30% of their budgets on health and education, and they get this money from taxes. With monetism, central banks could guarantee some funds for these areas, reducing the tax burden significantly. A UBI program would also make taxes unnecessary for some other welfare programs, including a portion of retirement transfers, so another big chunk of taxes becomes unnecessary. Overall, if central banks fund a continuously increasing UBI transfer, as automation spreads, governments would require far less in taxes.

This does not mean that most of current taxes should disappear. For example, monetism could yield a system with much lower taxes on income, while continuing to tax companies on employees' salaries, with the rationale that the tax provides more incentive to automate jobs.[20]

TAXING UNDESIRABLE ACTIVITIES

Sales taxes can also limit the consumption of tobacco and alcohol, as well as environmentally unfriendly practices, but more generally we should tax any activity that reduces universal sustainable well-being.

We pay an impressive price for some of these activities. In 2012, a study estimated the annual global cost of armed conflicts to society at $2.1 trillion and the cost of smoking was about the same. We pay $2.0 trillion a year for the consequences of obesity.[21] All together, these cost us $6.2 trillion annually, or about 7% of global GDP.

The cost in lives is more frightening. The WHO reported in 2017 that tobacco kills up to half of its users, or 7 million people each year. Moreover, 890,000 of these deaths are of nonsmokers exposed to smoke, and nearly 80% of the world's 1 billion smokers live in low- and middle-income countries.[22] Every year, the use of alcohol kills 2.5 million people, including 320,000 young people between 15 and 29.[23] Obesity increases the risk of death from cardiovascular diseases and cancer, the two major causes of death, claiming about 24 million deaths (or 50% of the total) in 2015 according to WHO.[24]

And taxes are effective to alter behaviors underlying these issues. For example, taxation seems to have been the most effective intervention to cut demand for tobacco, according to the WHO and the World Bank.[25]

In most cases, a sales tax (in the form of a value added tax, or VAT[26]) is the most appropriate form of taxation to reduce the demand of a certain product or service. It directly affects the specific activity only, is hard to evade, and is the least influenced by globalization, since physical goods must still pass through a physical border with a customs office. Other practices may require different taxes. Low homeownership with high rents, a pattern common in many high-income countries, could require specific taxes to keep wealthy individuals from hoarding the limited supply of real estate. For instance, a tax on physical wealth above a certain threshold of value could solve this problem.

Some countries have already pursued such policies. Norway has had a sugar tax since 1922 and increased it by 83% in 2018.[27] In 2017, Singapore collected much of its tax revenues from strategic taxes: about 20% from taxes on cars (which also limit the country's imports and traffic), 9% from property taxes, and 6% from gambling taxes.[28] Sweden has imposed a carbon tax now equivalent to about 130 USD per metric ton of CO_2 since 1980.[29]

On decarbonization in particular, governments could consider different tax regimes for companies that are net-zero emitters along their supply chain, as to steer all the companies in the supply chain to adopt carbon neutral practices. A report by the World Economic Forum and Boston Consulting Group shows that being carbon neutral would increase prices to consumers only moderately, between 1% and 4%.[30] Some certification and inspection mechanism and even a modest tax break to companies that are net-zero emitters (or tax-hikes to non-net-zero emitters) could make the trick here.

TAXING THE BIAS TOWARD DELAYING INVESTMENTS

A counter-inflation tax on companies' profits can spur companies to invest in growing supply and quality instead of just raising prices. Such a tax would prompt others to follow suit since companies that simply raise prices when more people seek its products will face higher taxes, and in the long term they will lose out to companies investing in growth. And in the case of monopolies, this tax can at least limit the benefits of monopolists.

To achieve this goal, the tax rate would have to be progressive, based on some metric of profitability. The term *progressive* refers to a tax rate that increases based on something else, in this case, the profitability of the company, and I would measure it with the Return on Equity (ROE).

Income taxes are typically progressive, as people with higher income pay a higher tax rate than people with lower income. The reasoning is that if you earn more you can contribute more. Most people on the right wing of the political spectrum do not like progressive taxes, because even with a flat tax rate, high-income people pay more in absolute terms. A progressive tax multiplies the amount for high earners.

Thomas Piketty proposes a progressive tax on wealth, with one justification being that capitalism gives an advantage to those who possess wealth. The greater one's fortune, the higher the returns on wealth, he said, so it is fair to tax the wealthier at a higher rate. His progressive wealth tax aims at making capitalism more inclusive. Collecting funds is a secondary goal.[31] This justification is convincing, as it neutralizes the unfair advantage of people with preexisting wealth.

The justification for monetism's progressive tax on ROE is similar to Piketty's. Companies have a common interest in increasing prices and a bias toward delaying investments, especially when the benefit materializes in the long term. In the European Union, for example, corporate investments were the last component of GDP that reached its pre-crisis level after the 2008 crisis.[32] Across OECD countries, companies are making extra profits and hoarding cash instead of increasing investments.[33]

We should tax these behaviors not so much with the aim of taking money from companies, but to compensate for their bias toward increasing prices. We could in fact give tax breaks to companies that invest more and achieve the same objective. Donald Trump's reduction of corporate taxes in 2017 was a lost opportunity: If he had only cut taxes to companies that reinvest a significant portion of their profits, he would have created the equivalent of a progressive tax on profits based on ROE.

Companies with high ROEs are those pricing their products significantly higher than their costs while not reinvesting the profits to provide more or better products in the future.[34] Sustained, elevated ROEs would be impossible if there was sustained competition—companies would compete vigorously and bring prices down. Sustained, high ROEs are a sign of a monopoly and a progressive tax on profits can nudge companies toward a less-flawed competition. One could call this progressive tax on companies' profits based on their ROE a *monopoly tax*.

We often consider ROE as a measure of a company's success in creating value for its customers, but this is another issue of capitalism that Mariana Mazzucato, among others, pointed out: We can't distinguish prices from value.[35] The two seem synonymous, but consider this: If a company had great marketers who could convince customers to overpay for a product, is the company creating value or extracting it? What if the customer had to get indebted and reduce funds for their children's education, because the social pressure to buy the latest iPhone just felt too strong? A progressive tax based on ROE would not make companies moral, but it would at least limit the benefits of charging prices that are unjustified by either the investments required to keep improving their products, or the risks involved.

Marketing can add a lot of value by understanding customers' needs and preferences and guide a company in providing the best solutions. But part of marketing is also about using advertising to convince people that a certain product is worth much more than it actually is. This latter activity is a zero-sum game, fattening big-tech companies with money for their ads and shifting value from consumers (who are made willing to pay higher prices) to companies. Innovation and productivity increase value creation for both customers and companies. Higher prices and the advertising needed to achieve them just transfer value from consumers to companies.

A progressive tax on ROE helps shift the balance away from price increments to investments, stimulating real growth in the process. If it is sufficiently progressive, it provides enough incentive to compensate for the risk aversion and present bias of companies that keep perfect competition a utopia. By imposing higher taxes on those companies with higher return margins, simply increasing prices becomes a losing strategy (at least in the long term) compared to investing to increase supply (and market share) or to conduct research and innovation to increase quality. In fact, companies that fail to invest will lose out against companies that do, as the latter receive the equivalent of a tax break for those investments. We don't need all companies to change their behavior at the outset. Once some competitors take advantage of the lower taxes linked to higher investments, they will force rivals to follow suit.

Take electric cars for example. The electric engine has been around for centuries; it's much simpler and with better performance than the combustion engine, but it took many decades for the automotive industry to really invest in it. What if automakers splashing in high profit margins had to pay much higher taxes unless they invested more of those profits? My hope is that this corporate counter-inflation tax will stimulate bolder or just earlier investments to accelerate progress rather than raise prices and sit on profits. We just needed one automaker—in this case, without monetism it took Elon Musk to found Tesla—for the whole industry to follow suit.

With this progressive tax on ROE, people will no longer hail the ROE as a sign of profitability, but as an indicator that a company is taking advantage of imperfect competition at the expense of society. This is not necessarily new.

At least among economists, land rents that were common throughout history are now (rightly) stigmatized as value extraction rather than value creation. The land is better off rented than idle, but rent payments are a form of extraction of value from what is generated by those putting the land to use. Profits due to monopolies are also stigmatized among economists. Housing rents are now considered similarly unfair. Piketty even called the profits from extraction of natural resources *rent*. Having worked in mining, among many other industries, I can't see why mining companies' profits should be rents and other industries' profits should have the higher status of *returns*. Returns on capital in general are a form of rent. The question is, what level of return is fair and provides the right incentive and what level is unfair, useless, or even harmful to society? A tax on ROE would force this democratic debate to happen.

This tax will have great repercussions in education as well. Marketing professors in business schools of the future would have to say something along these lines: There was once a loophole in capitalism, allowing companies to increase prices as much as the customer was willing to pay, and make more profit that way. This behavior led to inflation and made central banks limit credit, causing economic recessions. Then a progressive tax on ROE closed this loophole and pricing strategy lost significance. The art of marketing today is understanding what type of research and innovations to pursue to best meet consumers' demands. The teaching of microeconomics would have to expand from looking statically at price and quantity to considering investments and taxes, and the short-, medium-, and long-term impact of price and investment decisions on profits.

This counter-inflation tax also motivates investments in equity rather than in debt and companies with higher equity relative to debt would further stabilize the economy. Furthermore, this tax is targeted, as it automatically subtracts money from sectors of the economy with excessively high prices, but not from those with lower ones. And finally, the tax does not limit the profit that a company can make, or the drive for profit in general. The difference between the current flat tax rate on corporate profits and the progressive tax rate is that with the latter, companies can more easily achieve large profits through investments that make them grow in volume or quality, benefiting themselves and everyone else, rather than through inflated prices that harm consumers and socio-economic stability.

As with any new tax, there will be loopholes to fix. For instance, a small company could pay its few shareholders a massive bonus, thus avoiding the tax on profit. The taxation would also limit the incentive to take risks, and for this reason some exceptions and variations should be put in place for start-ups, small companies, and high-risk industries.

Taxing Short-Term Financial Transactions

While taxing financial transactions is not necessary to manage inflation in monetism, such a tax would both reduce undesirable activities and limit the bias toward delaying investments.

Thanks to modern technology, traders can now buy and sell many times within minutes at no or low transaction cost. The average holding period for a stock on the New York Stock Exchange has dropped from eight years to four months.[36] Some institutions employ machines instead of traders to automatically buy and sell financial assets, thus extracting money from society at little risk. Since speed is essential in these trades, companies invested $180 million to cut data transmission between New York City and Chicago by four milliseconds,[37] and $300 million to save six milliseconds between New York City and London.[38] The investment is profitable because trading companies can make billions out of arbitrage opportunities they can exploit only if they are faster than everyone else. Beside the unfairness of this situation, think of the time and money people have wasted by having to drill holes into mountains, with cables as straight as possible for the fastest transmission.

The rationale for maximizing the number of transactions is again the nebulous perfection of free markets. The more the transactions, the more market prices are accurate and the more confident people are to invest. Of course, economists have already proven this theory flawed.[39] No transaction costs simply create an opportunity for financial institutions to extract value from society and funnel it into the hands of bank directors or shareholders. These companies do so by employing tens of thousands of the brightest talents, with high-paying jobs that add limited (if any) value to society.[40]

The good news is that to stop the waste of talent, the extraction of value, and the induced short-term focus on CEOs, we only need to tax those financial transactions that are short-term focused, with the objective of arbitrage and speculation.

The bad news is that any such tax runs against the interests of individuals typically associated with the term Wall Street, and they would require massive pressure from public opinion. James Tobin was the first to propose a similar tax in 1972, which is commonly referred to as the Tobin Tax, but no one has ever implemented any variations of it.

Yet it would be one of the easy fixes of a major problem, and my proposal is quite drastic: a 100% tax on profits from speculation in capital markets,[41] when financial instruments are bought and sold on the same day. The tax rate would decline to the standard rate for instruments held longer, which could be a month if we wanted to maintain significant trading, or two years if we wanted to foster only longer-term investments. The main objective is not to collect funds but to avoid harm and waste. We are currently destroying value in numerous ways, such as by creating software to extract money from capital markets at no risk and concentrate it in the pockets of Wall Streeters or by putting short-term pressure on corporations and governments. We can only imagine what the talents now employed in speculative trading could have offered society, had we established this tax back in 1972.

And if some of the highly speculative banks and investors exit countries imposing this tax, good riddance. It leaves more opportunities for talent and long-term investors to advance useful projects. Companies engaged in the real economy will still be there and will find better investors that will allow them to focus on long-term value creation.

THE EMERGENCY COUNTER-INFLATION TAX

No system always works perfectly. The hope is that inflation remains low thanks to the company counter-inflation tax. But it may not. For instance, if we injected permanent money too fast, the economy could reach the maximum use of available resources at a particular time—its production potential—and demand would outrun supply. Even though we give strong incentives to invest, if demand is just too high for suppliers to keep up with, prices will increase, at a minimum because workers will be scarce and will demand a salary raise, increasing suppliers' cost base. Then what?

Part of the solution is still good inflation targeting. Central banks' role of price stability will be as important in monetism as in capitalism, just with more tools available. In the next chapter I will describe a possible future for central banks. Bottom line, there will still be adequate planning to avoid excessive inflation from the start.

As we know from historical failures in managing inflation (too high in the '70s, too low in 2010s), good planning and prediction can only get us so far. Inflation could still end up higher than desired. We need a good backup: an emergency counter-inflation tax that we can quickly impose on the sale of selected products.

This concept is similar to the way central banks manage inflation today. To slow or stop it, central banks remove money by increasing interest rates, and to spur growth they inject money by reducing rates. I am proposing a remedy that does exactly the same, but with taxes instead of interest. Higher or lower taxes can inject or extract money from the pockets of people, and again taxes work much faster than interest rates without deterring investments.

Compared to income or wealth taxes, sales taxes affect demand more directly and feel less confiscatory. In fact, you pay this tax only if you decide to buy a specific product. It is a direct link to purchasing behavior instead of a higher tax on salary or accumulated wealth.

Sales taxes can also be selective. We can raise the rates only on products and services that are actually causing inflation, and spare those that aren't. High inflation in certain industries can signal the lack of perfect competition.

The selective nature of sales taxes also addresses the fact that sales taxes are otherwise *regressive*. That is, they are the same for poor and rich alike, and hence affect the poor more. But if tax rates for basic products and services are much lower than the tax rates for non-basic or luxury ones, the overall system is not regressive. Instead, sales taxes become progressive. And to some extent this is already happening in many countries. In Italy, for example, taxes on books or bread are typically low while those on sports cars are higher and based on their engine power. In the UK, some items for children are exempt from sales taxes altogether. Again, a competent agency should ensure that the sales tax system is not regressive.

THE INFLATION TARGET

What target should we aim for in monetism? Should it be the 2%–3% that most economies seek today? Should we even have a target for inflation?

Gerald Epstein, an academic who has long researched this topic, believes inflation should be a constraint, not a target. He suggests *real economic variables*, such as employment and growth, should be targeted, but inflation is only a constraint, with no evidence that inflation rates below 20% have any negative effect on real economic variables.[42] I am of a similar view and I think we should be flexible with this target as we confront different economic situations. As things stand today, within the limitations of capitalism, we are clearly flirting too close to deflation and a higher inflation could help rebalance a few of the imbalances described.

Instead, with monetism we could even aim for 0% inflation. In fact, central banks set the current target of 2%–3% because deflation is much more dangerous than inflation. They have better tools to slow the economy than to restart it, especially when interest rates are close to 0%. With Pillar One of monetism, when demand is low central banks can give money directly to the people, which would immediately increase spending. A negative inflation is therefore no problem for monetism and even a 0% target could be an option. We can guarantee strong demand by the greater availability of money in society and we can prevent high inflation with counter-inflation taxes. With such powerful control mechanisms, the target matters less and we should probably stop talking about a target altogether.

It is still important to give some guidance on what inflation to expect, though, to allow people and companies to plan their futures based on a stable value of inflation. A 0% inflation target would be a very strong signal of price stability. It also reduces the nominal cost of capital, further motivating investments. And finally, workers' weak bargaining power has been making it less likely that wages will move upward with inflation. This is not the case for the wealthy, as housing and stock prices typically do rise with inflation. Having said that, in emergency situations such as an increase in the need to fight climate change with permanent money or to solve poverty, one could tolerate higher inflation, as long as it is still stable and under control. If a target was beneficial, it should be sensible and not dogmatic.[43]

Therefore, my proposal would be to define two ranges rather than one target. One range is a boundary; inflation should never be allowed to exceed it. If I was to give some arbitrary number, I would say that inflation should not be allowed to go below 0% or above 10%, but more research and work would be needed to make a less arbitrary proposal.

As for the second range, I would suggest a target range, which central banks could aspire to maintain unless something more important requires them to consciously choose to breach this range. Such a range would be narrower and would help businesses create their business plans, given inflation in the overall economy is often an input to make investment decisions. A narrower range would also give an indication to the central banks on when to start changing their policies, be that a change in emergency counter-inflation taxes, or reserve requirements, or interest rates. When the overall inflation breaches the target range, central banks would automatically have the mandate to change counter-inflation taxes on selected products, for example. (More on the governance of monetism in the next chapter.)

This target range could be set depending on what is the symbolic value that one wants to give. One option is to indeed target a range around 0% inflation, like between –2% and +2%. The argument for such a target would be that society finds continuously new ways for producing the same things at lower cost and, therefore, as long as companies also compete on prices, the inflation should be negative or, at most, zero. But the counterargument would be that this inflation level is below the inflation of most countries today, and below the lower bound of inflation at 0%. My proposal would be to build a range around the current inflation target, to allow more flexibility without causing much change. For most central banks of high-income countries this would mean a core inflation target[44] range of 1%–3% or 2%–4%.

The important thing on inflation targeting in monetism is, leave more flexibility within a broader range and define a narrower range beyond which central banks are authorized to change emergency counter-inflation taxes.

* * *

To summarize, the inflation management system in monetism is very different from what we have today. Today we base everything on the flawed assumptions about market efficiency: Rational people will demand loans only if they have rationally concluded that they can generate enough money to repay them. Such a system would guarantee a stable long-term inflation, while in the short-term, interest rates can correct for temporary overconfidence or risk-aversion biases.

But beyond the fact that people don't always make rational decisions, the concept of *long term* is only an idea, like *the future.* It is the dynamic balance of demand and supply that matters: the present. Tomorrow never comes until it becomes today, so all that matters is being able to manage the present and provide confidence about the future. With interest rates alone we can't reliably succeed at either. In an uncertain environment, things will continually go wrong in many possible ways.

Monetism is a much more present response, with its injections of permanent money and its counter-inflation taxes. It lets us better manage the economy with precise nudges, like changing counter-inflation taxes on specific products, rather than blanket, preventive moves like raising interest rates. Put differently, if you are piloting a boat at night and have only a hand-torch to light your way, would you rather be in a responsive motorboat or the *Titanic*?

And we *are* piloting a boat at night. Our society is undergoing unparalleled changes—globalization, automation, and climate change among others—and we are still unclear about what will happen. Monetism addresses this uncertainty, with UBI as a lifeline for those who may fall off the boat, and more and faster tools to steer the economy through the fast-changing balance of demand, supply, and the environmental hazards ahead of us. This strategy adjusts the economy with much more agility and effectiveness than aiming at a long-term theoretical equilibrium that, in reality, we never achieve. The emerging theories of complexity economics have indeed shown that this long-term equilibrium is a flawed assumption even from a theoretical standpoint. (More on this later.)

The next exhibit summarizes all of monetism's tools for managing inflation and the economy in general.

Tools	Use	Rationale in Monetism
Conditional transfers	⬆	• Increase selected investments
	⬇	• Reduce selected investments
UBI transfers	⬆	• Sustain aggregate demand against raising unemployment
	⬇	• Increase labor force participation in case of a resurge of employment needs
Emergency inflation taxes (VAT)	⬆	• Reduce aggregate demand or consumption of selected products
	⬇	• Increase aggregate demand or consumption of selected products
Company inflation taxes	⬆	• Incentivize aggregate investments over price increases
	⬇	• Reward lack of price increases and attract foreign capital
Interest rates	⬆	• Reduce debt and aggregate investments
	⬇	• Increase aggregate investments

Exhibit 10: Monetism's tools to manage the economy

THE HELICOPTER-DROP EXPERIMENT IN THE 21ST CENTURY

It's useful at this point to revise the helicopter-drop thought experiment that Milton Friedman introduced in 1969. What would happen if a flock of drones (updating the technology) delivered $1,000 to each citizen? The answer to this question can only be *it depends*.

Some citizens would use the money to repay existing debts. This portion of money would neither increase the money supply,[45] nor demand, nor inflation. Some people would save the $1,000, therefore expanding the money supply but not increasing consumption or inflation (though higher deposits may lead banks to lend out even more credit).[46] Other people would invest this money, potentially increasing the supply of goods and services and even reducing inflation.[47] The rest of the recipients will spend the money, increasing consumption and potentially inflation (in case suppliers have no extra capacity and/or prefer increasing prices instead of investing).

What would happen to the overall level of prices? The answer depends on many factors. The more people save and invest, the less inflation would grow and prices could even fall. The more people spend, the greater the pressure on inflation. But today, wealth is concentrating and causing higher savings rates; the wealthy don't even have the time to spend all they have, and many become Squirrels with no intention to ever reduce their stockpile. People are also living longer and need more savings to afford consumption for their increasing retirement years. Let's add trade to the picture. Some people will use money to buy foreign products. Others will invest money to manufacture products that go abroad. What happens to exchange rates? Again, it depends. And if central banks change reserve requirements or governments change tax policies, even more factors would be at play. The impact of a drone-drop of permanent money should always have this answer: It depends.

And if some inflation and currency devaluation did occur, would that be more problematic than higher unemployment, higher poverty, and perhaps populist parties gaining power and wrecking the economy and the global political stability?

Most of these decisions and trade-offs draw more on social and political considerations than economic ones. That brings me to the point I have been putting off until now but can no longer avoid. The governance of monetism.

How do we identify the right issues worthy of permanent money? How much should UBI transfers be? Who makes these decisions? Who acts as society's brain? And how should this brain work?

Chapter 15

Who Calls the Shots?

Governance options for monetism

A meditation teacher once described how a surgeon and a street robber use similar tools and perform similar actions but the outcome is completely different. The first cuts a person open with a knife to restore health. The second cuts a person open with a knife to take possessions and even life itself.

The point is that it's not words or actions that matter most but the intent behind them. So far, I have proposed new ways of using certain tools, but I postponed the discussion about who should use them. Who in society should be the equivalent of the doctor? How do we keep the robbers away?

More generally, I have not addressed how society should organize itself to make the decisions that monetism requires, which I will refer to as its governance.

Monetism requires ongoing governance. If it was just a simple set of rules that formed a new framework, the situation would be simpler. We could set up a task force or a commission and once the new rules are defined, it becomes a matter of execution. But decisions like the monetary sum of conditional transfers, which activities they fund, how much the UBI needs to be, and counter-inflation taxes will require continuous adaptation.

As such, a time-bound task force is not enough. Monetism needs a new governance model with checks and balances to ensure that any institution or person working on these topics serves the ultimate purpose of universal and sustainable well-being. There can be variations on the model, but the three key players that could be calling the shots are some form of government, central banks, and potentially new government-owned but independent technical institutions.

THE CURRENT STATE OF GOVERNANCE

Society needs governance because of the paradox of freedom: Full freedom for everyone equals lack of freedom for all. In less extreme situations we see what ecologist Garret Hardin called "tragedy of the commons," in which the unrestrained use of a common pool of resources by the population leads to their overuse and depletion, leaving everyone worse off.[1]

Environmental damage and overfishing are two examples he used. Game theory has well explained the difficulty in breaking free from these situations. In many situations, cooperative restraint leads to the best results for everyone, but if a few people don't cooperate, they wind up better off.

Think of people fishing out on the seas. If they all agree to limit their catch and keep the fish population within bounds, they can keep taking as many fish as the oceans can provide. But one person overfishing gets more benefit than the rest. Without enforced coordination and rules, everyone worries that others will not collaborate and most people will overfish. So everyone winds up worse off in the long term. That's what happened to the cod in the Gulf of Maine. Over the 10 years ending in 2017, cod numbers dropped by 80%.[2] These situations are plentiful, so we often need governance to prevent individuals' free decisions that ultimately hurt themselves and society as a whole.

But concentrating too much power in government bodies can backfire, since people with self-interest also run them. The absolute power of monarchs and dictators often led to extravagant pursuit of self-interest and in turn bred the revolutions of the 18th and 19th centuries in Western societies and the more recent Arab Spring. But as countries became more democratic, the *tragedy of the commons* shifted in part to governments, as to get reelected, politicians may make decisions that are popular in the short term but detrimental in the long term.

Furthermore, governments still allowed waste and corruption to proliferate. This is part of the reason that the neoliberal movement gained traction: It gave more power to people's free choice and let independent central banks control money management to limit government waste. The removal of the power to manage money has created a series of checks and balances: If a government wastes money, taxes or the public debt grow too high and the public will presumably elect new leaders.

We can summarize the lessons from the history of societal governance in two principles:

1. Certain activities and decisions require someone independent of short-term public pressure to avoid tragedy of the common situations.

2. Any concentration of decision-making power requires accountability to the public to prevent use of the power against the interest of society.

While these lessons are important, we identified many issues with our current governance in the first part of the book, in particular:

*   Central banks pursue a mandate with the potential to go against public well-being without unaccountability to the public.

*   Commercial banks and businesses in general are not accountable for many societal costs they cause and taxpayers foot the bill.

*   Governments in a global economy lack the ability to raise the taxes they need to provide public services while fixing market failures.

*   Both governments and central banks lack the tools to pursue their mandate effectively.

It is therefore not surprising that monetism requires a new governance, one that maintains checks and balances as per learning from the past but also one that does not limit the ability of governing institutions to pursue the universal well-being of its citizens. Monetism governance will have to enable the creation and allocation of permanent money to maximize sustainable well-being, while avoiding inflation.

One of the messages of this book is that, in a developed country, any social issue including homelessness, climate change, and poverty is not an inevitable economic circumstance but a political choice. Politicians in the 1980s and 1990s have been able to enforce their implicit choice upon our time through central bank mandates that even today's politicians have difficulties in changing. But when circumstances evolve, mandates and even constitutions need to be revised.

Before proposing a new governance enabled by and/or compatible with monetism, I will state three disclaimers.

First: I do not believe perfect governance exists for any country. Different nations already have different political structures and they should implement what best fits their culture and institutions. Here I will not prescribe a *best* governance, but rather show that many alternatives are compatible with monetism.

Second: The devil is in the details and describing full governance for society would be too technical for this book and would require expertise I do not possess. Some of these ideas could compel changes to laws and constitutions. Others will require new processes to appoint the heads of certain governing institutions. Overall, countries will need legal and regulatory changes. It will all be part of the invisible work that happens in governments that too few people appreciate. I will discuss only the guiding principles and leave the details to those unseen workers in the countries that implement a version of monetism.

Third: While I do appreciate that the public sector is oftentimes less efficient and more bureaucratic than the private sector, I do not believe that this fact leads to the conclusion that the role of governments in society should be minimal. The communist government that *owns, plans, micro-manages, and operates* is gone, and so is the equally dystopian neoliberal government that only *enforces the law to give everyone freedom.* Today all governments strategize, regulate, and, as a last resort, they operate. This is reality; the other extremes are dystopias.

I also don't believe that the public sector cannot be made efficient. There is no law of nature that establishes public inefficiency. Having advised both public and private organizations, the difference is often in the quality of people (and the salaries they receive for the jobs), and a performance-management system that ensures those who reach results are rewarded and those who do not are not (and those causing damage are laid off).

If you consider the governments of Singapore and Dubai, the first is well known for attracting the best talents of countries through varied means, like scholarships in prestigious education programs, and the latter has several performance targets that it continually monitors, with real consequences for poor performance. The government of China has a system where mayors are promoted based on their performance on targets set by the central government. When the Chinese government prioritized internet-based entrepreneurship and development of artificial intelligence and poured money into it, mayors unleashed their own local policies to promote R&D, AI training, and entrepreneurial activities, putting the country well on track to overcome the US in both innovation and AI, as per the Chinese government's targets.[3] These targets are elements of an effective performance management that exists in all well-run private companies. It is not a communist artifact.

I have also had the pleasure of knowing Nika Gilauri, the former prime minister of Georgia, which is another great example of a successful government transformation. In less than 10 years, he almost eradicated corruption and reformed the education system in his country through performance management. The worst teachers were fired or relocated every year, while the best received more money. He got rid of most corruption by motivating whistleblowers to report cases of it.[4] In the process, he managed to almost quadruple the GDP per capita of the country, from $1,200 in 2004 to more than $4,000 in 2012, notwithstanding the 2008 crisis. Since Georgia was in a desperate situation, he had no unions or lobbies that could prevent performance management.

These examples show that government institutions can be made efficient, but they just need a strong performance management system.

Moreover, while public sector institutions today face popular pressure to provide jobs and avoid firing public workers, with a UBI program all need for this featherbedding vanishes. Lazy or less-able people will know that institutions can fire them on the spot and replace them with more productive people. It won't even be as traumatic because they'll land in a resilient safety net. As the public sector is quite inefficient in most countries, we may actually need fewer people in governments, further reducing the need for taxes and giving more time back to citizens.

With these three disclaimers in mind, let's look at where monetism needs a new governance model.

GOVERNANCE NEEDS FROM MONETISM'S TWO PILLARS

I will approach monetism governance from the decisions and activities required by monetism's two pillars and associated programs and policies:

- Pillar 1a: Designing a UBI program funded with new permanent money and changing the UBI transfers as automation reduces the need for employment or new challenges increase the need for employment.

- Pillar 1b: Deciding which priorities to fund through conditional transfers, as well as the criteria and processes to allocate the funds.

- Pillar 2a: Balancing credit creation with the injection of permanent money to keep the overall money supply and inflation in check.

- Pillar 2b: Designing an agile taxation system to manage inflation and continually update tax rates[5] based on inflation dynamics.

Many of these activities are incompatible with the current governance. In fact, while central banks are responsible for inflation, they are not accountable to the public and, therefore, should not be responsible for allocating resources to economic activities or imposing new taxes. At the same time, giving the government back the ability to print money could lead to waste and poor popular choices that become tragedies of the commons. Except for balancing credit creation with the injection of permanent money, which fully falls to central banks, all other activities are in a gray area in which both the government and the central bank should be only partially responsible.

Let us go through them one by one and provide a few overall governance options for monetism.

PILLAR 1A. UBI

Universal basic income has the advantage that it distributes resources equally. The measure is also highly popular and hence there is less need for accountability to the public. The risk is that a government under short-term pressure will increase the UBI transfers beyond an optimal level. For this reason, while the design of the program should come from the government, popular will should have little or no influence in decisions on the transfer amount. Raising UBI too high before its time would cause a tragedy of the commons, with too many people enjoying their leisure and too few left to produce for society. Hence, there is a strong case for an institution that makes these decisions independent of public opinion and based on technical considerations.

An alternative view is that since UBI also has major political implications—for instance, affecting the balance between the power of employers versus employees and also the level of minimum living standards guaranteed to people—we should leave it to an institution accountable to the public. An intermediate solution might then be that the independent institution and the government both have to agree to any changes to UBI transfers.

Which independent institution would take on this role? The central bank is in a good position to, since 1) permanent money created by the central banks would fund UBI, 2) UBI affects inflation, the current mandate of central banks, 3) central banks already possess the technical skills to determine how a UBI transfer may affect the economy, and 4) UBI would run more smoothly if the central bank could directly open a free deposit account to all citizens of a country, something that many central banks are already considering in the context of creating a central bank's digital currency. The central bank would only be missing the information to ensure the identity and eligibility of recipients, as well as providing everyone digital access to their account in the central bank.

The UBI program ends up being compatible with the current governance and for this reason many have already asked why central banks do not already give permanent money to citizens instead of providing cheap credit to banks, governments, and corporations. The movement Quantitative Easing for People has been among the loudest advocates of this course of action for more than a decade.

PILLAR 1B. CONDITIONAL TRANSFERS

Prioritizing activities with permanent money is much more delicate than running a UBI program, because the choice of which topics to prioritize, and within them which projects to fund, is highly political and vulnerable to lobbying and corruption.

The temptation may be to leave these matters to democratic vote and ensure that any process related to the use of the funds is transparent and subject to public scrutiny. At the same time, direct democracy has some weaknesses.

Proposals to improve minority rights, for instance, have tended not to prevail in American elections. And voters have limited knowledge of public affairs so, for instance, most can't tell which industries would yield a competitive advantage in the global economy. We must make this task accountable to the public, but the people shouldn't direct it.

The same goes for the criteria for allocating conditional transfers. How do we distribute this funding? Is it an equity investment? A debt like buying green bonds and other types of bonds? Or a grant like the many research grants given to universities? And how can a project be evaluated against an alternative one?

How do we ensure against waste of these funds? Should a co-investment always be required? Should a public tender always be required?

The details of these issues, as well as the ongoing need to update the topics and allocate funds to different areas, require technical expertise and personnel dedicated to the task.

At the same time, since it is permanent money, whoever manages money and inflation should also take part.

Regarding conditional transfers, it is not obvious how the current governance could cope, nor what the best option could be.

At one extreme we would give all powers to a technical, independent institution that must listen to people's opinions but can then make its own informed decisions on issues such as which topics to prioritize, which projects to fund, and which bidder to select for each project. The survey mentioned earlier, for understanding determinants of people's well-being, would be one input into this complex decision-making process, but technical expertise should bridge the gap for the rest. And the necessary skills would go far beyond what we need to manage UBI. We basically need expertise from all areas of society. For this reason, an independent institution would require proficiencies and a mandate much broader than central banks have today.

At the other extreme, we could leave all power to governments. Governments already make these decisions whenever they provide subsidies or incentives. The European Commission has several programs that provide conditional transfers in diverse forms and to diverse industries, and is now about to distribute €750 billion of post-COVID-19 recovery funds to national governments conditional to achieving pre-agreed-upon milestones. They already have all the technical capabilities and the infrastructure. The limitation today is that governments need to collect taxes to fund these transfers. The downside is that several socially useful projects may go unfunded, but the upside is that it deters waste. At the voting booths, taxpayers normally will not forgive a big waste of their money. If governments were free to get permanent money for any purpose or project they deem a priority, the risk of waste increases as does the risk of a tragedy of the commons.

The Three Institutions for Conditional Transfers

What lies in between the two extremes? My view for governing conditional transfers is to have three institutions involved. 1) The central bank that has to agree on the overall amount of conditional transfer given, they have implications on inflation together with other choices such as the UBI transfers and the tax rates. 2) The government that would define the priorities topics, the share of funds of conditional transfers going to each topic, and set some goals to be measured against. 3) And a technical institution that is independent or semi-independent from the government would be responsible to allocate the funds to projects and bidders, in a way that maximizes the impact of these funds.

The European Union has a system not that dissimilar to what I described. It is not the central banks that define the size of the envelope but the joint work of the European parliament and the European council, both accountable to the public directly or indirectly. If funds were to come from the central bank, the ECB would also have to agree to this. The same institutions are responsible for determining the topics that can be funded with the EU budget. These topics have been revised several times and often require changes in the treaties, the equivalent of the constitution. And finally, it is the European Commission, a technical institution that is independent from national governments, that proposes the yearly budget and is then responsible to disburse the funds through different types of conditional transfers, oftentimes having to approve a project versus another or a bidder versus another, either directly or through partner national and regional fund managing authorities.

While this intermediate option is the most complex to design and implement, it probably strikes the right balance between the need for independence from short-term public pressures and the need for accountability to the public.

PILLAR 2A. SUBSTITUTION OF DEBT WITH PERMANENT MONEY

We can leave this task to whoever manages inflation and money, which in the current system is the central bank.

PILLAR 2B. AGILE INFLATION MANAGEMENT SYSTEM THROUGH TAXES

Like conditional transfers, this activity is highly political but also technical. As long as we use taxes solely to fund governments, they will have the conflicting goals of raising enough funds to provide the services and support societal needs but not so much that they take away money that people could use to get the services themselves, maybe from a private provider.

With a good portion of government funds coming from central banks, governments would likely set a level of taxation below what is required to maintain a stable inflation. Why raise more taxes if we do not need to? Yet taxation is highly political, as it takes from some people. The idea of giving taxes to an independent organization would be very difficult for the public to digest.

But we should differentiate the types of taxes in Pillar Two. As a reminder, the agile taxation system to manage inflation included 1) the reduction of most current taxes, 2) sales taxes on goods and services detrimental to a universal, sustainable well-being, 3) company counter-inflation taxes to motivate investments, and 4) emergency counter-inflation taxes on sales if inflation does occur.

Of these, we could leave anything political in the hands of governments and give central banks the only tool they need to keep inflation in check: the emergency counter-inflation taxes. This tax can be highly objective, and we already measure inflation at the product level. Hence, our decisions to change sales taxes on certain goods and services can be more objective than the current approach of changing interest rates.

In fact, since we can deploy emergency counter-inflation taxes in reaction to inflation rather than in anticipation of it, we can give the central banks this more useful tool, while keeping governments and companies in check.

The government would know that the greater the ineffectiveness in translating money into productive investments, the more the central banks will increase taxes on selected goods and services. Companies would know that if their industry is not investing, counter-inflation taxes on profits will hit them (the rates would be set by the government) and emergency counter-inflation taxes on sales might hit them too.

Another reason to have independent institutions like the central bank manage the emergency counter-inflation taxes is that it is an instrument for *emergency*. A decision to change the rate needs to happen right away, without being stuck between parties, coalitions, parliaments, and lawyers.

GOVERNANCE OPTIONS FOR MONETISM

If we now step back from each one of monetism's proposals and try to look at the system overall, we see four emerging governance options for monetism.

FATHER KNOWS BEST

The first is to give most of the new responsibilities to the government, leaving central banks with just its current tools plus the emergency counter-inflation tax.

Such governance is simple and similar to what we have today. Its biggest risk is obviously the reduced pressure to cut government waste, which might force central banks to make heavy use of the emergency counter-inflation tax.

Yet many nations could find this choice appealing. It would be the natural pick for any nondemocratic country, where even central banks and monetary authority are often not independent from the state. It could also be a good option for countries with highly competent and trustworthy governments. And it's the implicit choice if central banks start buying all government bonds and hold them permanently on the balance sheet, as Japan is doing and most other high-income nations have started after the combination of the 2008 financial crisis and the COVID-19 pandemic.

CALL SOCIAL SERVICES

The second option is to empty both the government and the central bank of most strategic decisions and activities and assign them to a new institution. The government would become a provider of public services and legislations while the central bank would simply ensure the stability of the banking system.

The new institution would have to be accountable to the public yet remain independent of public opinion. This approach could work well, but it is also the most vexing to achieve, especially given the tension between accountability and independence.

The institution would need employees who are more technical, objective, and meritocratically chosen than what happens in a democratic election. Its success would fully depend on its governance and organization design.

Choosing this institution would be a recognition that democracy in its current form is not good enough. Before reaching such a drastic conclusion, I would attempt to evolve out of capitalism while keeping solid democratic foundations, but again this is my personal opinion and others may well have good arguments for more technocracy.

LET THE CHILDREN PLAY

The third option is for true believers in free markets who want to minimize the role of institutions. Here, monetism would simply provide a generous UBI that greatly cuts back the credit creation from banks.

This version would recognize that leaving 95% of money creation to the free-market decisions of banks and borrowers is neither efficient nor egalitarian. Most people can't take out millions in loans to invest in assets, though institutional investors do it regularly.

Monetism would provide all the growth in the money supply that an economy needs through UBI transfer from the central bank to citizens who, with their spending and investing decisions, would achieve a better resource allocation than today.

I believe that, given human biases, this approach will not let us efficiently tackle issues such as climate change. Yet if it is the only one available for a society largely opposed to any institutional intervention, it is still better than what we have today.

MOM AND DAD CO-PARENTING

The fourth option—the one I would pick for most countries—is greater collaboration between the central bank and the government, splitting the activities of monetism between the two.

In general, the government would decide the allocation and priorities while the central bank would manage the total funds available, linking them to the effectiveness of their use. A second independent institution besides the central banks may need to be created to manage the conditional transfers, something of the likes of the European Commission in the European Union.

The government would thereby design the UBI program, but the central bank would have to approve any change to the amount of UBI transfers. The government would choose the topics and set goals for the conditional transfers, but the central bank would have to agree on the overall amount available and technical institutions would be defining and revising the mechanisms for allocating the funds and monitoring their impact.

The government would design and maintain the tax system, but the central bank would keep the government in check by imposing emergency counter-inflation taxes and influencing banks' credit creation. Ultimately, it will still be the central bank that decides how much permanent money it can issue in any given year: It would be the difference between the permanent money issued and the counter-inflation emergency taxes imposed, that will go back to the central bank.

With this system, the central bank has a say in all decisions related to the creation and allocation of permanent money and can still fulfill its role of managing inflation.

CHANGING THE NATURE OF CENTRAL BANKS

The success of this last governance option is based on effective collaboration between governments and central banks. For it to happen I suggest at least two changes to central banks: the name and the mandate.

FROM CENTRAL BANKS TO MONETARY AUTHORITIES

Society needs an institution to manage money. Calling this authority a *bank* can both generate distrust in citizens and give an aura of privilege to the banking sector. This institution's activities would also far exceed the deposit and lending activities of a traditional bank. It would play a far more important role in society than that of a *bank of banks*.

Furthermore, the word *bank* could develop different connotations in the foreseeable future. Central bank digital currencies and crowdlending could make banking a more marginal activity than it is today. It would almost be superfluous if there was so much equity in the system (thanks to injections of permanent money) that capital markets themselves (i.e., investment funds allocating equity to different companies) could take on the role of providing finance to companies, with similar expected returns as interests on loans. And if anyone has any doubts, most world-changing and life-improvement innovations come from start-ups funded through equity investors and research institutes funded by governments or philanthropists, not by bank loans.

The new name for a central bank could be monetary authority, reserve fund, or even money issuer—any term that makes it clear that money is something we create for the good of all. We no longer dig it up from the mines and we will no longer rely fully on banks.

THE MANDATE OF MONETARY AUTHORITIES

No central bank should have a mandate focused on managing inflation and ensuring financial stability, as the ECB and Bank of England currently do. The conflict of interest with serving society is too big given that a moderate change in inflation has much less impact on well-being than other changes.

A monetary authority focused on inflation can afford to reach its objective apart from the government and irrespective of the economic crises it may ignite. This is actually how central banks asserted their independence: by igniting the worst recession of the post-war period (until the 2008 crash).[6] The Fed under Paul Volcker beat inflation in the early 1980s but with a significant impact on the well-being of the unemployed.

The focus of central banks on price stability is itself a reasonably young historical experiment, given it was never the case before the 1980s.[7] And while central banks did their job well and kept inflation low, we should measure the success of this experiment based on other metrics, and both growth and well-being in the last 40 years have grown less than in the previous 40 or not at all.

Monetism provides central banks with new tools to overcome the trade-off between low unemployment and low inflation, hence we can aim at a mandate that makes the most of monetism, with much less risk of sacrificing our well-being to tame the inflation monster.

An unelected institution with the important responsibility of managing money must have a mandate aligned as much as possible with universal and sustainable well-being. While a monetary authority cannot generate it alone, the reality is that no one can. Within monetism, a monetary authority would have a stronger control of the overall money supply and a strong influence over the share of money supplied to the government, to people in a UBI program, or to banks. This is a big role and monetary authorities must be highly sensitive to well-being.

The mandate I propose for monetary authorities is a flexible one, responsive to a changing socio-economic context. It is, *to enable the government to pursue universal and sustainable well-being, as defined by the government, while ensuring inflation to stay within a predetermined range.*

Such a mandate would be broad and flexible. Today's rigidity around an inflation target of 2% is helpful to provide limitations, as well as comfort to the technicians of central banks. But rigidity creates problems and, in any case, central banks still have to make judgment calls.

The mandate I propose does not include the stability of the banking system. Central banks' role of lender of last resort might need revisiting to have a tighter control on banks' money creation, and saving banks might be in conflict with the proposed mandate. The slow pace of central banks in issuing digital currencies and in providing quantitative easing for the people while bailing out banks again and again are examples of this tension. These decisions are political, and one could argue they are not in the best interest of people's well-being.

In conversations I've had with senior central bankers, I learned they did consider and debated all options, including permanent money to people, but concluded that what they deployed after 2008 best aligned with their narrow mandate on inflation. What if their mandate was more open-ended and included people's well-being? Would they have chosen the same course? I doubt it.

With the mandate I propose, the monetary authority would make more judgment calls, but these would advance government strategies to pursue a universal, sustainable well-being. At the end of the day, if we want the politicians we elect to pursue a certain strategy, the monetary authority must enable it, while providing adequate checks and balances. Some small but positive movement in this direction is already happening, with the Bank of England and the ECB taking actions to ensure their monetary policies are aligned with the goal of curbing climate change.

Any government, at the start of its cycle, would agree with the monetary authority on a set of objectives, and the monetary authority would have the mandate of supporting them. The government would have to play its part, as it can use taxation to help the monetary authority manage inflation. Independence and separate mandates between central banks and governments have bred lack of coordination. They both have tools to help each other, but they don't use them because the goal lies outside their mandate. With a more appropriate mandate and the new tools at their disposal, central banks and governments could collaborate together more effectively and get better results.

In summary, it is very important to think carefully about who makes all the decisions required to implement and continuously manage monetism, a topic I referred to as *monetism's governance*. I proposed four governance options, each preserving some checks and balances that would avoid the mistakes of the past. I suggested that different political systems, cultures, and countries would choose different options, and I set my preference on the option seeing a monetary authority and a government collaborating while keeping each other in check.

In this book, I will assume that nations implement this governance option while noting that other options exist. Governance is important, but it is not the core of monetism, which is instead its framework to create and distribute the incentive of money to pursue sustainable well-being while fixing the human biases that lead to inflation.

Chapter 16

Monetism vs. Capitalism

Why propose a whole new system?

I'm often asked why I give a new name to the system, or framework,[1] I propose in this book. Given it is still founded on several of capitalism's principles, why not just propose a bunch of ideas to improve capitalism with a better monetary system?

My answer is twofold: A new name helps break free of the old habits of capitalism and the changes that monetism proposes break a lot of capitalism's foundational axioms. There are times for marginal improvements and times for quantum leaps, and this book has shown we need the latter. There are thousands of proposals to improve capitalism at the margin, but none would significantly improve everyday life and grasp most of the opportunities we have.

The laws of capitalism are too ingrained in most facets of society, in the invisible gears that most people do not see yet that affect everyone. It is like the force causing the Earth to rotate that no one perceives but we all depend on. I argue that putting money—instead of capital—at the center of our economic system is as consequential as Copernicus's theory that the Earth revolves around the sun. And if capitalism is as ingrained in our economic system as the idea that the sun revolves around a flat Earth was ingrained in our ancestors, we need all the help we can get to challenge the habits connected to capitalism. A new name can give an important extra push to think with a fresh and unbiased perspective.

But a new name is not just symbolic. Monetism breaks down and corrects at least five axioms of capitalism that no longer fit modern reality.

The first of these axioms: If a government needs to spend in a way that benefits society, it can convince citizens to pay the taxes for it and thus fix any market failure. We live in a global economy where money flows freely across borders and politicians are part of the wealthy elite most negatively affected by taxation. Society cannot rely on taxing the wealthy to fix market failures. Monetism corrects this problem.

The second axiom: People are rational and if free to operate they will pursue the most beneficial investments to maximize profit, which in turn maximizes value for consumers and therefore society at large. The implication is that, with full utilization of resources, government spending will crowd out this more desirable allocation of private sector resources and society will suffer. This axiom is at best arguable, since we are on the verge of a climate catastrophe, with poverty persisting, inequality continuing to rise, and many other social issues neglected. Markets for luxury products are booming, yet resources are lacking to temper climate change, provide high-quality education, and support the poor. Monetism provides them.

The third axiom: Capital is limited and money is just a by-product of capital. Monetism embodies the fact that it is money, often in the form of credit, that allows companies and governments to generate new capital—be that physical, human, or intangible (like a patent, a brand, etc).

The fourth axiom: People have unlimited needs that generate an unlimited demand for labor. The implication is that, as companies become more productive, workers and shareholders automatically benefit from higher wages and dividends that they will spend or reinvest, keeping the growth engine going. However, this isn't happening, and monetism addresses the two fundamental reasons: 1) the need for low- and middle-skill labor is not unlimited, given cheap foreign labor and technological advancements and as a result, shareholders capture an increasing share of value added; and 2) the wealthy don't have unlimited needs and only live 24 hours a day, consuming a much smaller share of their income. Therefore, as inequality grows, demand decreases. Increasing inequality thus leads to lower aggregate demand, and ultimately slower economic growth and need for labor.

The fifth axiom: Increasing the GDP translates into higher incomes across most of society and thus greater well-being. This premise is flawed in two ways in advanced economies: 1) the inflation-adjusted growth in national income only benefits a minority of citizens and 2) beyond a certain level, income becomes either uncorrelated or merely a minor determinant of well-being, depending on the definition of well-being.

In summary, if capitalism were a car, it would be heading in the wrong direction, toward higher average GDP instead of more inclusive and sustainable well-being, with an inefficient engine (market failures), a leak in the fuel pipes (income concentration becoming idle wealth), with the wrong fuel (capital rather than money) and a very stiff steering wheel and pedals (limited ability to raise taxes to fix market failures). The vehicle is still better than the wild horses of premodern societies or the LEGO car of communism, but the 21st century urgently demands an upgrade.

Many authors, researchers, and politicians have challenged one or more of these axioms and some have also proposed solutions.[2] Capitalism is being attacked from all different directions, but no one has yet tackled all these axioms at once and designed a coherent alternative. I think the new emerging framework I have proposed is sufficiently different from capitalism and sufficiently comprehensive to be granted the new name of monetism.

MONETISM IN ACTION

How would monetism change our way of life? Let's consider some important events that are likely in our near future and describe how monetism—in its full implementation—would manage them.

THE AUTOMATION OF ABOUT 50% OF PAID JOB ACTIVITIES

Automation is a normal process that has been an important source of prosperity, yet swift adoption of AI may pose significant challenges to the capitalist model.

In capitalism, rapid automation would see some people becoming permanently unemployed and others accepting lower salaries and working in poverty. Meanwhile, salaries would grow for high-level knowledge workers and owners of robots. Their higher incomes will not compensate for the lost consumption of a shrinking middle class, leading to fewer new jobs. Unable to tax the rich, governments would indebt themselves more and would be unable to provide sufficient stimulus to the economy or support to low-wage and unemployed people. A displacement of 50% of workers over a decade would be unthinkable and unsustainable in capitalism. A populist party would likely take power and either limit automation, heavily increase income taxes, or shift to a version of monetism. This scenario is arguably already at play in many OECD countries.

With monetism, however, a nation would continue incentivizing auto-mation while providing increasingly generous UBI transfers. Citizens would receive enough money to entice them to work less, helping the labor market to remain tight and wages to grow at the same pace as productivity. The future of work would be shorter working days, longer weekends, earlier retirements, more flexible and independent employment, and more volunteering and unpaid activities that people do as fulfilling hobbies. Between the UBI transfers and the higher wages from a tight labor market, aggregate demand would stay strong, driving the owners of robots to keep producing and automating more. Public debts would be unaffected as the UBI transfers would come from the monetary authority, which would be increasing the transfers to avoid the deflationary spiral already looming over most OECD countries.

FUNDING A PROGRAM WITH 50 YEARS OF LIFETIME VALUE BUT NO DIRECT FINANCIAL RETURNS

Imagine a large research program on a new technology to capture 90% of car-bon dioxide from the air, or to generate 100% of electricity through a new renewable process (nuclear fusion, for example). The challenge to fund these projects is that their direct financial return is uncertain; most would be failures and have no returns at all, and those succeeding would not provide meaningful social value until after several decades.

Capitalism offers few routes to fund such programs, and funding tends to be late and insufficient. With climate change, for instance, the private sector would only invest once social damage is already occurring and an investor can reasonably estimate the costs that governments would impose on companies emitting more carbon. Few governments would be able to fund these pro-grams, as their long-term value is not accounted as a new asset (government balance sheets do not have an asset side), while the cost would be fully incurred today, making the public-debt-over-GDP ratio appear higher. Governments can fund only a few of these long-term investments. Funding such a program through taxes would require convincing people to pay higher taxes, a strategy with limits especially for projects that only have uncertain benefits in the far future. This pattern of late investments occurs in all such long-term investments, with infrastructure, research, and early childhood education among the most underfunded areas.

With monetism, however, an issue like fighting climate change would be a national priority and the central bank would create money and assign it to development funds tasked to invest, lend, or grant the money to the most ambitious and/or technically attractive projects. The limits would be based on the availability of promising projects and competent people to complete them, which in turn can increase if we adequately invest in education and research. These programs would create new jobs and, in case of full employment and rising inflation, higher taxes would reduce money in circulation. The only side effect of achieving full employment with these long-term projects would be to limit the alternative short-term-focused ones, often for-profit activities (pursued by private companies) for which resources (including labor) would be scarcer.

GOVERNMENT DEBTS EXPLODING
ABOVE 200% OF GDP

Debts spike for most governments when they attempt to fix market failures such as poverty and climate change but can't raise taxes and can't run large trade surpluses.

In capitalism, such debt trajectories are a sign that governments cannot convince citizens to pay higher taxes, maybe due to a reputation for inefficient spending but also due to global tax competition. When the ratio of public debt-to-GDP rises above 100%, markets start losing confidence in the nation's ability to repay and hence demand higher returns. Governments in this situation enter a vicious cycle as the cost of interest grows more onerous. Some default on their payments. In other cases, the IMF comes in to provide loans and prevent the default while demanding significant reductions in government spending. The leadership in these governments often changes and the new government cuts the easy expenses, those the public won't feel immediately, such as in education, R&D, and infrastructure. In extreme conditions, governments also reduce spending that is easy to cut but painful for the population, such as social security. Growth would initially drop (with risks of social riots), but ultimately it would restart, albeit at low rates, given the cuts to education and other important long-term investments. This narrative has again been happening in many OECD countries with high public debts—except for Japan, which I claim is already taking a leaf from the monetism playbook.

In monetism, much more money will be permanent and debts will naturally be lower, both in the private and public sectors. Similar to Modern Monetary Theory, monetism recognizes that a government might have many reasons to run a deficit—such as a high propensity to save in the private sector, underutilization of resources, or unbearable market failures requiring an urgent fix—and fund it not only with debt but also by printing and injecting more permanent money. If excessive government spending causes excessive inflation, in monetism, a monetary authority would increase the rates of value added tax (VAT) I called emergency counter-inflation tax, and withdraw excess money circulating in the economy. Of course, a significant rise in VAT could still cause voters to replace a government, since they would feel the higher prices and turn against the government that inefficiently caused the inflation.

INFLATION INCREASING ABOVE TARGET

This occurrence has been rare in OECD countries since the 1980s because of the way capitalism manages inflation.

We discussed at length that, in capitalism, central banks would increase interest rates and try to induce banks to issue or renew fewer loans, often with the side effect of causing an economic crisis—potentially a financial crisis—and would hammer down both consumption and investments.

Monetism aims first at preventing inflation by creating a tax system where tax rates are lower for companies that invest a higher share of their profits. Monetary authorities would be more flexible in letting inflation fluctuate within a small range. Should inflation go beyond the range defined, the monetary authority would raise the VAT rates on the product categories showing inflation, with no impact on the rest of the economy, on interest rates, or on investments in general.

Only if commercial banks were creating more loans than desired would the monetary authority raise their reserve requirements. And at the first sight of an economic slowdown, the monetary authority could reduce VAT or increase UBI transfers.

The result is a system with a higher pace of investments and growth and an inflation-reduction approach that does not cause systemic crises.

MANAGING AN ECONOMIC RECESSION

This was also discussed in previous chapters, but in short, capitalism is stuck in a catch-22: Central banks can make debt cheaper so that more loans and money are created by banks and spent or invested by the borrowers, oftentimes leading to inflation in asset prices, be that houses or stocks. The inequality trap of capitalism does ultimately channel the new money into the bank accounts of the affluent while the debts are left to governments and the middle- and low-income households to repay with stagnating or declining real incomes, fueling the following recession.

In monetism, many crises would not occur in the first place, since the credit and debt in the system would be a fraction of today's levels. The catch-22 comes from the rigid tie between money, credit, and debts, and monetism breaks it. Average individual savings would also be much higher, cushioning people against economic uncertainty. And given that monetism runs a high-pressure economy that enables faster growth, governing institutions would likely have time to intervene before a slowdown becomes a recession. At the dawn of the slowdown, a monetary authority with a mandate and governance different from modern central banks would decide how to best create and inject new money, taking into consideration the cause of the recession and societal objectives.

FUNDING A LARGE CORPORATE INVESTMENT

Any company deciding whether to invest will look at the return it expects from the investment and compare that with the cost of the investment. If they have the money in their bank account already, they typically assign a *hurdle rate* that defines the costs of using that money. If they need to raise money, they will look at the cost that banks or private investors will charge.

One of the main activities of banking is deciding which companies are worth lending to and at what price, and such decisions are a core pillar of the capitalism resource allocation engine.

In capitalism, banks only create new money and give it to companies that they expect will create monetary value. Most banks assess the financials and strategies of companies to determine the price and amount of loans they are willing to provide. Private investors, often investing through institutional investment funds, behave similarly to banks, although some are more selective about the nature of the companies they invest in. The returns needed by investment funds is typically higher, given they have to collect equity—the financial savings of their investors—promising above-market returns, while banks can create deposits for free or at much lower costs if they need to borrow reserves.[3]

In monetism, the ratio of equity to debt in society would be much higher than today, but the costs of equity (from private investors) and debt (from banks) would be similar, with the cost of equity likely lower than today (because more equity is available) and the cost of debt higher (because banks would likely face higher reserve requirements and be able to create less credit). Companies would most likely face a similar cost of financing projects, potentially lower given the larger amount of equity and the likely lower amount of government debts, which typically absorbs much of the equity. Companies would therefore be more likely to approve investments earlier, especially given the higher market demand and the tax incentives that favor investments.

Investment funds would likely behave as they do in capitalism, but banks would have to increase their attention to the social impact of their investments. In fact, since all citizens could park their savings in a risk-free deposit account with the central bank, they would only deposit in commercial banks for investment purposes. Reporting requirements on how and where banks invest would lead them to align with depositors' preferences.

BUYING A HOUSE

The price of housing has undergone the highest inflation. One reason for this trend is the cheap and almost unlimited credit that banks provide to purchase housing, since they can repossess the house in the event of default. Most credit growth has indeed gone to real estate funding, creating a continuous growth in house prices.

In capitalism, as long as population grows and city life attracts more people, wealthy investors will keep buying domestic and commercial real estate spaces and renting them to families and small businesses that cannot afford a loan to purchase these assets. House prices will continue to rise, generating inflation directly and indirectly, since businesses pass the cost of rent to consumers. To buy a house, a middle-class worker needs a massive loan that takes decades to repay, with borrowers weighing whether 10 years added to a mortgage justifies a reduction in commute by 10 minutes. Since wages are growing more slowly than housing prices, the time to repay the mortgage would ultimately extend past the lifetime of a middle-class worker, with banks repossessing the house at the time of death, demanding repayments from the heirs, or not giving the loan in the first place.

Monetism recognizes that affordable housing is a major issue that requires government investments and taxation. Investments would increase the supply of houses by, for example, better connecting megacities to adjacent towns with investments in transportation, offering incentives to construction companies, or to remote workers moving into rural areas. Taxation could limit the benefits of buy-to-rent, eliminate the profits from reselling the same house (if not justified by improvements to the house), and make it more expensive to own multiple houses. As a result, the price of houses would gradually decrease, making them more affordable. Credit (mortgage rates) in monetism would be more expensive, but since people could save more thanks to more permanent money circulating in society and house prices would be lower, they would need a much smaller mortgage, compensating for a higher cost of the loan and ultimately reducing the time they need to repay it.

* * *

The following exhibit summarizes the difference between capitalism and monetism at managing these important events.

Event	Capitalism	Monetism
Automation of 50% of paid job activities	• Wages grow less than productivity • Unemployment, in-work poverty, and public debt growth • Lower aggregate demand reduces productivity growth	• UBI transfers increase, people work less, hourly wages grow with productivity • Central bank's balance sheet expands
Funding a program with 50 years lifetime but no direct financial returns	• Some programs funded late, some underfunded, some not pursued • Increasing public debts	• Programs addressing formal national priorities are eligible for central bank funding • Technical development funds assess programs
Government debts explode above 200% of GDP	• Potential default and likely replacement of government leaders • Austerity leads to easy-to-cut costs: long-term investments • Recession followed by low growth	• In case of rampant inflation, sales taxes raise automatically and government leaders are likely replaced • In case of low inflation, public debt is monetized by the central bank
Inflation increasing above target	• Regulatory rates increased, banks limit credit, companies invest less • Wages, prices, and the economy all grow slower • Difficult repayment of loans may cause a financial crash	• Inflation prevented through a corporate tax scheme that incentivizes overcapacity • In case of high inflation, sales taxes remove money without causing systemic crisis
Managing an economic slowdown or recession	• Regulatory rates lowered or quantitative easing in the extreme • Banks increase credit, restarting growth but fueling the next crisis • Fiscal stimulus based on ability to issue debt	• Recession would not happen due to lower dependence on credit and debts, and higher savings providing a buffer • In case of slowdown, a monetary authority would inject money, choosing the best channel given the situation
Funding a large corporate investment	• Funding approval and costs mostly based on risk-returns considerations • Cost of equity greater than cost of credit • Many investments not pursued due to high cost of funding	• Nature of investment acquires some importance beyond risk-return profile • Cost of equity = cost of debt and much lower than in capitalism • More investments pursued leading to higher growth
Buying a house	• Unlimited credit creation to buy houses fuels speculation and house inflation • Middle class takes longer to repay mortgage • Inflation of houses transmitted to the economy, slowing down real growth	• Higher cost of credit and taxes reduce opportunity to speculation • Higher savings and lower house prices compensate for higher difficulty in getting credit while decreasing the time to repay a mortgage

Exhibit 11: Societal impact of capitalism vs. monetism on selected events

COULD MONETISM HAVE PREVENTED THE 2008 CRASH?

It is difficult to pinpoint one root cause of the 2008 crisis across the Western world. Banks did lend too much money to home buyers who couldn't afford it, but many borrowers were unable to pay because of the inequality in society.

What role did limitations on the central banks play? They saw a bubble coming but could only act by increasing interest rates, which in turn raised the mortgage payments for borrowers who then defaulted and burst the bubble. How instrumental was the neoliberal exaltation of profit, and the greedy, blind search for it that led to borderline-fraudulent financial products that crumbled at the drop in house prices?

Throughout the world, and in the US particularly, house prices skyrocketed in the years preceding 2008. That fact signaled that the economy needed more houses—not surprising since there is still a growing population in the US. But the problem was that real estate companies were late to meet this rising demand and prices naturally increased.

Next, greed led the financial sector to give home loans to people unlikely to repay them, and sometimes they gave loans to buy multiple houses that kept increasing in value because supply could not keep up. The lenders were, of course, foolish in any long-term view since the situation resembled a Ponzi scheme. The more people wanted houses, the more prices would rise, and the lofty price of the collateral of the loan—the actual house—seemed to counterbalance the fear of non-repayment. As with all Ponzi schemes, the crisis began when more people wanted out—or defaulted and had to get out—than actual home buyers wanted in (cryptocurrency fans beware).

What is less known, though, is that the US government had seen the nation's problem with homeownership and moved to fix it by making it easier for low-income people to receive a mortgage.[4] This is the most capitalist way of fixing the issue: helping people to borrow. The theory was that banks would then lend as much as it makes rational sense to lend, new homeowners would work harder to repay their debts, and builders would be attracted by a booming sector and build more. (Student loans are another example of this pattern.) It is useful to highlight again that excessive credit to housing was one of the causes of house unaffordability in the first place, which again was a phenomenon that expanded with the deregulation of mortgage lending of the 1980s.[5] Similarly, costs of higher education are also moving upward: You throw money—even in the form of subsidized debt—to purchase a product that everyone wants, and its price is bound to increase.

In hindsight, it is easy to see some shortfalls of the government homeownership incentives (although the learnings haven't transferred to student loans and higher education). To start, we could have limited subsidized loans to people without a house and allowed the purchase of one house per family. In this way we would have prevented people from buying multiple houses and boosting demand beyond a level that builders could keep up with. Secondly, if we truly want to make homeownership more affordable, we have to make houses cheaper rather than letting people take out bigger loans. To make homes more affordable, we need more of them, and more innovation on housing, hence we should direct incentives to the actual production of houses and innovative construction processes.

With monetism, we could have avoided the crash, using both permanent money and counter-inflation taxes.

If house prices ever skyrocket out of control, with monetism we can impose an emergency counter-inflation tax to limit the purchase of them. For instance, we might tax the sale of existing houses, which would penalize flippers yet not slow the builders of new houses. Or we might temporarily tax only people purchasing a second house. In parallel, we could create temporary monetary incentives to builders—or cut taxes to them, thus spurring the construction of houses.

If cities are overcrowded and the demand continues rising for houses on limited land, we could use conditional transfers to incentivize the development of infrastructure to connect suburbs to the city or even different cities. We might then see the Hyperloop in operation. Cutting commute times would motivate people to demand houses outside the main cities and possibly to develop those areas. Incentivizing remote work that, thanks to COVID-19, has become the new normal for roughly half the population would also get people to buy outside cities, not only reducing prices but also reducing traffic and pollution.

These actions would need continual adjustment based on the extent of the homeownership problem. They would be phased out as home price inflation declines. This strategy makes no reference to debt. No credit bubble and no housing price bubble means no 2008 financial crash.

And even if there was a crash, with monetism, central banks could have permitted insolvent banks to go bankrupt as we mentioned earlier, re-created the deposits that the failing bank had, and restored confidence with a one-off transfer of permanent money to all people.

COULD MONETISM HAVE PREVENTED THE COVID-19 CRISIS?

I often mentioned epidemics among those events that can disrupt life and oftentimes cannot be stopped, together with natural catastrophes. Earthquakes, volcano eruptions, floods, and hurricanes are frequent events that we have learned to forecast, although unfortunately we only get few days to prepare, seconds in the case of earthquakes. While it's probably impossible to predict when a new strain of a deadly virus will emerge, it is possible to limit the probability of a pandemic like COVID-19. Maybe more importantly, if an epidemic occurs, monetism could help the affected population and economies better cope with it.

In monetism, stability is one of the four strategic directions to maximize people's well-being and likely justifies more funding to prevent deadly epidemics. I am unqualified to even guess how those funds would be best used, so I won't venture further on prevention. What I am qualified to explore is mitigation strategies for epidemics that governments can put in place.

In 2020, a new form of coronavirus later named COVID-19 had gradually spread to most countries in the world, infecting and killing millions and causing a sudden and large economic contraction. The magnitude and medium-term consequences of this pandemic are still unfolding as this book goes to press.

One obvious fact for most economists is that in all high-income countries, government funds were not a limitation. When it is a matter of life and death, be that a war, pandemic, or alien invasion, governments will always raise as much funds as are needed, simply because central banks can create money from thin air and inflation is less of a concern when you are facing possible death.

Within two months since the pandemic reached Europe and the US, governments announced stimulus packages for 10 trillion USD, three times as big as the stimulus after the 2008 crisis.[6] Central banks immediately enabled it. The Fed increased its balance sheet by 3 trillion USD between March and May 2020, three times as big as the injection immediately after September 2008. The ECB increased its balance sheet by 2 trillion euro between March and September 2020. But can governments quickly spend these funds? Do they have the right infrastructure in place? And where does the money that central banks are printing end up? People in central banks and government treasuries are scrambling because there is no framework or infrastructure to best allocate and spend the money. Here is where monetism would have helped the most.

If we look at the response of governments in high-income countries, we can distinguish four macro-policy directions. 1) The imposition of temporary regulations to limit the spread of the virus; 2) the strengthening of the health-care system to track the spread of the virus and tend to sick patients; 3) a set of policies to provide financial support to companies and people most disrupted by the pandemic; 4) a set of policies to restart economies. Monetism could have helped in all of these.

LIMITING THE SPREAD OF THE VIRUS

In January 2020, Chinese authorities completely locked down the city of Wuhan and other cities close to the epicenter of the first COVID-19 outbreaks. Most governments had to make the difficult decision of disrupting people's lives with some form of restriction, with the intent of limiting the outbreak. Preserving freedom, limiting economic repercussions, and preventing unnecessary deaths were the three elements to balance in such decisions.

With some diversity of approaches most governments chose some forms of lock-down. They prioritized saving lives; research on the Spanish influenza in 1917–18 suggested that economies that better manage the epidemic from a health care point of view would later see a faster economic recovery. The actions of the Chinese governments are a contemporary proof of this.

In summary, it was not too difficult a decision to choose the path of lock-down and other restrictions like wearing masks. Yet we witnessed different intensity of restrictions and some countries such as the US or Sweden barely imposed any, leading to hundreds of thousands of unnecessary deaths. The mortality rate in these countries was much higher than in countries imposing some form of lock-down.

While defending the right to individual freedom might have played a role in such decisions, and monetism would not interfere with that, limiting the economic consequences of lock-downs also weighed on these decisions, albeit ill-informed given historical evidence.

Had monetism been in place, these economic considerations would have had much less weight. In fact, monetism is flexible to a temporary fall in economic activities. If people are forced to stay at home, they are going to consume much less and so it is natural that much less production and employment are needed. In these situations, monetism would have temporarily increased the UBI transfers and kept them higher until people could get back to their normal lives.

This would not have solved the issue of companies risking bankruptcy, but governments have deployed other policies to avoid that and they could have done even more within monetism. In summary, with monetism, governments would have been less likely to prioritize economic resilience over people's lives in planning their restriction policies.

STRENGTHENING THE HEALTHCARE SYSTEM

As the outbreak spread, most governments realized their healthcare infrastructure had insufficient capacity to cope with the number of patients requiring intensive care. Especially in the most affected regions, new hospitals were built in record time and companies shifted their production to provide more medical equipment like ventilators and face masks. Healthcare workers had to work overtime and some programs even helped reskill people into healthcare professions not requiring a degree. In the span of a few months, healthcare systems were strengthened to cope with the crisis. What could monetism have done better?

Only a little here. Healthcare would have been a priority sector that could receive conditional transfers; therefore the healthcare system might have been stronger before the emergence of the pandemic. But with the exponential speed of contagion, there is no healthcare system that could have coped with such an increased demand.

Nonetheless, given monetism's focus on maintaining stability, a large fund would likely have been available to governments to get emergency funds in a matter of hours rather than weeks or months. The government would have just needed to declare a status of national emergency for selected government entities to tap into this fund and start disbursing it right away. While this may seem of little help, saving a couple of weeks to approve extraordinary healthcare expenses during a pandemic would still save lives.

SUPPORT TO FAMILIES AND
COMPANIES DURING A PANDEMIC

When the outbreaks expanded in March 2020, companies started laying people off or putting them on furlough. Unemployment in the US went from 4% to 15% in the span of a month,[7] while in the European Union with more barriers to laying people off, as well as more robust safety nets, unemployment has been steadily rising from 6.5% to 7.5% as of September 2020[8] and is projected to peak in 2021 at 11.2%.[9] Millions more had seen their working hours cut. And remember that many of these people have little or no savings, are paying rent or a mortgage, and have credit card debts. Millions fell below the poverty line. Imagine their anguish and insecurity, as well as their understandable anger.

The issue was too big not to tackle. Many governments increased unemployment cash transfers or extended their duration. The majority of US people received a cash transfer from the US government in April 2020 of up to $1,200.[10] In Italy, a good chunk of the population received €600 and several other governments sent money to their citizens.

Yet these are one-off transfers that had to be set up ad hoc. Many had to go through administrative processes to receive the transfers. In Italy, many people only received furlough transfers with delays of months.

If monetism had been in place, every citizen would already be receiving cash every week or month as UBI, and governments would have just had to approve an increase in these transfers or reroute furlough transfers through these accounts.

People would have had to find ways to spend their time at home instead of working, but without the stress of how to get to the end of the month. Many could have taken training, especially those unemployed, given that new jobs emerging after the COVID-19 crisis will likely require different skills, owing in part to the acceleration of digitization trends.[11] Other people may have had the mindset to activate for the community, volunteering at hospitals or engaging in whatever activities they felt worth their time.

Instead, we had a chunk of the population working remotely 12 hours a day to manage what COVID-19 was throwing at their companies, and another chunk stuck in involuntary unemployment wondering if their job will come back and calculating how long they could afford to pay for food and rent.

As for supporting companies, the situation is more complex. While survival of people is clearly a priority, survival of companies may or may not be beneficial. Of course, we cannot have all companies going bankrupt and within capitalism we can afford only a few companies going bankrupt in a given time period. The economic crisis that would otherwise follow—the usual vicious cycle of unemployment, less consumption, and less production—would be another tragedy.

But think about this: If people started working remotely and continued working remotely once the pandemic is in our rear-view mirror, do we still need so many airlines? If people increasingly buy online, do we still need so many physical stores? A shock such as COVID-19 is bound to change the way people live, their needs and preferences, and therefore which companies are more or less useful depending on what they do.

The philosophy of most governments has been to minimize the closure of those businesses that society would most likely need once the crisis is over. They focused especially on small enterprises, which are those that have fewer cash reserves to survive with lower revenues. And they allowed companies to suspend workers temporarily not needed with furlough schemes and work-share programs.

With monetism, governments would have behaved in the same way, but might have allowed more companies to go bankrupt. In fact, the least efficient companies often bankrupt first and their business is absorbed by more efficient competitors as part of creative destruction. Monetism would allow more of this given its lower dependency on full employment. While this always sounds traumatic within capitalism, think of it this way: Those people employed in inefficient businesses are just wasting their time. They can either work for more efficient companies and likely get paid better, or they can live off of UBI and other social security programs while they figure out a better way to spend their time.

POLICIES TO RESTART ECONOMIES

The last response of government was that of securing significant funds for the recovery. Fortunately, Keynesian theories to manage recession are once again mainstream and most governments seem poised to provide a significant stimulus to the economy. Yet there are still some concerns, which monetism would solve.

The first is that governments may do too little, which would lead to protracted low inflation and unemployment, an increase in suicide rates and crime, and the worsening of many other well-being metrics, as what happened post-2008. Doing too little would be linked to public debt considerations, which would be less important within monetism.

The second concern is that governments do not have the capability to inject a large fiscal stimulus in a rapid, optimal way. In most countries, there is no infrastructure to distribute cash transfers to citizens efficiently, and few government institutions have the business competence required to direct trillions of investments to the right places.

The speed and effectiveness of monetary policy is even less promising given it passes through commercial banks' lending policies.

There are some good signs that central banks are becoming more conscious of where their monetary stimulus ends up. The ECB, for example, is reconsidering the balance between market neutrality and the impact on climate change. Given much of their funds had gone to the carbon intensive sector, this is a positive development, though other central banks, including the US Fed, seem less attentive.

With monetism, the stimulus would restart the economy much faster because citizens would already have a bank account with the central banks and the infrastructure to provide conditional transfers would already be in place. Much of the stimulus would be one or more add-ons to the UBI transfers so that citizens could get money fast and spend it. Their expenditures would become companies' revenues, pulling the economy back based on whatever people demand.

And this is an important feature that allows for a true market-based recovery. If the stimulus is directed through banks, do banks have a crystal ball to know what citizens will demand post-COVID-19 and, therefore, which companies are worth more or less loans? They may have an idea, but remember that most credit goes to purchase assets and fueling bubbles. For example, in the US we can already see stock prices and house prices inflating due to easy, cheap credit while economic growth, employment, and inflation are still far from targets. Will the Fed raise interest rates and revert QE to limit these bubbles while stunting the economic recovery? Or will they let the instability build and fuel the next crisis?

Why not just give the stimulus to people and let them make their own spending choices? The consumption patterns will steer companies to meet the demand. This is more market-based than any allocations banks may do and it will happen faster. Let's not forget that it is demand that pulls economies today, and especially so after economic recessions.

My third and last concern for the post-COVID-19 recovery is that once we get back on our feet, sooner or later austerity policies may come back. The belief that public debts need to be repaid fully rather than continuously revolved is still predominant among many policymakers. And if central bankers will decide or be pressured into selling their holdings of public bonds, the interests that governments pay on those will increase and pressures to cut expenditures will further mount.

Austerity will lead to either higher taxes or less public investments and weaker safety nets, worsening of well-being metrics, and ultimately more economic stagnation. With monetism, most public debt would be either owned by the central bank or repaid with printed money by the central bank, and austerity discussions would become less convincing. The only legitimate reason for austerity would be high inflation. Austerity would lower inflation, allowing central banks to lower interest rates (or reserve requirements) and emergency counter-inflation taxes, and therefore have more resources distributed by the free market as opposed to governments. This argument is and will always be a valid one, although the burden should be on the austerity advocates to prove that government investments are less beneficial than bank-enabled ones.

BEYOND THE RIGHT AND LEFT DIVIDE

If there was one bias I could remove among all those afflicting our human brain, it would be the confirmation bias. We are quick to form opinions on the basis of limited information. Since our mind likes a certain consistency and coherence, it performs a magic trick—new evidence against these opinions hardly registers, barely reaching the part of the brain that learns. However, if the evidence supports our views, we heed this new evidence and our brain reinforces the belief before we even recognize the broader context of the new evidence.

Confirmation bias is most dangerous because it generates never-ending conflicts. People get locked in their own opinion cells and can't listen to, let alone tolerate, different points of view, never gaining enough curiosity to peek out from their own mental prison. So, we get never-ending wars and societies that fail to progress.

The situation grows even worse when two opposing sides engage in an endless ideological debate that leaves no room to consider alternatives that could please both sides. The debate and the fight against *the other side* becomes all that matters. It's us versus them. Opposing political parties almost never collaborate because it is more important to win than to improve society.

What if the fight between right and left is actually distracting everyone from more important issues and more effective ways to organize society? What if we are perpetually stuck in the face-off between left and right?

Philosopher Alasdair Macintyre argued that we live in an era in which we can't settle any debate when ideology is at play. If a claim of equality is at odds with a claim of liberty, it is difficult or impossible to have an objective or rational debate. Who can establish whether being equal is more or less important than being free? What does either of the terms actually mean? When we accept ideologies, we cannot evaluate ideas objectively and rationally because our brain assesses them based on their coherence with our preexisting beliefs.[12]

Here is an example of irrational ideology. Imagine that your partner has adopted a belief about closet doors. They insist that closet doors must never be left open when unused, yet say it's okay to leave the tube of toothpaste uncapped. There is no real rationale here, because capping the tube yields a pragmatic benefit—it keeps the toothpaste from drying out—while closing the closet door yields only an aesthetic benefit, if any. This is similar to an insistence on creating money through credit while ignoring the inflation-controlling power of permanent money.

As mentioned in Chapter 9, the clash between capitalist US and communist Russia created an ideological battlefield and after the former prevailed, ideologues came to quickly tag any policy that relies too much on government or on social justice as communist or socialist.

But a very broad spectrum of grays lies between black and white. A government that owns all private property and runs all major economic activities is not at all the same as a government that negotiates prices of healthcare services or funds strategic investments. Similarly, though a lawless financial sector was an important cause of the 2008 crisis, we should not embrace the ideology that anything related to banking, Wall Street, and capitalism is bad. Ideologies are simplifications of more complex situations. They make us lose nuance, precision in understanding diverse situations, and, often objectivity, breeding poor decisions as a result.

A key feature of monetism is that it is not a new ideology. While the title *Outgrowing Capitalism* seems to pick on capitalism, this is simply because capitalism is now the prevailing ideology that inhibits society from moving forward.

Monetism is a system to better leverage our financial tools so we can solve the real problems before us and achieve societal goals.

Think of monetism this way. You stand in line at your regular burger joint and prevaricate between the benefits of taste versus health. A rich and tasty double cheeseburger or a low-cal, low-fat salad. Fat tastes so good, but you just read that the WHO classified red meat as a cause of cancer. A low-fat salad is a healthy meal but doesn't quite satisfy your appetite. What do you sacrifice?

But what if you don't have to sacrifice? You have gotten so used to this burger joint and its menu that you don't even realize you have other choices, like that sushi place right across the street serving food that's both tasty and healthful.

I will conclude this chapter by showing that monetism lets you go to the sushi bar and please your palate in a nutritious way. Not because monetism is a new, better ideology that compels one kind of food over another. But because monetism is not an ideology.

Ideologies are blind alleys, ultimately. They are anti-pragmatic. They exaggerate one virtue out of a whole range of virtues, such as equality in communism. Most people in communist countries obtained equality, but they suffered dictatorships, gulags, poverty, and lack of freedom. Capitalism exalted freedom without recognizing preexisting inequalities that constrain freedom, as well as dignity, stability, and sustainability. Monetism is instead a practical recipe focused broadly on universal well-being and it offers policies that governing institutions can reasonably implement, to make better use of existing tools and improve society. It adapts to circumstances. It's the equivalent of suggesting you take your smartphone and look for a restaurant that best fits all your current desires, including taste, health, and whatever else you may feel on any given day.

Monetism is actually impartial regarding any of the left–right political debates. Whatever your views, monetism can bring significant benefits.

MONETISM WITHIN RIGHT-WING IDEOLOGIES

Monetism is still grounded on freedom and private ownership, the two cornerstones of capitalism. The only modification is that some governing institution has to do more to fix market failures, increasing its influence in the allocation of resources. In a very minimal implementation of monetism, with only UBI funded with permanent money from central banks, governing institutions would just shift some money creation from banks' lending to a direct citizen transfer.

This is a rather minor change to the foundations of capitalism. If voters from the right can't stand the idea of a system different from capitalism, we could call this *monetary capitalism* or *direct capitalism* or just *moneyconomics*, since all the virtues of capitalism remain.

But if you set aside any disappointment from changing a cherished name, you may appreciate the ways that monetism could support a right-wing political program. If we disregard right-wing politicians who are extremists or captured by business lobbies, a right-wing political program would tend to favor less government involvement in economic operations, lower taxes, less regulation to businesses, and more business opportunities. A version of monetism where most permanent money is distributed into a UBI program would achieve all the above goals.

Universal basic income would increase aggregate demand and create opportunities for businesses. With a generous UBI there would be less need to deploy often cumbersome government means-tested forms of social assistance or to restrict companies from releasing workers or to pursue automation. People would be in a position to truly bargain, given they have UBI to fall back on, but they may also accept lower wages for a job they like for the same reason.

If we consider conditional transfers as well, many public incentives and funds could be made available to business in the form of conditional transfers, an additional source of revenues.[13]

The tax system would require fewer overall funds and therefore fewer taxes. Inequality would be less of a problem with a generous UBI and there would be less pressure on taxing accumulated wealth.

And the counter-inflation taxes would only affect the monopolies and those few companies that are enjoying consistently above-market returns, often a signal of poor competition. And, of course, for companies that strangle employees and harm society, monetism will empower employees to quit and probably result in increased taxes for these companies. The taxation system I propose would likely target those getting most of their income from rent and speculation; monetism rewards people and companies that contribute to society, not those who take advantage of it.

For this reason, I would expect a version of monetism implemented by right-wing politicians to pursue fewer taxes on businesses than I suggested, but nonetheless it would be an improvement compared to starving the poor or the economy to minimize taxes on businesses and the wealthy.

MONETISM WITHIN LEFT-WING IDEOLOGIES

Given its similarities to the founding principles of capitalism, monetism might feel at odds for those who are closer to the communist ideology, and one might even say I am just dressing up capitalism in different clothes.

Those who argue that it is immoral to base our socio-economic system on competition are stuck with an unfortunate choice of words. *Competition* combines the benefits of having different organizations fulfilling different needs with different solutions—which we could call diversity of approaches—with the benefits of having these organizations striving to be as efficient and effective as possible—which we could call pursuit of excellence. Having private players compete, potentially with a public option to limit the monopolistic tendency of today's markets, has proven its worth and it's rather pointless to further question it.

Once those on the left leave behind any communist ideology, they could appreciate the many opportunities that monetism brings to their political programs. Left-wing political programs typically include stronger safety nets, the limitation of monopolies, action to reduce damage to the environment, and more funding to priority services such as health and education. Given many of these programs require funds and most left-wing politicians are averse to the idea of public debts left to future generations, left-wing programs typically include higher taxes, which diminish their appeal to voters who understandably don't like having money taken away from them.

Monetism can provide the funds to pursue the widely popular initiatives in left-wing programs, while avoiding having to raise as much in taxes. Furthermore, monetism is built on the idea of pursuing sustainable well-being, a goal much closer to left-wing ideologies than right-wing ones.

Universal basic income is in fact a program to get everyone above a comfort threshold, from Stage 1 to Stage 2. Left-wing politicians could argue that a job guarantee would be better suited to this, like MMT proponents suggest, but in the wider scheme of things, UBI versus guaranteed jobs becomes a bit of a same-but-different debate.

Conditional transfers are a tool to fund societal priorities, getting the public, private, and not-for-profit sectors to compete for access to these funds.

The counter-inflation tax system helps the fight against monopolies without putting off voters, including wealthy voters, who would not need to fear confiscatory taxes on their wealth.

On the other hand, monetism is much more attentive to allowing freedom of businesses to operate than the more extreme left-wing parties, including in their relationship with employees. Monetism would see less need to limit a business's ability to hire, lay off, pay, or automate, as long as a strong safety net gives employees the ability to refuse to work for conditions that don't allow life with dignity, and as long as business practices are not discriminatory among gender, race, religion, and so on.

If we want society to progress at full speed, we need to let companies be efficient and either lay off or reskill people they no longer need. Monetism directs some resources in certain areas of the economy and provides more purchasing power to increase demand of companies' products, but it's ultimately companies' innovativeness and productivity that will keep fueling progress.

Chapter 17

Not a Utopia

Underlying benefits and risks of monetism

I f you are an economist, you may still be skeptical about monetism and claim that I have been selling benefits impossible to deliver. I have claimed that with monetism we can avoid recessions and grow faster, even if monetism does not need economic growth. I have claimed that we can work less, cut taxes for everyone, even give money away.

In the following chart I have listed the most important benefits of monetism over capitalism, along its four strategic directions to pursue sustainable well-being.

A fair question is, Am I trying to sell candies to kids (citizens) while their parents (economists) are looking away? The answer is no. There is no sorcery behind monetism. We don't just print more money and make everyone magically happy. The benefits of monetism come from a faster growth of productivity and a redistribution of resources from activities that damage society to those that make it thrive.

Sustainable Progress	• Deters unsustainable activities and ensures funding to solve major societal issues • Incentivizes higher private sector investments and faster adoption of innovation's products • Makes society progress independent from economic growth and sustainable with robots working instead of people • Enables the government to fix market failures
Universal dignity	• Shifts all people above the comfort threshold through UBI and priority funds for education, health, and housing • Makes an increase in savings rates compatible with economic growth • Empowers people to reject low-paid undignified jobs and pursue occupations aligned with personal talents and motivation
Stability	• Avoids economic recessions by decoupling aggregate demand from wages • Decrease our dependency on debt and banks' unstable credit allocation processes • Ensures availability of funds for disaster prevention, relief, and reconstruction • Ensures more control on inflation without causing economic crises
Time to pursue happiness and life fulfillment	• Enables and fosters technological innovations reducing the need for employment • Removes the obligation of paid work to gain access to basic needs • Focuses government attention on most important drivers of well-being

Exhibit 12: Benefits of monetism vs. capitalism

THE ORIGIN OF MONETISM'S BENEFITS

The higher growth potential that monetism promises comes from Janet Yellen's concept of a high-pressure economy. Larry Summers and Antonio Fatás, among others, have long argued that weak demand leads to less investments and innovation, which in the long term harm the growth potential. Ensuring a higher demand with permanent money is enough to hasten progress. Running a high-pressure economy within the limitation of capitalism would lead to excess debt and potentially inflation, but monetism solves this problem.

Counter-inflation taxes would offer a further increase in the production potential. They would motivate companies to invest more than the current taxation system because they'd receive an equivalent of a tax break if they closed the year with moderate ROE levels. Higher and earlier investments can increase the rate of both progress and growth. Managing inflation through taxes also avoids recessions, which have been proven to not only affect the short-term but also the long-term growth potential.

More permanent money and greater collaboration between governments and central banks could stimulate investment in another way—by reducing the cost of equity. Governments that work well with central banks and don't waste resources thus causing inflation never need to default. The return on their bonds would be close to or even below the inflation rate, as it already is today for most high-income countries. That's not an appealing rate for investors. With fewer opportunities to earn money from government bonds and more abundant permanent money seeking places for investment, we'll see the funding of many projects that today go ignored, even if they only return 2% or 3%. Where else could investors put money? The average returns on capital will drop, but that is not bad news for society. It is bad news for people expecting 5% returns or more just by hiring a very good fund manager. Monetism would be more meritocratic and less prone to rents on existing wealth.

Aside from the potential for faster progress, the redistribution of resources that monetism implies would limit society's waste. Instead, we can dedicate resources to better uses or just free up time for people. The pointless use of resources is all around us.

We produce unhealthy food for people and then treat their health consequences. Poverty-related crime leads to wasted resources of police, lawyers, jail guards, and healthcare for victims. We have to clean up our environment, but the activity is a waste: We are the ones who damaged it in the first place, and continue to with full awareness.

Employees' lack of engagement leads to lower productivity and their anxiety and burnouts waste their time, the time of their employers, and the time of therapists. Wars waste unthinkable resources and human lives, even if they increase GDP (as do all the aforementioned activities).

Government welfare programs and complicated tax systems also waste people time in administering all this, which monetism can partially avoid.

And as consumers gain more purchasing power, they will shift their preferences toward higher quality goods, avoiding the waste from goods that cost less but don't last or cause later harm.

More generally, imagine we achieve a society in which everyone lives above the comfort threshold, pursuing well-being with enough free time to actually think about how they can fulfill their lives. Imagine a society where people don't face the stress and insecurity of survival. This society will have fewer wars, crime, legal disputes, violence—and you can add to the list. I'm not speculating. Wilkinson and Pickett have already shown statistical evidence that reducing a country's inequality is enough to cut crime and many other benign upshots.[1]

REVERSING PIKETTY'S INEQUALITY DOOM LOOP

Is monetism sufficiently different from capitalism to reverse Piketty's equation on inequality?

Piketty showed how in capitalism the returns on accumulated wealth (r) tend to always be higher than the growth rate of an economy (g). Depending on how much higher r is than g, inequality could either indefinitely increase or increase until it reaches levels even higher than today's inequality.

While monetism is more concerned with getting everyone above the comfort threshold than in reducing inequality, the topic of inequality is a very sensitive one and it would be important for monetism to also overcome this limitation of capitalism.

Here is one of my few divergences from Piketty: I believe that growth could be much higher and returns on capital much lower, even without resorting to taxation of wealth. In fact, I blame neoliberal capitalism for this concentration machine more than Piketty seems to.

Neoliberal capitalism has harmed growth, if we look at the longer trends and not just 1980–90. Piketty showed that US productivity was growing at 2.3% a year in the Keynesian era 1950–70 but only 1.4% in the neoliberal period of 1990–2012. These were two comparable periods in which the US was at the frontier of the technology and did not have to catch up with other countries.[2]

We've shown that inequality contributed to the 2008 crisis and to the secular stagnation that has been limiting the growth of the production potential at least since then, and possibly even earlier. Risk-aversion and present biases lead companies to invest and innovate less, but company counter-inflation taxes can fix these biases and reestablish a higher level of investment.

Furthermore, AI is coming to help on productivity. The McKinsey Global Institute forecasts that toward the end of the 2020s, companies will start reaping the benefits from investments in AI and productivity growth could again exceed 2% and reach even 3% per year, assuming sustained overall demand.[3] In summary, productivity growth could rise higher than the 1%–1.5% forecasted by Piketty.

As for the return on accumulated wealth, an important reason for high returns is the availability of risk-free returns. With government debts exploding after the implementation of the neoliberal recipe,[4] buying risk-free government bonds ended up yielding returns of 3%–6% above the rate of inflation. People and companies wouldn't bother with investments offering any less.

Any large company works with a *hurdle rate*: the minimum rate of return that would make the company pursue an investment. This rate is based on the returns that government bonds give for free (and 10-year US government bonds are typically the benchmark here), plus an additional component to compensate for higher risks in investing in a project versus buying government bonds.

As a result, companies pursue fewer investments than they would have with lower risk-free returns, making the average returns higher since only high-return projects get funding. The risk-free rate leads to higher returns but is a killer for investments and growth.

But with monetism, risk-free returns would be lower. If governments and central banks collaborate and avoid high inflation, there is no risk for governments defaulting on debts issued in their own currency and therefore interest rates on government bonds should tend toward the expected rate of inflation, or 0% in real terms.[5]

With diminished returns on accumulated wealth and a higher pace of growth thanks to higher investment and a high-pressure economy, we can reverse Piketty's equation. Growth can exceed the return on capital (g>r) and the increasing concentration of wealth would not plague monetism. Investors can still make a lot of money. But to do so, they must create new ways to benefit society rather than just extracting rents. If we consider that a UBI transfer from the central bank (similar to today's government transfers through deficit spending) is also a form of income that people can spend or save and can become private wealth, the right formula for Piketty would be ((g + pm) > r) where *pm* would be the value of permanent money injected every year as percentage of GDP. This equation is much more likely to occur and inequality would therefore not continuously increase in monetism.

And the equation could even hold if economies stopped growing (negative g). Imagine if, thanks to creative destruction, we are able to make some needs disappear and others fulfilled with new models at a fraction of the cost and resources needed. Many businesses may close down, returns on investments may even go negative, and deflation may trigger more injection of permanent money and keep $((g + pm) > r)$. I am far in the future now, but it's important to note that monetism does not lead to continuous wealth accumulation as capitalism does. Neither high-wealth taxations nor wars nor revolutions are needed to compress inequality in monetism.

NO NEED FOR AN INTERNATIONAL AGREEMENT

Piketty's proposal of a progressive tax on global wealth to fix inequality was considered utopian by the author himself. Even a local progressive tax on wealth would be hard to implement with free financial flows among countries, and would require significant global cooperation that is decades away.

Does monetism pose a similar problem? Do we need global coordination or closed borders for monetism to be viable?

Given that we live in a globalized economy—and I am a firm believer in the economic and social benefits of a connected world—we must ask this: Can monetism be implemented by a single country while keeping a free flow of goods and money between borders?

The answer is yes, although some may argue differently. One counterargument could be that companies and people could avoid and/or evade monetism's taxes. But this argument is moot, because this is already an issue within capitalism, and it's a much more detrimental issue given governments are much more dependent on tax revenues in capitalism. At least 366 of the companies in the Fortune 500 have at least one subsidiary in a tax haven, according to a 2017 report by the Institute on Taxation and Economic Policy.[6] One American and Danish study estimated that in 2015, €600 billion—45% of global corporate profit—went to tax havens, corresponding to €200 billion of tax avoidance. The US and the EU governments each lose about €60 billion this way every year.[7]

This is a serious problem for both advanced and developing nations, but while solving it is important, it does not make monetism less attractive than capitalism. It is an additional argument for monetism.

The only relevant counterargument for the viability of monetism in a global economy would relate to risks of a mass exodus of companies from a country that first implements monetism. Think of Venezuela, where Nicolás Maduro's dictatorship has changed the system for the worse and led to most companies leaving. Would a county implementing monetism risk a similar fate?

Assuming no incompetent or corrupt dictator takes the helm of any high-income country, companies would leave a country for two main reasons. The first is that it would become more profitable to serve the countries' citizens from abroad. The second is that the value of the currency of the country would be unpredictable and/or continuously depreciate.

CORPORATE PROFIT IN MONETISM

Most companies operate in countries where they sell rather than only ship or deliver to, for many reasons: physical proximity in case problems arise, customs taxes, credibility with suppliers and customers, impossibility of delivering some services remotely (e.g., health care), and many more. The point is leaving a market is not something most companies can afford to take lightly.

Would monetism's counter-inflation taxes be so disruptive as to convince companies to leave en masse? The answer is no, and the opposite might be true for most companies. In fact, monetism overall requires lower taxes to fund governments, so the average business is much more likely to pay lower taxes than in many other countries.

Value added taxes (as a basis of the emergency counter-inflation taxes) would have to be equally paid by both companies operating within the country and those shipping goods or delivering services remotely.

Progressive taxes on ROE could be a real concern for companies in two ways: if they are unpredictable or too high. Regarding predictability, governments should guarantee the stability of those taxes, but that is basically what they do today. If taxes keep changing, companies can't devise reasonable business plans, and in monetism, as well as in capitalism, it is important to keep taxation stable and communicate changes ahead of time.

As for higher taxes, would progressive ROE taxes actually be higher than the taxes companies pay today? It is hard to discuss the exact tax rates outside the context of a broader government budget, but I envision a tax rate of approximately 0% for low ROE values and perhaps up to 50% for high ROEs. Let's say the tax rate is equivalent to the ROE, so a 1% ROE yields a 1% tax on profit and a 50% ROE yields a 50% tax on profit and is the maximum rate. These tax rates are either lower than today's corporate tax rates of other countries or, for high ROE levels, they would be higher but they still leave profits in the pockets of companies. Of course, companies with high ROEs could always go to tax havens, but that is already happening and governments have started to notice and fight back.

The remaining issue regards whether a company would even exist if monetism erased its opportunity to make very high profit margins. This is the case for some high-risk companies. Indeed, high ROEs are typically associated with 1) successful innovative start-ups, 2) small businesses, 3) high-risk businesses, and 4) oligopolies and monopolies. Of these, monetism would want to penalize oligopolies and monopolies, while not damaging the other three. To achieve this goal, we can create a separate tax system for companies that are young, small, or high risk. This adjustment is minor, considering how monetism simplifies today's tax system that abounds with exceptions and deductions.

CURRENCY VALUE IN MONETISM

To adequately explore this topic we would need to get a better understanding of international trade, currencies, and exchange rates, which would quickly get too technical for this book. In fact, an appropriate question is whether the currency value actually matters in high-income countries or whether it's just background noise. If it does matter, a second question would be whether monetism would lead to any meaningful change in the currency value. I will limit myself to only a quick answer here.[8]

In high-income countries the currency value doesn't matter much; it serves primarily as a mechanism to avoid trade imbalances (exports much higher than imports or vice versa) from remaining protracted,[9] which would mean that a country's population continues producing for consumption in other countries. In developing countries, one needs to pay more attention to currency values; whether they're ready for monetism requires more debate than I can address in this book.

Even assuming that the currency value did matter, monetism would not necessarily lead to a devaluation in any different way than the growth of bank credit or quantitative easing would.

Having addressed the sustainability of monetism in a globalized world, I do not want to give the impression that fully open borders are another taboo that can't be challenged. Barriers to trade (tariffs and nontariff barriers) may be necessary to ensure the implementation of forward-looking polices (think of carbon taxes, stricter sustainability regulations, etc). Without barriers, companies in countries adopting such policies would be penalized with competition from companies in countries that have much lower standards. Open borders have many benefits, but there is a spectrum of openness and the optimal solution depends on multiple considerations.

OTHER RISKS AND MITIGATION STRATEGIES

Shifting to a new socio-economic system comes with challenges and risks and it's important to know them up front and devise adequate mitigation strategies. Much of the risk lies in the magnitude of change, which we can mitigate by introducing monetism in a smooth and incremental way, and I'll describe such a gradual approach in the last part of this book.

Yet there are other risks that ordinary people and economists would raise. Some are easy to manage but others need attention. Here I'll cover seven risks, two related to the governance, three to technical aspects, and the last two to people's nature.

FIRST GOVERNANCE RISK: MONETISM GIVES MORE POWER TO CORRUPT AND INEFFICIENT GOVERNING INSTITUTIONS

We touched on this topic earlier, yet this will be a major criticism from those defending deregulation and unrestrained free markets. I have three answers to it.

First, any of the governance options proposed maintain checks and balances on governments. Second, people underestimate the success that the independent central banks have achieved, free from political pressure. Third, if one is vehemently against any form of government involvement, a simpler version of monetism would be to just introduce UBI and limit credit creation. This solution would be as independent from governing institutions as the system today, except for the decision of defining an amount of UBI and equivalent reduction of credit creation.

As we have discussed, capitalism's strategy of relying on commercial banks and the free demands for loans is multidimensionally flawed. If there is one thing we can comfortably state, it's that central banks have shown that they can go against governments' short-term interests thanks to their independence. This was true when Paul Volcker killed both inflation and economic growth in the early 1980s, when Ben Bernanke raised interest rates and burst the massive housing bubble in 2008, and in the late 2010s when Mario Draghi fended off German pressure to raise interest rates before core inflation and wages showed a robust recovery.

Any of the governance options proposed for monetism would keep the system of checks and balances. And if governments still somehow manage to waste money—which they already do today—people will see the central banks raising emergency counter-inflation taxes. These taxes will make people pay more for products and if the majority of people are affected by these taxes, they will oppose the government inefficiency.

Again, no governance option is perfect on its own. People are imperfect and governance alone can't fix everything. Yet the checks and balances are still there with monetism.

SECOND GOVERNANCE RISK: SOCIETY WILL LOSE CONTROL OVER PRINTING PERMANENT MONEY

This is the most common challenge to anyone who has proposed printing money and giving it to people in a permanent form. Most people suggesting permanent money, monetary finance, or helicopter money recommended it as a last resort one-off tool. However, the economy needs a continuous infusion of some form of money to enable growth and we have two alternatives: credit (and debt) and permanent money.

Mainstream economics supports the injection of debt over permanent money with the rationale, as we've seen, that debt is an anticipation of future value creation, forcing borrowers to actually create that value to repay the debt. Distributing permanent money without any obligations, money could just be spent and not lead to value creation. If we stop here, debt looks much better than permanent money, and that is why mainstream economics supports it.

But let us dig deeper. As we have discussed, the value the borrower creates to repay the loan comes from someone else in society who has received a loan.

Any profit making, or value creation, depends on other players in the economy taking debt and paying for goods and services at prices higher than costs. This creates a loop in our economy: Demand, supply, value creation, profit, everything depends on the continuous growth of credits and debts that for-profit banks create and allocate.

At the same time, there is no theoretical or practical evidence that permanent money—allocated by a combination of a government and an independent central bank in advanced economies—would spin out of control. However, credit creation and allocation from banks is systematically out of control.

Let's start with the theory. The superiority of credit over permanent money is only for those loans that stimulates private investments. With this kind of loan, accountability is important to ensure that borrowers don't waste limited resources by investing money in projects that society does not want. The superiority of debt is unfounded for stimulating consumption (of any player) or for government investments. These two do not create monetary returns but directly satisfy needs.

Using loans to stimulate demand of investments with negative net present value[10] (NPV negative) only creates a domino effect. The repayment of such loans, which I'll call A, cannot come from returns on A loans because that money is spent, not invested for profits. The repayment depends on 1) new "B" loans linked to investments by someone else in the economy that create a value larger than the value of A loans, and 2) the redistribution of the value added from investments through B loans to the people having to repay A loans. This loop may or may not happen. Perhaps companies never take out B loans and if they do, the value added may not be redistributed to reach the borrowers of A loans, and society remains prone to defaults and crises.

Here's a concrete example: Suppose John buys a house, a car, and a fridge and pays for them through debt (A loans). The standard assumption is that there will be a company creating enough value in the next two to four decades to pay John a salary with which he can repay the loans. If we break down this assumption, we find multiple premises that collectively are often wrong, generating defaults and crises. In fact, in order for John to have a job with a salary to repay his A loans, there must be a company that obtains more debt (B loans), finds ways to generate extra value from that debt, and uses part of the value added to pay John a salary. If John's employer had enough funds that it didn't need the B loans, the value added would still depend on some other society players who took on a B loan and bought the goods of John's company.

But what happens when banks just stop providing loans, A or B? What if John's company goes bankrupt? What if new technology makes his skills irrelevant? What if his company starts creating value abroad and employs Lucy Wong instead of John?

The same complications affect governments, which in fact continually increase their public debts under the implicit assumption they will be able to tax part of the value indirectly created through their investments and expenditures, and thus repay the loans. Yet they have no chance to fully repay them, as they cannot raise taxes on the people who are accumulating the value added from investing through B loans (this goes back to our discussion on the difficulties on taxing the wealthy). This domino effect is at the base both of the need for permanent growth in capitalism and of the cycles in the economy when banks get it wrong.

On the other hand, we can print money and give it directly to people to cover basic needs, and to the government or private companies to invest in societal issues that often do not lead to profit. There is no need for repayment and no domino effect but only the overall risk of inflation, which monetism tackles with reserve requirements to reduce credit creation and with counter-inflation taxes.

The other theoretical failure of mainstream economics is that the theory only holds when looking at one single loan over its life cycle.[11] This may seem fine on paper, but it doesn't represent reality. In the real world, millions of loans are constantly being created, used, and repaid; billions of people are making purchases; and millions of companies are making decisions on salaries, hiring, and firing. All of it happens every year, every month, and every day. It is the combination of all these acts that generates a certain availability of money and a certain balance in the supply and demand of goods. If this combination leads to an excess, a shortage, or a poor allocation of money, month after month, society is left with higher inflation or lower economic growth. The commitment of a borrower to repay a loan in the long term is no guarantee of an optimal balance of supply and demand, which is dynamic and varies day by day.

If all companies and people had a crystal ball when taking out loans and knew exactly when they could repay and how the economy would act for the duration of the loan, then the free-market debt allocation could be efficient. We clearly don't have this kind of foresight. For instance, your ability to repay a loan also depends on future decisions of other players to take or not take loans. No one can anticipate this factor.

By letting governments and monetary authorities quickly inject permanent money and remove it through counter-inflation taxes, we can give them greater agility in controlling the unforeseeable monthly and yearly balance between supply and demand.

So, from a theoretical standpoint, the combination of injecting permanent money and changing counter-inflation taxes is superior to injecting debt because 1) it makes the economy more stable, as it is independent of the ability of people and governments to repay loans used to fuel demand or NPV negative investments, and 2) it provides better control of the dynamic balance of supply and demand.

Let us shift now to practical evidence. Which one has gone out of control in history: the loan creation process of commercial banks, or the creation of permanent money by governments and central banks? As we discussed, it's the former. Control over credit creation is partly in the hands of central banks, but *mostly* with commercial banks, which have lost that control many times, yielding both excesses and shortages.

History shows how debt allocation from commercial banks is doomed to give us periodic busts that reset the system. Both Adair Turner and Mervyn King have explained that, in the current regulatory environment, banks will always create too much credit and take excessive risks in good times, and too little in bad times. These are the cause of business cycles. Unfortunately, no one listened to them even after they raised the alarm.

It's like when your computer crashes and not knowing why, you just switch it off and on. That tactic often works pretty well, but the problem never goes away and at some point, you just have to buy a new computer.

Control over printing permanent money has been lost only in specific situations: 1) in some advanced economies in the beginning of the last century, such as Germany, before central banks were independent and in combination with a shock in the ability of the country to produce, or 2) in developing countries such as Zimbabwe and Venezuela, where high-quality, independent central banks are not in place and governments are deeply corrupt and dysfunctional. In all these situations, governments printed money without any limitation or criteria and put it to unproductive uses, such as financing the military.

No country has really tried injecting a controlled amount of permanent money through modern governments and central banks, except to some extent Japan in the last two decades, which successfully injected a massive amount of money, directed it to good uses, and kept inflation around 0%.

There is hence no theoretical or practical evidence that a modern economy would lose control over printing permanent money, while there is plenty of theoretical and practical evidence that the banking system periodically does.

FIRST TECHNICAL RISK: EMERGENCY COUNTER-INFLATION TAXES VIA A VAT WILL DIRECTLY INCREASE PRICES, SO THEY'LL INCREASE INFLATION

If the central bank increased the sales tax on sports cars by 10%, one would intuitively expect that the suppliers would just add the 10% to the price, thus creating inflation.

On the other hand, economic theory holds that suppliers price cars to maximize profit, normally as much as most customers are willing to pay for them, and so a higher price would make them lose customers. Suppliers would likely have to price below 110% of the prior amount, though the overall price may still be higher.

Research is not conclusive on which of the two alternatives is more accurate, since at any point it is hard to determine how much inflation is increasing due to a change in VAT or for other reasons. An IMF paper seems to suggest that the impact on prices of an increase in VAT would be less than the increase in the VAT rate itself.[12]

The key thing to notice, though, is that an increase in VAT does not generate a continuous cycle of increasing prices, profits, wages, and prices again, which is exactly what central banks want to avoid. In fact, a VAT is different from other price increases because it does not generate new income.[13] It actually extracts money from society, and hence its overall impact is deflationary.

From personal experience, I have seen how some private companies set prices: Their ability to understand the price customers are willing to pay is quite good. Large companies often make investments in understanding the price elasticity (that is, how much customer buying changes if the price goes up or down) of different segments of the population, which means that most companies will increase their prices if there is room to do so.

The consequence is that prices closely track what customers are willing to pay. A higher VAT will erode a good portion of that profit that companies are opportunistically making through pricing. And if companies fully pass the VAT through to consumers, they signal that they had more room to increase prices, and would likely have done so in years to come.

In sum, while it is possible that the VAT could actually cause a short-term rise in after-tax prices, in the long term it limits a potential outburst of inflation in a specific product category. And as a reminder, targeting VAT at a specific product category avoids cutting credit across the board, which would limit demand and investments across all economic activities.

SECOND TECHNICAL RISK: GIVING AWAY PERMANENT MONEY WOULD TECHNICALLY BANKRUPT THE CENTRAL BANK

Central banks treat money much as they did in the time of the gold standard. Back then, money was just a piece of paper providing liquidity, which required backup with gold or some other asset, the real wealth. Balance sheets of central banks still talk that way. In fact, all central banks hold tons of gold as physical assets to ultimately back the money they issue, even though these amounts are far from enough to support all their money in circulation.[14]

When central banks print money, they create an asset and a liability on their balance sheet. What is the meaning of the liability, though? Is it that if someone claims something in return for his money, the central bank must provide it? What is the purpose of it, since no one uses gold for transactions anymore and everyone uses money? What is the central bank going to provide? People these days want money; they don't want gold. This convention of booking a liability when central banks print money makes it unthinkable to give away permanent money. It would send the equity of the central bank in the negative.

But that's just an ancient accounting convention we can change. A recent paper argues that central banks should account their money creation as profit, thus creating new equity and no liability.[15] This approach would be consistent with international accounting standards.

If we start recognizing a profit every time central banks create money and a loss when they destroy it, we can distribute permanent money without booking a loss on the central bank balance sheet.

Even if we don't change the accounting convention, work-arounds are still available. Central banks could in fact buy a permanent bond issued by the government, which would become an asset in central banks' balance sheets and prevent a reduction in equity. For UBI, central banks could provide free instruments to people, like a UBI voucher, which the banks could then buy back at a price equivalent to the UBI transfer, and then keep the UBI voucher on their balance sheet.

If this sounds outrageous to you, I'm not surprised. But it is not much different from buying gold and keeping it permanently locked in vaults. The difference is that society could actually use the gold instead of keeping it locked in vaults. A piece of paper like a UBI voucher is useless to society and would just maintain the current accounting convention.

The alternative I propose is obviously simpler: to recognize that central banks do create a profit when they print money and that this profit increases their equity. The distribution of the profit would then finance the distribution of permanent money in whatever way the government and the monetary authority agree to disburse it.

In summary, there is a technical, ancient accounting convention that seems incompatible with permanent money. Yet work-arounds are available, and updating the old accounting system would be even better.

THIRD TECHNICAL RISK: WHEN THE WORLD NO LONGER NEEDS GROWTH, AN INJECTION OF PERMANENT MONEY IS BOUND TO CAUSE INFLATION

This critique is partially correct, even though one could argue that as long as the population does not shrink, we will always come up with better products and services that command higher prices. So even if we consume the same amount of stuff, quality and price could rise and so would GDP and the need for more money.

But even without GDP growth, every year the value of our assets will likely increase, thanks to, for instance, renovations and new buildings on vacant lots and any new assets that are produced but not consumed. We'll need more money to exchange more valuable wealth. Yet we might indeed reach a point where there is no need to have more money in circulation.

But if this happens, monetism has an automatic mechanism to siphon away excess money from society: counter-inflation taxes. And implicit in this approach is a gradual redistribution of wealth. In fact, if all people get new permanent money to buy products and services that have been produced primarily by robots, we have to subtract money from somewhere in the system. Counter-inflation taxes will automatically take money by taxing companies that have large ROEs and people with greater purchasing power through VATs on the products they buy. This will be the case unless all the new permanent money ends up in more savings, or if higher taxes are collected from unhealthy and dangerous activities, taking away all the permanent money injected in the year.

FIRST HUMAN-RELATED RISK: MONETISM OPENS THE DOOR TO OPPORTUNISM AND FREE RIDING

If I get a basic income without working, why should I work? And if I know that there is free money out there, wouldn't I try to get my hands on it? After all, it's free money, so I'm not harming anyone. These are thoughts that could flow into people's minds once we put monetism in place. I think this problem is less of a reality than some might imagine.

First of all, we already face this problem with current forms of welfare, which only help people who are unemployed or poor. Individuals receiving government subsidies can get used to them and avoid getting a job from fear of losing these benefits. The smarter ones, or rather the most unfair to their fellow citizens, might work in the black market and receive both government benefits and additional income on which they pay no taxes.

And those safety nets that force people to accept a job offer or lose benefits do not really avoid these issues. Most of those folks perform so poorly that they are back on unemployment benefits soon enough. These issues would not exist in a UBI framework as people receive benefits regardless of employment status.

Furthermore, we can limit the UBI transfers in a way that people would actually not want to be jobless, or at least not before we can afford robots to send people into early retirement. Martin Ford writes, "Our fear that we will end up with too many people riding the economic wagon, and too few pulling it, ought to be reassessed as machines prove increasingly capable of doing the pulling."[16]

As for those who take advantage of conditional transfers to the government, the problem would be much smaller than the tax evasion we see today in most countries. In 2007, the global shadow economy was at 31% according to the World Bank. In OECD countries, it was 13.5%.[17] These numbers are incredibly high. They place a heavy burden on the shoulders of taxpayers, who pay higher taxes to compensate for those who don't. How could monetism, which requires fewer taxes to function, be worse than what we have? For that to happen, people in the government would have to steal so much money that they couldn't possibly hide it from investigations. People can evade taxes much more easily than government employees can steal money and the volumes in question are not even comparable.

Nonetheless, the risk of people wasting money through conditional transfer is real and I want to highlight it. Yet we can limit it by tightening the monitoring and penalties for these frauds—frauds that already happen today but indeed could be larger the more money is given through conditional transfers.

SECOND HUMAN-RELATED RISK: AS PEOPLE GAIN GREATER INDEPENDENCE AND FREE TIME, IT WILL BECOME IMPOSSIBLE TO CONTROL THEIR BEHAVIOR

In a system where few people can accumulate savings and most must work 40 hours a week for 40 years just to meet basic needs, it is very easy to control the population, since 1) everyone is busy and has little free time to challenge the system, 2) monetary fines can steer behavior, and 3) if you don't have a job, you have to do whatever someone asks you to in order to meet your needs. This is the reality of capitalism with a debt-based monetary system.

If we shift to monetism, people will gradually have more free time and possibly enough savings to pay fines and say no to bad jobs. If you are a government or someone with a lot of wealth, you might prefer the current system, since it makes managing the masses easier and wealth has more power. If you are part of the masses, you obviously do not, and you'd like the freedom of monetism. This may be risky, though, as the line between anarchy and freedom is often blurred.

Rutger Bregman thinks that the problem of filling leisure time will not lead to more crime or drug abuse. History is on his side, since it is poverty that increases those risks.[18] But let's assume that Bregman is wrong and people have a tendency to do stupid and harmful things when they have leisure time. We can mitigate this risk too.

Take Switzerland. Most of its citizens are relatively wealthy, not because they have a system much different from others, but because they did not go through two world wars. Partly because of their neutrality, they attracted massive amounts of money from around the world and they had good institutions that made the most of those advantages.

In Switzerland, people don't yet have much free time, but if they did, the government could easily cope with this. Some cantons in Switzerland make fines proportional to wealth (speeding tickets have exceeded $200,000 in some cases[19]) so that monetary penalty is still a good enforcement mechanism.

Jobs that citizens refuse end up going to migrants, as they do in most places in the world, and as they will for many decades ahead. By the time the world runs out of migrants needing to work, we will likely have automated most jobs and we won't need to force people to work anymore.

But more importantly, we can use UBI as an incentive to avoid crimes. If the UBI legislation has provisions for removing or suspending people who commit serious crimes, or redirecting payment in other situations—for instance, giving the UBI of drug addicts to rehabilitation communities—then UBI can become an additional tool to motivate people to act in a responsible way. Of course, money will be less of a source of power to the wealthy, but that is an unethical drawback of our current system. Weakening the equation of *money = power* is an advantage of monetism, not a risk.

To summarize, the perceived need for control over people may be one of the reasons we are still stuck with capitalism and a debt-based monetary system. In monetism, with everyone above the comfort threshold, losing control over people becomes less of a problem. And we can mitigate it further with monetary fines proportional to wealth or suspension of UBI transfers.

* * *

In this chapter we showed that monetism is not an ideology, conflicting with the existing ones, and not an unachievable utopia. It is also not magic or vague promises, since we traced its benefits back to the source: a faster pace of innovation, higher productivity, and a better distribution of real resources. The huge benefits far outweigh the few risks, especially since capitalism is currently on a path toward implosion under the weight of inequality, unsustainable debts, AI, globalization, and climate change, to mention just a few.

When thinking of risks, one should always consider them relative to maintaining the status quo or even changing too little. Think of the racial or gender disparities in the US, as well as in many other countries. If you look at the documentaries of racial injustice in the US in the 1970s, it's scary how little has changed since then. And at the pace at which we are moving on gender equality, we'll only close it in 100 years.[20] Can we afford this slow pace of action on reforming capitalism?

Even blindly believing the ideology that monetism would risk higher inflation and higher government involvement, is that scenario worse than passively walking into an environmental catastrophe and having populists take over governments to redistribute wealth? A landslide is coming at us and the shift to monetism will no longer be a choice. There is no reason to keep traditional capitalism: not for well-being, not for growth, not for progress, not for the environment. The old excuse that there is no better alternative no longer applies.

Yet the changes from monetism will pervade every aspect of society. The magnitude of the change is itself a risk and we'd be reckless to downplay it and proceed full speed toward implementation. Fortunately, all the reforms that monetism proposes can be introduced gradually. We can begin to introduce UBI with low amounts and the same is true for conditional transfers and for the substitution of current taxes with the system of counter-inflation taxes. Small changes will obviously have a slower impact, but slower impact toward a sustainable socio-economic model is better than failing at the transition, or maintaining the status quo.

In the final part of this book, we'll discuss how we can smoothly transition to monetism, as well as what roadblocks are in the way. Who will oppose monetism? Who should help governing institutions implement it? And why has no one proposed a holistic alternative to capitalism since Karl Marx? Why have economists been playing at the margins, debating minor tweaks to a system as suboptimal as capitalism?

V.
ROADMAP

We are operating on the core of society here. Shifting from capitalism to monetism is not a simple beauty treatment—it's more like specialized neurosurgery. Even though there's not much to radically change, the brain is a vastly complex system. Inadequate planning or an overeager hand on the scalpel can still risk significant and possibly enduring pain. On the other hand, doing too little risks not removing the tumor. Society is used to changing too little: How long have we been fighting against gender or racial discrimination? Yet so much change is still ahead of us. How can we get the right balance between changing too quickly and too slowly? How can we shift to monetism painlessly? Do we need surgery at all or could we embark on a longer rehabilitation program that yields the same result with neither pain nor risk?

Chapter 18

Blind in the Ivory Tower

Obstacles in the road: Interest groups that may oppose monetism

We are not done yet! Monetism needs an implementation road-map. We want to start with the less controversial and more urgent aspects of monetism so we can grasp the benefits early while avoiding unnecessary disruptions. The world is full of bright ideas, but they cannot get anywhere if they are impractical or too risky. In Italy we have a saying that goes *tra il dire e il fare c'é di mezzo il mare*, which translates to something like *between saying and doing lies the ocean*.

But a roadmap for shifting to monetism cannot consist of just a sequence of steps. Large systemic transformations require first a deep understanding of the stakeholders of this transformation. Who will be opposed to monetism and how can we overcome their objections? Given the complexity of society, are econo-mists up to the task of guiding society through this change? And what type of economists and economic institutions do we need?

Before outlining the steps required to implement monetism in the next chapter, we will first need to understand who will likely oppose monetism and who can advise governing institutions in implementing this shift.

Let's start with the opponents of monetism: Who would want to maintain the status quo? Who benefits from a debt-laden, highly unequal system that requires permanent growth?

Money is like a magnet that can move almost anything in our society. Imagine you had a world made out of metal. Those who were first to build the biggest magnet (accumulated most money) and those who can produce and destroy magnets (grant or revoke loans) have an immense power to move things around. But it is also unthinkable that we never addressed creating and allocating magnets but instead left it all to the free market.

It is therefore wealthy individuals and the banking industry who benefit most from the status quo, but it is the economic discipline—the institutions and individual economists that can influence policymakers and economics students—that should place more attention to the design of our monetary system and continuously challenge its adequacy.

MERCHANTS OF DEBT

Banks enjoy enormous power through their role in distributing loans in society. The more debt they pump into the system, the more money they make, and when they take excessive risks, inject too much debt, and crash the economy, governments have to bail them out. So great is their role in the current credit-based system that they normally only ever see the upside of risk.

What situation could be better for banks than this economic system that can't function without ever-increasing debts and a government forced to bail them out when too many people can't repay them? The banks resemble a king who can eat and digest food faster than his chefs can cook it, yet instead of him gaining weight and developing chronic diseases, his chefs do. Such a scenario is only imaginable in fiction—and the banking system.

After central banks initiated policies of quantitative easing, commercial banks have been getting an unprecedented amount of free money. Many central banks have been creating and lending money to banks at negative interest rates (i.e., paying them to take central banks' money) to stimulate higher lending.[1] And we discussed how the Fed had to offer positive interest payments to banks (again, give them money) to incentivize parking the excess reserves that the Fed had itself created during quantitative easing operations.

This is not to say that banks are behind the design of this monetary system, but it is undeniable that they benefit from society's dependence on them.

These hidden benefits would look outrageous to the average person living below the comfort threshold. Why would society give billions in free money to banks and their wealthy shareholders and employees, when it could distribute that same amount of money to people instead? If all people had the same understanding of the banking system that central bankers and some economists have, they would be up in arms. Maintaining the unfair status quo is a serious hazard to social stability.

But banks also face challenges from the instability of society. Banks lost an incredible amount of money in the 2008 crisis, and while they managed to preserve a large portion of past earnings, they also don't benefit from lots of people defaulting on loan repayments. Standard commercial banks benefit from a system dependent on debt but not from one that is so unequal as to lead many borrowers to renege on repayments.

There is a subgroup of banks that indeed gain from both the debt and the inequality and instability of our economy: investment banks and their traders. If you add up all investment funds and hedge funds and you give them the name *Wall Street*, you have the lobby that draws the most benefit. The higher the debt in the system, the more those who can access cheap debt can manipulate prices of assets, possibly in collaboration with rating agencies, as we saw in the 2008 financial crisis.[2] But even within the law, the higher the volatility (linked to instability), the more the experienced traders in these companies (or algorithms for automatic trading) can extract money from society. If the price of a stock or a bond fluctuates X%, traders can make a multiple of X%. If it fluctuates 5X%, traders can make much more money. Those losing out are the less experienced investors, typically middle-class folks who can't afford to pay experienced fund managers and traders. They'll invest directly or seek support from inexperienced employees in their bank and lose money when the capital markets crash and earn little when they boom.

Within our societies, banks and especially investment banks are interested in keeping a debt-based and highly volatile form of capitalism.

The conspiracy theorists think these interests are influencing government decisions. I sincerely hope not, but the large amount of public debt that institutional investors (many of whom are investment banks) have in their hands opens the door to this possibility and it is one more reason to implement monetism. By injecting permanent money into society and reducing the public debt, the banking interests will have less influence over elected politicians.

History gives us many examples of governments protecting banking interests. The Chicago Plan to exit the Great Depression would have stripped the banking industry of its influence by forcing commercial banks to hold in reserves as much money as they lend, limiting to a fraction their ability to create new deposits.[3] Had we adopted it, we could have avoided the 2008 financial crisis. But the only part of that plan ever implemented was the separation between commercial and investment banks, which many countries later removed, then restored, and now again have placed under scrutiny. The banking lobby has been able to keep this lone policy change on the table, while the most important parts of the Chicago Plan rarely appear on the political agenda, even after a second recession within a century caused by the same issues of financial exuberance and inequality.

It is difficult to believe that the banking lobby is not interfering in policymaking, especially concerning the monetary and banking system. With monetism, bank profits would decrease with the reduction of overall debt and we would let poorly managed banks fail like any other company in the marketplace. Whether banks are interfering or not, the risk is too high not to preemptively mitigate this, and the only way to break free of the banking lobby is to have a system that is less dependent on banking credit.

Cryptocurrencies shed light on the issue, but they aren't workable. The nationalization of some banks would be a solution, but it has often backfired in the past, even though in China the government now owns the largest banks in the world. China has effectively eliminated the emergence of a banking lobby at odds with the public interest by limiting many banking activities from being performed by private interests. China has recently made news by forcing an Alibaba-affiliated company to stop their deposit and lending business.[4] To an inexperienced eye, this is just bureaucratic communism, but to someone who understands that allowing deposit creation is equal to allowing money creation, a move to limit private money creation requires deeper considerations. It is yet too early for history to tell which approach to banking is less harmful to societies, given the Chinese financial industry is almost fully publicly owned.

My hope for high-income Western societies, where nationalizing all banks would be impractical and unthinkable, is that the power of banks will naturally decrease when central banks introduce their own digital currencies. As mentioned in Chapter 8, central banks' digital currencies (CBDCs) would enable people to directly hold central banks' money without having a bank account. As more people take money out of banks and put it into digital wallets that give them a bank account in the central bank, commercial and investment banks would become expendable. People would only keep money in a commercial bank for investment purposes. The existence of money outside of banks in a permanent form (other than physical cash that today is an impractical minority of the money supply) will lead banks to have less influence over central banks and governments.

China is about to launch its central banks' digital currencies and Sweden seems to be following very soon. This change is not part of monetism, but it is an important enabler to monetism and an act that would limit the power of banks to obstruct the shift to a system less dependent on debt.

It is important for the public to understand the benefits of a shift to CBDCs, a change that would make everyone's deposits more secure while forcing a revolution in the banking industry.

THE ONE PERCENT

The second group of people benefiting from the status quo is the wealthy. They have power akin to male rhinos at watering holes during the dry season— they control a scarce resource that most others seek. They get rent from housing or government bonds without risk. And without lifting a finger, they can achieve even higher returns by simply investing in riskier ventures. They just have to pay a good fund manager to diversify their investments and their risky ventures can become safer than most of those you or I have access to.

The fact that governments are forced to issue interest-bearing bonds that wealthy individuals can buy as a risk-free investment deserves particular attention. Stephanie Kelton has quite eloquently highlighted how among US policymakers everyone agreed on the need to have less public debt but no one wanted to give up on the opportunity to invest in government bonds.[5] The two are exactly the same thing: You can't have one and not the other.

The wealthy can afford to have many poor people work for them at relatively low cost. Is a very unequal system much different from slavery? A key feature of slavery is the lack of freedom over one's time, which comes with many human rights violations we have fortunately overcome in most of the world. But how free are poor people, really? Is there much free choice between the insecurity of joblessness and the need to take whatever job can put a roof over my head and food on my table?

In Italy, there is a phrase, *slave of the system*. You hear it often because many people find themselves in this unfortunate situation where their *free choice* has a limited set of options, none of which is desirable. And this condition gets worse as jobs become scarcer while piles of wealth grow higher.

Again, it's worth considering that none of the founding fathers of capitalism or even neoliberalism ever supported a purely individualistic society. Adam Smith wrote extensively on morals and Milton Friedman and Friedrich Hayek both supported a basic income guarantee. The wealthy, who could influence politicians, seem to have supported the half of the neoliberal recipe that seemed pleasing to them, lobbied for it, and neglected the rest.

The wealthy also gain the advantages of global investment. In the past, they had to physically control a country in order to invest there, which led to wars and colonialism. Now they can extract high returns from foreign nations without war.[6] Once a low-income country agrees to free movement of money, the wealthy can invest there and gain higher returns. If the wind changes, they can move their funds somewhere else. If the wealthy truly incurred a higher risk on these investments, one could be sympathetic and deem investing in low-income countries a good thing for global development. But this is often not the case. Their *hot money*[7] yields questionable benefits to low-income countries, providing high returns that flow out of those countries, sometimes so rapidly the economies are plunged into default or recession and are forced to rely on an IMF bailout.[8]

But the wealthy also face a less happy long-term prospect. While they may be privileged today, they could be in trouble tomorrow when fewer people can afford the offerings of their companies that may go bankrupt. They will also not be pleased when the widening chasm of inequality leads to more crime and unrest, since they'd have to invest time, energy, and emotion in protecting their safety and wealth. They probably would be unhappy if it led to more retrograde populism. And they would not like it if people in low-income countries blamed foreign influence for impoverishing their nations and started committing terrorist acts.

In the long term, a more equal distribution of wealth and a guaranteed minimum standard of living can benefit both the wealthy and less wealthy. It is therefore important that rich individuals like Bill Gates, Mark Zuckerberg, Warren Buffett, and many others have recognized the problem and will bequeath most of their wealth to charity. But they would not need to do so with monetism. Accumulating wealth is fine as long as it does not prevent others from doing so. Today, excess savings from the wealthy lower overall spending, but with monetism this would just trigger stronger injections of permanent money.

Everyone can benefit at the same time within monetism. Banks will have lower volumes of debt to manage, but they will also deal with fewer nonperforming loans.[9] Wealthy people can accumulate money as the supply of money can grow and there is no need to impose confiscatory taxes to sustain aggregate consumption.

And such high taxes on the wealthy are increasingly discussed among politicians and pointed to as a possible solution by economists and economic institutions. In the aftermath of the COVID-19 crisis, if governments choose to follow the ill-advised route of austerity, it is unlikely they can implement it by forcing more hardship on people. The recent history of this hardship on the European PIIGS[10] is still vivid in people's minds and they would be up in arms if austerity hit them again. Without injecting permanent money as monetism would suggest, the only solution would be high progressive taxes on wealth and income. Capitalism as we've known it is just outdated, and clinging to it in this way will ultimately hurt the wealthy, giving Marx his small revenge.

IS IT ALL A CONSPIRACY?

With all the benefits that monetism could bring and all the problems highlighted in a debt-based inequality-ridden capitalism, why is society taking so long to change direction? Is there some conspiracy that wants to preserve the status quo? With so many conspiracy theories on the rise, could there be some truth behind some of them?

Because I happen to have believers of some conspiracy theories among my relatives and friends, my stance toward them is one of sympathetic pity rather than anger. The system is broken and people have the right to be angry in their own way. However, believers of conspiracy theories lack an understanding of the most basic features of complex systems, such as a multinational company, a government, or the banking system.

Before civilization understood the forces affecting nature, we created and believed in many gods—of the sun, of death, of the oceans, and so on. It is only natural that people with no understanding and no real influence on changing the system would think and believe in conspiracies.

But considering myself someone who understands in some depth the world of business, banking, and government (and believe me, I have no self-ish interest other than finding time to enjoy life), I can confidently say that a conspiracy of some small group of people deciding the fate of all human beings is just impossible.

People have challenges coordinating and agreeing on small decisions like joint expenses in co-owned buildings. Large companies struggle with internal silos where the left hand doesn't know what the right hand is doing. A global conspiracy where some people from multiple countries agree and coordinate the millions of decisions that millions of society players continuously take, which end up affecting the outcomes for everyone, is just unrealistic.

Lobbies may indeed bear some responsibility for the unfortunate design of our current system, and many will likely oppose aspects of monetism. Indeed, there are many economists and historians suggesting that lobbies were behind the rise of the neoliberal drift of capitalism[11] and are still engaged in *marketing* (economics) ideas to policymakers and to the public.[12] But lobbies don't mean there is a conspiracy. Lobbies protect their interests and try to exercise influence. They have affected some political decisions and supported one view of economics over its alternatives, but these are complex topics that the lobbies themselves don't fully understand. And there are thousands of lobbies, too.

The time for big conspiracies and revolutions has passed for high-income countries and only by reforming the system from within, is it possible to move forward rather than falling dangerously backward as the four years of the Trump administration exemplify.

To understand the failures in adapting our system to the changing circumstances, we need to start looking into those that, within the system, society trusted with the responsibility to design, challenge, and improve our socio-economic system.

An important cause of our inability to see outside the cage of capitalism lies, in my view, with the economics discipline itself.

TRADITIONAL ECONOMISTS

When you have millions of people learning economics from thousands of professors and society ends up with such a suboptimal socio-economic system, the discipline should peer into its core and figure out what went wrong.

If you build a structure on three pillars and one weakens, you reinforce and perhaps replace it. Traditional economists are those who promoted and then defended the foundations of neoliberal capitalism, but none of its pillars stands today.

Not the first pillar—people don't always behave rationally and they lack the information and skill to accurately forecast the probability of future events.

Not the second—the free pursuit of self-interest does not naturally lead to perfect competition among companies, in which the most capable win by providing the best goods and services at the lowest price.

And not even the third, the core of economics itself—a higher value of goods and services, measured by GDP, is not necessarily conducive to societal progress and greater well-being.

If GDP was the problem, we'd choose a different metric, or just focus on median GDP per capita, and the whole structure could still stand strong. But what about the other pillars? We know that perfect competition has limited resemblance to the way businesses operate and people are riddled with biases and just can't foresee the future. The structure is doomed to fall and patch jobs are insufficient. You change architects and build a better foundation for a new structure.

I do not expect traditional economists to be as forthcoming and open-minded as to engage in such a deep rethink of their discipline and their view of society. Traditional economists will be one of the groups most opposed to monetism, since it brings many economics taboos to light and even embraces them. Understand that I am generalizing. This book would have been impossible without the work of great economists and many—including Nobel laureates—have been highly critical of established economic thinking. More and more economists are critical of the status quo, yet the field's inertia stands firm.

Overcoming the opposition to monetism from traditional economists will probably be the biggest challenge for monetism to become reality. In fact, while policymakers don't rely much on economists when implementing policies—economists are often too theoretical to get in the weeds of the real world—they do rely on (mostly) traditional academic economists for the theoretical foundation of anything that could affect the socio-economic fabric of society. If traditional economists oppose monetism from a theoretical perspective, it will be difficult for policymakers to embrace monetism.

And traditional economists have a strong interest in challenging monetism.

TRADITIONAL ECONOMICS AND
CELESTIAL SPHERES

In the 16th century, astronomer Copernicus developed a treatise, "On the Revolution of Celestial Spheres," suggesting that the Earth rotates around the sun and not the other way around. The challenge to the previously held belief led to supporters of such a theory, such as Giordano Bruno, to be burned at the stake as a heretic.[13]

In the modern world, traditional economists have built a complex set of theories that are consistent with each other, most of which are centered on the idea that economies are in some form of equilibrium. Some shocks may move this equilibrium, but there are some invisible forces that continuously push the economy toward an equilibrium, a bit like gravity. You may toss a ball toward the sky and briefly win against the force of gravity, but the ball will inevitably fall back down toward its equilibrium.

Monetism supports a different view of economics that sees the economy as a continuously changing and chaotic system that has no equilibrium, or at least a continuously changing one, like the weather.

Imagine you have to care for a goldfish in its bowl. The system has an equilibrium and the best strategy to make the fish thrive is to minimize shocks to the system. There is no need for any sophisticated strategy or complicated tools. You just need to keep the room temperature stable, feed the fish, and occasionally change the water.

But imagine you have to care for the species living in the oceans on Earth. There are so many forces affecting them that it's much more complex to manage. Your solution scope spans from "do nothing, anything you do is meaningless," to "care for every individual specimen of all species and try to control the tides." Both extremes are suboptimal. The free-market response of "do nothing" is probably closer to what is feasible (and that's why modern societies are founded on market principles and not on communist ones), but you still want to avoid oceans' acidification and overfishing, and protect some of the species from extinction, which requires a more sophisticated strategy.

Traditional economics thinks of an economy as a simple fish bowl where we need to minimize shocks. New complications in the real world wouldn't change the care routine: Just focus on absorbing shocks to the fish bowl and all will be well. Permanent changes in society, such as automation, climate change, or the aging of the population, would just move the equilibrium; there would be no need to design a more sophisticated strategy or change the system.

To a traditional economist, the proposals of monetism would be either unnecessary or dangerous, as they would introduce shocks to a system that's in equilibrium, or are outside the scope of economics. Asking economists to recognize that we do in fact need a strategy, new tools like injecting permanent money and agile inflation taxes, and a continuous set of decisions that governing institutions (and not just central banks) need to take to help society adapt would be like asking the Catholic Church in Copernicus's time to acknowledge that the Earth revolves around the sun. This would likewise be an acknowledgment that what was sold as the only economic truth—the general equilibrium theory of traditional economics—is actually flawed, and the cathedral of equations in macroeconomic models, as well as much of the economic research focused on those equations, is actually meaningless.

Frightened by the consequences of a revolution within the economic disciplines, traditional economists keep defending assumptions and models that are as wrong as the assumption that the sun revolves around the Earth. Ostracizing heterodox economists from the important debates and economic journals is the equivalent of excommunication for the Medieval church.

Traditional economists have first built a structure on three pillars that are flawed, but they also developed that structure into a full cathedral. Changing the foundation of a cathedral—just like changing a central assumption of a complex theory—is no easy task. A lot of dependencies may make the whole structure crumble. The admission that the foundation needs changing would be extremely painful for traditional economists.

Similarly to the Church no longer being able to claim that everything they say is the eternal truth, traditional economists would have some credibility issues of their own.

TRADITIONAL ECONOMICS AND MONETISM

Given I expect obstruction from traditional economists, it is useful to frame the perimeter of society that economics typically covers, the perimeter that monetism covers, and how to read economists' views on something that goes much beyond economics.

I will introduce one final analogy to illustrate how traditional economics is only a relatively niche topic when taking the perspective of society and the lives of every individual (past and future) living in it; therefore, it should be considered as one minor opinion relevant for a portion of the much larger problem of improving well-being of all citizens.

Let's think of society as a large company. Citizens would be equivalent to the company's shareholders, who are represented through elected officials (in democratic countries, at least), the same way a board of directors represents companies' shareholders.

A chief executive officer (CEO) is appointed by the board, similarly to how a prime minister or president is elected. Given the CEO (or president) has only 24 hours in a day and cannot be an expert in all disciplines, they typically organize their company (or government) in different units, functions, and departments.

A typical company would have functions to manage operations (producing things), logistics (distributing things), marketing and sales (defining what products customers want and selling them), and finance (getting the money to run the company).[14] The CEO would also have either a strategy department or would hire strategic advisors to ensure that the company is aware and ready to adapt to emerging trends to maximize profits for its shareholders.

In society, with citizens being the shareholders, monetism starts by challenging the overarching goal of society, stating that average GDP or average income is suboptimal: first, because some shareholders (citizens) get increasingly more than others, and therefore averages are inadequate to represent the situation of the majority, and second, because income itself becomes unimportant for high-income people and high-income countries.

As discussed in this book, economists proposed GDP not because they believed that it is the best goal for maximizing society's well-being, but because it is a metric they can measure and it has shown *some* correlation to some definition of well-being, especially for low-income people and low-income countries. Well-being economists exist and scholars from other disciplines are looking into metrics that can better describe the overarching goals for society, but these are beyond the scope of traditional economics. Any discussion on what society should optimize is therefore outside the scope of traditional economics departments, who cannot adequately advise policymakers.

But what is the focus of traditional economics then? What is the role of the discipline in society? And is this the right role, given so many have high expectations from the economics discipline?

If we go back to the analogy of society as a large company, traditional economics has mostly been focusing on operations: how to maximize the production of things. Economics has started covering logistics, looking into distribution of income and wealth, especially now that inequality is such a large issue. It has also restarted to be interested in finance, but only recently. Most economists today went to universities post-1980s, and the economic discipline had already lost interest in money and banking. This situation has only started to shift since the 2008 crash. Many people and policymakers were surprised by the economists' inability to foresee any dangers from within the banking industry.

Economics does not cover marketing, aside from holding that society does not need marketing: There is no need to understand what society needs, because society will need whatever its citizens will be willing to pay for, and the market will therefore provide it in pursuit of profits.

Economics also does not cover strategy, aside from stating that society does not need one. Society only needs to allow the companies in the free market to compete, which will enable them to become more productive year after year. The strategy of society for economics is just good operations: by becoming more productive year after year, society will produce more and citizens will be better off.

This *operation-based strategy* goes together with capitalism. As we have discussed in Chapter 11, it was a good strategy when every country was very poor and producing close to nothing, and increasing productivity was all that mattered. Just focus on supply and everything else would fall into place.

And continuing with the analogy of society as a company, a small business or a start-up is often constrained by its operations. Improving productivity can be important for these early-stage or small businesses, similarly to how productivity matters a lot for developing countries.

But for high-income countries, as well as large established companies, operations and productivity start becoming less important. Any large company can raise the capital or access a loan and expand production, similarly to how a highly productive economy can always raise debt or print money and channel the extra people (currently unemployed or employed but not creating much value in their current role) toward new production (potentially requiring upskilling or reskilling). When the marketing department shows customer needs are changing and the company develops a new product, operations follow suit. If a trend will reshape the industry, the strategy department may decide to shut down certain operations and open new ones, and again operations follow suit. Should society not do the same then and reshuffle operations to deliver what citizens want or pursue new strategic initiative to tackle trends like climate change?

If we think high-income societies are akin to large companies, then we have a few things to learn from them.

First, it is strategy and marketing that guide operations: You only produce what customers want, rather than assuming they want more of the same. Few businesses would survive without marketing or strategy. In society, if citizens' well-being no longer grows with production (and income and the associated consumption), then the priority in society should shift away from simply maximizing production. Citizens don't benefit from just more of the same. Monetism's proposal of allocating resources toward climate change mitigation or education or health care or poverty alleviation or whatever other priority would therefore be justified, even if society indeed reached full employment and fewer resources would be available for whatever the market is currently producing.

Second, if there is an investment that the CEO and the board of a company approve, finance is not a limitation. Companies will be able to convince shareholders to invest more money or get banks to lend it. In society, I have shown that we can do much more than we're currently doing, as modern societies have central banks that can create as much money as they deem appropriate. The debate would be among the shareholders and board members (citizens and their elected representatives) to decide what investments are worth. Money doesn't have to be a limit. The real limit is only in the real resources society has and the knowledge to mobilize them in highly productive ways.

In summary, economics has generally succeeded in their main focus, which is managing operations. In high-income countries, we have become so productive that the focus can shift from operations to other neglected departments: finance (money creation and management), logistics (distribution of money, income, and wealth), marketing (understanding what citizens need to grow well-being), and strategy (how to continue to progress in the face of upcoming threats and opportunities such as climate change and automation).

Monetism takes the CEO or the shareholders' perspective, not that of the head of operations. It asks questions and advances proposals that are beyond the field of traditional economics.

But even for those topics where monetism enters the field of operations, monetism changes too many rules of the game for traditional economics to apply. The division between monetary policy and fiscal policy blurs in monetism, given that creating and giving away money (without attaching it to loan contracts) falls between monetary and fiscal policy, as they are defined today. Monetism also proposes changing the mandate and tools of central banks. Traditional macroeconomic models do not really have institutions in them, so they can't model how a change in governance would affect society or the economy. The goal of GDP and income in monetism is also secondary to universal well-being, so how can GDP- and employment-focused traditional economics apply?

Fundamentally, monetism is a solution in line with a completely different economic theory than the traditional one. Economists conceiving the economy as an equilibrium system naturally veer toward understanding different laws that point toward that equilibrium. If instead one takes the view of complexity economics, conceiving societies and economies as chaotic systems with radical uncertainties, then any simplistic laws of economics like the Phillips curve or deterministic models such as general equilibrium models have little relevance. What becomes more important is to have several tools, policy options, and the guidance to pick the right combination depending on the economic *and* social circumstances of the moment. Monetism is a more sophisticated strategy than the capitalists' and operations-focused approach of "let the free market produce whatever citizens are willing to pay for" that traditional economists support.

Ultimately, it is therefore society that should decide whether monetism highlights a better strategy than capitalism to thrive in the 21st century and beyond, not traditional economists. For this reason, I wrote this book for the public and not for economists. If the public at large wants some version of monetism, economics should either shift their focus beyond operations and debate monetism from a strategic, marketing, financial, and logistical angle or stick with operations and do the same that chief operating officers (COOs) would when a new strategy from their CEO lands on their table: restructure the operations to deliver it.

WHAT CAN WE TRUST ECONOMISTS WITH?

I have been referring to *traditional economics* to highlight the general and prevailing direction that the discipline seems to be pointing to. But in economics

as in everything else in life, we should go beyond averages. The economics discipline is the poster child of a house divided against itself. Those most critiquing
the discipline of economics are economists themselves, and most of the research
I have been using to create and argue for monetism comes from economic
research, oftentimes at the edges of the mainstream economic thinking, and
sometimes outright heterodox views (nonetheless advanced by highly qualified
academic and nonacademic economists).

More fundamentally, renowned economists including many Nobel laureates and mainstream institutions have been challenging the very foundations
of traditional economic thinking, their models, and their assumptions: the
Copernicus-type of challenge.

After the 2008 recession, Nobel laureate Joseph Stiglitz complained that
many economists used models that assume that "demand had to equal supply—
and that meant that there could be no unemployment," and "all individuals
were assumed to be identical, and this meant that there could be no meaningful
financial market. So who would be lending to whom?"[15]

Similarly, Piketty wrote that since the 1970s, economists "have probably
relied too much on so-called representative agent models, in which each agent
is assumed to earn the same income and to be endowed with the same amount
of wealth."[16]

Intriguingly, economists have known for decades that they use unrealistic
assumptions and rely too much on math models that poorly represent society. Back in 1994, for instance, economist Paul Ormerod compared believing
in the model of competitive equilibrium—that is, perfect competition among
companies—to living in Alice's Wonderland, given the hundred years of economic history showing the opposite.[17]

A paper from the Bank for International Settlements (BIS), the central bank
of central banks, summed up the problem. It observed that banks played no role
in the macroeconomic models before the 2008 crash and that economists were
still looking in the wrong places. "Let's say that we are trying to measure tide
height at the beach," its analysts wrote. "We know that the sea is filled with fish,
and so we exhaustively model fish behavior, developing complex models of their
movements and interactions. Finally, we have a model of the fish that we are
able to simulate and compare to the data from monitoring the fish themselves.
The model is great. And the model is useless . . . we are focusing on the fish
when we should be studying the moon."[18]

In an interview in *The Wall Street Journal* titled "Why Central Bankers Missed the Crisis," the head of the BIS research department strongly denounced the simplistic assumptions describing the relationship between economic variables and economists' disinterest in better understanding the impact of finance and banking on the real economy.[19]

It sounds counterintuitive. Economists are not dumb. How could they base serious conclusions on such unrealistic models? One explanation could be that people with higher cognitive skills are more affected than others by the *ambiguity aversion bias*: They cannot cope with uncertainty.[20] This can explain why economists are desperate to model the economy with a deterministic equilibrium, forcing them to use simplistic assumptions and excluding whole portions of the economy—like banks—from their models. They just can't cope with the radical uncertainty of society.

Ambiguity aversion is a fundamental issue that affects society at large, as it is part of human nature. It leads most people to see things as black or white and look for one-size-fits-all solutions. For example, markets are beneficial; therefore markets are perfect and everything needs to be market-based. The reality is that most of the time the optimal solution is somewhere in the gray area and the optimal will be different for different countries and circumstances.

That's why those IMF policies, WTO rules, and EU treaties that are based on strict golden rules are set up for failure. Humans struggle to cope with diversity, variability, and uncertainty. Therefore, we create rigid rules, but unfortunately we have to face reality.

In *The Origin of Wealth*, Eric Beinhocker presents the work of several scholars, both within and outside of economics, pointing to a new approach to economic thinking under the label of *complexity economics*. In his work, he shows how most of the real, hard sciences like physics or biology find traditional economics deeply flawed, given how the assumptions of their deterministic equilibrium models are at odds with reality. One can call something *science* if it simplifies reality but not if it distorts it. Complexity economics is still a niche within the world of economics, although the Institute for New Economic Thinking (INET), a relatively new economic institution that was founded partly to challenge traditional economics, is working hard to create a *new economics* based on it. Some of its grantees have developed much more realistic models that helped to understand the 2008 housing bubble, modeling real-life people and showing how the bubble could have been avoided with good regulations.[21] Of course, these models can't explain the whole economy, because the whole economy is just impossible and too complex to model all at once. As mentioned, this is a completely different view of economics, which looks more at events that matter in real life rather than chasing physical laws where the laws of physics don't apply.

TIME FOR A KUHNIAN REVOLUTION FOR ECONOMICS?

Thomas Samuel Kuhn was a philosopher of science who studied the history of science and tried to understand how scientific progress came about. He advanced a theory—controversial at the time—that scientific progress does not happen only with the discovery of a truth being added to the previous body of truth. He proposes an alternance of phases, one in which a discipline builds enough consensus around a framework, or paradigm, and scientists cumulatively build on it, and another phase of scientific revolution where the framework is instead revisited.[22] Economics has cumulatively built its cathedral over the three pillars that represent an initial framework that turns out to be flawed.

According to Kuhn, it is in the cumulation of sufficiently worrying puzzles that can't be solved by the discipline, which he called *anomalies*, that creates an opening for a scientific revolution. Kuhn explained the tension between the conservatism of those who need to *protect* the consensus of the discipline around the founding framework (paradigm) and those trying to innovate.[23] This tension is nowhere stronger than in the discipline of economics, so much so that economists have started taking a distance from the discipline by referring to it as *traditional economics*—something separate and archaic compared to what they (and I) write about.

As we consider all the critiques to traditional economics and the very possibility that the discipline is in the midst of its Kuhnian scientific revolution, a relevant question for the future of modern societies is whether we can entrust much to the economics discipline in its current form. If economists are a house divided, busy with theoretical debates of questionable utility and with an emerging consensus at odds with reality, do we really want them to look beyond operations and into finance, logistics, marketing, and the strategy of society? Or should we just recognize that a new discipline with its own institutions should emerge, maybe starting from those niche economists who are working with scientific principles and real-world observations?

As an outsider, I find it is difficult to attempt an answer to this. But some people at the core of the economics discipline seem to be raising doubts that traditional economics should be entrusted with something as important as guiding society to improve well-being of the citizens of the world.

THE STATE OF THE
ECONOMICS PROFESSION

Steven Payson is the executive director of the Association for Integrity and Responsible Leadership in Economics and Associated Professions. In *How Economics Professors Can Stop Failing Us* (2017), he suggests traditional economists are "living in their La La Land."[24] He took no sides in any economic debate, yet he exposed the inner dynamics of the world of academic economics, which raises concerns over the adequacy of the discipline to have any large influence on the design of our socio-economic system. Here are the three interwoven issues he highlighted:

1. Greater focus on the statistical process rather than applicability to the real world

2. Mistaking the means (academic publication) for the end (improving society)

3. Lack of interest in morals

To these, I add a fourth concern, that the economics discipline is ill-equipped for strategic thinking:

4. A keener focus on explaining the past than preparing for the future

Let's quickly go through these.

1. Focus on the statistical process

A great deal of what matters in academic economic publications is whether the finding is statistically significant and the process has enough mathematical complexity. Yet statistical significance depends on the choice of data and samples used, and to model a phenomenon, one must make certain assumptions to simplify it. Nothing is wrong with this idea in principle, but we have a problem when economists strategically choose the data sample to achieve statistical significance, or when their simplifying assumptions lead their models to describe La La Land instead of reality.[25]

The classic model of *Homo economicus*, the rational omniscient being at the basis of most traditional economic thinking, is particularly vulnerable. A famous paper showed the results of experiments performed in 15 different cultures to see whether people behaved like the self-interested, rational *Homo economicus*. Every culture systematically violated the model.[26] One of the authors, Harvard anthropologist Joseph Henrich, ultimately did find a situation where *Homo economicus* usefully predicted behavior: chimpanzees in simple experiments.[27]

Thomas Piketty explained in the introduction to his masterpiece that he left the US because he "did not find the work of US economists entirely convincing." He realized he knew too little about the world's problems, even as he was writing a thesis that involved complex math theorems. "Yet the profession liked my work. . . . The profession continued to churn out purely theoretical results without even knowing what facts needed to be explained. And it expected me to do the same."[28]

This penchant leads the discipline away from solid ground. Economics, Piketty writes, "has yet to get over its childish passion for mathematics and for purely theoretical and often highly ideological speculation, at the expense of historical research and collaboration with the other social sciences. Economists are all too often preoccupied with petty mathematical problems of interest only to themselves." Hence, the discipline cultivates irrelevance. "This obsession with mathematics is an easy way of acquiring the appearance of scientificity without having to answer the far more complex questions posed by the world we live in."[29]

The heavy-lifting math causes another serious problem: It has helped make most papers written by economists incomprehensible to others, including researchers in related fields and policymakers themselves. It is not surprising that economics in the US has largely isolated itself from other disciplines. Only 42% of economists agree that they need to understand the world through a multidisciplinary lens, the lowest percentage among the disciplines, and far below psychologists (79%) and sociologists (73%).[30] Traditional economists are affected by *expertitis*: They think the economy is too complex for outsiders to understand and are therefore uninterested in anything they have to say that relates to the economy.

This nonchalance about the wider world has had significant consequences. According to Angus Deaton, for example, mainstream development economists have historically neglected the importance of political institutions when recommending steps to develop low-income countries.[31] It's no wonder their efforts backfired.[32]

Yet economists offer advice with self-assurance. We all suffer from the *overconfidence bias,* or as my professor Neil Bearden would put it, "We overestimate the precision of our knowledge." Mark Twain once said, "It ain't what you don't know that gets you into trouble. It's what you know for sure that just ain't so." He could have been referring to economics, especially if he'd seen the head of the Fed Alan Greenspan lauding the stability of the financial system and its complex financial instruments, just two years before these instruments brought the economy to its knees in 2008.[33]

Keynes predicted that economists would have marginal importance in society, since production levels would be high enough for everyone to enjoy leisure time. Though we're not fully there yet, the sterility of much economics discourse may bring us closer to his forecast. Other disciplines focused on improving universal well-being could receive a greater share of the research grants that now go to traditional economists.

2. Mistaking the means (publication) for the end (improving society)

When Steven Payson was in a position to set requirements for accepting an economics paper, he told each submitting author to explain in 250 words why the work would be important. After many complaints, he had to end this simple step, as most economists do not know how to answer that. They basically have no reason for writing a paper other than to publish it in a prestigious journal.

This would not be a problem if economics journals decided which paper to publish based on its relevance for society. They'd reject the submissions that didn't improve the world, and economists would soon orient their work in that direction. According to Payson, though, economic journals do not provide a service to society, but to the authors who need to publish for career progress. As such, most journals look at the authors first and then the potential to receive citations—the way economic journals are ranked—and the amount of advanced math in the paper.[34]

Apparently, applicability to world problems is secondary within the discipline of economics, because what matters for career advancement are citations and publications.

Payson proposes that we change the incentive system of economics pro-fessors.[35] But while this improvement is long overdue, it may not occur if economists themselves find the task just beyond their reach.

Ann Pettiford thinks that a better understanding cannot come from uni-versity economists. "Departments of economics are overwhelmingly stuffed by 'classical' and 'neoclassical' economists," she writes. "These have no firm foun-dation in monetary theory on which to develop appropriate policies. . . . And microeconomists who study economic processes in detail, and often in isola-tion, wrongly draw macroeconomic conclusions from such processes."[36]

Indeed, money, banking, and finance are almost completely absent from basic economic studies. Most economists to this day believe that economies need to save before investing, while in real life, banks make the opposite true. It is thanks to banks' credit expansion that companies can receive loans in an amount that is higher than savings from previous years. More loans mean more investments, which create the opportunity for the economy overall to save more. Money and banking are topics that economists have considered not cool enough to warrant important publications, although every company and most individu-als have to deal in real life with money and banks. The fact that most economists have neglected them since the 1980s is mind-boggling.

I find it grotesque that the discipline of economics itself is an example of a market failure, with thousands of economics researchers unable to guide policy makers in shaping a better society. As in free-market capitalism, many econo-mists have sought the immediate and self-interested rewards of publication and ignored the larger, genuine problems of society.

Most economists do not even think that warning against market failures is their job. "There is no profession on Earth," says Payson, "where there is so great a discrepancy between the incredible responsibility that society right-fully expects of the profession, and the minimal level of responsibility that most members of the profession appear to have."[37]

John Rapley goes further, comparing economics to a religion[38] whose mem-bers defend a belief codified in complex models with axiomatic assumptions that only heretics would question. With a similar reference in mind, Adair Turner calls the unorthodox idea of permanent money, which he has been sup-porting for over a decade, "the devil."[39]

One topic I also find concerning is that it's common to find multiple papers and articles with minor disagreements among scholars, while there is a huge misalignment between the prevailing economic consensus and what politicians and the general public believe to be true. For example, the consensus that government austerity in times of crisis and high unemployment is the worst policy a government can implement is almost as established within economics as the science behind climate change.[40] Yet while climate change is recognized, politicians and the public still do not understand that the government is not a household, and that in times of crisis it needs to run deficits (or print money). Going back to the analogy of society as a company, the CEO needs the big picture and the *so what* from its employees. Instead, economists send thousands of pages of details that no one cares about, which convey only confusion and disagreement. The CEO can only use their own common sense and wait for economists to agree on the high-level message.

I want to underscore this: We have tens of thousands of brilliant economists and no one saw the 2008 crisis coming, and our politicians and citizens still haven't figured out something as basic as the fact that public debts are not to be repaid but continuously revolved.

We have thousands of brilliant minds that are stuck doing economic research and debating theories while we actually have a society that needs guidance on real-world problems. It is okay for the physics discipline to spend time on theories of black holes: Physical laws are rather immutable and physics doesn't have a role in advising how to organize real-life societies. The discipline of economics seems to be interested in doing physics-like theoretical research, although society looks up to the discipline to guide policymakers in pursuing sound socio-economic policies.

Fortunately, after many decades of economic and financial crashes, other sciences are entering and revitalizing economics. Psychology, sociology, and evolutionary biology, among other disciplines, have infiltrated this realm and shown that we can better understand the real world by acknowledging our cognitive biases rather than relying on oversimplifying assumptions. It is also reassuring that six Nobel Prizes in economics have gone to behavioral economists[41]—psychologists competing in the economics market.

The 2017 Nobel Prize for Richard Thaler was particularly important, not only because of his open critique of *Homo economicus*, but also because his work went beyond the theoretical, continuing the path that Daniel Kahneman and Amos Tversky started decades earlier. He used behavioral economics to study *nudges* to help people make better decisions—such as about sound health or investment options, and saving enough for retirement.[42]

Branko Milanovic is optimistic about the future of economics, claiming that the 2008 crash led to a shift from the old paradigm of the "income-maximizing agent with perfect information" to a new "heterogeneity- and inequality-based paradigm" that will look at differences between people beyond their similarities.[43]

The Bank for International Settlements has expressed similar optimism. In a 2012 paper it seemed to demand more accurate models and focus on the impact of debt on our economy. We "need to have a rationale for debt as distinct from equity," it said, and added, "We need to understand why the predominant financial contract is a loan or a bond rather than equity. In fact, we need a clear understanding of the optimal debt/equity ratio for the economy as a whole. We know that high levels of debt can lead to disaster for a society, but beyond notions from crude empirical work, we don't have any idea what the right level of debt is. A rich enough macro/monetary/financial model will tell us the answer."[44]

The Bank is moving in the direction suggested by monetism, which proposes solutions to reduce debt and increase equity.

But I am not sure I share the same optimism on the ability of the academic profession to steer its economists beyond the focus of publication toward improving society. In fact, if mistaking the means for the end applies to economics publications, it also applies to the objective of society, which remains the amoral GDP.

3. Lack of interest in morals

Responding to US protests against South Africa's apartheid, a prominent economics professor built a model showing that apartheid was economically inefficient. It appears that ethical issues catch economists' interest only if they have an impact on economic efficiency.[45] Economist George DeMartino argues that the field is ethically deficient overall, and Piketty wraps up his masterwork by saying that instead of the term *economic science*, "I much prefer the expression 'political economy,' which may seem rather old-fashioned but to my mind conveys the only thing that sets economics apart from other social sciences: its political, normative, and moral purpose."[46]

While people have raised moral issues since the late 19th century, the American Economic Association has always held that they did not require attention.[47]

This attitude seems to have side effects. In a study dating back to 1993, the authors collected various experiments and surveys showing students and professors of economics were more likely to free ride and less likely to collaborate.[48] Psychologist Tom Stafford notes about such findings, "If we tell students that it makes sense to see the world through the eyes of the selfish rational actor, my suspicion is that they are more likely to do so."[49] There is now sufficient evidence on both the fact that the economic discipline attracts more selfish students and that studying economics makes students more selfish.[50]

In summary, the discipline that should most influence the shape of our society is not much guided by morals, and the rational agent of *Homo economicus* was implicitly made selfish. The more this discourse prevails, the more we hear "greed is good," "the business of business is making money for shareholders," and "people are poor because they deserve it." These narratives are destroying the fabric of society, a fabric that has been built over millennia of increasing collaboration among individuals.

Morals, altruism, and collaboration are at least as much a part of human nature as self-interest and have been foundational to societal progress, although capitalism-reinforced self-interest has long undermined these. A system such as neoliberal capitalism (which became a political ideology but had emerged from economic theory) that promotes, rewards, and even celebrates self-interest will naturally self-implode into the chaos and misery that we find in animal societies: a fight for survival. And it is traditional economics that keeps providing the justification for such an amoral and self-centered system of capitalism.

4. Focus on the past rather than the future

The use of statistics has a major flaw: You need to collect data over a long time to get reliable insights. Before 2008, many economists were busy watching housing prices increase 10% per year and they assumed it would continue forever,[51] instead of trying to understand causes, consequences, and potential mitigation strategies to avoid a price bubble.

While the laws of thermodynamics will still be true a million years from now, economies are in flux minute by minute. They arise from the shifting interactions of billions of people of different cultures and ages, and millions of companies producing new products and services. Fashions sweep the world and disappear. Every day about 380,000 people are born and about 160,000 die worldwide.[52] New companies can completely redefine industries and sometime societies. The classic economic variables—such as prices, employment, wages, profits, savings, and distribution of income and wealth—vary constantly. And given the unprecedented changes society is going through today, talks of immutable laws and equilibria feels like putting cast-iron clothes on a growing child.

If we don't stop thinking that we have a magic economic theory and models that fit any country at any time in history, we are doomed to fail dramatically.

The combination of unlimited variables with changing values yields what Mervyn King calls *radical uncertainty*. To cope with such, we have to consider the long-term trends that will shape the future of the economy, understand their implications for society, and prepare ourselves with tools and policies to deal with the uncertainty. In short, we need a strategy that continuously adapts to our changing society.

The strategy needs the lessons of the past, but it must look to the future. Economics is bound to analyze past data and established theories, but we also need psychology to ground economics in reality and strategists to add purpose and long-term vision. Such a task goes beyond traditional economics, and looking at the state of the profession today, it seems sensible that economics be only a small contributor to a new discipline that looks more holistically at social progress.

Similar to the name *monetism* signaling a break with the outdated capitalism, although significantly building on it, a new discipline with a new name could signal a break with traditional economics, which seems to have reached the end of its usefulness for society.

A NEW INTERDISCIPLINARY APPROACH TO IMPROVE OUR SOCIETIES

If I believe (and I do) that monetism is the type of holistic rethink that is most needed to further improve society and the lives of its citizens, I sure hope that more people will advance many more monetism-like proposals or improve and elaborate on some portions of monetism. I am not claiming I've arrived at the ultimate answer here. I hold a strong opinion that any systemic socio-economic reform needs to include a review of money and inflation management, but certainly better alternatives can be developed as to how to do so and how to reshape the governance of society. I do claim, though, that with this book I tackled the problem of *holistically and creatively rethinking society with the purpose of improving outcomes for its citizens*, which many more people should be thinking about as a profession rather than a side project.

What is it that enabled me to create monetism that traditional economists lack? Monetism is basically a mix of strategy and processes that I created looking at future trends and using an interdisciplinary approach. I therefore believe we need an interdisciplinary approach to improve society rather than a new discipline.

My first intuition that money was mismanaged came from my major in engineering, and science of operations in particular. My ability to develop a holistic, forward-looking strategy comes from my profession of strategy consultant. Recognizing the incompatibility of capitalism with inequality, automation, and climate change came from research that roamed among psychology, environmental sciences, and management, as well as economics. It is after seeing people being happier and more relaxed in poor countries than at home that I began questioning the appropriateness of GDP as a societal objective. And my confidence that capitalism was flawed came from real-life work with both governments and private companies.

In summary, monetism came from a combination of different disciplines and diverse points of view of society: government versus businesses, rich versus poor, theoretical versus practical. We need to create a way for people to receive an interdisciplinary education with a good mix of theoretical and practical experience, as well as a good understanding of and appreciation for diversity and ambiguity.

We need people who are able to think outside the box and see the big picture, or we are going to end up stuck with capitalism, discussing the shades of silver of the car door handle when we should be rethinking whether we want a car. Educational institutions providing standard economics courses should really consider turning economics into a new interdisciplinary course of study.

In fact, could it be that we have been asking too much of economics alone, and economists have not been humble enough to ask for help? This is my explanation for the poor design of our socio-economic system: Society is extremely complex and very few people have the interdisciplinary competence, the holistic point of view, and the spare time to actually design an alternative.

Most people look at one portion of the problem based on their specialty. It's like the parable of the blind men and the elephant—with each blind person describing the only part of the same animal that they can touch. Politicians look at politics, economists look at the economy, and bankers look at banking. These people try to improve society from their own area of expertise and it is just impossible for them to think of something as big as rethinking society to improve people's well-being.

And to be fair to the discipline of economics, the problems of our current system have come to light only recently. The system seemed to be doing well enough, so why change it? But we're now seeing why. Since the 1980s, two cracks have opened in capitalism's foundations: productivity growth not trickling down to wages and globalization limiting governments' ability to raise enough taxes to fix market failures. The combination of the third and fourth industrial revolutions also emerged recently, with both opportunities and disruptions. Climate change is only now exploding in our hands. Wealth accumulation had paused until the 1980s, then came back with a vengeance.

Many people have only now started to think that capitalism is broken. In fact, soon we may have hundreds of studies from the academic world about the topics I am writing about.

As I prepare to finish this book, a report by advocacy group Positive Money suggests that we go beyond economic growth and use sovereign money (another name for permanent money) instead of debt.[53]

Robert Skidelsky, a well-known London School of Economics professor, has contested the mainstream view that money and government should play minimal roles.[54]

Steve Keen, an economics professor at the Kingston University London, is homing in on the role of money and debt in our economy, finding an almost perfect correlation between unemployment and the slowdown of money creation in the form of private debt.[55]

Yanis Varoufakis started to describe a hypothetical future without capitalism that has many similarities with monetism.[56]

Stephanie Kelton proposed "deficits that matters," describing a set of society priorities that require priority funding, which can come from central banks creating money,[57] again a proposal in line with monetism.

And many more economists in general are going beyond the narrow scope of economics as the *operations of society* and are covering topics such as well-being, sustainability, and financial stability, with INET being an active economic institution trying to mobilize and support these economists.

Throughout the book I have used evidence from this breed of *renegade economists* who are willing to shake the box in which most traditional economists have comfortably nested. Maybe it has just taken time for people to innovate in this space—and the time has now come.

But we are at least a decade late and many of you reading this book are likely doing less than you could. Myself included.

OPENING THE WINDOWS OF THE IVORY TOWERS

Earlier I compared a shift to monetism to brain surgery. One does not go into brain surgery unless it's really needed, and the decision-makers in the world are all healthy patients. Politicians, academics, and senior members of organizations are in State 2—above the comfort threshold. They are not sick. Why, then, would they push for surgery?

Contrary to doctors whose brains are not affected when they perform surgery on their patients, policymakers and the lobbies that influence them live in the same society that would require surgery. They decide whether society needs surgery, but they are healthy and comfortable in the status quo. They neither feel the pain nor live with the consequences of not having surgery. Loss-aversion bias (losses hurt more than gains of the same proportion) and status quo bias (aversion to change and uncertainty) are at play again here. Why embark on significant change reforms if we are already comfortable?

If we call these groups the *elites*—those who have the strongest influence on our society—we need to realize that they tend to live far removed from the rest of the population and their problems, especially from the harsh lives of less fortunate people. They've never had to skip a meal for lack of money or deal with back pain after spending the night sleeping in a car or, for the least fortunate, on a park bench.

Poverty and unemployment only reach the ivory tower in the shape of numbers and statistics, which don't scream as loud as the mother of a suicidal unemployed son and don't cut as deeply as the impoverished family member who can't afford healthcare. At home we can hear these screams and must live with the concerns, but in the ivory tower, we just look at numbers that, on average and in the long term, don't look dramatic, often even concerning. Poverty is unavoidable, economists think, and unemployment can be tolerated for a while.

Even if the majority of people have a high sense of urgency and desire for change, those who call the shots don't—not because they consciously do not want to, but because they just don't experience the same emotions and sense of urgency of those who need more radical change. As a result, society continues to change too slowly for the majority of the population.

There is ample evidence that the concerns of anyone who is not in the affluent 10% of Americans has no influence on policymakers.[58] Part of the reason in my opinion is simple: Policymakers are mostly in the top 1% of wealthy Americans and they hang out among them and with some folks who are in the top 10%, hearing them out in social gatherings. The problems and opinion of these folks are completely different than those who are not in the affluent 10%. Policymakers will look at statistics and meet with the rest of the population, but they do not have a genuine emotional connection with them. The ivory tower gets visitors from the affluent 10%, but they rarely leave the tower to experience what's happening outside.

People above the comfort threshold, those at State 2, are naturally biased into thinking that the world out there—including those living in State 1—does not need urgent change, because they themselves don't and they have few if any emotional relationships with people in State 1.

If you wonder why central bankers didn't take the risk of giving money to people instead of to banks after 2008, why would they? It was not their family members who were poor or unemployed. Yet, even after the 2008 debacle, why aren't we doing more to limit the root causes of recessions: debts and inequality? Could it be because none of the policymakers will lose their jobs over those problems? Recessions are just outside their control, right?

Between countries it is the same. Why were the pro-austerity politicians in the eurozone so deaf to the calls of most economists demanding fiscal stimulus, the opposite of austerity? Because it was not their problem. They actually did run stimulus programs in their own countries. They just did not want more indebted countries to do the same and postpone repayments. As you recall, we already discussed the increase in suicide rates linked to these decisions.

Those doing well are relatively blind to the suffering that does not touch them. They have grown complacent, incapable of changing their views, let alone thinking outside the box. It is unsurprising that populist parties are succeeding. Democracy doesn't necessarily lead to progress.

What I hope we can all do is open the windows of our ivory towers and be more attentive and less judgmental to the challenges of those who society hasn't served.

Improving democracy goes much beyond my competence and the scope of this book, but I really hope someone can make our democracies more inclusive and diverse. We can't have the majority of people in parliament, senate, and in policymaking roles coming from the top 1%, nor do we want their children in those roles. The pace of change will not be sufficient for those with incomes in the bottom 50%, and there are many smart and capable people in this group who should be more numerous among policymakers.

IN SUMMARY

Banks, the wealthy, and traditional economists have vested interests in opposing monetism, and for the economists, recognizing the benefits of monetism would lead to a significant rethink of the whole economics discipline.

We discussed that traditional economics mostly concerns the *operations* of society, the ability to produce more, while high-income countries need to step back and take a CEO's perspective, shifting societal strategy away from traditional growth and focusing more on what people need to grow their well-being and cope with emerging trends such as automation and climate change.

We also realized that the economics discipline is a house divided and is highly inadequate to be responsible for guiding society in its next phase of development—be that monetism or any other better system that can substitute for obsolete capitalism. I encouraged educational institutions to consider substituting economics with a more interdisciplinary approach to provide society with people with the right skills, knowledge, and mindsets to continuously think about how to adapt our society to changing real-life circumstances.

Ultimately, I suggested that there is no conspiracy theory guiding our governments or monetary structures. Our system is just too complex, we have asked too much from economics, and policymakers naturally have less urgency and willingness for radical change—not because they are evil, but simply because they do not feel the same struggles and sense of urgency of the majority of the population.

In the hope that this will put into perspective the challenges that these groups could bring against monetism, as well as shaking policymakers from their state of complacency, I will move forward in the next chapter to suggest *how* to introduce monetism in society in a way that balances the need for radical change with the sensibility of not disrupting a system that has brought significant prosperity.

Chapter 19

Step One, Step Two, Step Three

Pragmatic suggestions for bringing monetism to you

onetism will not appear from night to day. It will take time and incremental steps. Where should the initial impulse for monetism begin? Should a country start its implementation or can single cities attempt it? Could monetism work as an international system? And, critically, who should bring it about and how?

The shift should not be a traumatic operation. There is a sense of urgency, but we shouldn't rush headlong into total change. We'd just create disruptions and surprise domino effects. If you go to a hospital you might first get painkillers, then medications, and at some point, you may end up in the operating theater to eradicate the problem and get you back in full health. At each stage, the doctor has assessed your progress and chosen the best next step. We should take the same approach with today's capitalism. We can introduce monetism in phases, gaining many benefits even at the outset with minor changes (similar to painkillers) and proceed when ready to do so.

STAGES OF MONETISM

I foresee four stages for developing monetism within a nation: bracing for impact, stabilizing growth, refocusing businesses, and repurposing society.

STAGE 1: BRACE FOR IMPACT

The easiest and more urgent portion of monetism is an infrastructure that allows central banks to provide permanent money for every citizen. We need it to mitigate the next recession—especially now that COVID-19 ignited one— and it is a precondition for implementing UBI.

This infrastructure requires the central bank to—

- Obtain identifying information on all citizens from the government.

- Open a free bank account for each citizen.

- Ensure the central bank mandate explicitly allows for the distribution of permanent money to citizens as a tool to manage inflation.

- Establish an instrument, or accounting mechanism, to give people permanent money without reducing the equity of the central bank.[1]

If you work for a central bank, this should be your priority from here on. There is no controversy about setting up this infrastructure, as it's simply an optional tool that, at this stage, central banks may never use. Even if we wanted to hang on to capitalism, we need this additional tool to better face crises. With the COVID-19 response it has become clear that with such an infrastructure in place it would have been much easier to send money directly to people. Also, such an approach could become a conventional monetary policy tool for central banks when commercial banks just don't want to lend more money. Again, why give free money to banks so that they can create more debt instead of giving free permanent money to people?

If there is a desire to proceed further, the central bank and the government should also set up a *monetism task force* to plan the overall shift. Its first objective should be to agree on the introduction of a partial UBI, defining the initial transfer amount, the other social protection programs—if any—it could substitute for, and a framework to raise or lower UBI transfers based on changes in unemployment, inflation, propensity to save, income distribution, and other macroeconomic variables. For the sake—and to the delight—of economists, this will require a model.

STAGE 2: STABILIZE GROWTH

Central banks, by now converted into monetary authorities, start injecting enough permanent money to enable growth without additional credit (increasing reserve requirements in parallel to avoid credit growth). As the economy becomes less dependent on banking credit (and debt), it grows more stable. We don't need complex new governance for this step, but it would require a change in the mandate of central banks into the monetary authorities no longer acting as lenders of last resort.

The money supply has historically equaled about ⅔ of GDP,[2] increasing beyond ⅘ of GDP after the COVID-19 crisis. Let's say we target a nominal GDP growth of 6%–8%; we could inject permanent money for at least 5% of GDP and allocate it between a partial UBI and the existing development funds (such as for clean energy) as conditional transfers. Different countries will have different growth potentials and targets, and should also establish different targets for monetary expansion. The monetary authority and governments would decide how much goes to UBI and how much to conditional transfer through development funds.

The money thus injected would end up in multiple areas of the economy and have diverse effects on the overall money supply and inflation dynamics.

Central banks can develop models to forecast where the money will end up and the many possible alternative human behaviors and situations, but they will not know for sure which will prevail. It is thus even more important that central banks continue monitoring the money supply, as well as factors like inflation, wages, income distribution, savings rates, and unemployment, and decide if they should inject more or less permanent money, as well as how much to change banks' reserve requirements and/or interest rates.

My suggestion would be to start injecting more permanent money than the economy needs to grow, and increase reserve requirements as to decrease the amount of credit and debts. In time, reserve requirements will have to grow to limit credit creation and I would continue until reaching reserve requirements of 50% of banks' loans. If, as per my hypothesis, the increase in permanent money will lead to higher savings and more abundant equity, thus reducing the need for loans, central banks could proceed, inject more permanent money, and gradually reach 100% reserve requirements.

STAGE 3: REFOCUS BUSINESSES

We can implement this stage together with the previous one. Refocusing businesses means introducing a) the progressive tax on companies' profits based on ROE while increasing the flexibility of the labor market (that is, leaving companies free to release people if they cannot find a use for them—similar to the current situation in the US or Denmark); b) more taxes on unhealthy activities; c) more funds for innovation on selected activities (such as fighting climate change); and d) establishing and funding independent research programs to both accelerate creative destruction (such as lower-cost clean energy or drugs) and create more transparency over important aspects of our lives potentially misaligned with business interests (such as the impact of nutrition on health or of industrial fishing on the environment).

This stage does not require much redesign in the governance. Just 3a, the counter-inflation corporate taxes based on ROE, would be a requirement to implement stage 4 of monetism.

STAGE 4: REPURPOSE SOCIETY

By this point, we may have stabilized the economy, limited our impact on the environment, unleashed significant and useful growth from the private and public sector, and even prepared people to cope with a future with less employment.

Yet until society agrees on all the governance changes and details that monetism needs and establishes the emergency counter-inflation tax mechanism, once we achieve 100% reserve requirements in Stage 2, we would have to limit the injection of permanent money to an amount that is counterbalanced by roughly an equivalent reduction in credit (and debt). This factor would limit both the UBI transfers and the conditional transfers for useful societal projects.[3]

We would have to, that is, unless the monetary authority and government collaborate so well that governments effectively manage inflation with taxes and, in exchange, the central bank injects more and more permanent money. Yet if we were to put structure around this and make such collaboration continuous and enshrined into law, we would need a) the monetism task force to propose a governance solution (along the lines suggested in Chapter 15); b) the broader society to agree with it and possibly add it to the constitution; and c) governing institutions to operationalize the governance with processes, new institutions, and employees to carry out monetism activities. It could take several years, but only then can we be comfortable and be prepared to introduce a full UBI when automation allows, and as many conditional transfers as we need to fix priority social issues. This time lag is not a problem, since as I've noted several times, we don't need a full UBI right now and by Stage 2 of monetism we could already implement a modest negative income tax or a partial UBI.

In France, the program Revenu de Solidarité Active (RSA) is already similar to a negative income tax, with more than €500 per month for a single person with no income, and a gradual reduction of transfers for people with some income with reduction profile that maintains the incentive to earn every extra euro.[4] Given the complexity of the eligibility criteria, the program is likely more expensive to administer than an unconditional negative income tax, and France is financing it with conventional taxes.

While these four stages describe a high-level roadmap that any country with its own central bank can implement, a version of monetism can also be implemented locally or globally.

LOCAL MONETISM

As I am closing this book, the municipality of Maricà in Rio De Janeiro is trying a version of monetism. It has a UBI funded through a new digital currency injected as permanent money.[5] If the EU or the US cannot agree on adopting monetism, individual states or even cities could take this course of action.

The Mumbuca, the new currency of Maricà, is pegged 1-to-1 with the *real*, the currency of Brazil. Given the increased volume of commerce from its introduction, the municipality has increased the UBI transfers from 10 to 20 Mumbucas a month (about $3–$6). It also pays a supplementary income to low-income families of 110 Mumbucas.[6]

As with all local community currencies, people can use the Mumbuca only within the community, the city of Maricà in this case. If inflation were to heighten local prices and bring in more imports, the local currency could not sustain its value. Yet it can provide the flexibility to pursue different monetary and social policies for states without their own central bank. And if the local community can collect taxes, it can put the system of counterinflation taxes in place, and thus there is no reason why monetism would not work at a more local level.

While communities could better tailor local currencies to their needs, it is clearly a duplication of effort to set up multiple currencies and multiple decision-making bodies to manage them. And the competencies people need to manage monetism are not that easy to come by. We are talking about hundreds if not thousands of highly educated individuals with high salaries.

Cities may indeed struggle should they attempt to implement monetism, but in Italy and states as large as California there is plenty of expertise to run a parallel currency. Legal constraints with the federal government or with the European Union may be the main barrier, but let's not forget that laws and treaties are made and changed by men and women.

The European Union treaties in particular were created on the premises of flawed and outdated economic beliefs and are due for a revision anyway. Allowing member states to manage their own currencies in parallel to the euro would hardly be the end of the euro, which would continuously be legal tender in all member states. It would rather add the flexibility needed by countries with diverse circumstances so that they fully benefit from the euro and the European Union and reduce the arguments for exiting them.

At a minimum, a voucher-based partial UBI or one-off stimulus, with vouchers recognized by a state or country, could be an easy policy for implementing Stage 1 of monetism in countries without their own currency, and this move alone could go a long way to respond to economic crises and provide more security to citizens.

GLOBAL MONETISM

Capitalism is a global issue. According to Piketty's estimates, the 0.1% richest people already own 20% of global wealth, and if the returns on their wealth reach 6% and global growth stays at 2%, they will own 60% of global wealth in 30 years. He points out that this would trigger a violent political reaction.[7] The backlash against globalization is already a sign of this.

Earlier we discussed a portion of the global governance that fell apart in 1971: the international monetary system based on the gold standard. We have never reintroduced a new monetary agreement between countries, except for some fair-trade agreements broadly recognized as insufficient and now being reformed.

But as we've seen throughout the book, the monetary system is not just a small wheel in the giant scheme of free-market capitalism. Money is *the* incentive. It gets people and organizations to work for the most important goals. And we now have fundamental worldwide challenges, of which minimizing climate change is only one.

The United Nations (UN) has periodically set development objectives: the Millennium Development Goals for 2015 and now the Sustainable Development Goals (SDG) for 2030. It has multiple institutions working on these goals and among these, two institutions form the global equivalent of a central bank and a development bank: the IMF and the World Bank.

Similarly to individual countries, neither the IMF nor the World Bank is creating money and directing it toward these challenges. They have ample room for lending and the IMF even has the mandate to create Special Drawing Rights (SDR)—the closest we have to a global currency—but neither organization is creating and distributing money in a global UBI, nor directly funding projects with global benefits. Why not? Well, the challenges are similar to those of each country: What about global inflation? Who decides which projects are worth funding?

This latter question would require a difficult level of agreement among countries, which I only imagine possible if a giant asteroid is directed toward Earth and we need to find a way to destroy it. Other projects would be too complex to agree upon. Imagine we find immense mining potential on the moon: Who does it belong to? Who should pay for the extraction and transportation to Earth? And what happens to those countries mining the same materials on Earth, which would now see the prices fall due to extra supply from the moon?

We took decades to agree on a target for limiting climate change, but the agreement still has no teeth and no guarantee that it will solve the one existential issue we currently face.

While I am myself pessimistic that much of monetism can be achieved through the UN at the global level, I believe there is some hope for some components of monetism. As the COVID-19 pandemic unfolds there seem to be advanced discussions on whether the IMF could issue 650 billion USD in new SDR and make it available to all IMF countries to help fight the pandemic.[8] Should this happen, it could be an important step toward monetism, albeit still on a very exceptional basis. My highest hope is for a small global UBI, with a global currency and newly printed permanent money every year and distributed to every adult in the world. The amount might be symbolic for high-income countries but could be life-changing for people in developing countries. With a bit more optimism I could see global permanent money printed (or destroyed) every year to compensate (or tax) countries based on their net carbon footprint. Countries would then start valuing their forests and oceans more and take carbon emission and carbon capture more seriously. With even more optimism, I could see today's international organizations funded by a global currency with again newly printed permanent money. Today, these organizations are funded by UN member states and are naturally more attentive to the views of their biggest donors. If funding comes from a global currency continuously created by the IMF, for example, then voting rights should be revisited, decisions should be more inclusive. Unfortunately, this action would leave the biggest donors—the US *in primis*—unhappy for the loss of influence, and this might be the reason that several proposals for a global currency never came close to becoming a reality.

A global currency in parallel to national currencies is an idea that was first proposed at Bretton Woods by John Maynard Keynes and revisited by economists Joseph Stiglitz and Bruce Greenwald. The main goals of their proposals were to enable international trade by reducing exchange-rates risks and the dependence on any individual currency (today mostly the US dollar), and avoiding the accumulation of massive foreign reserves.[9]

While these goals are important, they take a back seat when compared to directing resources to eradicate global poverty, fighting climate change, or any other global issues. Nevertheless, a global currency and global monetism, as utopic as it might be, could meet both goals.[10] With increasing issues that have to be tackled in a global way, a global currency becomes increasingly important. It's time to reopen this debate and launch a new Bretton Woods–like task force to start charting the course for a new global monetary system.

UBI OF 5% OF GDP FUNDED WITH PERMANENT MONEY

Although I presented a path to implement monetism in four incremental stages, it's useful to advance also a concrete proposal that can be debated and implemented immediately by policymakers. It would of course not cover all of monetism but be a good springboard.

My proposal is for the central bank of a country to create the equivalent of 5% of GDP of the national currency, split it among every adult person in the country, and distribute it in a central bank account that each adult citizen is automatically entitled to. Without changing anything else, central banks will then manage interest rates and reserve requirements to achieve their inflation and employment targets (for those who have them).

At a more local level, the same could be done with a voucher system, and at the global level the same could be achieved with a global currency issued by the IMF. Five percent of GDP worth of new money, global, national or local/ voucher currency, would be distributed to each adult.

At the Eurozone or US level, 5% of GDP would be €170 or $350, respectively, per adult per month,[11] enough to provide some security but insufficient to fully cover basic needs, yet a significant floor that people can rely on, with the only potential—but not certain—cost to society being a slightly higher interest rate on bank loans.

If this was to be considered at the global level with a global currency created and distributed by the IMF, 5% of GDP in UBI would lead to about 100 international USD a month per adult.[12] In poor countries that is enough to afford basic needs (UBI pilots typically pay less than 50 USD a month). It might cause some local inflation and higher imports, but it could also result in a lot of local economic activity and security. Given recipients would be getting an international currency (or global currency), the impact on the local currency value from higher imports would be limited.

Capitalism has brought great progress. It's now time to take full advantage of what humanity can do and pursue bold initiatives to leap toward a new level of universal and sustainable well-being.

Epilogue

Will We Be Frogs in the Pot?

Growing sprouts of hope

We started the journey of this book realizing that the majority of people, both in high- and low-income countries, spend most of their lives below the comfort threshold, and naturally focus on securing their basic needs for the rest of their lives before truly living fully in the pursuit of their fulfillment.

When considering proposals like UBI that would rapidly lift everyone above the comfort threshold, we hit the challenges of governments' inability to tax and an obsolete design of our monetary system with too much responsibility and power in the hands of private commercial banks.

We traced the issue to an overemphasis on the perfection of free markets and we found that capitalism as a backbone for organizing society has become obsolete to face challenges such as aging of the population, automation, AI, and climate change, among many others.

Capitalism has broken its promises, especially since the neoliberal shift in the 1980s that, without any evidence, has started an experiment of extreme market-based religion that created higher divisions and inequities. It is now a cage limiting society's ability to leapfrog into a higher level of evolution where all people can live above their comfort threshold for most of their lives. More concerningly, it is on a path to implosion in secular stagnation and inequality, unable to even achieve its equally outdated goal of maximizing GDP. If the frog is trapped in a cage and the cage is in the pot, it has no chances of escaping the pot of warming water.

Societies of high-income countries have outgrown capitalism and are now ready for a new phase where most of what people need can be provided with highly automated processes and some human labor. People can gain more freedom as to how to use their time in a mix of paid and unpaid activities. Goals such as protecting the environment, providing universal access to good quality and modern education and health care, and advancing more research takes priority over producing golden toothbrushes for those who can afford them. The main goals for societies are changing, and so should the process to allocate resources, with some priority channels (aside from taxes and government spending) that can complement markets and banks.

We therefore defined sustainable and universal well-being as the overarching societal goals with four strategic directions: sustainable progress, universal dignity, stability, and time to pursue life fulfillment.

We designed monetism as an alternative to capitalism, based on the two pillars of starting to create and inject permanent money for a UBI and for selected priorities and better managing inflation with a new agile taxation system, repurposed for tackling inflation instead of for fundraising purposes.

We looked at how different countries could choose different governance options, as well as what programs are worth printing money for and who can best design and maintain the system of counter-inflation taxes.

We also foresaw some risks from a shift to monetism that do not seem to be higher than the risks of changing too little too late. All major steps forward for society looked controversial or even crazy at the outset, including ideas such as abolishing slavery, universal suffrage, and gender and race parity.

We traced the cause of inertia in reforming capitalism both to some interest groups that might be opposed to monetism, but more importantly to limitations in the economics profession that would need a much more interdisciplinary and practical approach to guide policymakers into reforming society.

Ultimately, we proposed pragmatic steps and policies to gradually shift to monetism in four stages.

THE FROG MIGHT ACTUALLY
ESCAPE THE WARMING POT

Had I concluded this book before the COVID-19 crisis, my outlook would have actually been more pessimistic. The challenge of fighting a pandemic has brought back warstyle monetary policies whereby central banks have opened the tap and printed unprecedented sums of money, injecting them in whatever way their mandates allowed.

In the UK, the treasury was allowed a larger credit line at the Bank of England (BoE), whereby they can just spend money that will be created into existence by the BoE.[1] Other central banks kept more conventional distribution channels, buying government bonds or paying banks to take central banks' money under the condition that the money be lent and not stored as reserves. Some governments including the US are considering—or already started—issuing 100-year bonds, which, at such low interest rates, are close to being permanent money.[2]

This is actually a loose form of monetism. We can keep relying on obsolete mandates and accounting systems and on the discretion of central bankers, or we can put structure around the monetary system and define when central banks can create money and who they should give it to. Equally important is to shift from using money printing only after a crisis hits to using it to prevent one.

China seems to be experimenting more than Western economies. The People's Bank of China (PBOC) already adopted tools beyond interest rates to cope with the evolving macroeconomic context and will likely resort to monetism's tools when appropriate.[3] Chinese state-owned banks can already issue permanent bonds that the PBOC can convert to money, therefore a form of permanent money. And the PBOC is testing its central bank digital currency and a digital wallet for citizens. Maybe Chinese authorities will be reluctant to give UBI to people, and state-owned banks will misallocate loans as much or worse than privately owned banks would. But China has never been shy about experimenting with money, and this is what's important.

What we learn from evolution is that without mutations and trial and error, species won't be able to adapt to the changing environment and are more likely to go extinct.

My hope is that in the Western world as well, it will become clear that the world has changed and there are some societal challenges that we cannot just wait for the markets to fix. We can hope that the combined challenge of

COVID-19, poverty, inequality, and climate change will convince policymakers and institutions of the need of a system redesign, with some fresh thinking that extends beyond traditional economics.

There are many signs that the world is naturally moving from capitalism to monetism. Governments are spending more for welfare to protect those left behind. UBI pilots or partial implementation are springing up, including in Finland, the Netherlands, Stockton in California and several more cities across the US, Ontario in Canada, Kenya, India, and many more places. Quantitative easing programs are getting bigger and lasting longer, while interest rates have at times gone in negative territory, showing that debt is unsustainable.

After quantitative easing expanded the balance sheets of central banks and reduced the interest rates on government debts, many economists are less concerned about government debts. In a speech to the presidency of the American Economic Association, former IMF chief economist Olivier Blanchard argued that, given that interest rates are now much lower than nominal GDP growth, governments could easily afford more debt.[4]

This is the obvious consequence of central banks buying more government bonds, which is nothing more than a patch to capitalism that goes in the direction of implementing monetism in a reactive and uncoordinated way.

If we connect different papers written by IMF staff members, we could argue that monetism is becoming respectable even there. The IMF holds that inequality is limiting growth,[5] that a system using permanent money like the Chicago Plan would increase the stability of our economy,[6] that skyrocketing household debts are undermining future growth and stability,[7] and that limiting inflation is much less of a problem today.[8]

In May 2019, the UK Parliament declared a climate change emergency, a move similar to what I described as the definition of national priorities. In the meantime, head of the Bank of England Mark Carney has acknowledged that climate change will become a financial risk, and dozens of central banks have joined the Network for Greening the Financial System.[9] Not much has happened yet, but it looks like a promising start toward using money creation to fight climate change, one of the biggest wins of advocacy group Positive Money and one of the core recommendations of this book. The Biden administration has approved an unprecedented stimulus that includes one-off cash transfers but also some ongoing tax credits distributed as monthly cash transfers to each family with children.[10] This is not UBI, but we are moving toward it. Both Spain and New Zealand announced plans to move toward a four-day workweek, a good step to free up more time for nonpaid activities. We are slowly moving in the right direction.

But getting to monetism in this passive way may be incredibly painful, as we suffer through the uncertainty of our jobs and look to central banks to put patch after patch on our system.

This approach is fine for those well-off, including most policymakers: Take one step at a time and only if things go really south, try to jump two steps. But the risk appetite of the elites to reform society is much lower than that of most citizens, especially those unemployed, or at risk of losing their jobs and even their homes. It is important that institutions have some detachment from emotions and act rationally. But it's not rational to neglect the suffering that a pure reactive approach would cause. Working with equations that omit the human suffering component is an act of neglect that particularly traditional economists need to take responsibility for.

If policymakers don't want to reform as fast as people's overall need, then the only solution is for the well-off to pay the higher taxes whenever a crisis occurs. One cannot pretend to pull back the reins on socio-economic reforms and not pay the costs that inaction causes. Ultimately people's patience and resilience hit their limit, which historically did not end well for either society or the elites.

Getting sick every other year is painful, and if we treat the patient too late, they might die. Our planet takes a long time to respond to treatment; it is taking decades to close the ozone hole, for instance. No one knows the extent of unavoidable damage from climate change. Can we afford incrementalism? Monetism is the vaccine to avoid the pain and sickness altogether and we can take it before getting irremediably sick.

If there is something that you do not like about monetism, don't throw it all away. If you don't like UBI, we can still use permanent money to fund other priorities and reduce the dependency on debt and on the banking system. If you don't like the taxes I proposed, we can think of other taxes. At its core, monetism is a system that uses money creation to fix market failures. Beyond that, multiple variants can achieve this goal. This book does not claim to present the sole or ultimate solution, but it will hopefully strike a significant blow to the cage of capitalism, opening many minds to consider better ways of organizing society and giving a chance for the frog to escape from the slowly warming pot. If society doesn't start dismantling the cage of capitalism, we will end up like the fabled frog, not because we do not realize the danger but because we are constrained in our escape routes by the cage of capitalism.

It takes many studies, critiques, and debates to make societal change happen. I started writing this book thinking I was among one of the few linking the issues of inequality, capitalism, and a debt-based monetary system. Then I discovered hundreds of academics and other thinkers complaining about these topics. Modern Monetary Theory (MMT), while largely neglecting the role of banks in the economy and downplaying the risks of blank checks to governments, is as close as one can get to monetism. Proponents of MMT have already started to become mainstream and they advise senators and presidential candidates in the US. New York representative Alexandria Ocasio-Cortez helped popularize the Green New Deal in the US, an ambitious and expensive program to tackle climate change and other social issues, funded through either monetary finance or a 70% income tax on the ultra-rich. She fully understood the only two options to find the money to finance priority programs.

Maybe Trump's election could turn out to have been the shock bringing new energy into politics and economic reforms. The damage to the international reputation of the US, to international collaboration, and the social normalization of lying, ignorance, selfishness, intolerance, and narcissism—to name but a few—will likely outlast Trump. But those coming after him in the US and across the world could have the courage to truly transform our societies for the better.

We should all stay tuned and reengage in political life. The next few years could set in motion exciting changes for all of us.

WHAT CAN I DO?

Some of us might be able to directly impact or influence portions of our socio-economic system, and to these people I hope monetism has provided inspiration and food for thought. But no individual can ignite, let alone mobilize, the evolution of society beyond capitalism. I have felt completely powerless, seeing the challenges with my own eyes, yet unable to even recommend some of the changes I believe are needed. A single systemic reform can have negative consequences if not complemented with a holistic rethink. You have in your hands that holistic rethink, and now you know that society needs to and can evolve beyond capitalism. And the more people who know and talk about these possibilities, the sooner they become our reality.

And whether we like it or not, it is governments that have—to their merit—enabled capitalism to emerge and develop, and only the most senior government officials can ignite the next evolution of society toward monetism, or whatever better system we may be able to craft. These folks only react to contributions to their political campaign and to an overwhelming public opinion that demand this level of change. So I ask you to make this book yours—own it—and start engaging in new narratives that follow an #OutgrowingCapitalism logic rather than one of #FixingCapitalism.

You may also find the narrative of free-market capitalism pervading in most of the movements that might be closer to you. Winning over gender disparities must go past the narrative that it's just the free market that determines promotions, wages, and opportunities. That's capitalism at work again. It is unconscious human biases that reinforce and perpetuate gender disparities and the power of men in making these decisions. If we want to fix a preexisting power imbalance and bias, we need stronger policies than "letting the free market play its course, and if women are really equal then they'll ultimately be recognized as so with promotions and higher wages." The narrative in all these situations should be one that acknowledges that there are preexisting power dynamics and cognitive biases ingrained in people and the system and, therefore, the system must change. This is true for Black Lives Matter, Me Too, and the many movements that are trying to change power dynamics or ingrained biases in society.

Make this narrative yours: We need to rectify unbalanced power dynamics and correct ingrained biases in society. This is your answer to the notion that the free market and choice of individuals will lead to the best outcomes. This advertised freedom is only available to those with the power to make decisions and choices and is at odds with the lack of freedom of those impacted. Capitalism is not and has never been about freedom.

Change, however, always starts within ourselves, as individuals.

> "As a man changes his own nature, so does the attitude of the world change towards him. . . . We need not wait to see what others do."
>
> —Mahatma Gandhi

The first step to change is introspection in our own lives and acknowledging the values that drive us. It is far too easy to get trapped in the rat race and be mindlessly driven by the notion of success that has been defined for you by your peers, your parents, and even Hollywood. To escape, you need to orient your life toward your idea of success and separate this from the amount of money you make or what the Jones' are doing. Understand what you truly need—what constitutes enough—to live a fulfilled life, independent of what society thinks. And when you have enough money and are in Stage 2 (above the comfort threshold), look for a way to contribute to others or society at large and try to understand whether and why that pursuit gives you purpose. If it doesn't, learn from it and look for new priorities. By doing this, you will gain more clarity around your own life purpose and you'll likely be happier and more fulfilled. You will be successful, by your own definition.

CAN THE SYSTEM SHAPE PEOPLE OR DO PEOPLE SHAPE THE SYSTEM?

In October 2013, I embarked on a 10-day silent meditation retreat, an intense experience that happened to clarify my idea of living a life with purpose. Life for me has become an opportunity to better myself and become as selfless as one can be. I think individual selflessness is at the core of everything, especially a well-functioning society. That is not an easy task, though, and it is even harder for people below the comfort threshold.

It would take a whole new book to explain what lies beneath the previous paragraph, but the point I want to make is this: The basic reason I have written this book is not to fix economies but rather to overcome the obstacles that society imposes on citizens, obstacles that prevent them from becoming more selfless and pursuing a more purposeful life. Monetism is my response to these barriers.

Yet one might take the opposing view of the cause-effect relationship. One might claim that people's self-interest and lack of morality have crafted capitalism and caused society's issues, and not the other way around. People simply created the society that represents them and their values, and only by changing these values can we hope to create a more inclusive and compassionate society. It's because people are what they are that we are stuck with capitalism and unwilling to move forward to monetism.

If this view is right, a switch to monetism—or any newer system—would likely bring only temporary improvements, as when a chemical company introduces stronger pesticides or a security company designs a stronger firewall, pests will grow resistant to the new pesticides and cyberthieves will figure out how to crack the code again.

Even if monetism did give people a higher sense of security, more free time, and the opportunity to pursue happiness and life fulfillment, if people's values are misaligned with the new society, they won't put the extra freedom to good use. Instead of helping the neighbor or tackling other large societal issues, they'll turn against each other in an egocentric pursuit of supremacy.

While this pessimistic view of humankind is unfortunately the prevailing narrative, there is actually convincing evidence that morality, as an innate quality of humans, and cooperation have been major drivers of survival first and prosperity now. And there are multiple examples where the constraints of a system lead caring people to make unfair decisions, be that in courts, schools, organizations, or governments. As I review this chapter for the last time, I am actually stuck working for free during my unpaid leave and without health insurance in the middle of COVID-19. This unfair outcome has nothing to do with the many caring colleagues who have been helping with my transfer. It is only caused by the system, which in this case is a mix of migration laws and bureaucracy within my employer.

Yet we cannot dismiss this question: Is it a flawed system that constrains virtuous people or flawed people that shape a flawed system? The answer is probably that both are correct, and given traditional economics and capitalism have exalted and rewarded self-interest and dismissed morality, it is important we take direct action to develop virtuous people.

While parents and religious institutions nurture morals, some clear, shared values are desirable in all people in a society, independent of religious belief. For these, education could play a much larger role than it does today.

We develop our personality, morals, and social behavior in the years up through youth, and they become increasingly hard to change in adulthood. The right time to cultivate people's moral sense is in their first 20 years of life, and people spend much of this time at school.

Unfortunately, most education systems across the world are not concerned with morals. We have premised policy on the GDP—a suboptimal objective—so it's not surprising that we may have also built the education system on suboptimal premises. A shift to a more value-based education could be as important as everything else I have written in this book.

TOWARD VALUE-BASED EDUCATION

When Bhutan introduced Gross National Happiness (GNH) as its main objective, it also developed a new GNH school curriculum with subjects like mindfulness, empathy, self-awareness, coping with emotions, communication, interpersonal relationships, creative thinking, critical thinking, decision-making, and problem-solving. Such courses increased children's well-being *and* their academic achievements.[11]

If with monetism we also shift to a sustainable and universal well-being as a societal objective, we should also upgrade our education system.

The concept of value-based education (VBE) is actually being tested and studied. At the West Kidlington School in the UK, VBE programs have had a positive impact on all educational measures, including academic achievement. This result occurred despite the fact that the population under study had traditionally underperformed at school. Emotional stability was another benefit, together with greater awareness of the wider community.[12]

In Australia, the federal government launched a values education program in 2003 and expanded it, reaching 100,000 students and 10,000 teachers between 2005 and 2010. Benefits included improved student learning, happier teachers and students, a calmer school, more academic diligence, increased attentiveness, a greater capacity to work both independently and more cooperatively, and, finally, improved student well-being.[13]

The International Baccalaureate (IB) now counts millions of alumni and more than 5,000 schools in more than 150 countries and, although not explicitly a "value-based" education system, among the attributes of the children they aim to develop you can find *caring, principled, reflective, open-minded,* and *balanced.*[14] These attitudes and values would go a long way in developing better people for a better future.

These education models often cost more, but in line with monetism's principles, education should receive more money because we can't compromise with universal access to high-quality education.

We need to change our economic system to one that gets all people above the comfort threshold, but we also need to create an education system that helps each individual become more self-aware and caring so that they can make the most of their time, fulfill their lives, and contribute to reshaping society.

Pursuing these two goals will be my way of living a fulfilling life. What is your way going to be?

Acknowledgments

There are three groups of people I need to sincerely thank from the bottom of my heart. Without these people, this book would not have been possible.

The first group includes all the researchers, journalists, activists, think tanks, and institutions that have funded the incredible body of research on which this book is based. *Outgrowing Capitalism* has no primary research because so much already exists out there. Thank you for all your hard work that allowed me to dive in, digest, and leverage your learnings.

The second group includes my friends and family near and far who nudged me along, offered encouragement, and supported me throughout this process. They came with brutally honest feedback and suggestions on the title, storyline, and cover design. Again. And again. Special thanks to my sister, Laura, for obliging my numerous requests for images; although in the end I only used a couple.

The third group includes all those who went through the entire manuscript at some point during its seven-year evolution and contributed to progressing the content or style. To Howard Tomb who held the mirror up to me and told me I was too Italian and needed a ghostwriter if I wanted the book to go anywhere; to Dan McNeill who convinced me to completely rewrite the storyline and then proceeded to help rewrite the book, cover to cover, and made the narrative more suitable for the non-technical audience; to Antonio Fatas who read and reread multiple versions and helped me understand and connect to the debates in economics relevant to *Outgrowing Capitalism*; to Rik Kirkland who nudged me for the final round of significant changes in response to the COVID-19 pandemic and to radically change the ending; to Sven Smith who helped reframe my thinking in certain parts and encouraged me to look into Kuhnian scientific revolutions; to Jonathan De Jonck and Peter Gout for commenting on every other page of the manuscript and saving me from some Kafkian analogies; to Dina Badawy and my publicity team at Finn Partners who helped share my work with the world; to the Greenleaf and Fast Company Press teams who put this book in your hands.

A heartfelt expression of gratitude to my dad, Maurizio, who relearned English so that he could read a very early (and very mediocre!) manuscript, and, despite this, continued to encourage me to pursue my writing.

And to my partner, Kristie, who listened to me talk about this book longer than any human should have to listen to another, edited parts of the manuscript along with various articles along the way, tolerated my busy evenings and weekends, and kindly forced me to do everything I could to make this book a success.

Thank you for your faith in this book and in me.

Notes

Introduction: You Think Society Is in Danger and Then You Get Donald Trump

1. Defined in America as people below the poverty line, which was about 13,000 USD a year for an individual and 25,000 USD for a family of four, in 2018 BLS Reports, "A Profile of the Working Poor, 2018," US Bureau of Labor Statistics, July 2020, https://www.bls.gov/opub/reports/working-poor/2018/home.htm#technical-notes

2. Lane Kenworthy and Ive Marx, "Discussion Paper Series: In-Work Poverty in the United States," IZA Institute of Labor Economics, March 2017, http://ftp.iza.org/dp10638.pdf

3. Cameron Huddleston, "Survey: 69% of Americans Have Less Than $1,000 in Savings," GoBankingRates, December 16, 2019, https://www.gobankingrates.com/saving-money/savings-advice/americans-have-less-than-1000-in-savings/

4. US Department of Education, National Center for Education Statistics, "Tuition Costs of Colleges and Universities," *Digest of Education Statistics*, 2019, https://nces.ed.gov/fastfacts/display.asp?id=76. Reference to four-year-college cost in 2017–18, multiplied by the four years.

5. Carl Benedikt Frey and Michael Osborne, "The Future of Employment: How Susceptible Are Jobs to Computerisation?" University of Oxford, September 17, 2013. https://www.oxfordmartin.ox.ac.uk/downloads/academic/The_Future_of_Employment.pdf

6. Martin Ford, *The Rise of the Robots: Technology and the Threat of a Jobless Future*. 2015.

7. Thomas Piketty, *Capital in the Twenty-First Century*. 2013.

8. Richard Wilkinson and Kate Pickett, *The Spirit Level: Why Equality Is Better for Everyone*, 2009.

9. Daniel G. Huber and Jay Gulledge, "Extreme Weather and Climate Change: Understanding the Link and Managing the Risk," Center for Climate and Energy Solutions, December 2011.

10. That's just a parable. Dropped in boiling water frogs die, and heated slowly from cool water they get more frantic in attempts to escape. See Karl S. Kruszelnicki, "Frog Fable Brought to a Boil," *Conservation*, March 3, 2011, http://www.conservationmagazine.org/2011/03/frog-fable-brought-to-boil/

11. Coral Davenport, "Major Climate Report Describes a Strong Risk of Crisis as Early As 2040," *The New York Times*, October 7, 2018.

12. Julian Robinson, "The Horrifying Human Zoos: Shocking Photos Reveal How Zoos Around the World Kept 'Primitive Natives' in Enclosures as Westerners Gawped and Jeered at Them Just 60 Years Ago," *Daily Mail*, March 2017.

13. Anne Trafton, "How the Brain Controls Our Habits: MIT Neuroscientists Identify a Brain Region That Can Switch Between New and Old Habits," MIT News Office, October 2012.

14. Since the fall of the gold standard, the quantity and value of money are not dependent on the quantity and value of gold. The book will later discuss the consequences of the fall of the gold standard.

15. Mervyn King, *The End of Alchemy: Money, Banking and the Future of the Global Economy*, March 2016.

16. "A Conversation with Lord Adair Turner," Private Debt Project, http://privatedebtproject.org/view-articles.php?An-Interview-With-Lord-Adair-Turner-6

17. Rutger Bregman, *Utopia for Realists: How We Can Build the Ideal World*, 2017.

I. WELL-BEING

Chapter 1: Two Happy Marriages, Seven Satisfying Jobs, and One Fulfilled Life, Please

1. Most of this section draws from multiple studies summarized in the book International Differences in Well-Being, 2010.

2. Ed Diener, Daniel Khaneman, William Tov, and Raksha Arora, "Income's Association with Judgements of Life Versus Feelings," chapter 1, *International Differences in Well-Being*, 2010.

3. The next four in order were: "I wish I hadn't worked so hard," "I wish I'd had the courage to express my true feelings," "I wish I had stayed in touch with my friends," and "I wish I had let myself be happier." Bronnie Ware, *The Top Five Regrets of the Dying: A Life Transformed by the Dearly Departing*, May 2012.

4. Individual studies are often inconclusive and partially influenced by the ideas of the author. I will try to be as objective as possible, consider many studies available, and give you the gist of the final answer.

5. "Volunteering in the United States—2015," US Bureau of Labor Statistics, February 25, 2016, https://www.bls.gov/news.release/pdf/volun.pdf

6. James K. Harter and Raksha Arora, "The Impact of Time Spent Working and Job Fit on Well-Being Around the World," chapter 13, *International Differences in Well-Being*.

7. Bronnie Ware, *The Top Five Regrets of the Dying: A Life Transformed by the Dearly Departing*.

8. Brent D. Rosso, Kathryn H. Dekas, and Amy Wrzesniewski, "On the Meaning of Work: A Theoretical Integration and Review," *Research in Organizational Behavior*, vol. 30, October 2010, pp. 91–127.

9. efinancialcareers white paper, June 2014.

10. Joe Pinsker, "Which Jobs Have the Highest Rates of Depression? Give That Bus Driver a Hug," *The Atlantic*, December 22, 2014.

11. "Global Talent Monitor Report," CEB, www.cebglobal.com/human-resources/global-workforce-insight-report.html.

12. "Global Talent Monitor Report," CEB, www.cebglobal.com/human-resources/global-workforce-insight-report.html.

13. The Indeed Job Happiness Index 2016: Ranking the World for Employee Satisfaction. http://blog.indeed.com/hiring-lab/indeed-job-happiness-index-2016/

14. "Careerbuilder 2014 Survey," http://www.careerbuilder.com/share/aboutus/pressreleasesdetail.aspx?ed=12%2F31%2F2014&id=pr797&sd=1%2F9%2F2014

15. "Workplace Survey American Psychological Association Harris Interactive," March 2012.

16. Michael Lewis, *The Fifth Risk*, 2018, p. 106.

17. Vincent S. Flowers and Charles L. Hughes, "Why Employees Stay," *Harvard Business Review*, July 1973.

18. "Job Mobility in the European Union: Optimising its Social and Economic Benefits," Danish Technological Institute, final report, 2008.

19. John F. Helliwell and Shawn Grover, "How's Life at Home? New Evidence on Marriage and the Set Point for Happiness," National Bureau of Economic Research, December 2014.

20. Alois Stutzer and Bruno S. Frey, "Does Marriage Make People Happy, or Do Happy People Get Married?" *The Journal of Socio-Economics*, vol. 35, issue 2, April 2006, pp. 326–347.

21. Bella DePaulo, *Singled Out: How Singles Are Stereotyped, Stigmatized, and Ignored, and Still Live Happily Ever After*, October 2007.

22. Paul R. Amato, "The Consequences of Divorce for Adults and Children," *Journal of Marriage & the Family*, 2000.

23. Xenia P. Montenegro, "A Study of Divorce at Midlife and Beyond," *AARP The Magazine*, May 2004.

24. Todd K. Shackelford, David P. Schmitt, and David M. Buss, "Universal Dimensions of Human Mate Preferences," *Personality and Individual Differences*, vol. 39, issue 2, 2005, pp. 447–458.

25. "Marriage and Divorce Statistics," Eurostat.

26. Pamela Engel, "MAP: Divorce Rates Around The World," *Business Insider*, May 25, 2014.

27. Andrew Francis-Tan and Hugo M. Mialon, "'A Diamond Is Forever' and Other Fairy Tales: The Relationship Between Wedding Expenses and Marriage Duration," SSRN, September 15, 2014.

28. Jeffrey Dew, "Bank On It: Thrifty Couples are the Happiest," The State of Our Unions, 2009.

29. Lauren M. Papp, E. Mark Cummings, and Marcie C. Goeke-Morey, "For Richer, for Poorer: Money as a Topic of Marital Conflict in the Home," *Family Relations*, vol. 58, issue 1 (2009): 91–103.

30. Sonya Britt, John E. Grable, Briana S. Nelson Goff, and Mark White, "The Influence of Perceived Spending Behaviors on Relationship Satisfaction," *JFCP Research Journal*, vol. 19, issue 1, 2008.

31. Jeffrey Dew, "Bank On It: Thrifty Couples Are the Happiest," The State of Our Unions, 2009.

32. Paul R. Amato and Stacey J. Rogers, "A Longitudinal Study of Marital Problems and Subsequent Divorce," *Journal of Marriage and the Family*, 1997.

33. Chrisanna Northrup, Pepper Schwartz, and James Witte, *The Normal Bar: The Surprising Secrets of Happy Couples and What They Reveal about Creating a New Normal in Your Relationship*, January 2014.

34. For stats on women in marriage, see: Fawn Weaver, *Happy Wives Club: One Woman's Worldwide Search for the Secrets of a Great Marriage*, 2010. For stats on money in marriage, see: "Top 10 Qualities We Look for in a Lover (Plus 10 Things We Don't Care About)," October 2012. Based on a survey of 700,000 users of eHarmony. Also: Thomas R. Lee, "Factors That Make a Difference in Marital Success," Utah State University, 2001.

35. Fredric Neuman, "Why People in a Bad Marriage Stay Married: At Least, the Reasons They Give for Staying Married," *Psychology Today*, July 13, 2014.

36. Brittany Wong, "The Top 10 Reasons People Stay In Unhappy Marriages," *Huffington Post*, updated December 6, 2017.

37. Carol L. Graham and Stefano Pettinato, *Happiness and Hardship: Opportunity and Insecurity in New Market Economies*, December 2001.

38. A linear scale is simply 1, 2, 3, 4, and so on. A logarithmic scale is exponential, and instead we might see 2, 4, 8, 16. The sequence is 2, then 2 squared, then 2 cubed, and so on. You can see how it expands the scale. The Richter earthquake scale is logarithmic, as is the pH scale in chemistry.

39. Carol Graham, Soumya Chattopadhyay, and Mario Picon, "The Easterlin and Other Paradoxes: Why Both Sides of the Debate May Be Correct," chapter 9, *International Differences in Well-Being*, 2010.

40. Angus Deaton Income, "Health and Well-Being Around the World: Evidence from the Gallup World Poll," *Journal of Economic Perspectives*, 2008.

41. Example: Two sets of numbers might both average out to 50. But if one had numbers between 1 to 100 and the other between 45 and 55, the first would have more variance.

42. Richard Layard, Guy Mayraz, and Stephen Nickell, "Does Relative Income Matter? Are the Critics Right?" chapter 6, *International Differences in Well-Being*, 2010.

43. Ruut Veenhoven, "How Universal Is Well-Being?" chapter 11, *International Differences in Well-Being*, 2010.

44. John F. Heliwell, Chris Barrington-Leigh, Anthony Harris, and Haifang Huang, "International Evidence on the Social Context of Well-Being," chapter 10, *International Differences in Well-Being*, 2010.

45. Ronald F. Inglehart, "Faith and Freedom: Traditional and Modern Ways to Happiness," chapter 12, *International Differences in Well-Being*, 2010.

46. Ed Diener, Daniel Khaneman, William Tov, and Raksha Arora, "Income's Association with Judgments of Life Versus Feelings," chapter 1, *International Differences in Well-Being*, 2010.

47. This distinction especially stands out when measuring life satisfaction with the tool called the Cantril Ladder, which leads people to compare their situation to others.

48. Ed Diener, Daniel Kahneman, William Tov, and Raksha Arora, "Income's Association with Judgments of Life Versus Feelings," chapter 1, *International Differences in Well-Being*, 2010.

49. Daniel Kahneman and Angus Deaton, "High Income Improves Evaluation of Life But Not Emotional Well-Being," Center for Health and Well-Being, Princeton University, 2010.

50. Lindsey Fendt, "Why Costa Rica Is One of the Happiest Countries in the World," *Huffington Post*, September 6, 2018, https://www.huffpost.com/entry/costa-rica-happiness-well-being_n_5b6184a8e4b0de86f49c7611

51. Daniel Gilbert, *Stumbling on Happiness*, 2006.

52. Among the low-income countries, those with higher income have citizens who are, on average, more satisfied with their lives than citizens of lower-income countries.

53. Richard A. Easterlin, "Does Economic Growth Improve the Human Lot?" in *Nations and Households in Economic Growth: Essays in Honor of Moses Abramovitz*, 1974.

54. Betsey Stevenson and Justin Wolfers. "Economic Growth and Subjective Well-Being: Reassessing the Easterlin Paradox," Brookings papers on economic activity, 2008.

55. Richard Wilkinson and Kate Pickett, *The Spirit Level: Why Equality Is Better for Everyone*, 2009.

56. Richard Layard, Guy Mayraz, and Stephen Nickell, "Does Relative Income Matter? Are the Critics Right?" chapter 6, *International Differences in Well-Being*, 2010.

57. Absolute income has a coefficient of 0.6 for predicting well-being, but if relative income is included, its coefficient is 0.69 and the absolute income coefficient becomes negative.

58. Rafael Di Tella and Robert MacCulloch, "Happiness Adaptation to Income Beyond "Basic Needs," chapter 8, *International Differences in Well-Being*, 2010.

59. Richard Layard, Guy Mayraz, and Stephen Nickell, "Does Relative Income Matter? Are the Critics Right?" chapter 6, *International Differences in Well-Being*, 2010.

60. http://www.lifetothefullest.abbott/

61. Matthew 19:24.

62. Luke 10:35.

63. Buddhist Cultural Centre, Sri Lanka, http://www.lanka.net/bcc/

64. The Qur'an 261 (translated by Al Baqarah).

65. The Qur'an 92 (translated by Aal Imraan).

66. John F. Heliwell, Chris Barrington-Leigh, Anthony Harris, and Haifang Huang, "International Evidence on the Social Context of Well-Being," chapter 10, *International Differences in Well-Being*, 2010.

Chapter 2: Gazing Up at the Comfort Threshold

1. Saul McLeod, "Maslow's Hierarchy of Needs," *Simply Psychology*, December 29, 2020, https://www.simplypsychology.org/maslow.html

2. Abraham Maslow, *Motivation and Personality*, 1954.

3. Abraham Maslow, "Critique of Self-Actualization Theory," *The Journal of Humanistic Counseling*, 29, no. 3 (1991): 98–126.

4. My uncle has more or less successfully lived for some time by fishing and bartering using smoked trout—but do not try this at home.

5. "Poverty Rate," OECD Data, https://data.oecd.org/inequality/poverty-rate.htm, accessed on November 13th 2020.

6. Geoffrey Gertz and Homi Kharas, "Beyond Neoliberalism: Insights from Emerging Markets," Global Economy and Development at Brookings, April 2019.

7. Taylor Tepper, "Most Americans Don't Have Enough Savings to Cover a $1K Emergency," Bankrate, January 18, 2018, https://www.bankrate.com/banking/savings/financial-security-0118/

8. Chris Weller, "28% of Americans Say They Couldn't Handle an Emergency Expense of Just $10," *Business Insider*, May 17, 2017, https://www.businessinsider.com/personal-finance/emergency-expenses-work-survey-2017-5?r=US&IR=T

9. James Rufus Koren, "Most Americans Aren't Financially Healthy Despite Booming Economy, Survey Finds," *Los Angeles Times*, November 2, 2018.\, http://www.latimes.com/business/la-fi-financial-pulse-20181101-story.html

10. "Report on the Economic Well-Being of U.S. Households in 2017," Board of Directors of the Federal Reserve System, May 2018.

11. "One in Three People Unable to Face Unexpected Financial Expenses," Eurostat, May 5, 2020, https://ec.europa.eu/eurostat/web/products-eurostat-news/-/DDN-20200505-1?inheritRedirect=true#:~:text=In%20the%20European%20Union%20(EU,or%20a%20car%20in%202019

12. Sheldon Danziger, Koji Chavez, and Erin Cumberworth, "Poverty and the Great Recession," The Russell Sage Foundation and The Stanford Center on Poverty and Inequality, October 2012.

13. Shu-Sen Chang et al., "Impact of 2008 Global Economic Crisis on Suicide: Time Trend Study in 54 Countries," *British Medical Journal*, September 2013.

Chapter 3: Universal Basic Income: Too Good to Be True?

1. Whenever these services are not provided for free by the government.

2. Philippe Van Parijs and Yannick Vanderborght, *Basic Income: A Radical Proposal for a Free Society and a Sane Economy*, March 2017.

3. Chris Weller, "Iran Introduces a Basic Income Scheme, and Something Strange Happened," World Economic Forum, May 31, 2017, https://www.weforum.org/agenda/2017/05/iran-introduced-a-basic-income-scheme-and-something-strange-happened/

4. Rutger Bregman, *Utopia for Realists: How We Can Build the Ideal World*, March 2017.

5. Van Parijs and Vanderborght, *Basic Income: A Radical Proposal for a Free Society and a Sane Economy*.

6. Ioana Marinescu, "No Strings Attached: The Behavioral Effects of US Unconditional Cash Transfer Programs," Roosevelt Institute, May 2017, http://rooseveltinstitute.org/no-strings-attached/

7. NIT transfers money to the unemployed or those with income below a certain threshold, defining the income levels at which the benefits decrease. Like UBI, an NIT guarantees a basic income while maintaining the incentive to gain more money through work, at any income level. NIT differs from UBI: People get the cash transfer at the end of the month rather than the start, and NIT is like UBI but with an implicit tax equivalent to the cash transfer on people with an income above a certain threshold. A UBI program and a change of income tax rates could be made equivalent to a NIT.

8. Scott Santens in "What is There to Learn From Finland's Basic Income Experiment? Did It Succeed or Fail?" offers a good analysis to understand the preliminary results.

9. The first year of the pilot shows small but non-statistically significant increases while the second year shows small and statistically significant increases, but some changes in active labor market policies may or may not have affected the results. Either way, the impact was marginal and not in the direction of lower working hours. https://julkaisut.valtioneuvosto.fi/bitstream/handle/10024/162219/STM_2020_15_rap.pdf?sequence=1&isAllowed=y. For an assessment of the final results of the Finland UBI in English see https://www.mckinsey.com/industries/public-and-social-sector/our-insights/an-experiment-to-inform-universal-basic-income

10. Up to $48,000 a year in 2013 USD, for a family of four. See Ioana Marinescu, "No Strings Attached: The Behavioral Effects of U.S. Unconditional Cash Transfer Programs," Roosevelt Institute, May 2017, http://rooseveltinstitute.org/no-strings-attached/

11. Louis Doré, "Finland Is Giving Each Citizen a Universal Basic Income and It's Changing Lives," *Independent*, February 14, 2018.

12. Axel Marx and Hans Peeters, "Win For Life: An Empirical Exploration of the Social Consequences of Introducing a Basic Income," http://www.compasss.org/wpseries/MarxPeeters2004.pdf

13. See the report from the Overseas Development Institute reviewing more than 200 cash transfer programs in developing countries. Report available at https://www.odi.org/sites/odi.org.uk/files/resource-documents/11316.pdf

14. "Increasing Maize Productivity and Food Security in Swaziland," Technoserve, Swaziland, 2013.

15. "Pilot Project," 2020, http://www.bignam.org/BIG_pilot.html

16. Francesca Bastagli, Jessica Hagen-Zanker, Valentina Barca, Ranja Schmidt, Luke Harman, and Georgina Sturge, "Cash Transfers: What Does the Evidence Say? A Rigorous Review of Programme Impact and of the Role of Design and Implementation Features," Overseas Development Institute, July 2016.

17. "A Growing Number of People Think Their Job Is Useless. Time to Rethink the Meaning of Work," QS Global Education News, February 22, 2018.

18. Ioana Marinescu, "No Strings Attached: The Behavioral Effects of US Unconditional Cash Transfer Programs," Roosevelt Institute, May 2017, http://rooseveltinstitute.org/no-strings-attached/

19. Rutger Bregman, Utopia for Realists: How We Can Build the Ideal World, March 2017. See also evidence collected by the World Bank: Sudhanshu Handa et al., "Myth-Busting? Confronting Six Common Perceptions about Unconditional Cash Transfers as a Poverty Reduction Strategy in Africa," October 2018, and by Think Tank OBI: Francesca Bastagli et al., "Cash Transfers: What Does the Evidence Say? A Rigorous Review of Impacts and the Role of Design and Implementation Features," July 2016.

20. Mariana Mazzucato, The Entrepreneurial State: Debunking Public vs. Private Sector Myths, 2013, https://marianamazzucato.com/entrepreneurial-state/

21. Martin Ford, The Rise of the Robots: Technology and the Threat of a Jobless Future, 2015.

22. Linda T. Kohn, Janet M. Corrigan, and Molla S. Donaldson, "To Err is Human: Building a Safer Health System," Institute of Medicine, November 1999, http://www.nationalacademies.org/hmd/~/media/Files/Report%20Files/1999/To-Err-is-Human/To%20Err%20is%20Human%201999%20%20report%20brief.pdf

23. Ford, The Rise of the Robots: Technology and the Threat of a Jobless Future.

24. A partial UBI is typically referred to as an unconditional cash transfer of an amount not sufficient to cover basic needs.

25. Jessica Wiederspan, Elizabeth Rhodes, and H. Luke Shaefer, "Expanding the Discourse on Antipoverty Policy: Reconsidering a Negative Income Tax," Journal of Poverty, vol. 19, issue 2, February 2015, pp. 218–238.

26. Michalis Nikiforos, Marshall Steinbaum, and Gennaro Zezza, "Modeling the Macroeconomic Effects of a Universal Basic Income," The Roosevelt Institute, August 29, 2017.

27. Van Parijs and Vanderborght, Basic Income: A Radical Proposal for a Free Society and a Sane Economy.

28. IMF Fiscal Monitor, Tackling Inequality, October 2017.

29. Andrew G. Berg and Jonathan D. Ostry, "Inequality and Unsustainable Growth: Two Sides of the Same Coin?" IMF staff discussion note, 2011.

30. OECD, "In It Together: Why Less Inequality Benefits All," 2015, http://dx.doi.org/10.1787/9789264235120-en

31. Joseph Stiglitz, The Price of Inequality: How Today's Divided Society Endangers our Future, 2014.

32. "Overhaul Tax for the 21st Century," The Economist, August 11, 2018.

33. Referring to the study from Djavad Salehi-Isfahani and Mohammad H. Mostafavi-Dehzooei. "Cash Transfers and Labor Supply: Evidence from a Large-Scale Program in Iran," Journal of Development Economics, Elsevier, vol. 135(C), pp. 349–367.

34. David Autor Anna Salomons, "Is Automation Labor-Displacing? Productivity Growth, Employment, and the Labor Share," National Bureau of Economic Research, August 2018.

35. John Lanchester, "After the Fall: John Lanchester on the Decade of Doom That Followed the 2008 Financial Crash," The Times, September 8, 2018.

36. Salehi-Isfahani and Mostafavi-Dehzooei, 2018. "Cash Transfers and Labor Supply: Evidence from a Large-Scale Program in Iran."

37. Frederic Laloux, *Reinventing Organizations*, 2016.

38. John Vidal, "The Tribes Paying the Brutal Price of Conservation," *The Guardian*, August 28, 2016.

Chapter 4: Funding UBI in a Globalized and Unequal World: Piketty's Dilemma

1. Thomas Piketty, *Capital in the Twenty-First Century,* April 2014.

2. Thomas Piketty, *Capital in the Twenty-First Century.*

3. Richard Wilkinson and Kate Pickett, *The Spirit Level: Why Equality Is Better for Everyone*, 2009.

4. There are other issues linked to wealth concentration that I will cover later when speaking of the flaws of capitalism. For example, if wealth can buy elections or skew the decisions of policymakers, wealth concentration is a problem per se.

5. David Fine, James Manyika, Pal Erik Sjatil, Karim Tadjeddine, Tilman Tacke, and Maggie Desmond, "Inequality: A Persisting Challenge and Its Implications," McKinsey Global Institute, June 26, 2019, https://www.mckinsey.com/industries/public-and-social-sector/our-insights/inequality-a-persisting-challenge-and-its-implications

6. Thomas Piketty, *Capital in the Twenty-First Century.*

7. Thomas Piketty, *Capital in the Twenty-First Century.*

8. "US Federal Individual Income Tax Rates History, 1862–2013 (Nominal and Inflation-Adjusted Brackets), Tax Foundation, October 17, 2013, https://taxfoundation.org/us-federal-individual-income-tax-rates-history-1913-2013-nominal-and-inflation-adjusted-brackets/

9. Thomas Piketty, *Capital in the Twenty-First Century.*

10. Annette Alstadsæter, Niels Johannesen, and Gabriel Zucman, "Who Owns the Wealth in Tax Havens? Macro Evidence and Implications for Global Inequality," National Bureau of Economic Research, September 2017.

11. According to IMF, 17 countries in the G20 have reduced corporate tax rates since the mid-1990s, lowering the average from about 35% to 26%, https://www.imf.org/external/np/g20/pdf/2018/031518.pdf

12. Tony Czuczka, "IMF Warns Trump's Tax Overhaul Could Fuel a Global 'Race to the Bottom," Bloomberg, February 2018.

13. Thomas Piketty, *Capital in the Twenty-First Century.*

14. Idle as in "no one cared to put it to use and therefore no one is benefitting." Land consciously dedicated to conservation purposes is not idle, but a third home in California not rented and empty for 350 days a year is idle, as well as land that landowners do not have time to rent out, sell, or develop.

15. Winston S. Churchill. "The Mother of All Monopolies," 1909, https://www.cooperative-individualism.org/churchill-winston_mother-of-all-monopolies-1909.htm

16. He assumes a 0% tax rate for wealth below one million euros, 0.5% between one and five million euros, and 2% for wealth above five million euros. Thomas Piketty, *Capital in the Twenty-First Century*, April 2014.

17. Bob Lord and Chuck Collins, "Opinion: Donald Trump's Abuse of the Conservation Easement Tax Loophole Shows How the Tax Code Favors the Ultrarich," MarketWatch, October 21,2020, https://www.marketwatch.com/story/donald-trumps-abuse-of-the-conservation-easement-tax-loophole-shows-how-the-tax-code-favors-the-ultrarich-11603301585

18. "Macron Slashes France's Wealth Tax in Pro-Business Budget," *Financial Times*, October 24, 2017, https://www.ft.com/content/3d907582-b893-11e7-9bfb-4a9c83ffa852; Iven De Hoon, "France Wants Back Its Rich People," No More Tax, https://nomoretax.eu/france-wants-back-rich-people/

19. "Debt % of GDP," International Monetary Fund, http://www.imf.org/external/datamapper/DEBT1@DEBT/ADVEC/FAD_G20Adv

20. "Life Expectancy and Healthy Life Expectancy Data by Country," World Health Organization, http://apps.who.int/gho/data/node.main.688?lang=en

II. MONEY

Chapter 5: The Tennis Game of Money

1. David Clarke, "Poll Shows 85% of MPs Don't Know Where Money Comes From," PositiveMoney, October 26, 2017.

2. In his book, *Debt: The First 5,000 Years*, anthropologist David Graeber traces the origin of money and its use across most times as credit, people keeping tabs on each other. Governments invented money to pay soldiers for war and later collect taxes from citizens of conquered lands.

3. Richard Nixon, "Address to the Nation Outlining a New Economic Policy: "The Challenge of Peace," August 15, 1971. Online by Gerhard Peters and John T. Woolley, The American Presidency Project.

4. Robert L. Hetze, "Germany Monetary History in the First Half of the Twentieth Century," *Federal Reserve Bank of Richmond Economic Quarterly*, vol. 88, issue 1, Winter 2002.

5. C. N. Trueman, "Hyperinflation and Weimar Germany," The History Learning Site, May 22, 2015, https://www.historylearningsite.co.uk/modern-world-history-1918-to-1980/weimar-germany/hyperinflation-and-weimar-germany/

6. Robert L. Hetzel, "German Monetary History in the First Half of the Twentieth Century."

7. This is true depending on the definition of money. If we define money as M0 (physical currency and coins in circulation) or M1 (M0 plus demand deposits and checkable accounts easily converted into cash), then the velocity of money can grow significantly, thanks to bank activity creating deposits and credit. If we define money as M2, which

includes banks' deposits and credit, then the velocity cannot grow indefinitely. When I talk of money, unless specified, I'm talking about M2.

8. Richard J Evans, *The Third Reich in Power*, 1933–1939, 2005.

9. Roger Lowenstein, "The Nixon Shock," *Bloomberg Businessweek*, August 4, 2011.

10. Falling prices ignite a chain of issues: Producers cannot easily reduce their cost of goods and especially the wages they pay employees, except by firing them and hiring new (cheaper) ones, which would entail retraining, mistakes, lost productivity, and many other costs. Many companies would lose money and shut down, causing more unemployment, which would further depress spending, prices, and production. It is impossible to grow an economy with decreasing prices.

11. Mervyn King, *The End of Alchemy: Money, Banking, and the Future of the Global Economy*, p.76.

12. Allyn Young, "The Mystery of Money," *The Book of Popular Science*, The Grolier Society, 1924, revised 1929.

13. Kenneth J. Robinson, "Depository Institutions Deregulation and Monetary Control Act of 1980, Federal Reserve History, March 1980, https://www.federalreservehistory.org/essays/monetary-control-act-of-1980

Chapter 6: How Money and Banks Work Today

1. Werner, R, "Can Banks Individually Create Money Out of Nothing? The Theories and the Empirical Evidence," *International Review of Financial Analysis*, 2014.

2. Mervyn King, *The End of Alchemy: Money, Banking and the Future of the Global Economy*, March 2016.

3. Mervyn King, *The End of Alchemy: Money, Banking and the Future of the Global Economy*. After the 2008 crisis, central banks' monetary easing has reduced this ratio in most countries but commercial banks' deposits still form the vast majority of the money supply.

4. Technology would be part of both capital and entrepreneurship and given knowledge and technology are today more important than capital, I want to change the terminology as well.

5. How do GDP and GNI differ? The latter includes the balance of transfers of interests and dividends. The difference is typically negligible, with notable exceptions like Ireland, which thanks to a favorable corporate tax, has had a GDP much higher than GNI, since companies with headquarters in Ireland distribute their profits to shareholders outside the country. Technically, they are producing in the country, but citizens of Ireland receive little income from this activity.

6. The author acknowledges and supports homosexual relationships, but since the majority of people have a mother and a father, the author assigned roles this way.

7. For instance, the shareholders of the Central Bank of Italy have historically been other commercial banks, whose shareholders are private individuals.

8. Central banks make money through the interest on money they lend to other banks or their gain from purchasing interest-bearing assets like government bonds.

9. In Italy in 2015, for example, private shareholders received dividends of 340 million euros, while the government received 3.17 billion euros.

10. Andrew Jackson and Ben Dyson, "Modernising Money: Why Our Monetary System Is Broken and How It Can Be Fixed," PositiveMoney, 2012.

11. Central banks can set the rate at which banks can borrow money from other central banks, and they can purchase and sell assets to influence the interest rates at which banks lend money to each other.

12. With a higher margin, banks can afford more borrowers defaulting and still be profitable

Chapter 7: The Unsolved Money Puzzle

1. Mohamed A. El-Erian, *The Only Game in Town*, 2017, p. 42.

2. "Federal Open Market Committee," the group of 12 that makes decisions about interest rates and the money supply.

3. Mohamed A. El-Erian, *The Only Game in Town*, p. 42.

4. Mervyn King, *The End of Alchemy*, 2016, p. 86.

5. Josh Ryan-Collins, Tony Greenham, Richard Werner, and Andrew Jackson, *Where Does Money Come From?*, 2011, p. 23.

6. Jonathan Quick and Bronwyn Fryer, *The End of Epidemics*, 2018, p, 199.

7. Ajita Atreya, Susana Ferreira, and Erwann Michel-Kerjan, "What Drives Households to Buy Flood Insurance? Evidence from Georgia," *Ecological Economics*, vol. 117, September 2015, pp. 153–161, https://repository.upenn.edu/cgi/viewcontent.cgi?article=1359&context=fnce_papers

8. Luigi Zingales, *A Capitalism for the People*, 2013.

9. Justin Fox, "How Shareholders Are Ruining American Business," *The Atlantic*, July/August 2013, https://www.theatlantic.com/magazine/archive/2013/07/stop-spoiling-the-shareholders/309381/. See, e.g., Andrea Beltratti and Rene M. Stulz, "Why Did Some Banks Perform Better During the Credit Crisis?" European Corporate Governance Institute, July 2009, http://citeseerx.ist.psu.edu/viewdoc/download?doi=10.1.1.464.5022&rep=rep1&type=pdf

10. Government Accountability Office, "Financial Regulatory Reform: Financial Crisis Losses and Potential Impacts of the Dodd-Frank Act," January 2013.

11. Colin Roche, Kenneth Haar, and Stan Jourdan, "ECB Cash Injections for Polluters Must Stop, 70 NGOs Demand," Corporate Europe Observatory, March 8, 2017, https://corporateeurope.org/pressreleases/2017/03/ecb-cash-injections-polluters-must-stop-70-ngos-demand

12. Laurie Macfarlane, "Most 'Wealth' Isn't the Result of Hard Work. It Has Been Accumulated by Being Idle and Unproductive," *Evonomics*, November 2017, http://evonomics.com/unproductive-rent-housing-macfarlane/

13. "A Conversation with Lord Adair Turner," Private Debt Project, http://privatedebtproject.org/view-articles.php?An-Interview-With-Lord-Adair-Turner-6

14. Turner cites a study by Jorda, Schularick, and Taylor showing the proportion of banking credit going to real estate in 14 advanced economies has been growing throughout the last century, now peaking at more than 50%. Available here: https://www.frbsf.org/economic-research/files/wp2014-23.pdf

15. Òscar Jordà, Katharina Knoll, Dmitry Kuvshinov, Moritz Schularick, and Alan M. Taylor, "The Rate of Return on Everything, 1870-2015," National Bureau of Economic Research, December 2017.

16. I am simplifying here. The returns of 7% also included rent income but are also real, therefore note of inflation. I assume an average inflation of around 3% per year over the period that is roughly equivalent to the portion of rent income in the 7%. I also consider negligible improvements to the house beyond maintenance that is already netted from returns. The 7% returns after inflation can therefore be approximated to the average price increase of houses or its inflation.

17. This index measures the average inflation in a country by weighing price increases in thousands of products and services that the typical consumer might buy.

18. "G20 Consumer Price Index," Eurostat: Statistics Explained, http://ec.europa.eu/eurostat/statistics-explained/index.php/G20_consumer_price_index

19. Given the UK and the EU do not include the rent forfeited by people living in their own house in the CPI, housing weight is much lower than that of other countries, likely underestimating inflation and limiting comparability between countries.

20. Rana Foroohar, "The Fed Has Exacerbated America's New Housing Bubble," *Financial Times*, March 2019.

21. Francesco Manaresi and Nicola Pierri, "Credit Supply and Productivity Growth," International Monetary Fund, May 17, 2019, https://www.imf.org/en/Publications/WP/Issues/2019/05/17/Credit-Supply-and-Productivity-Growth-46894

22. Gerald Epstein, "Central Banks as Agents of Economic Development," Political Economy Research Institute, September 2005.

23. David Archer, "Roles and Objectives of Modern Central Banks," in Issues in the Governance of Central Banks, Central Bank Governance Group, May 18, 2009, p. 22. https://www.bis.org/publ/othp04_2.pdf

24. European Central Bank, "Monetary Policy," https://www.ecb.europa.eu/mopo/intro/html/index.en.html

25. "The Federal Reserve's Dual Mandate," Federal Reserve Bank of Chicago, April 30, 2018, https://www.chicagofed.org/research/dual-mandate/dual-mandate

26. Mohamed A. El-Erian, *The Only Game in Town*, p. 43.

27. Andrew E. Clark, "Work, Jobs, and Well-Being Across the Millennium," in Ed Diener and Daniel Kahneman, eds., *International Differences in Well-Being*, March 2010.

28. Martin Sandbu, "The Hidden Costs of Macroeconomic Moderation," *Financial Times*, November 2018

29. Bryan Taylor, "The Death of the Zimbabwe Dollar," Global Financial Data, https://www.globalfinancialdata.com/gfdblog/?p=3098

30. "Venezuela Annual Inflation Hits 24,600 Percent in May: National Assembly," Reuters, June 11, 2018, https://www.reuters.com/article/us-venezuela-economy/venezuela-annual-inflation-hits-24600-percent-in-may-national-assembly-idUSKBN1J71YB

31. Patricia Laya and Andrew Rosati, "Venezuela's 2018 Inflation to Hit 1.37 Million Percent, IMF Says," Bloomberg, October 8, 2018, https://www.bloomberg.com/news/articles/2018-10-09/venezuela-s-2018-inflation-to-hit-1-37-million-percent-imf-says

32. "BOJ Now Holds 40% of Japanese Government Bonds," *Nikkei Asian Review*, February 2017.

33. "Parameters and Transformations," European Central Bank Statistical Data Warehouse, https://sdw.ecb.europa.eu/quickview.do?SERIES_KEY=117. BSI.M.U2.N.R.LRE.X.1.A1.3000.Z01.E

34. Richard Vague, "Rapid Money Supply Growth Does Not Cause Inflation," *Macroeconomic Theory*, December 2, 2016, https://www.ineteconomics.org/perspectives/blog/rapid-money-supply-growth-does-not-cause-inflation

35. This description does not consider another type of inflation, which arises from an increase in the cost of inputs. An oil crisis or a widespread drought could increase inflation simply because it increases the prices of oil and food commodities, which are common inputs for a variety of products. Companies would attempt to raise prices to maintain their margins. Central banks cannot handle this kind of inflation. One could argue that tackling climate change could reduce the threat of both oil crises and natural catastrophes like drought. But once a drought or oil shock happens, central banks cannot do much to mitigate the impact on price inflation, and if they tried, they would probably cause even more harm.

36. It wouldn't happen for existing loans with fixed interest rates.

37. See for example: "Special Report: Competition. America v Europe: The big picture" by The Economist, November 2018; or *Playing To Win: The New Global Competition For Corporate Profits*, by the McKinsey Global Institute, September 2015; or Mai Chi Dao and Chiara Maggi, *The Rise in Corporate Saving and Cash Holding in Advanced Economies: Aggregate and Firm Level Trends*, December 2018, IMF.

38. Commercial banks need to change their lending conditions, and companies have already invested, and many investments cannot be reversed. As people realize their debt is now more expensive, they decide to consume less, and so on.

39. As I write, the US Federal Reserve is increasing interest rates and they reached 2.0%–2.5% in September 2018, by which time inflation was 2.28%, down from 2.95% in July. Quantitative easing in Europe is also being reduced.

40. Price growth because of higher quality does not affect inflation but rather increases the value of production.

41. When a product has higher quality at the same price, real production increases, even if supply stays the same. Most real growth in developed countries now happens through quality increase rather than supply increase.

42. European Business: Overcoming Uncertainty, Strengthening Recovery. McKinsey Global Institute. May 2017.

43. Barry Z. Cynamon and Steven M. Fazzari, "Inequality, the Great Recession, and Slow Recovery," Cambridge Journal of Economics, vol.40, issue 2, March 31, 2015, pp. 373–399, https://academic.oup.com/cje/article-abstract/40/2/373/2605561?redirectedFrom=fulltext

44. As part of conventional monetary policies, central banks buy short-term government bonds in various kinds of open market transactions. The money they pay the bond sellers ends up increasing commercial banks' reserves. The central bank can buy more

or less of these bonds, and when it buys more, commercial banks have less need to borrow from each other or from the central bank, hence the overall cost of their funding—the target interest rate—decreases. In quantitative easing, central banks buy other kinds of assets, including long-term government bonds (affecting the long-term interest rates on them), as well as asset-backed securities and corporate bonds. As a result of this policy, from December 2007 to May 2017, the Fed's assets quintupled, from $882 billion to $4.47 trillion. Stephen D. Williamson, "Quantitative Easing: How Well Does This Tool Work?" Federal Reserve Bank of St. Louis, third quarter 2017, https://www.stlouisfed.org/publications/regional-economist/third-quarter-2017/quantitative-easing-how-well-does-this-tool-work.

45. Allyn Young, "The Mystery of Money," *The Book of Popular Science*, The Grolier Society, 1924, revised 1929.

46. Edward I. Altman, "Bankruptcy with a Twist," *Forbes*, November 12, 2008, https://www.forbes.com/2008/11/11/gm-bankruptcy-government-oped-cx_ea_1112altman.html#405393c04a6a

47. Paul Ingrassia, *Crash Course*, 2010, p. 236, p. 260.

48. "A Giant Falls: The Bankruptcy of General Motors," *The Economist*, June 4, 2009, https://www.economist.com/node/13782942

49. The reason companies like General Motors do seek debt is that, if their businesses go well, they can enjoy the same returns with lower stockholder equity, increasing the overall ROE.

50. Moritz Schularick and Alan M. Taylor, "Credit Booms Gone Bust: Monetary Policy, Leverage Cycles and Financial Crises, 1870–2008," *American Economic Review*, vol. 102, issue 2, April 2012, pp. 1029–61.

51. Adair Turner, "Debt and Demand," Project Syndicate, January 2014.

52. For a comprehensive analysis, see: Adair Turner, *Between Debt and the Devil: Money, Credit and Fixing Global Finance*, October 2016.

53. I am simplifying here: Banks don't revolve all debt. For example, companies can issue bonds that are underwritten by non-banking financial institutions.

54. Global Debt Monitor, Institute of International Finance.

55. Some debt is also between non-bank society players, like individuals or pension funds buying government bonds. These forms of debt do not need to be revolved by banks.

56. Bob Bryan, "The Verdict: A Comprehensive Look Back at Obama's Jobs Record," *Business Insider*, January 6, 2017, https://www.businessinsider.in/the-verdict-a-comprehensive-look-back-at-obamas-jobs-record/articleshow/56381385.cms

57. Gavin Jones, "Italy's Election Pledges Are a Debt Time Bomb, Economists Warn," Reuters, February 15, 2018, https://www.reuters.com/article/us-italy-election-debt/italys-election-pledges-are-a-debt-time-bomb-economists-warn-idUSKCN1FZ1HJ

58. IMF: World Economic Outlook (WEO) Database, April 2019.

59. Adair Turner, "Debt Déjà Vu," Project Syndicate, October 6, 2015, https://www.project-syndicate.org/commentary/demand-crisis-radical-measures-by-adair-turner-2015-10?barrier=accessreg

60. Board of Governors of the Federal Reserve System, "Changes in US Family Finances from 2013 to 2016: Evidence from the Survey of Consumer Finances," Federal

Reserve Bulletin, September 2017, https://www.federalreserve.gov/publications/ 2017-September-changes-in-us-family-finances-from-2013-to-2016.htm

61. Christopher Carroll, Jiri Slacalek, and Kiichi Tokuoka, "The Distribution of Wealth and the Marginal Propensity to Consume," ECB Working Paper Series, no. 1655, March 2014.

62. Economist Edward Wolff refers to "the rather staggering debt level of the middle class in 2016." "Has Middle Class Wealth Recovered?" paper presentation at the ASSA Meetings, LERA Session N3, "Dimensions of Wealth Inequality," January 6, 2018, https://www.aeaweb.org/conference/2018/preliminary/paper/5ZFEEf69

63. Leo Sun, "A Foolish Take: Here's How Much Dent the Average U.S. Household owns," *USA Today*, November 20, 2017, https://www.usatoday.com/story/money/ personalfinance/2017/11/18/a-foolish-take-heres-how-much-debt-the-average-us- household-owes/107651700/

64. "The Global Secular Savings Stagnation Glut: Why Are Savings Piling Up in Slow- growing Countries?" *The Economist*, April 3, 2015.

65. Matt Egan, "Apple, Google and Microsoft are hoarding $464 Billion in cash," CNN, July 19, 2017, http://money.cnn.com/2017/07/19/investing/apple-google-microsoft- cash/index.html

66. "Opportunity for Europe: The Case for Helicopter Money," Presentation of the McKinsey Global Institute to the Peterson Institute for International Economics conference on income inequality, 2015.

67. "Monti's Medicine," *The Economist*, December 8, 2012, https://www.economist.com/ news/finance-and-economics/21567936-mario-monti-has-restored-italys-credibility- much-more-must-be-done-restore.

68. "The Rotten Heart of Finance: A Scandal over Key Interest Rates Is About to Go Global," *The Economist*, July 7, 2012, https://www.economist.com/node/21558281

69. "Barclays, UBS among six top banks fined nearly $US6bn for rigging foreign exchange, Libor rates," ABC News, May 20, 2015, http://www.abc.net.au/ news/2015-05-21/us-britain-fine-top-banks-nearly-6-bn-for-forex-libor-abuses/ 6485510

70. "Supplementary Convention on the Abolition of Slavery, the Slave Trade, and Institutions and Practices Similar to Slavery," United Nations, April 30, 1957, http://www.ohchr.org/EN/ProfessionalInterest/Pages/SupplementaryConvention AbolitionOfSlavery.aspx

71. Martin Ford, *The Rise of the Robots*, quoting Emmanuel Saez, "Striking It Richer: The Evolution of Top Incomes in the United States," *Pathways*, Stanford Center for the Study of Poverty and Inequality, Winter 2008, pp. 6–7, updated June 30, 2016, https://eml.berkeley.edu/~saez/saez-UStopincomes-2015.pdf

72. Chris Isidore, "Why Saving Is Killing the Economy," *CNN Money*, February 12, 2009.

73. Myles Udland, "People Weren't Supposed to Be Saving This Much Money—And Now It's a Problem," *Business Insider*, October 6, 2015, https://www.businessinsider.com.au/ savings-rate-increases-as-interest-rates-fall-2015-10

74. Jaewoo Lee, Pau Rabanal, and Damiano Sandri, "US Consumption after the 2008 Crisis," IMF staff position note, January 2010.

Chapter 8: Time for Permanent Money?

1. Adair Turner, *Between Debt and the Devil: Money, Credit and Fixing Global Finance*, October 2016.

2. "All Cryptocurrencies," CoinMarketCap, https://coinmarketcap.com/all/views/all/

3. Ann Pettifor, *The Production of Money: How to Break the Power of Bankers*, February 2017.

4. Andrea M. Antonopoulos, *Mastering Bitcoin: Unlocking Digital Crypto-Currencies*, December 2014.

5. As in, the value of transactions in cryptocurrencies could be a proxy to estimate the value of illegal activities.

6. In fact, the central bank would know the value of all deposits people held in its digital currency and conventional payment technologies would be sufficient to complete a payment.

7. Delphine Strauss, Look at issuing digital currency, IMF head tells central banks, November 2018, Financial Times.

8. "RBA: We have no plans to create digital AUD. No demand, no point," June 2018.

9. Committee on Payments and Market Infrastructures, Markets Committee, "Central Bank Digital Currencies, March 2018, https://www.bis.org/cpmi/publ/d174.pdf

10. "The Sardex Factor: When the financial crisis hit Sardinia, a group of local friends decided that the best way to help the island was to set up a currency from scratch," *Financial Times*, September 2015, https://www.sardex.net

11. Sara Calvo and Andres Morales, "Exploring Complementary Currencies in Europe: A Comparative Study of Local Initiatives in Spain and the United Kingdom," Living Minca Working Papers, September 2014.

12. Octavio Groppa, "Complementary Currency and Its Impact on the Economy," *International Journal of Complementary Currency Research*, November 26, 2013, https://ijccr.net/2013/11/26/complementary-currency-impact/. See also: "Italy's B2B Cashless Sardex Currency Set to Take on the World," DW, https://www.dw.com/en/italys-b2b-cashless-sardex-currency-set-to-take-on-the-world/a-45300395

13. Think of globalization. The creation of a global community has also increased the imbalances, with companies now accessing billions of consumers and multiplying their profits, the value of their companies, and the wealth of their shareholders.

14. Dylan Matthews, "More Than 50,000 People Are Set to Get a Basic Income in a Brazilian City," *Vox*, October 30, 2019, https://www.vox.com/future-perfect/2019/10/30/20938236/basic-income-brazil-marica-suplicy-workers-party

15. Larry Summers, "US Economic Prospects: Secular Stagnation, Hysteresis, and the Zero Lower Bound," Business Economics, vol. 49, issue 2, (2014); Antonio Fatás, Lawrence H. Summers, "The Permanent Effects of Fiscal Consolidations," National Bureau of Economic Research Working Papers, June 2016.

16. For instance, commercial banks cannot pass negative interest onto depositors for long, since there is a broad consensus that people would quickly move their money elsewhere or hoard cash. And if banks cannot charge interest on deposits but have to pay interest to the central bank, they would lose money by holding deposits instead of earning it.

17. Lukasz Rachel and Lawrence H. Summers, "On Falling Neutral Real Rates, Fiscal Policy, and the Risk of Secular Stagnation," Brookings, March 7, 2019.

18. Adair Turner, *Between Debt and the Devil: Money, Credit and Fixing Global Finance.*

19. Willem H. Buiter, "The Simple Analytics of Helicopter Money: Why It Works – Always," *Economics*, vol. 8, August 2014. 2014–28.

20. Eric Labaye, Sven Smit, Eckart Windhagen, Richard Dobbs, Jan Mischke, and Matt Stone, "A Window of Opportunity for Europe," McKinsey Global Institute, June 2015.

21. Frank Van Lerven, "Recovery in the Eurozone: Using Money Creation to Stimulate the Real Economy," PositiveMoney, December 2015.

22. PositiveMoney, http://www.qe4people.eu/

23. Ben S. Bernanke, "What Tools Does the Fed Have Left? Part 3: Helicopter Money," Brookings, April 2016, https://www.brookings.edu/blog/ben-bernanke/2016/04/11/what-tools-does-the-fed-have-left-part-3-helicopter-money/

24. Leika Kihara, "Japan Sinking Deeper into De Facto Helicopter Money," Reuters, August 2016.

25. I choose Italy because it makes a good comparison country to Japan, as they share similar demographics—an aging and declining population. They also share similar attitudes toward household debt.

26. We will see later, though, why Japan is actually one of the economies that least needs UBI. With such low unemployment and an aging population, fear of joblessness is rather unwarranted. In fact, unless productivity significantly increases, Japanese citizens will have to keep working long hours to sustain their aging population. A minimum wage combined with standard unemployment benefits could be a better solution in Japan, motivating companies to invest in automation to avoid the cost of employees. A UBI may make more sense only when unemployment starts to rise.

27. Unless imports grow more than exports, and then some savings become foreign savings.

28. Jonathan Woetzel et al., "Bridging the Global Infrastructure Gap," McKinsey Global Institute, June 2016.

29. Isabel V. Sawhill, "America's Two Most Troubled Sectors: Health and Education," Brookings, July 2013, https://www.brookings.edu/opinions/americas-two-most-troubled-sectors-health-and-education/

30. "Whose Money Is It? Martin Wolf (FT) on Public Money Creation," Sustainable Finance Lab, November 22, 2016, https://sustainablefinancelab.nl/kennisbank/whose-money-is-it-martin-wolf-ft-on-public-money-creation/

31. "Money and Government: A Challenge to Mainstream Economics," The London School of Economics and Political Science, Public Lectures and Events, September 17, 2018, https://www.lse.ac.uk/lse-player?id=4505.

32. Yanis Varoufakis, "The Promise of Fiscal Money," Project Syndicate, August 2017.

33. This explanation is oversimplified and I will give you an adequate view of globalization later in the book.

34. Beardsley Ruml, "Taxes for Revenue Are Obsolete," *American Affairs*, vol. 8, issue 1, January 1946.

35. William R. Allen, "Irving Fisher and the 100 Percent Reserve Proposal," University of California, October 1993.

36. Ann Pettifor, *The Production of Money: How to Break the Power of Bankers*.

37. Jaromir Benes and Michael Kumhof, "The Chicago Plan Revisited," IMF working paper, August 2012.

38. See for example: Yeva Nersisyan and L. Randall Wray, "Does Excessive Sovereign Debt Really Hurt Growth? A Critique of This Time Is Different, by Reinhart and Rogoff."

39. See, for example: Thomas I. Palley, "Money, Fiscal Policy, and Interest Rates: A Critique of Modern Monetary Theory," *Review of Political Economy*, vol. 27, issue 1, 2015.

III. CAPITALISM

Chapter 9: Divorce Without Alimony: The Love Story of Capitalism and Government

1. Daniel McFadden, "Free Markets and Fettered Consumers," *The American Economic Review*, vol. 96, no. 1, March 2006, p. 7.

2. This is just an illustrative example. On mining in particular it is debatable whether natural resources should belong to a private company, a government and its people, or even to the global community.

3. Hamid R. Davoodi, "IMF Survey: Swaziland's Economy Stagnates; Financial Reforms Needed," IMF African Department, July 2008.

4. Kevin Sieff, "Zimbabwe's White Farmers Find Their Services in Demand Again," *The Guardian*, September 2015.

5. Moisés Naim and Francisco Toro, "Venezuela's Suicide: Lessons from a Failed State," *Foreign Affairs*, Nov/Dec 2018.

6. "South Korea: The Government Role in Economic Development," June 1990, http://www.country-data.com/cgi-bin/query/r-12298.html

7. Shin-Haing Kim, "Finance and Growth of the Korean Economy from 1960 to 2004," *Seoul Journal of Economics*, 2007.

8. The policy mix that allowed Asian countries to develop at the fastest pace in history is contested. My view will be available on the book's website.

9. Thomas Piketty, *Capital in the Twenty-First Century*, April 2014.

10. "Economy in the 1960s," Shmoop.com.

11. Philippe Van Parijs and Yannick Vanderborght, *Basic Income: A Radical Proposal for a Free Society and a Sane Economy*, March 2017.

12. Christian A. Davis, *Imagining Basic Income as an International and Domestic Policy to Wealth Inequality*, master's thesis, City University of New York, January 2017.

13. Jacques Rodriguez, "From Public Charity to Putting the Poor to Work," Book and ideas, October 2, 2014, https://booksandideas.net/From-Public-Charity-to-Putting-the.html

14. Rutger Bregman, *Utopia for Realists: How We Can Build the Ideal World*, March 2017.

15. A recent study by the Fed confirmed that the relationship in the Phillips curve no longer seems to exist. See Matthew Boesler, "Phillips Curve Doesn't Help Forecast Inflation, Fed Study Finds," Bloomberg, August 2017.

16. Bureau of Labor Statistics, "Employment Status of the Civilian Noninstitutional Population, 1942 to date," May 2008.

17. "Charting the Labor Market: Data from the Current Population Survey (CPS)," US Bureau of Labor Statistics, August 7, 2020, https://www.bls.gov/web/empsit/cps_charts.pdf

18. J. Bradford Delong, "Why Low Inflation Is No Surprise," Project Syndicate, January 2018.

19. Dàniel Olàh, "If You Look Behind Neoliberal Economists, You'll Discover the Rich: How Economic Theories Serve Big Business," *Evonomics*, October 2017, http://evonomics.com/look-behind-neoliberal-economist-youll-discover-rich-economic-theories-serve-big-business/

20. Jonathan D. Ostry, Prakash Loungani, and Davide Furceri, "Neoliberal Capitalism: Oversold?" Finance & Development, IMF, June 2016.

21. To this day, private sector value added is accounted including the costs of labor, amortization of assets, and the profit generated. The same activity done by the public sector is accounted by the cost of public wages, without considering asset utilization or the profit, given there is no price or profit in public provision of service.

22. Ed Diener, Daniel Kahneman, and John Helliwell, *International Differences in Well-Being*, February 2010.

23. Joseph Stiglitz, *The Price of Inequality: How Today's Divided Society Endangers Our Future*, 2014.

24. Rick Wartzman, "We Were Shocked: RAND Study Uncovers Massive Income Shift to the Top 1%," *Fast Company*, September 14, 2020, https://www.fastcompany.com/90550015/we-were-shocked-rand-study-uncovers-massive-income-shift-to-the-top-1?fbclid=IwAR1M9qubuJOSNKaCvhsuOEo6frJ9_m2P4xOQ4IYkPtPD8dGtvZLQo5wbe_0

25. Thomas Piketty, *Capital in the Twenty-First Century*, April 2014.

26. taxfoundation.org

27. Growth rates are CAGR in constant USD. Results are similar when using FRED or World Bank Data and by counting the decade from the last year of the previous decade (e.g., 1969) or the first year of the decade (e.g., 1970).

28. Branko Milanovic, *Global Inequality: A New Approach for the Age of Globalization*, 2016.

29. Angus Deaton, *The Great Escape: Health, Wealth, and the Origins of Inequality*, 2013.

30. "OECD employment outlook 2018"

31. Angus Deaton, *The Great Escape: Health, Wealth, and the Origins of Inequality*, 2013.

32. Thomas Piketty, *Capital in the Twenty-First Century*, April 2014.

33. "Is Growth at Risk?" IMF Global Financial Stability Report, October 2017.

34. George Monbiot, "Neoliberal—The ideology at the root of all our problems," *The Guardian*, April 2016.

35. Walter Scheidel, *The Great Leveler: Violence and the History of Inequality from the Stone Age to the Twenty-First Century*, 2017.

36. Branko Milanovic, *Global Inequality: A New Approach for the Age of Globalization*, 2016.

37. Edward N. Wolff, "Household Wealth Trends in the United States, 1962 to 2016: Has Middle Class Wealth Recovered?" *The Russell Sage Foundation Journal of the Social Sciences*, vol. 2, issue 6, 2016, pp. 24–43.

38. Branko Milanovic, *Global Inequality: A New Approach for the Age of Globalization*, 2016.

39. "Is Growth at Risk?" IMF Global Financial Stability Report, October 2017.

Chapter 10: Flaws in the Core: Cognitive Biases and Broken Promises

1. Andrew Pierce, "The Queen Asks Why No One Saw the Credit Crunch Coming," *The Daily Telegraph*, November 2008.

2. Robert Shiller, "Richard Thaler Is a Controversial Nobel Prize Winner—But a Deserving One," *The Guardian*, October 2017.

3. Richard H. Thaler and Cass R. *Sunstein, Nudge: Improving Decisions About Health, Wealth, and Happiness*, April 2008.

4. Richard H. Thaler and Cass R. *Sunstein, Nudg: Improving Decisions About Health, Wealth, and Happiness*.

5. A. Wilke and R. Mata, in *Encyclopedia of Human Behavior* (Second Edition), 2012.

6. Solving the Productivity Puzzle, McKinsey Global Institute February 2018.

7. Rana Foroohar, *Makers and Takers: The Rise of Finance and the Fall of American Business*, May 2016.

8. Richard H. Thaler and Cass R. *Sunstein, Nudge: Improving Decisions About Health, Wealth, and Happiness*, April 2008.

9. Joseph E. Stiglitz, "America Has a Monopoly Problem—and It's Huge," *The Nation*, October 2017.

10. World Economic Outlook, April 2019, chapter 2, IMF.

11. Preeti Varathan, "In Just Two Hours, Amazon Erased $30 Billion in Market Value for Healthcare's Biggest Companies," *Quartz*, January 2018.

12. Mariana Mazzucato, interview to INET presenting her book *The Entrepreneurial State*, available at https://www.ineteconomics.org/perspectives/videos/the-government-as-entrepreneur

13. John Nichols and Robert W. McChensey, *Dollarocracy: How the Money and Media Election Complex Is Destroying America*, 2013.

14. Branko Milanovic, *Global Inequality: A New Approach for the Age of Globalization*, 2016.

15. Thomas Piketty, Emmanuel Saez, and Stefanie Stantcheva, *Optimal Taxation of Top Labor Incomes: A Tale of Three Elasticities*, 2011.

16. Angus Deaton, *The Great Escape: Health, Wealth, and the Origins of Inequality*, 2013.

17. Sabrina Siddiqui, Ben Jacobs, and Lauren Gambino, "Senate Approves Most Drastic Changes to US Tax Code in 30 Years," *The Guardian*, December 2017.

18. Jennifer Fitzgerald, "To Fix Health Care, We Need to Expand Medicaid, Not Cut It," CNBC, February 2018.

19. Annie Nova, "Trump's Budget Would End Student Loan Forgiveness Program," CNBC, February 2018.

20. Branko Milanovic, *Global Inequality: A New Approach for the Age of Globalization*, 2016.

21. Branko Milanovic, *Global Inequality: A New Approach for the Age of Globalization*.

22. Elizabeth Anderson, *Private Government: How Employers Rule Our Lives (and Why We Don't Talk About It)*, May 2017; James Livingston, *No More Work: Why Full Employment Is a Bad Idea*, October 2016.

23. Didier Jacob, "Extreme Wealth Is Not Merited," Oxfam America, November 2015.

24. Chris Hayes, *Twilight of the Elites: America After Meritocracy*, June 2013.

25. Angus Deaton, *The Great Escape: Health, Wealth, and the Origins of Inequality*, 2013

26. The Opportunity Index 2015, cited by Shawn Bohen and Gerald Chertavian, "Restoring the Capitalist Promise: Opportunities in the US," in Dominic Barton, Dezso Horvath, and Matthias Kipping, eds., *Re-Imagining Capitalism*, 2016.

27. Miles Corak, *Income Inequality, Equality of Opportunity, and Intergenerational Mobility*, University of Ottawa, July 2013.

28. "The State of Human Development," United Nations Human Development Report, 1998.

29. "Education for All: Global Monitoring Report," UNESCO, July 2015.

30. Rima Assi, Hana Dib, David Fine, and Tom Isherwood, "Rethinking Resilience: Ten Priorities for Governments," McKinsey & Company Public & Social Sector Insights, November 30, 2020, https://www.mckinsey.com/industries/public-and-social-sector/our-insights/a-government-blueprint-to-adapt-the-ecosystem-to-the-future-of-work?cid=other-pso-twi-mps-mps-tsp-2003-i10a&sid=5e6f90d4f713da1002c32533&linkId=84432770

31. Shalini Unnikrishnan, Cherie Blair, "Want to Boost the Global Economy by $5 Trillion? Support Women as Entrepreneurs," Boston Consulting Group, July 30, 2019, https://www.bcg.com/en-ch/publications/2019/boost-global-economy-5-trillion-dollar-support-women-entrepreneurs

32. "The Power of Parity: How Advancing Women's Equality Can Add $12 Trillion to Global Growth," McKinsey Global Institute, September 2015, https://www.mckinsey.com/~/media/mckinsey/featured%20insights/employment%20and%20growth/how%20advancing%20womens%20equality%20can%20add%2012%20trillion%20to%20global%20growth/mgi%20power%20of%20parity_full%20report_september%202015.pdf

33. George Marshall, *Don't Even Think About It: Why Our Brains Are Wired to Ignore Climate Change*, August 2014.

34. Adair Turner, "The Limits of Carbon Pricing," Project Syndicate, November 2016.

35. Alyssa Baker, "A History of Solar Cells: How Technology Has Evolved," July 2016, Solar Power Authority, https://www.solarpowerauthority.com/a-history-of-solar-cells/

36. I recommend The Great Escape by Angus Deaton and Utopia for Realists by Rutger Bregman. Or Google "26 charts and maps that show the world is getting much, much better," where the author presents statistics on several metrics that most of us would agree help measure the success of a society.

37. James Manyika, Gary Pinkus, and Monique Tuin, "Rethinking the Future of American Capitalism," McKinsey Global Institute, November 12, 2020, https://www.mckinsey.com/featured-insights/long-term-capitalism/rethinking-the-future-of-american-capitalism?cid=other-soc-fce-mgi--oth---&sid=41322720 82&linkId=104315833&fbclid=IwAR3O6AHaPd3VWHKKWHlIFTzEHN cKxqrXj59ik4iJqKFZ0VYglnbK_XGyDW4

38. Fabrizio Roncone, "Terremoto, Il Crollo di Amatrice e la Scuola Antisismica che si è Sbriciolata," Il Corriere Della Sera, August 2016.

39. Ajay Kapur, Niall Macleod, and Narendra Singh, "Plutonomy: Buying Luxury, Explaining Global Imbalances," Citigroup, October 2005.

40. Martin Ford, The Rise of the Robots: Technology and the Threat of a Jobless Future, 2015.

41. Robert Shiller, "Why Robots Should Be Taxed if They Take People's Jobs," The Guardian, March 2017.

42. Cara McGoogan, "South Korea Introduces World's First 'Robot Tax,'" The Daily Telegraph, August 9, 2017, telegraph.co.uk.

43. Jonathan D. Ostry, Prakash Loungani, and Davide Furceri, "Neoliberalism: Oversold?" Finance & Development, IMF, June 2016.

Chapter 11: It's a New World: Production Now Depends on Distribution

1. Dunja Mijatovic, "Report of the Commissioner for Human Rights of the Council of Europe," November 2018.

2. From here, the economic identity that yearly investments equal yearly savings, although many economists that neglect the role of finance in the economy think savings come from citizens' savings. Instead new savings come into existence as soon as a new deposit is created by a bank responding to a demand for a loan.

3. Jürgen Osterhammel, The Transformation of the World: A Global History of the Nineteenth Century, 2014, p. 171.

4. See: Andrew G. Berg and Jonathan D. Ostry, "Inequality and Unsustainable Growth: Two Sides of the Same Coin?" IMF staff discussion note, 2011, Fiscal Monitor, "Tackling Inequality," October 2017.

5. OECD, In It Together: Why Less Inequality Benefits All, OECD Publishing, Paris, 2015, http://dx.doi.org/10.1787/9789264235120-en

6. Josh Bivens, "Inequality Is Slowing US Economic Growth," Economic Policy Institute, December 12, 2017, https://www.epi.org/publication/secular-stagnation/

7. Lukasz Rachel and Lawrence H. Summers, "On Falling Neutral Real Rates, Fiscal Policy, and the Risk of Secular Stagnation," Brookings Papers on Economic Activity, BPEA Conference Drafts, March 7–8, 2019, https://www.brookings.edu/wp-content/

uploads/2019/03/On-Falling-Neutral-Real-Rates-Fiscal-Policy-and-the-Risk-of-Secular-Stagnation.pdf

8. "Solving the Productivity Puzzle," McKinsey Global Institute, February 2018.

9. Antonio Fatás, "Do Business Cycles Cast Long Shadows? Short-Run Persistence and Economic Growth," *Journal of Economic Growth*, vol. 5, issue 2, Spring 2000, pp. 147–62.

10. Markus Lorenz, Ralph Lässig, Jonathan Brown, Brian Myerholtz, "Winners Are Green, Smart, and Digital," Boston Consulting Group, December 11, 2020, https://www.bcg.com/en-ch/publications/2020/machinery-industrial-automation-megatrends

11. Antonio Fatás and Lawrence Summers, "Hysteresis and Fiscal Policy During the Global Crisis," *Wall Street Journal*, October 2016.

12. Jeff Cox, "Yellen: Fed Might Want to Run a 'High-Pressure Economy,'" CNBC, October 2016.

13. "Transcript of Chair Powell's Press Conference," December 11, 2019, https://www.federalreserve.gov/mediacenter/files/FOMCpresconf20191211.pdf

14. Labor force participation has started to increase in the US from 2015 until the COVID-19 crisis. "Labor Force Participation Rate," FRED Economic Data, https://fred.stlouisfed.org/series/CIVPART

15. Alicia Sasser Modestino, Daniel Shoag, and Joshua Ballance, "Downskilling: Changes in Employer Skill Reequirements Over the Business Cycle," February 29, 2016, https://scholar.harvard.edu/files/shoag/files/downskilling_paper_final.pdf

16. Robb Mandelbaum, "Nick Hanauer Wants You To Know Everything You Know About Economics Is Wrong," *Forbes*, January 2018.

17. Jane Wakefield, "Foxconn Replaces '60,000 Factory Workers with Robots,'" BBC News, May 2016.

18. Carl Benedikt Frey and Michael Osborne, "The Future of Employment: How Susceptible Are Jobs to Computerisation?," University of Oxford, September 2013.

19. "A Future That Works: Automation, Employment, and Productivity," McKinsey Global Institute, January 2017.

20. Thomas Meakin, Jeremy Palmer, Valentina Sartori, and Jamie Vickers, "Winning with AI Is a State of Mind," McKinsey Global Institute, April 30, 2021, https://www.mckinsey.com/featured-insights/artificial-intelligence/notes-from-the-ai-frontier-modeling-the-impact-of-ai-on-the-world-economy

21. Martin Ford, *The Rise of the Robots: Technology and the Threat of a Jobless Future*, 2015.

22. Max Roser, "Employment in Agriculture," Our World in Data.

23. "Jobs Lost, Jobs Gained: What the Future of Work Will Mean for Jobs, Skills, and Wages," McKinsey Global Institute, November 2017.

24. Approximately 690,000 employees work in the top seven smartphones brands that accounted for 80% of the market shares in 2020. Even assuming all of them are in the smartphone business units of these companies, and assuming these companies only generate ⅓ of the smartphone value chain while the rest is generated by their suppliers with similar productivity, you still get an estimate for the employment in the full value chain of 2.5 million people.

25. According to World Bank data, 65% of the global population is between 15 and 64 years old.

26. US Bureau of Labor Statistics, 2016.

27. See for example, Erik Brynjolfsson and Andrew McAfee, The Second Machine Age, 2014, and Cyrille Schwellnus, Andreas Kappeler, and Pierre-Alain Pionnier, "Decoupling of Wages from Productivity: Macro-Level Facts," OECD, January 2017. Or Andrew Sharpe and James Uguccioni, "Decomposing the Productivity Wage Nexus in Selected OECD Countries," 1986–2013, July 2016, International Productivity Monitor.

28. See for example, Daron Acemoglu and Pascual Restrepo, "Automation and New Tasks: How Technology Displaces and Reinstates Labor," March 2019, and Andrew Sharpe and James Uguccioni, "Decomposing the Productivity Wage Nexus in Selected OECD Countries," 1986–2013, July 2016, International Productivity Monitor.

29. Most economists studying the impact of AI on inequality report that AI adoption will increase inequality. See a collection of studies in the report https://www.mckinsey.com/industries/public-and-social-sector/our-insights/a-government-blueprint-to-adapt-the-ecosystem-to-the-future-of-work

30. Kai-Fu Lee, "AI superpowers: China, Silicon Valley, and the New World Order," 2018.

31. Kai-Fu Lee, "AI superpowers. China, Silicon Valley, and the New World Order," 2018.

32. Carl Benedikt Frey and Michael Osborne, "The Future of Employment: How Susceptible Are Jobs to Computerisation?" September 2013, University of Oxford, https://www.oxfordmartin.ox.ac.uk/downloads/academic/The_Future_of_Employment.pdf

33. OXFAM International, "Reward Work, Not Wealth," January 2018, https://www.oxfam.org/en/research/reward-work-not-wealth

34. L. Randall Wray, "Alternative Paths to Modern Monetary Theory," chapter 2 of Modern Monetary Theory and its Critics, World Economic Association Books.

35. For the economists among you, the equation Savings = Investments and the narrative that banks allocate existing savings is misleading. Many are led to believe that only thanks to savings we have investments. But this is inaccurate. It is thanks to investments that we have savings. New investments that are part of GDP are those for which someone has produced something of value that someone else will not consume. Most of these investments require a monetary transaction that can come from previous stocks of money, from previous wealth converted into money through its sale or from its use as collateral for a bank loan, or from a new bank loan that does not require any collateral. When looking at funding larger investments year after year, the monetary transactions increase in value and the money can come from only two sources. The velocity of existing money increasing or new money created by banks. Given the "velocity" of M2 cannot increase indefinitely and it is rather constant except for its fall in times of crisis, new money creation has to play a big role. And the right time sequence is the creation of credit and money first, and then its use as investments by companies.

36. Dominic Barton, Dezso Horvath, and Matthias Kipping, Re-Imagining Capitalism, 2016.

37. Luigi Zingales, *A Capitalism for the People: Recapturing the Lost Genius of American Prosperity*, 2012.

38. Angus Deaton, "How Inequality Works, Project Syndicate," December 2017.

IV. MONETISM

Chapter 12: Stepping Back: What Should Monetism Accomplish?

1. J. Steven Landefeld, Brent R. Moulton, Joel D. Platt, and Shaunda M. Villones, "GDP and Beyond: Measuring Economic Progress and Sustainability," Bureau of Economic Analysis, US Department of Commerce, October 2009.

2. Jean C. Buzby, Hodan F. Wells, and Jeffrey Hyman, "The Estimated Amount, Value, and Calories of Postharvest Food Losses at the Retail and Consumer Levels in the United States," United States Department of Agriculture, February 2014.

3. Asa Stenmarck et al., "Estimates of European Food Waste Levels," Fusions, March 31, 2016, https://www.eufusions.org/phocadownload/Publications/Estimates%20of%20 European%20food%20waste%20levels.pdf

4. That is the volume of economic transactions that happen without the knowledge of tax authorities. For accounting of these transactions in GDP statistics see Friedrich Schneider, Andreas Buehn, and Claudio E. Montenegro, "Shadow Economies All over the World: New Estimates for 162 Countries from 1999 to 2007," The World Bank, July 2010.

5. "US Health System Ranks Last Among Eleven Countries on Measures of Access, Equity, Quality, Efficiency, and Healthy Lives," The Commonwealth Fund, April 2014.

6. Given these services aren't sold for a price, employees' salaries are the only thing that gets accounted in GDP.

7. When private hospitals or universities price their service, the price includes the cost of employees but also the cost of infrastructure and the profit margin on top of the costs.

8. Thomas Piketty, *Capital in the Twenty-First Century*, April 2014.

9. "The Trouble with GDP," *The Economist*, April 2016.

10. Ed Diener, Daniel Kahneman, and John Helliwell, *International Differences in Well-Being*, February 2010.

11. Richard Wilkinson and Kate Pickett, *The Spirit Level: Why Equality Is Better for Everyone,* 2009.

12. "The Trouble with GDP," *The Economist*, April 2016.

13. Anthony B. Atkinson, Thomas Piketty, and Emmanuel Saez, "Top Incomes in the Long Run of History," *Journal of Economic Literature*, vol. 49, issue 1, 2011.

14. For precision, it would be the Gross National Income (GNI), similar to GDP except for countries where much of the value of production (GDP) is then distributed as dividend abroad and GNI is typically lower. Once you have GNI, this is equivalent of the sum of yearly income of all people in the country. From the individual incomes, one can calculate the median income, which is equivalent to the median GNI.

15. Kate Raworth, *Doughnut Economics: 7 Ways to Think Like a 21st Century Economist*, February 2017.

16. Thomas Piketty, *Capital in the Twenty-First Century*, April 2014.

17. Thomas Piketty, *Capital in the Twenty-First Century*, April 2014.

18. Branko Milanovic, *Global Inequality: A New Approach For the Age of Globalization*, 2016.

19. Thomas Piketty, *Capital in the Twenty-First Century*, April 2014.

20. Public debts might decrease as a percentage of GDP, but they always increase in absolute value as long as we have a growing economy.

21. Unless taxes focused on the wealthy, which would just reduce their savings, but we would be back with Piketty's utopia.

22. As a reminder, any incremental income (or negative income) for wealthy people generates a low change in their consumption behavior because the limit to their consumption is they only have 24 hours a day to consume. Less wealthy people would instead change their consumption more because their limitation is money to afford consumption and not the time to consume it. This is the concept of marginal propensity to consume an additional unit of income.

23. "Labor Force Participation Rate in OECD Countries. 15–64 Year-Olds. % in the Same Age Group. 1960–2016," https://Data.OECD.org

24. Eric Chivian and Aaron Bernstein, eds., *Sustaining Life: How Human Health Depends on Biodiversity, Center for Health and the Global Environment*, 2008.

25. Eric Chivian et al., "Extinction Risk from Climate Change," *Nature*, 2004.

26. "The Extinction Crisis," Center for Biological Diversity, https://www.biologicaldiversity.org/programs/biodiversity/elements_of_biodiversity/extinction_crisis/

27. George Marshall, *Don't Even Think About It: Why Our Brains Are Wired To Ignore Climate Change*, August 2014.

28. "Production and Consumption of Ozone-Depleting Substances," European Environment Agency, March 2017, https://www.eea.europa.eu/data-and-maps/indicators/production-and-consumption-of-ozone-2/assessment-3

29. "NASA Study: First Direct Proof of Ozone Hole Recovery Due to Chemicals Ban," NASA, January 4, 2018, https://www.nasa.gov/feature/goddard/2018/nasa-study-first-direct-proof-of-ozone-hole-recovery-due-to-chemicals-ban

30. "Health Effects of Ozone Depletion: Skin Cancer," Ozone-hole.org.uk

31. "The Cost of a Polluted Environment: 1.7 Million Child Deaths a Year, Says WHO," Public Health, Environmental and Social Determinants of Health (PHE), issue 90, March 2017.

32. Antonia Gawel, "Pollution Is a Silent Killer: Here's How We Can Stop It," World Economic Forum, November 2017.

33. State of Global Air 2017, Institute for Health Metrics and Evaluation's Global Burden of Disease Project, in collaboration with the Health Effects Institute.

34. "Press Release: The Lancet Commission on Pollution and Health," Global Alliance on Health and Pollution, October 2017.

35. George Marshall, *Don't Even Think About It. Why Our Brains Are Wired To Ignore Climate Change*, August 2014.

36. Kate Raworth, *Doughnut Economics: 7 Ways to Think Like a 21st Century Economist*, February 2017.

37. Rebecca Riffkin, "Climate Change Not a Top Worry in US," Gallup News, March 2014.

38. "What Worries the World," Ipsos Public Affairs, May 2018, p. 6, https://www.ipsos.com/sites/default/files/ct/news/documents/2018-05/what_worries_the_world_2018.pdf

39. George Marshall, *Don't Even Think About It: Why Our Brains Are Wired To Ignore Climate Change*, August 2014.

40. George Marshall, *Don't Even Think About It: Why Our Brains Are Wired To Ignore Climate Change*, August 2014.

41. George Marshall, *Don't Even Think About It: Why Our Brains Are Wired To Ignore Climate Change*, August 2014.

42. George Marshall, *Don't Even Think About It: Why Our Brains Are Wired To Ignore Climate Change*, August 2014.

43. Adam Vaughan, "IEA Warns of 'Worrying Trend' as Global Investment in Renewables Falls," *The Guardian*, July 2018.

44. https://www.iea.org/reports/world-energy-investment-2020/key-findings

45. David Coady, Ian Parry, Louis Sears, Baoping Shang. "How Large Are Global Fossil Fuel Subsidies?" World Development, March 2017.

46. "Bhutan's 2015 Gross National Happiness Index," Center for Bhutan Studies and GNH Results, November 2015.

47. Tyler Protano-Goodwin, "Bhutan Becomes the World's First Carbon Negative Country," Global Vision International, 2016.

48. "World Energy Investment 2020," International Energy Agency, July 2020, https://iea.blob.core.windows.net/assets/ef8ffa01-9958-49f5-9b3b-7842e30f6177/WEI2020.pdf

49. "How's Life?" OECD Better Life Index, http://www.oecdbetterlifeindex.org

50. Douglas Beal, Enrique Rueda-Sabater, Shu Ling Heng, "Why Well-Being Should Drive Growth Strategies," Boston Consulting Group, May 28, 2015, https://www.bcg.com/publications/2015/public-sector-sustainability-2015-sustainable-economic-development-assessment

51. "World Happiness Report 2017," World Happiness Report, March 20, 2017, http://worldhappiness.report/ed/2017/

52. Rosaria Amato, "Oltre il Pil: Gli Indici di Benessere Saranno le Nuove Isure della Crescita," *La Repubblica*, November 2017.

53. Kate Raworth, *Doughnut Economics: 7 Ways to Think Like a 21st Century Economist*, February 2017.

54. Florence F. Luo et al., "Impact of Business Cycles on US Suicide Rates, 1928–2007," *American Journal of Public Health*, April 2011.

55. David Stuckler at al., "The Public Health Effect of Economic Crises and Alternative Policy Responses in Europe: An Empirical Analysis," *The Lancet*, July 2009.

56. Stephen Morrell et al., "Suicide and Unemployment in Australia 1907–1990," *Social Science & Medicine*, vol. 36, issue 6, March 1993.

57. S.S. Chang et al., "Was the Economic Crisis 1997–1998 Responsible for Rising Suicide Rates in East/Southeast Asia? A Time-trend Analysis for Japan, Hong Kong, South Korea, Taiwan, Singapore and Thailand," *Social Science & Medicine*, April 2009.

58. Elizabeth Brainerd, "Economic Reform and Mortality in the Former Soviet Union: A Study of the Suicide Epidemic in the 1990s," *European Economic Review*, 2001.

59. Nikolaos Antonakakis and Alan Collins, "The Impact of Fiscal Austerity on Suicide: On the Empirics of a Modern Greek Tragedy," *Social Science & Medicine*, vol. 112, July 2014.

Chapter 13: First Pillar: Harvesting the Money Tree

1. Lizzie Dearden, "Theresa May Prompts Anger After Telling Nurse Who Hasn't Had Pay Rise for Eight Years: 'There's No Magic Money Tree,'" *Independent*, June 3, 2017, https://www.independent.co.uk/news/uk/politics/theresa-may-nurse-magic-money-tree-bbcqt-question-time-pay-rise-eight-years-election-latest-a7770576.html

2. Although recently commercial banks do get free money from central banks through the interest that the central bank pays to those banks parking the trillions of extra money that central banks injected during quantitative easing operations (more on this later). As explained earlier, QE is not permanent free money but just the substitution of a financial asset (e.g., a government bond) with the corresponding value in money, which will be reverted when the assets expire.

3. Maria D. Fitzpatrick and Timothy J. Moore, "The Mortality Effects of Retirement: Evidence from Social Security Eligibility at Age 62," Center for Retirement Research at Boston College, August 2016.

4. Among them: Andrew J Oswald, Eugenio Proto and Daniel Sgroi, "Happiness and Productivity," Journal of Labor Economics, vol. 33, issue 4, 2014; Mike Renahan, "Want to Be Productive? Learn to Love Your Job," Hubspot, January 2016; John Baldoni, "Employee Engagement Does More Than Boost Productivity," *Harvard Business Review*, July 2013; Kevin Kruse, "Why Employees' Engagement? (These 28 Research Studies Prove the Benefits)," *Forbes*, September 2012.

5. Seraphima Kennedy, "When I worked for KCTMO I had nightmares about burning tower blocks," *The Guardian*, June 2017.

6. See for example: Nicholas Gruen, "Why Central Banks Should Offer Bank Accounts to Everyone," Evonomics.com.

7. "The Great Decoupling," interview, *McKinsey Quarterly*, September 2014. Available at https://www.mckinsey.com/industries/public-sector/our-insights/the-great-decoupling

8. Philippe Van Parijs and Yannick Vanderborght, *Basic Income: A Radical Proposal for a Free Society and a Sane Economy*, March 2017.

9. Ann Pettifor, *The Production of Money: How to Break the Power of Bankers*, February 2017.

10. Ariel Fiszbein and Norbert Schady, "Conditional Cash Transfers Reducing Present and Future Poverty," The World Bank, 2009.

11. Valentina Raggiu, "Mio Padre Stava Morendo e al 118 Rispondeva Solo un Disco," *La Repubblica*, August 2017.

12. James J. Heckman, "Skill Formation and the Economics of Investing in Disadvantaged Children," *Science*, vol. 312, June 2006; and James J. Heckman et. al.,"A New Cost-Benefit and Rate of Return Analysis for the Perry Preschool Program: A Summary," July 2010.

13. "Reskilling in European Industry: Preparing the Workforce for Tomorrow," The European Round Table for Industry, July 1, 2020, https://ert.eu/wp-content/uploads/2020/07/ERT-Reskilling-in-European-Industry-Paper_July2020-1.pdf

14. Ann Pettifor, *The Production of Money. How to Break the Power of Bankers*, February 2017.

15. One destabilizing event not mentioned here is war. Besides the fact that we should avoid wars at all costs, I believe a world with monetism would reduce the need for growth, as well as people's discontent, and hopefully reduce reasons for war. Having said that, conflicts have often led to printing permanent money, which is an unproductive use of money and monetism brings no innovation to war finance.

16. Nicky Wolf, "Alaskan Village Votes on Whether to Relocate Because of Climate Change," *The Guardian*, August 16, 2016.

17. WHO's list of bacteria for which new antibiotics are urgently needed is at: http://www.who.int/mediacentre/news/releases/2017/bacteria-antibiotics-needed/en/

18. "Climate Change And Infectious Diseases," WHO, http://www.who.int/globalchange/environment/en/chapter6.pdf

19. Martin Ford, *The Rise of the Robots: Technology and the Threat of a Jobless Future,* 2015.

20. "Notes from the AI Frontier: Modeling the Impact of AI on the World Economy," McKinsey Global Institute, September 2018; "Will Productivity and Growth Return after the COVID-19 crisis?" McKinsey Global Institute, March 2021.

21. Anahad O'Connor, "How the Sugar Industry Shifted Blame to Fat," *The New York Times*, September 12, 2016.

22. "Q&A on the Carcinogenicity of the Consumption of Red Meat and Processed Meat," World Health Organization, October 2015, http://www.who.int/features/qa/cancer-red-meat/en/

23. Edward Group, "20 Health Benefits of Fasting for Whole Body Wellness," Global Healing Center, June 2017.

24. Rutger Bregman, "Look at the Phone in Your Hand—You Can Thank the State for That," *The Guardian*, July 2017.

25. Arthur Allen, "For Billion-Dollar COVID Vaccines, Basic Government-Funded Science Laid the Groundwork," *Scientific American*, November 18, 2020, https://www.scientificamerican.com/article/for-billion-dollar-covid-vaccines-basic-government-funded-science-laid-the-groundwork/.

26. "Public Options Are the Key to Restoring the Middle-Class Life," *Financial Times*, May 6, 2019, https://www.ft.com/content/42915ad4-6cc3-11e9-9ff9-8c855179f1c4

27. Andreas Kluth, "mRNA Vaccines Could Vanquish COVID Today, Cancer Tomorrow," Bloomberg, January 9, 2021, https://www.bloomberg.com/opinion/articles/2021-01-09/pfizer-moderna-mrna-vaccines-could-vanquish-covid-today-cancer-tomorrow?cmpid=socialflow-facebook-business&utm

Chapter 14: Second Pillar: Taming the Inflation Monster with Taxes

1. Janet Yellen, "Inflation, Uncertainty, and Monetary Policy Remarks," at Prospects for Growth: Reassessing the Fundamentals, 59th Annual Meeting of the National Association for Business Economics, Cleveland, Ohio, September 2017.

2. Higher inflation would automatically reduce the burden of old debts and make past savings less valuable in terms of new income. That would happen as long as salaries grow higher than inflation, which might have been true after World War II, when inflation solved the issue of the high public debts during war, but it is far from certain given the current imbalance of bargaining power between employers and employees.

3. Government employees' salaries are considered a proxy for their value added to society, hence they are just added to the total of the value of goods produced and services delivered in the year.

4. Steve Keen, "Reducing Debt via a Modern Debt Jubilee," Patreon, May 7, 2021, https://www.patreon.com/posts/reducing-debt-50972822

5. Although it is not permanent money, as central banks can always sell the assets and would destroy the money they get from the sale, as long as the money circulates, the impact on the banking system is the same as if there were more permanent money.

6. Although the effectiveness of reserve requirements has been called into questions given as a lender of last resort, banks can always get loans from the central bank. Nonetheless, increasing reserve requirements would enable to absorb liquidity and force banks to borrow form the central banks at an interest rate that the central banks can set.

7. At 100% reserve requirement, a bank would only be able to create deposits and loans for a value equivalent to the value of central bank digital currency they have attracted from citizens or companies, which would sit at the central bank as reserves.

8. J. Bradford Delong, "Why Low Inflation Is No Surprise," Project Syndicate, January 2018.

9. Core inflation is a measure of inflation that excludes energy and commodity prices, so to avoid global events such as an oil crisis or droughts, which are beyond any central bank control, that influence central banks' monetary policies.

10. Stéphane Dupraz, Emi Nakamura, and Jón Steinsson, "A Plucking Model of Business Cycles," National Bureau of Economic Research Working Paper, June 2021, https://www.nber.org/papers/w26351

11. Antonio Fatás and Lawrence H. Summers, "The Permanent Effects of Fiscal Consolidations," discussion paper no. 10902, Centre for Economic Policy Research, October 2015.

12. Antonio Fatás, "Do Business Cycles Cast Long Shadows? Short-Run Persistence and Economic Growth," *Journal of Economic Growth*, Spring 2000.

13. Chang-Jin Kim and Charles R. Nelson, "Friedman's Plucking Model of Business Fluctuations: Tests and Estimates of Permanent and Transitory Components," *Journal of Money, Credit and Banking*, 1998.

14. Stéphane Dupraz, Emi Nakamura, and Jón Steinsson, "A Plucking Model of Business Cycles," National Bureau of Economic Research Working Paper, June 2021, https://www.nber.org/papers/w26351

15. Antonio Fatás, "Self-fulfilling Pessimism: The Fiscal Policy Doom Loop," Vox EU & CEPR, September 28, 2018.

16. See also: Philipp Heimberger and Jakob Kapeller, "'Output Gap Nonsense' and the EU's Fiscal Rules," Insititute for New Economic Thinking, January 27, 2020, https://www.ineteconomics.org/perspectives/blog/output-gap-nonsense-and-the-eus-fiscal-rules

17. Claudia Fontanari, Antonella Palumbo, and Chiara Salvatori, "Why We Need New Measures of Potential Output—and What They Tell Us," Institute for New Economic Thinking, May 16, 2019, https://www.ineteconomics.org/perspectives/blog/why-we-need-new-measures-of-potential-output-and-what they-tell-us.

18. Abba P. Lerner, "Functional Finance and the Federal Debt," *Social Research*, vol. 10, issue 1, July 24, 2021, https://www.jstor.org/stable/40981939?seq=1

19. Stephani Kelton, *The Deficit Myth: Modern Monetary Theory and the Birth of the People's Economy*, 2020.

20. As a reminder, monetism wants to maximize the time people spend on voluntary activities. Paid employment is a signal that people might want to do something else with their time, if they could afford not to work. Picking up garbage and cleaning toilets are probably activities that no one would miss if society managed to fully automate. If people performed an activity only if they are paid for it, in monetism it would be a sign they'd rather do something else. Imposing higher taxes for salaries in jobs that no one wants to do could be part of monetism, so that those jobs are automated faster. One would think that the market would naturally lead the salaries for these jobs to be higher (think of garbage collectors or cleaning toilets), but we discussed that the labor market is broken: If you need a salary to survive, you do any job you can get for whatever salary you are offered.

21. "Overcoming Obesity: An Initial Economic Analysis," McKinsey Global Institute, November 2014.

22. "Tobacco: Fact Sheet," World Health Organization, updated May 2017, http://www.who.int/mediacentre/factsheets/fs339/en/

23. "Global Strategy to Reduce Harmful Use of Alcohol," World Health Organization.

24. "The Top 10 Causes of Death: Fact Sheet," World Health Organization, updated January 2017, http://www.who.int/mediacentre/factsheets/fs310/en/

25. Prabhat Jha and Frank J Chaloupka, "The Economics of Global Tobacco Control," BMJ, 2000, bmj.com

26. A value added tax is a tax at every point in the supply chain where there is a sale. A company that mines rare Earth elements, for instance, would pay this tax on a sale to the company that makes a part for a smartphone.

27. Briony Harris, "Will a Sugar Tax Help Reduce Obesity?" World Economic Forum, March 2018.

28. Samuel Ee, "S$9.2b to come from car taxes and COE premiums in FY2017," *Business Times*, February 2017; Angela Tan, "IRAS collected S$47b in tax revenue in FY2017; up nearly 5% from a year ago," *Business Times*, August 2017.

29. Samuel Jonsson, Anders Ydstedt, Elke Asen, "Looking Back on 30 Years of Carbon Taxes in Sweden," Tax Foundation, September 23, 2020, https://taxfoundation.org/sweden-carbon-tax-revenue-greenhouse-gas-emissions/#:~:text=rate%E2%80%94EU%20 ETS.-,Sweden%20levies%20the%20highest%20carbon%20tax%20rate%20 in%20the%20world,gas%20emissions%20by%2027%20percent

30. "Net-Zero Challenge: The supply chain opportunity," World Economic Forum, January 2021, http://www3.weforum.org/docs/WEF_Net_Zero_Challenge_The_ Supply_Chain_Opportunity_2021.pdf

31. Thomas Piketty, *Capital in the Twenty-First Century*, April 2014.

32. AMECO database, European Commission, May 3, 2018, ec.europa.eu; for more, see "European Business: Overcoming Uncertainty, Strengthening Recovery," McKinsey Global Institute, May 2017.

33. Mai Chi Dao and Chiara Maggi, *The Rise in Corporate Saving and Cash Holding in Advanced Economies: Aggregate and Firm Level Trends*, December 2018.

34. In fact, if the high-gross profit margins are justified by the need to sustain high investments, the returns after considering the depreciation of investments such as assets and R&D should be lower.

35. Mariana Mazzucato, "Capitalism's Greatest Weakness? It Confuses Price with Value," World Economic Forum, May 2018.

36. Lynn Stout, *The Shareholder Value Myth: How Putting Shareholders First Harms Investors, Corporations, and the Public*, 2012.

37. Christopher Williams, "The $300m cable that will save traders milliseconds," *The Telegraph*, September 2011.

38. Tom Leonard, "How Super-fast cable networks allow City flash boys to fleece your pension of billions," *Daily Mail*, April 2014.

39. Lynn Stout back in 2003 had already collected several studies showing the demise of the hypothesis of market efficiency, with evidence of pricing anomalies, demand inelasticity, excessive volatility, delayed information response, and consistently superior traders. Lynn Stout, "The Mechanisms of Market Inefficiency: An Introduction to the New Finance," Cornell Law Faculty Publications, Paper 450, 2003. The IMF has also questioned the effectiveness of markets in pricing stocks and bonds, announcing in 2017 that there was "Too Much Money Chasing Too Few Yielding Assets" and hence "Credit and Market Risks Are Increasingly Being Mispriced. IMF, "Global Financial Stability Report October 2017: Is Growth at Risk?" https://www.imf.org/en/ Publications/GFSR/Issues/2017/09/27/global-financial-stability-report-october-2017

40. As examples, Mervyn King writes, "The Dodd-Frank Act passed in the US in 2010 contains 2300 pages. . . . In Britain, the Prudential Regulation Authority and the Financial Conduct Authority have combined rulebooks exceeding ten thousand pages. Such a complexity feeds on itself, and . . . results in the employment of several hundred thousand people. To employ such a large number of talented people to cope with complex regulation constitutes a large 'dead-weight' cost to Society." Mervyn King, The End of Alchemy: Money, Banking and the Future of the Global Economy (New

York: W. W. Norton, 2016). Nobel laureate Angus Deaton states, "There is widespread suspicion that some highly profitable financial activities are of little or no benefit to the population as a whole, and may even threaten the stability of the financial system—what investor and businessman Warren Buffett called financial weapons of mass destruction. If so, the very high payments that come with them are both unjust and inefficient. The heavy recruitment of the best minds into financial engineering is a loss to the rest of the economy, likely reducing innovation and growth somewhere else." Angus Deaton, The Great Escape: Health, Wealth, and the Origins of Inequality, 2013.

41. Only capital markets can be subjected to such tax, as money markets must continuously make transactions to satisfy people's and businesses' demand for different currencies, as well as for central banks and banks to lend money to each other. Some of these are of a speculative nature, but there is no alternative to this in a world with variable exchange rates.

42. Gerald Epstein, "Rethinking Monetary and Financial Policy: Practical Suggestions for Monitoring Financial Stability While Generating Employment and Poverty Reduction," Employment Sector, Employment Working Paper no. 37, 2009, https://www.ilo.org/public/english/employment/download/wpaper/wp37.pdf

43. As we introduce UBI, for instance, it could be expected that jobs that are chronically underpaid would have to be paid more, as people gain freedom to negotiate fairly. The same is true if permanent money is directed to increase salaries of teachers and nurses, currently, which are underpaid given their wages are often set by governments that can't afford to raise them. Their wages have no link to the value they add to society, likely much higher than what they are paid for. As wages adjust, inflation may indeed have to rise for some products. If wages eat too much into companies' profits, prices will have to grow, a natural readjustment from decades of underpaying for certain goods and services. If inflation moves toward 4%–5% or even 10% for a decade or so, that is not a dramatic problem if one knows how to manage it.

44. Core inflation removes the changes in the prices of commodities and energy, which are often outside the control of any central banks and beyond the dynamic of any individual country.

45. The increase in the M0 portion of the money supply would be offset by the same reduction of credit.

46. This would not happen if governments increased reserve requirements.

47. Again, some secondary use of money—say, the wages paid for people employed by companies investing, or the profits made by the investor—could ultimately increase demand and avoid deflation.

Chapter 15: Who Calls the Shots?

1. Garret Hardin, "The Tragedy of the Commons," Science, 1968.

2. David Abel, "A Milestone in the War over the True State of Cod," Boston Globe, April 3, 2017.

3. Kai-Fu Lee, AI Superpowers. China, Silicon Valley, and the New World Order, 2018.

4. More information on the transformation appears in his book Economic Transformation and Government Reform in Georgia, 2004–2012.

5. That is, company and emergency counter-inflation tax rates and tax rates on unhealthy and unsustainable practices.

6. "Who Beat Inflation?" *The Economist*, March 2010.

7. Gerald Epstein, "Rethinking Monetary and Financial Policy: Practical Suggestions for Monitoring Financial Stability While Generating Employment and Poverty Reduction," Employment Sector, Employment Working Paper no. 37, 2009, https://www.ilo.org/public/english/employment/download/wpaper/wp37.pdf

Chapter 16: Monetism vs. Capitalism

1. Monetism is a new system as it changes systemic components of capitalism, such as the financial system, the role of taxation, the need to work for a living, and the overarching goal of society, to name a few. But it can also be seen as a framework to rethink the role of existing elements of society, be that taxes, work, money, etc. I consider monetism both a framework to guide policymaking and the system that emerges from it following the framework proposed.

2. For example, Piketty, the IMF, and the OECD have addressed the inability of governments to raise taxes due to a global tax competition. Hundreds of economists have challenged the perfect rationality model and identified market failures. Mervyn King, Ann Pettiford, and Steve Keen, among others, have long complained about the way we are managing money. Hundreds more economists have engaged to show that the benefits from automation and globalization are concentrating and that the limited purchasing power of the middle classes is reducing economic growth. Many authors, academics, businessmen, and politicians have proposed ways to fix this, including many exponents of UBI. Kate Raworth, Piketty and Wilkinson, Joseph Stieglitz, the OECD, and many others have also proposed to go "beyond GDP" as core societal metrics.

3. Interest rates for banks in high-income countries to borrow these reserves have been negative or zero for most years after 2008.

4. Jo Becker, Sheryl Gay Stolberg, and Stephen Labaton, "Bush drive for home ownership fueled housing bubble." New York Times, December 2008.

5. See for example, Free exchange: Home economics, by *The Economist*, November 2018.

6. Rima Assi, Hana Dib, David Fine, and Tom Isherwood, "Rethinking Resilience: Ten Priorities for Governments," McKinsey & Company Public & Social Sector Insights, November 30, 2020, https://www.mckinsey.com/industries/public-and-social-sector/our-insights/the-10-trillion-dollar-rescue-how-governments-can-deliver-impact

7. Bureau of Labor Statistics, "The Employment Situation," US Department of Labor, June 2021, https://www.bls.gov/news.release/pdf/empsit.pdf

8. "Euro Area Unemployment at 8.3%," Eurostat news release, September 2020, https://ec.europa.eu/eurostat/documents/2995521/10663786/3-30102020-CP-EN.pdf/f93787e0-0b9a-e10e-b897-c0a5f7502d4e#:~:text=The%20EU%20unemployment%20rate%20was,office%20of%20the%20European%20Union

9. Emma Dorn, Bryan Hancock, Jimmy Sarakatsannis, and Ellen Viruleg, "COVID-19 and Education: The Lingering Effects of Unfinished Learning," McKinsey & Company, July 27, 2021, https://www.mckinsey.com/industries/public-and-social-sector/our-insights/safeguarding-europes-livelihoods-mitigating-the-employment-impact-of-covid-19

10. The eligibility criteria were set to 75,000 USD for the full 1,200 and individuals with income up to 99,000 USD received a portion of the transfer. Given the gross median income in the US is below 35,000 USD, the majority of US adults received the cash transfer. https://www.irs.gov/newsroom/economic-impact-payments-what-you-need-to-know

11. In interviews of senior human resources representatives of more than 20 companies in Europe a few months after the pandemic, I heard in all of them a shared combination of concern for the lack of digital skills and excitement for their digitization agenda for the following years being implemented in months.

12. Alasdair MacIntyre, *After Virtue*, 3rd edition, March 6, 2007.

13. Imagine also the increased innovation if conditional transfers end up going to venture capital—and therefore equity investments in start-ups—as opposed to the current system of most money creation happening through banks, and therefore in loans that inflate asset prices.

Chapter 17: Not a Utopia

1. Richard Wilkinson and Kate Pickett, *The Spirit Level: Why Equality Is Better for Everyone*, 2009.

2. Thomas Piketty, *Capital in the Twenty-First Century*, April 2014.

3. "Notes from the AI Frontier: Modeling the Impact of AI on the World Economy," McKinsey Global Institute, September 2018.

4. In the US for example, the public-debt-to-GDP ratio was close to 30% at the end of the 1970s and is now more than 100%.

5. This is already happening thanks to central banks' Quantitative Easing.

6. Andrew DePietro, "Where Are the World's Best Tax Havens? The Paradise Papers Exposed Some of These Offshore Tax Havens," GoBankingRates, November 2017.

7. Thomas Tørsløv, Ludvig Wier, and Gabriel Zucman, "€600 Billion and Counting: Why High-Tax Countries Let Tax Havens Flourish," Stanford Economics, November 2017, https://economics.stanford.edu/events/600-billion-and-counting-why-high-tax-countries-let-tax-havens-flourish

8. You can find a more extensive treatment on the book's website.

9. Trade imbalances often are protracted too long, exactly when countries' currencies do not change in value in line with their trade balances. This is possible because the currency value is also affected by the flow of currency for investment purposes, or because countries with different trade balances have pegged their currencies together. Protracted trade imbalances can be a real problem, especially if the deficit countries are those developing countries that are also borrowing in a foreign currency.

10. Net present value is today's value of expected cash flows minus today's value of invested cash. Analysts assume that investments with a positive NPV will yield a profit and those with a negative NPV will not.

11. A quick reminder of their theory: Debt creates accountability as a borrower will ask for a loan only if at the end of its life cycle, he can repay the loan and the interest

and have some money left. This accountability mechanism ensures that banks create money only for value-adding activities.

12. Alina Carare and Stephan Danninger, "Inflation Smoothing and the Modest Effect of VAT in Germany," IMF, July 2008.

13. John F. Due, "Excise and Sales Tax as Anti-Inflationary Measures," *The Annals of the American Academy of Political and Social Science*, vol. 326, November 1959, pp. 79–84.

14. The value of gold is still extremely low compared to the amount of money in circulation, and again, we define the value of gold in monetary terms. Gold just provides a feeling that something exists to back up money, but it couldn't do so if people actually stopped trusting money. The idea that it's a backup is irrelevant anyway, because with a fiat currency there is no link between money and gold, and hence people have no workable alternative to trusting money.

15. Biagio Bossone and Massimo Costa, "The 'Accounting View' of Money: Money as Equity (Part I)," *World Bank* blog, May 2018.

16. Martin Ford, *The Rise of the Robots: Technology and the Threat of a Jobless Future*, 2015.

17. Friedrich Schneider, Andreas Buehn, and Claudio E. Montenegro, "Shadow Economies All Over the World: New Estimates for 162 Countries from 1999 to 2007," The World Bank, July 2010.

18. Rutger Bregman, *Utopia for Realists: How We Can Build the Ideal World*, March 2017.

19. "Switzerland Millionaire Hit by Record Speed Fine," BBC News, January 2010.

20. "Global Gender Gap Report 2020," World Economic Forum, December 16, 2019, https://www.weforum.org/reports/gender-gap-2020-report-100-years-pay-equality

V. ROADMAP

Chapter 18: Blind in the Ivory Tower

1. "ECB Scales Back Rise in Bank Support after Policymaker Pushback," *Financial Times*, December 10, 2020, https://www.ft.com/content/d3127f93-efe3-4070-913a-147c2d5e0662

2. See "Moody's $864m Penalty for Ratings in Run-up to 2008 Financial Crisis," The Guardian, January 2017; and Barry Grey, "Standard and Poor's credit rating agency charged with fraud in sub-prime mortgage ratings," Global Research, February 2013.

3. With monetism we also inject permanent money, but without the 100% reserve banking requirement.

4. Alison Tudor-Ackroyd and Enoch Yiu, "Ant Group Removes Small Banks' Online Deposit Products from Its Platform As It Toes the Line with China's New Fintech Rules," *South China Morning Post*, December 18, 2020, https://www.google.ae/amp/s/amp.scmp.com/business/banking-finance/article/3114500/ant-group-removes-small-banks-online-deposit-products-its

5. Stephanie Kelton, *The Deficit Myth: Modern Monetary Theory and the Birth of the People's Economy*, June 2020.

6. Branko Milanovic, *Global Inequality: A New Approach for the Age of Globalization*, 2016.

7. Hot money refers to money that moves very quickly to maximize returns and provides no guarantee for a country that those moneys will support development in the medium or long term.

8. For more on monetism in low-income countries, see my website www.outgrowingcapitalism.com.

9. That is, debtors unable to repay their debts.

10. Acronym for Portugal, Ireland, Italy, Greece, and Spain.

11. See: Dániel Olah, "If You Look Behind Neoliberal Economistss, You'll Discover the Rich: How Economic Theories Serve Big Business," *Evonomics*, https://evonomics.com/look-behind-neoliberal-economist-youll-discover-rich-economic-theories-serve-big-business/. See also: Robert Kuttner, "Neoliberalism: Political Success, Economic Failure," *The American Prospect*, June 25, 2019, https://prospect.org/economy/neoliberalism-political-success-economic-failure/

12. Anat Admati, "There Is No Economics without Politics," *Evonomics*, December 6, 2019, https://evonomics.com/political-economy-blind-spots-and-a-challenge-to-academics/?fbclid=IwAR3F0Y7E_tRb5BfDzWlyNETq1nglJ9qKfbf_YxkArWR5WUBorAvbeECM9gw

13. Nancy Atkinson, "Once a Heretic, Copernicus Now Re-Buried with Catholic Honors," *The Christian Science Monitor*, May 24, 2010, https://www.csmonitor.com/Science/Cool-Astronomy/2010/0524/Once-a-heretic-Copernicus-now-re-buried-with-Catholic-honors

14. There may be many other functions, but the most important for this analogy are these.

15. Joseph Stiglitz, "Needed: A New Economic Paradigm," *Financial Times*, August 2010.

16. Thomas Piketty, *Capital in the Twenty-First Century*, April 2014.

17. Paul Ormerod, *The Death of Economics*, May 1994.

18. Stephen G. Cecchetti and Enisse Kharroubi, "Reassessing the Impact of Finance on Growth," BIS working paper 381, July 2012.

19. Joseph C. Sternberg, "Why Central Bankers Missed the Crisis," *The Wall Street Journal*, November 2018.

20. Victor Stango and Jonathan Zinman, "We Are All Behavioral, More or Less: A Taxonomy of Consumer Decision Making," National Bureau of Economic Research, November 2020, https://www.nber.org/system/files/working_papers/w28138/w28138.pdf

21. Eric Beinhocker, "How the Profound Changes in Economics Make Left Versus Right Debates Irrelevant," *Evonomics*, https://evonomics.com/the-deep-and-profound-changes-in-economics-thinking/?fbclid=IwAR2I7EkSD88uZrLc-ZC2E5YpQYjGbb206d8hFhw1V2GjUtRh4cZbOZB85As

22. *Stanford Encyclopedia of Philosophy*, Thomas Kuhn, first published Friday, August 13, 2004; substantive revision Wednesday, Oct 31, 2018, https://plato.stanford.edu/entries/thomas-kuhn

23. *Stanford Encyclopedia of Philosophy*, Thomas Kuhn.

24. Steven Payson, *How Economics Professors Can Stop Failing Us: The Discipline at a Crossroad*, 2017.

25. Steven Payson, *How Economics Professors Can Stop Failing Us: The Discipline at a Crossroad*, 2017.

26. Joseph Henrich et al., "In Search of Homo Economicus: Behavioral Experiments in 15 Small-Scale Societies," *The American Economic Review*, 2001.

27. David Sloan Wilson, "Scientists Discover What Economists Haven't Found: Humans," *Evonomics*, July 2016.

28. Thomas Piketty, *Capital in the Twenty-First Century*, April 2014.

29. Thomas Piketty, *Capital in the Twenty-First Century*, April 2014.

30. Gary Saul Morson and Morton Schapiro, "Why Economists Need to Expand Their Knowledge to Include the Humanities," World Economic Forum in collaboration with Project Syndicate, August 2017.

31. Angus Deaton, *The Great Escape: Health, Wealth, and the Origins of Inequality*, 2013.

32. For more on this, see my website: www.outgrowingcapital.com

33. Dirk J. Bezemer, "'No One Saw This Coming': Understanding Financial Crisis Through Accounting Models," research report from the University of Groningen, 2009.

34. Steven Payson, *How Economics Professors Can Stop Failing Us: The Discipline at a Crossroad*, 2017.

35. Steven Payson, *How Economics Professors Can Stop Failing Us: The Discipline at a Crossroad*, 2017.

36. Ann Pettifor, *The Production of Money: How to Break the Power of Bankers*, 2017.

37. Steven Payson, *How Economics Professors Can Stop Failing Us: The Discipline at a Crossroad*, 2017.

38. John Rapley, *Twilight of the Money Gods: Economics as a Religion and How It all Went Wrong*, July 2017.

39. Adair Turner, *Between Debt and the Devil: Money, Credit and Fixing Global Finance*, October 2016.

40. With austerity I refer to running budget surpluses or small deficits. Austerity as "optimizing expenditures and avoiding waste" can always be good, but in recessions, within the constraints of capitalism, governments need to run large budget deficits to avoid resources in the economies being underutilized, with negative long-term implications. No economist without a political agenda will support running budget surpluses in times of crisis. The few who tried have brought forward flawed economic papers that have been discredited, similar to climate change deniers. See here for an example: https://www.ineteconomics.org/perspectives/blog/the-myth-of-expansionary-austerity.

41. Robert Shiller, "Richard Thaler Is a Controversial Nobel Prize Winner—But a Deserving One," *The Guardian*, October 2017.

42. Richard H. Thaler & Cass R. Sunstein, *Nudge: Improving Decisions About Health, Wealth, and Happiness*, April 2008.

43. Branko Milanovic, *Global Inequality: A New Approach For the Age of Globalization*, 2016.

44. Stephen G. Cecchetti and Enisse Kharroubi, "Reassessing the Impact of Finance on Growth," BIS working paper 381, July 2012.

45. Steven Payson, *How Economics Professors Can Stop Failing Us: The Discipline at a Crossroad*, 2017.

46. Thomas Piketty, *Capital in the Twenty-First Century*, April 2014.

47. George DeMartino, "Harming Irreparably: On Neoliberalism, Kaldor-Hicks, and the Parentian Guarantee," Video presentation at the 15th Annual Summer Institute for the History of Economic Thought, University of Richmond, August 2015.

48. Robert H. Frank, Thomas Gilovich, and Dennis T. Regan, "Does Studying Economics Inhibit Cooperation?" *Journal of Economic Perspectives*, Spring 1993.

49. Tom Stafford, "Does Studying Economics Make You More Selfish?" BBC, October 2013.

50. Adam Grant, "More Evidence That Learning Economics Makes You Selfish," *Evonomics*, https://evonomics.com/more-evidence-that-learning-economics-makes-you-selfish/?fbclid=IwAR0Mfe1CJJ_yQNfotKy_nWqoD75x6PvFmW4RdGT2SWNTsHxxcAFha1UiEbk

51. Steven Payson, *How Economics Professors Can Stop Failing Us: The Discipline at a Crossroad*, 2017.

52. Hannah Ritchie, "How Many People Die and How Many Are Born Each Year?" Our World in Data, September 11, 2019, https://ourworldindata.org/births-and-deaths.

53. "Escaping Growth Dependency: Why Reforming Money Will Reduce the Need to Pursue Economic Growth at Any Cost to the Environment," PositiveMoney. January 2018.

54. Robert Skidelsky, *Money and Government: A Challenge to Mainstream Economics*, September 2018.

55. Steve Keen, "Note To Joe Stiglitz: Banks Originate, Not Intermediate, And That's Why Aggregate Demand Is Stuffed," *Forbes*, January 2016.

56. Yanis Varoufakis, "Imagining a World without Capitalism," Project Syndicate, December 27, 2019, https://www.project-syndicate.org/commentary/imagining-a-world-without-capitalism-by-yanis-varoufakis-2019-12

57. Stephanie Kelton, *The Deficit Myth: Modern Monetary Theory and the Birth of the People's Economy*, June 2020.

58. Thomas Ferguson, "Affluent Authoritarianism: McGuire and Delahunt's New Evidence on Public Opinion and Policy," Institute for new Economic Thinking, November 2, 2020, https://www.ineteconomics.org/perspectives/blog/affluent-authoritarianism-mcguire-and-delahunts-new-evidence-on-public-opinion-and-policy?fbclid=IwAR1CRO05wXjbkShGKZDGAS9ifO6aNVK78TxrIjk2pshPTQOjF_rsIMp2ZVA

Chapter 19: Step One, Step Two, Step Three

1. An even better alternative to the last would be for the government to approve a change in the central bank regulations that let them book a profit when creating permanent money and a loss when distributing it.

2. Money supply defined as M2, compared to nominal yearly GDP.

3. Otherwise we would either end up with inflation or with a high banking reserve requirement, which leaves little room for banks and borrowers (that is, the free markets) to create credit.

4. "RSA: Providing Income Security and Supporting Return to Work," ILO, 2017, available at https://www.social-protection.org/gimi/gess/ RessourcePDF.action?ressource.ressourceId=53361

5. Bryan Tierney, "BRAZIL: Maricá Approves Changes in Basic Income Program," Basic Income News, July 2017, Original article in Portuguese at https://odia.ig.com.br/ rio-de-janeiro/2017-06-28/moeda-social-de-marica-e-premiada.html

6. Bryan Tierney, "BRAZIL: Maricá Approves Changes in Basic Income Program," Basic Income News, July 2017, Original article in Portuguese at https://odia.ig.com.br/ rio-de-janeiro/2017-06-28/moeda-social-de-marica-e-premiada.html

7. Thomas Piketty, *Capital in the Twenty-First Century*, April 2014.

8. "IMF Executive Directors Discuss a New SDR Allocation of US $650 Billion to Boost Reserves, Help Global Recovery from COVID-19," International Monetary Fund, March 23, 2021, https://www.imf.org/en/News/Articles/2021/03/23/ pr2177-imf-execdir-discuss-new-sdr-allocation-us-650b-boost-reserves-help-global-recovery-covid19

9. Joseph E. Stiglitz and Bruce Greenwald, "Towards a New Global Reserve System," *Journal of Globalization and Development*, vol. 1, issue 2, 2010, https://enotus.com/ wp-content/uploads/2018/04/Towards-a-New-Global-Reserve-System.pdf

10. I will stop the discussion on global monetism here, given the need to get technical on currencies, exchange rates, and international trade.

11. That is, 5% of about 11 trillion euros of GDP divided among about 290 million adults in the eurozone, and 5% of about 21 trillion USD GDP divided by about 255 million adults in the US.

12. Assuming about 140 trillion international dollars of GDP and 5.8 billion adult population.

Epilogue: Will We Be Frogs in the Pot?

1. "Bank of England to Directly Finance UK Government's Extra Spending," *Financial Times*, April 9, 2020 https://www.ft.com/content/664c575b-0f54-44e5-ab78-2fd30ef213cb

2. Alex Harris and Emily Barrett, "US Weights Selling 50- and 100-Year Bonds after Yields Plummet," Bloomberg, August 16, 2019, https://www.bloomberg.com/news/ articles/2019-08-16/u-s-treasury-to-do-market-outreach-again-on-ultra-long-bonds-jzejo2qu?utm

3. Example of PBOC policies can be found in the article "How China Copes With Capital Flight; As growth slows and tariffs threaten, the central bank now strives to prevent a sharp slide in the yuan," by John Greenwood and Steve H. Hanke, The Wall Street Journal, November 19, 2018, https://www.wsj.com/articles/ how-china-copes-with-capital-flight-1542672901

4. Olivier Blanchard, Public Debt and Low Interest Rates, Presidential address to the American Economic Association, available at https://www.aeaweb.org/webcasts/2019/aea-presidential-address-public-debt-and-low-interest-rates

5. Andrew G. Berg and Jonathan D. Ostry, "Inequality and Unsustainable Growth: Two Sides of the Same Coin?" IMF staff discussion note, 2011.

6. Jaromir Benes and Michael Kumhof, "The Chicago Plan Revisited," IMF working paper, August 2012.

7. Is Growth at Risk? Global Financial Stability Report of October 2017, IMF.

8. https://blogs.imf.org/2021/02/19/structural-factors-and-central-bank-credibility-limit-inflation-risks/?fbclid=IwAR2LN5CxVkdFIg39Lkc4Q5KhQ4nLuUikmax Qtx-DGecwo-q6hWas9_abUW8.

9. Gillian Tett, "Central Banks Are Taking Up the Climate Challenge," *Financial Times*, April 2019.

10. Robert Kuttner, "Biden's Child Tax Credit as Universal Basic Income," *The American Prospect*, March 16, 2021, https://prospect.org/economy/bidens-child-tax-credit-as-universal-basic-income/?fbclid=IwAR12HaLcz9CwgA9BLdPZT4F-sKWOnW9vgBkv 4fXdu2dUOjpiKQZ72wz8lME

11. Alejandro Adler, "Gross National Happiness and Positive Education in Bhutan," University of Pennsylvania, April 2015.

12. Neil Hawkes, "Values and Quality Teaching at West Kidlington Primary School," chapter 7 in Terry Lovat and Ron Toomey, eds., *Values Education and Quality Teaching: The Double Helix Effect*, 2009.

13. "Giving Voice to the Impacts of Values Education: Final Report of the Values in Action Schools Project," Department of Education Employment and Working Relations (DEEWR), Melbourne: Education Learning Services, October 2010.

14. "Benefits of the IB," International Baccalaureate, https://www.ibo.org/benefits/

Index

About the Author

Since his humble beginnings on the outskirts of Milan, Marco Dondi has established his career and expertise as a strategy consultant with over a decade of experience in advising CEOs and government officials on economics, economic development, banking, education, adult training, and people development.

Marco holds an MBA (INSEAD, 2012) and a master's in management, economics, and industrial engineering (Politecnico di Milano, 2009).

At 28 years of age, Marco went on a Vipassana meditation retreat and re-emerged from a quarter-life crisis with a renewed sense of purpose. Since then, he has been on a mission to challenge and reform the social conventions that hinder people from their pursuit of a fulfilling life—capitalism being the biggest culprit.

When he's not working or writing, Marco reenergizes by taking part in various sports on water or snow, creating and cooking Italian and Asian dishes, and continuing to indulge in his childhood passion for wild mushroom foraging.

Marco has worked and lived in 4 continents and visited over 60 countries. He currently calls Geneva home, where he lives with his partner, Kristie, and their ragdoll cat, Panko.